BROADCASTING LAW AND FUNDAMENTAL RIGHTS

Broadcasting Law and Fundamental Rights

RACHAEL CRAUFURD SMITH

CLARENDON PRESS · OXFORD
1997

Oxford University Press, Great Clarendon Street, Oxford OX2 6DP

Oxford New York

Athens Auckland Bangkok Bogota Bombay
Buenos Aires Calcutta Cape Town Dar es Salaam
Delhi Florence Hong Kong Istanbul Karachi
Kuala Lumpur Madras Madrid Melbourne
Mexico City Nairobi Paris Singapore
Taipei Tokyo Toronto
and associated companies in
Berlin Ibadan

Oxford is a trade mark of Oxford University Press

Published in the United States
by Oxford University Press Inc., New York

British Library Cataloguing in Publication Data
Data available

Library of Congress Cataloging in Publication Data
Data available
ISBN 0–19–826221–3

1 3 5 7 9 10 8 6 4 2

Typeset by Cambrian Typesetters, Frimley, Surrey
Printed in Great Britain on acid-free paper by
Bookcraft Ltd., Midsomer Norton, Somerset

For My Parents

Acknowledgements

This book is a revised version of my doctoral thesis which I defended at the European University Institute, Florence, in October 1994. I should like to thank in particular my supervisor Professor Bruno de Witte for his unfailing support and perceptive direction and Professor Eric Barendt for his encouragement and constructive comments over the years. I should also like to thank the other members of my jury: Professors Paola Carrozza, Luis María Díez-Picazo, and Vincent Porter. The staff at the Institute proved unfailingly helpful, particularly those in the library, who obtained for me many of the materials drawn on in this book.

Mention must also be made of all those who have helped to launch this book into print, in particular Richard Hart, Kate Elliott for her careful editing, Michaela Coulthard, and the staff at Oxford University Press.

Finally, special thanks are owed to Mary Hoose and also to Sean Smith who read, and made helpful suggestions on, earlier drafts of this work. If nothing else this book is a testament to their remarkable patience and generosity of spirit.

RACHAEL CRAUFURD SMITH

Contents

Abbreviations

The principal case reports and official journals referred to in this book
have been abbreviated in the following manner:

AC	Appeal Cases (Law Reports, UK)
All ER	All England Law Reports
ALR	Australian Law Reports
Bull. EC	*Bulletin of the European Communities*
CMLR	Common Market Law Reports
Crim. LR	Criminal Law Review
Coll.	Collection of Decisions of the European Commission of Human Rights
D & R	Decisions and Reports of the European Commission of Human Rights
ECR	European Court Reports (Reports of the Court of Justice of the European Communities, Luxembourg)
EHRR	European Human Rights Reports
F Supp.	Federal Supplement
F 2d.	Federal Reporter (Second Series)
Foro it.	Foro italiano
GU	Gazzetta Ufficiale della Repubblica Italiana
Giur. cost.	Giurisprudenza costituzionale
Giur. it.	Giurisprudenza italiana
Gius. civ.	Giustizia civile
JO	Journal officiel de la république française
L Ed. 2d	Lawyer's Edition
NI	Northern Ireland Law Reports
OJ	Official Journal of the European Communities
QB	Queen's Bench Division (Law Reports, UK)
Rec. Cons. constit.	Recueil des décisions du Conseil constitutionnel
Rec. déc. Cons. d'Etat	Recueil des décisions du Conseil d'Etat
S Ct.	United States Supreme Court Reports
SC	Court of Session Cases
SLT	Scots Law Times
US	United States Reports
WLR	Weekly Law Reports
Yearbook	Yearbook of the European Convention on Human Rights

Table of Cases

Table of French Cases

Table of Italian Cases

Table of United Kingdom Cases

Table of United States Cases

Introduction: An Expanding Judicial Role in a Multi-channel Environment

Courts are in the business of considering concrete disputes, concrete problems; rarely will they turn their skills to hypothetical questions, and only when these have a direct bearing on the case in point. The courts in resolving these disputes, tied in to a given place, a given time, do not simply take note of the world 'as it is' but shape the world 'as it is to become', setting up a continuous dialogue, a slow evolution. Thus it is that we can fully understand the role of judges and courts, or indeed their absence from the field, only against a backdrop of the social, political, technological, and regulatory conditions of the time. Nowhere is this clearer than in the gradual recourse to law in the audiovisual sector, and the backdrop, the reality against which courts were initially called to react, was that of a highly monopolized industry, in many instances state-owned or subject to extensive state control.

The widespread consolidation of public broadcasting monopolies across Europe in the immediate post-war period served initially to insulate the broadcasting world from judicial scrutiny. Broadcasting was widely seen as an institution acting *for* 'the state' or *for* 'the people', pursuing generalized goals of national education and cohesion—it was not something *of* the people, to be appropriated by individuals or run for profit, as the fierce debates in Britain of the early 1950s over the introduction of commercial broadcasting so clearly highlight.[1] In a world in which the political and social ground rules seemed firmly enough established, private enterprise was given little encouragement, beyond the prospect of future profit (initially at least quite uncertain), to challenge the existing status quo. European governments, which often considered the audiovisual media to be part of the legitimate 'spoil system' of political power, tended to be unreceptive to the suggestion that commercial operators be given a share of the broadcast market. Even in Britain, where commercial broadcasting was initiated in the early 1950s and where pressure from the industry achieved a wide margin of success, the Conservative leadership was ultimately won over to the private broadcasting cause on the basis of an agreement to leave radio, which was then the most established and

---

[1] On this see B. Sendall (1982) i, iii.

respected medium, out of consideration.[2] The introduction of commercial competition was thus carefully restricted to the television sector.

Given the political reluctance to open broadcasting to market forces, it is hardly suprising that in a country such as Italy, which combines a parliamentary system notorious for its internal machinations and delaying tactics with a constitutional system which provides for judicial challenge to existing laws, commercial actors have seen in the courts an effective mechanism for precipitating change. Recourse to the courts has taken a number of different forms: one approach has been to apply for a broadcasting licence from the relevant administrative agency and proceed to challenge its rejection in court, calling into question the state monopoly or other regulatory provisions on constitutional grounds. Another has been to set up an unlicensed station, seek to avoid closure for as long as possible, while attacking tenaciously in court any attempt by official bodies to disactivate the service, hoping thereby to expand viewer expectations and create a positive climate within the population in favour of change.

Such strategies have not, however, been universally available to commercial operators: whether courts are prepared to overturn statutory provisions limiting market entry or imposing onerous operating restrictions will depend on the constitutional context in which they operate. In a country such as Britain, where the docrtrine of parliamentary sovereignty has traditionally precluded judges from reviewing primary legislation,[3] courts of law have played a very limited role in shaping the audiovisual environment. Instead, it has been in countries such as France and Italy, where particular rights and interests are constitutionally guaranteed, that judges have been able to develop their own guidelines for audiovisual regulation. Yet even here early attempts to break new legal ground proved generally unsuccessful. The seeds of doubt sown by such actions took root only slowly: a careful observer would have seen that the broadcasting industry, deeply enmeshed in the political and cultural institutions of the nation state, was a singularly unattractive subject for constitutional courts, anxious to consolidate their position in the face of continuing political suspicion and hostility. But from the initial challenges of the 1960s the pressure on the conceptual wall demarcating the audiovisual and judicial fields intensified, for these legal skirmishes with state control heralded merely the first stage of judicial involvement in the audiovisual sector. An involvement which encouraged, as a protective reflex, politicians and professional broadcasters to attempt to clothe the old order with new, more socially acceptable, controls, rather than reject outright the prevalent

---

[2] B. Sendall (1982) i, x.
[3] A doctrine which has had to be modified in the light of the UK's membership of the European Community and the supremacy of Community law over domestic legislation.

reality of state control. In taking these first, enforced steps of re-evaluation, however, the status quo came to seem merely contingent, no longer carved in stone, and, with the inviolability of the established order shaken, private enterprise sought to push this contingency still further into final judicial rejection.

With the demise of state monopolies, the entry of commercial operators, and a growing diversification in both delivery systems and services, courts are now being called to respond to a range of new and very different questions. In a situation in which a monopoly company is either owned or regulated by the state formal, legally scrutinizable, rules may well be minimized. Regulation may be devolved directly to the industry itself, which then develops its own extensive system of internal rules and procedures.[4] Such provisions tend to be highly specialized and leave significant room for professional judgement, factors which discourage judicial scrutiny. An open market, on the other hand, will require 'more regulation than a monopoly market, especially if it is to emerge from a hitherto monopoly state'.[5] A competitive market environment calls for a particular regulatory regime to control the formation of dominant companies or cartels and to prevent generally uncompetitive activities. In the audiovisual sector there will also be questions relating to the allocation of licences, the exclusionary use of copyright, and third-party access in an increasingly vertically integrated industry. The move from a monopolized to a competitive market will inevitably lead, therefore, to an increase in regulation—it will lead precisely to the introduction of *market* regulation.

But what of those regulations governing programme content itself: will these too expand in the brave new world of the 'information society'? In 1989 two commentators on the audiovisual industry, Howkins and Foster, predicted a decrease in regulations aiming to uphold public broadcasting standards and a move to lighten the regulatory burden on commercial protagonists can be detected. The British government, for example, in its 1988 White Paper proposals for the audiovisual media outlined a leaner form of 'light touch' regulation, more suited, it was argued, to an increasingly competitive environment:[6] a vision realized in the 1990 Broadcasting Act. A move to fewer, but more formalized, rules and standards is also to be expected where an industry expands to allow in new entrants on whom long-established and highly complex systems of self-regulation cannot easily be grafted.

A preference for fixed programme quotas and franchise auctions undoubtedly renders the broadcasting world more open to legal scrutiny,

---

[4] See, e.g., the BBC Producers' Guidelines, published by BBC Information.
[5] J. Howkins and M. Foster (1989), 22.
[6] Home Office (1988).

just as it marks a parallel move away from extensive administrative discretion. As it becomes more difficult for political factions to control or manipulate particular regulatory bodies there may be a preference for the adoption of 'objective standards' and greater judicial oversight. Thus the system of franchise auctions, adopted in the 1990 British Broadcasting Act, was in part designed to limit the allocative discretion of the Independent Television Commission.[7] Although there remained an element of evaluuative juggling under the 1990 system, the emphasis on financial entitlement and market allocation encouraged some high-bid franchise losers to challenge the ITC's rejection of their tenders in court.[8]

The franchise system still stands at the centre of broadcasting policy, offering extensive scope for political control and the regulation of radio and television content. A shift in the oversight of spectrum use from political or administrative organs to the judiciary through, for example, the adoption of a judicially supervised regime of spectrum 'property rights' would constitute a significant transfer of power. This point was not lost, Thomas Hazlett suggests, on American politicians in the early days of popular broadcasting.[9] Hazlett argues that judicial moves to apply common law 'homesteading' principles to solve the problem of station interference prompted quick governmental action and the establishment of the Federal Radio Commission (FRC), charged with awarding licences 'in the public interest'. To have left spectrum allocation in the hands of the courts would have destroyed the central justification for the various content and access requirements which came to complement the adminis- trative process of FRC licensing: '[t]he fact was that the policy debate was led by men who clearly understood—and articulated—that interference was not the problem, interference was the opportunity'.[10] But spectrum shortage has been used more widely across Europe as a justification for government intervention in a field which raises complex issues of freedom of speech and expression; it is not, therefore, a mere matter of accident that, as the cogency of those arguments turning on the limited availability of broadcast frequencies has come increasingly into question, so the attacks on state regulation have multiplied. With the old political justifications for audiovisual regulation under mounting technical and ideological attack, courts of law have been called to develop their own ground-rules for the broadcast media adapted to the social and industrial circumstances of the late twentieth century.

Despite this regulatory shift from political and administrative organs to the courts, the main lines of broadcasting policy continue to be determined

[7] The procedures adopted by the IBA when awarding the ITV franchises in 1980 were criticized as being arbitrary and obscure. For discussion of the awards see A. Briggs and J. Spicer (1986).   [8] For details see T. H. Jones (1992).
[9] T. W. Hazlett (1990).   [10] *Ibid.* 162.

in the political arena. Moreover, there remains an enduring political and social allegiance to the maintenance of programme 'standards' and a lasting preference for industry-specific regulators to monitor them, largely by-passing the courts. In Britain, for example, an attempt was made to deal with increasingly vocal criticisms of broadcasting standards by the establishment of a new, if toothless, watchdog body, the Broadcasting Standards Council, now merged with the Broadcasting Complaints Commission to form the Broadcasting Standards Commission.[11] Nevertheless it is now apparent that neither political nor administrative actors can set new rules and regulations for the broadcasting sector without giving due consideration to how these will be received by courts of law. National broadcasting policy is increasingly being formulated in the shadow of judge-made law and, for Member States of the European Community, that law is to an ever greater extent being established by the European Court of Justice in Luxembourg.

What theory of the role of broadcasting in society do the courts then offer us in our rapidly changing technological environment, and to what extent have they drawn upon or rejected popular perceptions of the mass media? What are the institutional and ideological limits to their involvement in this field, and how successful has this involvement been? In considering these questions three interlinking issues have been isolated, issues with which courts of law have increasingly been called to grapple and which are central to any conception of the role of broadcasting in society:

(a) *Who* should be granted rights to use the available Hertzian frequencies or to lay cable networks in order to offer audiovisual services to the public? The debate here has centred on whether both public and private actors should be allowed to own radio or television stations.

(b) *How many* public and/or private actors should be allowed access to the broadcasting market? In the past this question has been asked predominantly in the national context, but the growth in transfrontier radio and, more recently, television services has highlighted its international dimensions.

(c) *On what terms* should these actors be allowed to pursue their various activities? In particular, must they allow other individuals or organizations air or cable time, and to what sort of programme requirements may they legitimately be subjected?

---

[11] For details see Home Office (1988) 34–5, the Council obtained statutory recognition in the 1990 Broadcasting Act. It may, however, be noted that s. 162 of the 1990 Act also extended the provisions of the Obscene Publications Act 1959 to television and radio broadcasting. The Broadcasting Standards Commission was established in Pt. V of the 1996 Broadcasting Act.

It will be immediately apparent that these three questions are by no means unrelated, for the various issues interlink and overlap in important ways. The terms imposed under (c), for example, may well vary with the number (b) and nature (a) of the authorized broadcasters. Structure and product are inextricably linked, such that any meaningful regulation of the audiovisual media must give consideration to both aspects.

The present study seeks to examine how these questions have been dealt with in a number of distinct judicial systems. At the national level, the courts of three European countries have been selected, those of France, Italy, and the United Kingdom, each with a very different constitutional framework. Although the French and Italian constitutions, unlike the British, make provision for judicial review of primary legislation, the scope afforded judicial scrutiny is very different in the two countries. In France, the Conseil constitutionnel is limited to examining the constitutionality of a legislative proposal prior to its final adoption, there is no possibility of reviewing legislation already on the statute book. In Italy, it is open for a litigant to argue that an existing law is unconstitutional in the course of ordinary judicial proceedings and where the judge is convinced that the issue raised is not manifestly unfounded and is relevant to the case in point he or she will refer it on to the Corte costituzionale for resolution. The main focus of the study of French and Italian decisions does in fact centre on the rulings of these two constitutional courts which have proved both able and willing to set guiding objectives for the audiovisual media.

The United Kingdom, lacking a written constitution and constitutional court to oversee its implementation, has not experienced the same judicial standard-setting for the audiovisual sector. Judicial involvement in the regulatory dialogue is largely missing from the British picture and the setting of audiovisual policy has remained firmly in the political domain, day-to-day supervision being vested in industry-specific regulatory bodies. The nature of industrial conflict is, however, changing rapidly and, as the focus for debate moves away from private access to the spectrum to the way in which market power may be used to restrict competition, courts across Europe, including those in the United Kingdom, will increasingly be called on to consider whether radio and television services should be treated simply as industrial commodities like any other, or distinct activities, the cultural and political functions of which call for specific provision.

Nor is it any longer possible to study such domestic legal systems in isolation from the wider European and international context: the growth in cross-border transmission has left the nation state poorly equipped to deal with many of the audiovisual issues which now arise. Faced with these challenges the European Community and Council of Europe have become important actors in the audiovisual field, and no consideration of national regulation would be complete without examining the developing case law of the European Court of Justice and the European Court of Human Rights. Although the decisions of these courts have, for the purposes of exposition, been considered separately their links with, if not incorporation into, the domestic legal orders should not be forgotten, particularly in the Community context.

The book is divided into three parts. Part I explores the early regulation of the broadcasting industry and contrasts this with the regulatory system established for the printed press. Why was the lightly regulated, competitive press model thought inappropriate for the new media of communication and why was state control established with so little apparent opposition? In Part 2 I examine the all-important structural framework for judicial intervention in the various legal systems under consideration, and provide a brief summary of the main constitutional and treaty provisions which have a bearing on the audiovisual media. Part 3 charts the early involvement of the courts as commercial operators sought to challenge the dominance of state monopolies and gain access to the broadcasting market. There follows an exploration of how judges have attempted to resolve the tensions between the freedom of expression and the principle of pluralism. Some of the concrete implications of these provisions are then considered before a concluding assessment is made of the potential advantages and disadvantages of judicial intervention in the audiovisual sector. The approach taken throughout has been a deliberately broad one for, as we have already noted, judicial pronouncements on the mass media can be fully understood only in the wider context of the aspirations and capabilities of other influential operators: the politicians, industry-specific regulators, the hard- and software industries, advertisers, and last, but by no means least, the viewing and listening public itself. Some time has therefore been given to an examination of the development of the audiovisual media and the various conceptions of broadcasting which evolved with it: conceptions which continue to resonate in judicial decisions to this day. It is with this development that the present study opens.

PART 1

The Early Development of Broadcasting Regulation. Fifty Years in the Political Domain

1

The Search for a Structure: Uncertain Origins and the Rejection of the Press Model

In this new situation the liberal answer loses most of its relevance, since to support, in any way, the existing and emergent organisation of the press is to underwrite a form which is certain by its own powerful internal criteria, to rationalise in the direction of profitability rather than of range.[1]

During the early decades of this century the regulations adopted across Europe to control the fledgling radio industry were far from uniform. National radio services evolved gradually, often in a piecemeal fashion, and, given the initial novelty of popular broadcasting, time was needed for diverse interest groups—the broadcasting and electronics industries, politicians, the listening public—to grasp its capabilities and future potential. It appears that the initial regulatory choices had little to do with elevated issues of human rights or 'fundamental freedoms' and were motivated more by a desire to further the national electronics industry, or by concerns over radio's social and political influence. Indeed, it was a recognition of the important role played by radio as a propaganda tool during the Second World War which helped confirm governments in their exclusion of private enterprise from the broadcasting sector. To place the post-war development of radio and television in context we must therefore turn back the clock to examine the play of forces which ensured that state monopoly became the paradigm model for radio regulation within Europe: a model which was to dominate the audiovisual media for another half century.

1. LEGAL FOUNDATIONS AND EARLY REGULATION

The legal foundation for state control was present, if not immediately acted upon, virtually from the inception of sound radio. In Britain such control

---

[1] R. Williams, (1978), 19.

had been entrusted to the Post Office by the 1904 Wireless Telegraphy Act which required those wishing to set up a wireless telegraph station to obtain a licence from the Postmaster General.[2] In Italy Article 1 of Law 395 of 1910 comprehensively reserved to the government 'the establishment and exercise of radio telegraph and telephonic equipment and, more generally, all equipment within Italy or its colonies, whether on land or sea, employing electricity for long-distance effects without relying on cable transmission'. It is of interest to note that the same Article also empowered the government to grant *authorizations* to third parties for the use of radio frequencies, indicating that monopoly was not initially considered an inevitable choice: there is no reference to an 'exclusive' concession. Indeed, the then Minister of Posts observed during the parliamentary discussion over the proposed legislation that Article 1 did not specifically mention the term 'monopoly', but simply made provision for the government to grant concessions to private individuals. The government, it was claimed, had no intention of monopolizing radio along the lines of the telegraphic industry.[3] Somewhat later, the French financial law of 30 June 1923 applied the provisions of the 1851 law on telegraphic communications to radio, giving the French government a similar power either to appropriate completely the use of the available radio waves or to grant licences to selected third parties.[4]

Although each of these provisions left open the possibility that the state might grant a number of private concessions and thus reject the prevalent example of the monopolized telegraphic industry, radio and telegraph were initially considered to be functionally very close.[5] The reasons underlying careful state supervision of the telegraph sector are not difficult to discern. Telegraph was seen as an important tool, not merely in the domain of private communications, for its speed and secrecy rendered it of invaluable assistance to the military and emergency services. It also played an essential role in the regulation of transport services, particularly rail; was used to convey official directives or noteworthy information around the national territories; and facilitated links with distant colonies.[6] To have left so vital a form of communication in the hands of private, profit-seeking entities may have seemed an unduly risky strategy.[7]

---

[2] Halsbury (1985), ilv, 177, 178, 288.   [3] F. Monteleone (1976), 13.

[4] The 1851 *décret sur les lignes télégraphiques* had provided that no telegraphic line could be established or used for the transmission of correspondence except by the government or with its authorization. The 1923 legislation simply extended this to the 'emission and reception of electric radio signals of all types'.

[5] J.-L. Libois (1983).

[6] The London–Calcutta telegraph line was completed, for example, in 1870.

[7] The risk of commercial irresponsibility was highlighted by the Marconi company's direction to its wireless operators to respond only to those emergency calls sent from Marconi

At its inception radio had generally been considered, first and foremost, a partial replacement for the telegraph: attractive, in that there was no need for costly wires (impossible anyway for air or sea communication); unattractive, in that radio messages could be listened to by anyone who had the will and the reasonably basic electronic means to do so. In the early 1920s radio's potential for popular broadcasting was consequently considered by military and postal services alike to be very much of secondary interest, if such potential was recognized at all.[8] Early legislation covered both aspects of radio, its individual relay and general broadcast capabilities, in a more or less undifferentiated fashion, and it was easy for those factions, hostile to private development of the new medium, to confuse the two and draw an analogy with the telegraph, for the most part under direct state control.

In many countries the PTT's and military services were opposed to the development of popular radio services, fearing that they could interfere, as they occasionally did, with more important communications. In Britain the Post Office reluctantly used its powers to grant only the most restrictive of broadcasting licences to the Marconi company. Initial permits were of a 'temporary' or 'experimental' nature, limited to periods as short as a mere half-hour a week, and imposed such irksome obligations as suspension of transmission every seven minutes to enable the operator to listen out for official messages.[9]

In both Italy and Britain the power to license radio broadcasters was quickly employed to limit the private broadcasting market through enforced monopolization. Thus in 1924, after only a brief experimental period, it was decided to grant an exclusive popular broadcasting licence to a single Italian company, the Unione Radiofonica Italiana. The two main broadcasting companies already in existence—one of which, 'Radiofono', represented the pervasive interests of the Marconi group, the other, 'Società Italiana Radio Audizioni Circolari', was intended to spearhead the American interests of Western Electric into the Italian wireless industry— were invited to unite to form a single company. This compromise offered,

---

installations. Attempts were made to deal with unscrupulous commercial behaviour of this type at the international level: the final protocol of the 1903 Berlin Conference, in part organized to respond to the monopolistic ambitions of the Marconi company, had provided that coastal stations were bound to receive and transmit telegrams from or to ships at sea regardless of the wireless telegraphic system employed on board. Although Great Britain and Italy abstained, the Marconi company, under public pressure, was later to countermand this protectionist practice. See J. G. Savage (1989), 32–3.

[8] R. Williams (1979), 265, suggests that it is 'difficult now to realise how marginal it then seemed'.

[9] S. W. Head (1985), 57; T. Burns (1977), 6. Certain exceptions to military suspicion of popular broadcasting can, however, be found. In France, for example, General Gustave Ferrié was instrumental in the development of both military and civilian radio broadcasting.

at least in the early stages, a secure financial basis for the new industry, placated the main protagonists, and left a single broadcasting body more easily subjected to state supervision.

A similar market contraction had been acted out two years earlier in Britain, where, under pressure from the Minister of Posts, Neville Chamberlain, the British Broadcasting Company was established as the sole licensed radio broadcaster. The new company's shares were divided among the leading radio manufacturing companies which hoped that the provision of a regular programme service would boost the sales of wireless sets. Thus, in both Britain and Italy, concrete encouragement was given to the new radio industry, while, at the same time, centralized control was facilitated and use of the limited broadcast spectrum was carefully contained. Financing the enterprise, whose worth was by no means yet established, was conveniently left to private initiative, backed by indirect public support through the imposition of taxes on wireless receivers and licence fees.[10]

Such early moves to monopolization were by no means universal, however, and in France private stations, funded by advertising, competed with the state service. The first French private station 'Radiola' commenced broadcasting in 1922, and by 1928 there were thirteen private stations in existence. It was, however, intended that these private stations would gradually be phased out in favour of a national state network, and no new private companies were granted licences after 1929. Nevertheless, private broadcasting continued until the German occupation of 1940, and private stations even lived on precariously in Vichy France, though they were closely supervised, with ownership restricted to proven supporters of the Vichy regime. It was only after the liberation that all private licences were finally revoked, in March 1945.

Nor was the French element of private enterprise a unique phenomenon, for monopoly, despite the 'limited airwaves' and initial technical short-comings, was neither a necessary nor even obvious choice.[11] A number of clear alternatives were well established prior to the Second World War. The Dutch pillarized radio system, for example, with its separate stations

---

[10] In Italy significant sectors of private industry came under state direction through its purchase of company shares, blurring the divide between public and private ownership. Radio was no exception for, by 1927, the broadcasting company URI was no longer able to meet the financial demands of a national service and a new entity was set up, the Ente Italiano per le Audizioni Radiofoniche (EIAR), with greatly increased capital investment. Shares in EIAR were eventually to fall under the control of the state holding company IRI 'the principal vehicle at the disposition of fascism for intervening directly in the economy and the world of finance': F. Monteleone (1976), 75.

[11] R. Williams (1979), 265, has noted that 'technology, even in its early stages of development, was in no way determinative'.

run by distinct religious and political groups, quickly took shape at the commencement of sound broadcasting, a natural evolution from the equally pillarized press. This structure was in turn grafted onto the Dutch television service when it started regular broadcasts in 1951. Similarly, the American system of competitive private enterprise was well known in Europe, if only as a model to be rejected.[12]

Given, first, the *restriction imposed on private enterprise* through the enforced monopolization of the programming industry and prohibition or limitation on advertising time and, secondly, the apparent *potential within state-regulated monopolies for neutralizing those voices in society falling outside the governing or establishment consensus*, it may seem striking that the monopolization of the industry was carried out with a minimum of public and political dissent. Even more suprising in that, by the inception of regular radio broadcasting in the early 1920s, that other form of 'mass' communication, the newspaper, was emerging in many countries after the battles of the nineteenth century as a bastion of competitive private enterprise—free at least from the worst excesses of enforced government censorship, if not continuing political control.

To answer the question why the 'press model' was not adopted it is necessary to consider both how closely that model mirrored the reality of the newspaper industry in the countries under consideration and whether, where that model was in operation, it was thought to be a successful one, worthy of emulation, by those charged with policy-making in the new field of radio. It appears that by the time reality finally began to match the paradigm 'free press' model the popular press was being widely dismissed in establishment circles as pandering to vulgar tastes and sensationalist comment. Hardly, then, the structure best suited for a new mass medium over which politicians were increasingly anxious to exert at the very least a containing measure of control.

2. THE PRINTED PRESS AND THE EVOLUTION OF A THEORY: FROM FREEDOM OF EXPRESSION TO THE FREEDOM TO INFORM

Britain is often cited as a country which recognized comparatively early on a press right to freedom from prior restraint, in that the restrictive Licensing (Printing) Act of 1662 lapsed in 1695 and was not renewed.[13]

---

[12] For details on the Dutch system see S. W. Head (1985), 109. In connection with the American broadcast model it should be noted that advertising was not automatically accepted as a solution to the problem of broadcasting finance and in the 1920s it was 'often condemned even by radio champions such as Herbert Hoover': see T. W. Hazlett (1990), 167. R. B. Horwitz (1989), 115, states that only in 1925 did advertising come to be seen as inevitable.   [13] Halsbury (1985) viii, 553.

This did not, however, stem from any magnanimous wish to liberate the press, for there was every intention at the time to produce a new, indeed more effective, piece of legislation. Nevertheless, the problems endemic to the old system, which had left in circulation a considerable quantity of unlicensed seditious material, and the difficulties inherent in ensuring the passage of a new bill on the matter through Parliament, led to the adoption in 1712 of an alternative strategy—the introduction of stamp duty. Stamp duty was a tax levied on each sheet, or half-sheet, of newsprint, and was coupled with a tax levied on every newspaper advertisement. The introduction of stamp and advertisement duties stemmed both from financial considerations and a continuing desire to check what were considered to be the worst press abuses. Stamp duty was an attractive way of raising revenue and, as the levy was increased, conveniently served to price newspapers out of the pockets of the urban artisans, whose minds were thought better turned to their tasks at hand than dabbling in discussion of political affairs beyond their station or sphere of influence. Political debate was a popular pastime in eighteenth-century London and the coffee houses overflowed not merely with customers for their fluid refreshment but with merchants and citizens anxious to glean what news they could from the many pamphlets and papers made available on the premises.

In France press censorship was official policy until the Revolution of 1789, 'the existence of a "thought police" was the normal state of affairs'.[14] After the Revolution, and despite the bold assertions of Article 11 of the 1789 Declaration of the Rights of Man, the newly-acquired press freedoms were, however, gradually whittled away, particularly with the advent of hostile Napoleonic rule. It was only in the late nineteenth century, culminating with the law of 29 July 1881, that the central constraints imposed upon the press—the need for prior authorization and stamp duty levies—were finally abolished. A similar pattern of practical repression, set against a backcloth of apparent legislative guarantees, can be detected in nineteenth-century Italy. An advance towards recognition of the press's protected status had been made with the Edict on the Press passed in March 1848, and these guarantees were subsequently extended to the unified Italy. By virtue of this enactment the right to publish was, at least in theory, open to all without the need for prior administrative authorization. In reality, however, extensive administrative interference was the order of the day, with sequestration, suspension, or more subtle forms of newspaper harassment common occurrences.[15]

---

[14] D. Roche, 'Censorship and the Publishing Industry', in D. Roche and R. Darnton (eds.) (1989), 3. For a discussion of the impact of the subsequent 1881 press law see R. Barbrook (1995), 7–8.   [15] V. Castronovo, *et al.* (1979), 7 ff.

This piecemeal and patchy liberalization was forged against a developing and hotly-contested theory of the press's role in society. Attitudes to the press in eighteenth-century England varied considerably. Some deemed it to be irrelevant to the determination of political questions—matters of policy were beyond the reach of fickle public opinion—while others regarded it a shining defender of the public welfare, there being 'nothing that concerns the attention of a private man so much as the actions of persons in the administration of public affairs'.[16] Gradually, however, a liberal belief in the efficacy of a free exchange of ideas in promoting social progress, if not truth itself, began to gain ground, backed as it was by religious and philosophical dissenters seeking to escape from the straightjacket of prior state censorship and imposed orthodoxy.

An early, though at the time largely ignored, plea for greater liberty of the printed word was made in 1644 by John Milton in his now famous tract 'Areopagitica'. This, a century and a half later, was to prove the inspiration for Mirabeau's 'Sur la liberté de la presse' which was to become one of the 'most militant and widely circulated calls for the freedom of the press after 1789'.[17] For Milton 'true' knowledge required not merely a parroting of authority but critical examination of the basis for one's beliefs. God had given man the gift of reason, a gift rendered sterile and empty without the opportunity to weigh opposing arguments and choose between good and evil.[18] He also introduced a competitive element to his argument in Areopagitica—that truth would ultimately be revealed 'in a free and open encounter'—which was to influence more than one generation of philosophers pursuing a similar enquiry into the role of censorship in society. Thus, in the eighteenth century, Voltaire and Rousseau, while viewing the day-to-day offerings of the periodical press as lamentably ill-informed and riddled with ignorance, considered those countries in which a free exchange of ideas was prohibited to be prey to the worst vices of superstition and barbarism. But concern over the deleterious effects of rote censorship was not limited to the forward-looking philosophers of the age: even a man so centrally involved in royal censorship as Chrétien-Guillaume de Malesherbes, director of the French monarchy's book-trade office from 1750 to 1763, came to defend a reduction of preventive censorship in order to foster a free and ultimately enlightening competition of ideas.[19] By the mid-nineteenth century John Stuart Mill was arguing that

---

[16] This quote, from a 1728 edition of Mist's *Weekly Journal*, is taken from J. Black (1987), 120. Black discusses these and other opposing viewpoints in his fifth ch. 'The Press and the Constitution'.   [17] R. Birn (1989), 64.

[18] J. Keane (1991), 12. Keane suggests that early proponents of press freedom adopted four main approaches, focusing variously on theological, natural rights, utilitarian, and truth-revealing arguments.

[19] R. Birn (1989), 50 ff. See also C. Bellenger *et al.* (eds.) (1969), i.

free speech was essential not only for the discovery and proper understanding of 'the truth' but also for the knowing rejection of what was wrong, activities he held to be beneficial to the individual and society alike.[20]

During the late eighteenth and early nineteenth centuries freedom of expression began to receive concrete legal recognition in provisions such as Article 11 of the 1789 French Declaration of the Rights of Man and the First Amendment to the American Constitution of 1791. But the varied beliefs which underpinned such assertions, whether focusing on the benefits to the community from an open debate or on the individual nature of the enterprise *'come fatto spirituale, come manifestazione empirica della forza costruttiva del libero pensiero individuale'*,[21] appear to this day to conjure up an ideal forged as much against, rather than by, the prevailing reality.

First, many newspapers were not simply, or even primarily, conveyors of political ideas: the rallying theory of the 'free press' had little if anything to say on the more mundane and essentially uncontentious aspects of press activity. For example, English newspapers of the eighteenth century provided a varied diet of official and business news, readers' letters, advertisements, sporting information, crime reports, and entertaining, frequently bawdy, stories. If the battle for 'press freedom' focused quite naturally on the political and radical press, the sector most at risk from censorship and repression, other press activities benefited from its liberal philosophy: thus advertisement tax was abolished in Britain in 1853, two years before the ultimate abolition of stamp duty in 1855 and paper duty in 1861.

Secondly, if newspaper production started life as an artisanal occupation, newspapers were often very far from mere vehicles to propagate the views of their individual proprietors. For owners who did not go into print to peddle a particular religious or political line the financial incentives to 'turn political' were considerable—such papers sold well and stood to gain from political patronage. Jeremy Black has suggested that in England 'profit

---

[20] J. S. Mill (1982 edn.); D. Kelley and R. Donway (1990), 71, suggest that Mill's utilitarianism can be used to legitimate a degree of state intervention in the mass media which would be rejected by those adopting an 'inherently individualist' view of rights: '[h]is substitution of a collectivist for an individualist teleology marks the watershed between classical and modern liberalism.'

[21] A. Baldassarre (1986), 579—'as a spiritual fact, the empirical manifestation of the constructive force of free individual thought'. In Italy the newspaper industry was undoubtedly slow to shed its artisanal, if not family, dimensions. Press circulation continued to be hampered by high levels of illiteracy, slow technological development, and a poor communications network: see V. Castronovo *et al.* (1979), 13, 66. By the late 19th century newspapers in France and Britain, however, were attaining sizeable dimensions. In 1873 the comprehensive circulation for 555 Italian daily papers was 797,520 copies while in 1880 the Parisian press alone was looking to a circulation of 2 million.

played a large role in the decision to take a political stance, as it was generally accepted that this was more popular'.[22] Newspapers were not simply the products of individual political allegiance; even in the eighteenth century certain exemplars were undoubtedly forged in a calculating spirit of financial enterprise and opportunism. By the mid-Victorian period associations between papers and particular political factions in Britain had reached such a level that 'freedom of the press' was construed 'as the freedom to make a political choice', that is, to choose to ally with a particular political party and its policies:[23] a far cry from the constructive force of 'free individual thought' to which Antonio Baldassarre makes reference.[24]

Thirdly, those restraints on the press which were gradually removed, in line with the liberal theory of press freedom as freedom from prior restraint, were essentially the pre-publication restrictions of administrative authorization and stamp duty levies; many post-publication restraints remained or were brought into force as the old licensing systems fell into disuse. In England, that supposed bastion of the free press, allegations of blasphemy, sedition, and even treason were used to keep the press in check, particularly in the aftermath of the Napoleonic War.[25] John Stuart Mill in his book 'On Liberty', noted that 'the law of England, on the subject of the press, is as servile to this day as it was in the time of the Tudors'.[26] Although Mill felt there to be little danger that political discussion in the press would be repressed by such laws, save in times of exceptional civil unrest or peril, he noted with some dismay the then recent addition to the statute book of the 1855 Government Press Prosecutions Act which created a new statutory offence of 'circulating what was deemed an immoral doctrine, the lawfulness of tyrannicide'. The chilling nature of these provisions, given the state of English jails and legal delays, should not be underestimated.

In Italy the liberalizing Edict on the Press of 1848 also envisaged the continuing containment of 'abuses'. These embraced such wide-ranging activities as instigating offences against religion, the sovereign and ruling family, foreign heads of state, and diplomatic personnel, as well as against

---

[22] J. Black (1987), 131. See also S. Koss (1981), 38.

[23] S. Koss (1981), 3. Though Pat O'Malley (1981), 72, argues that by 1850 the 'capitalist' sector of the British press was returning profits which took it 'well out of the financial reach of government bribes'.   [24] A. Baldassarre (1986), 579.

[25] For a commentary on press repression in the 18th century see J. Black (1987), 151 ff., who paradoxically suggests at 155 that, given the proportion of unattributed, potentially defamatory articles and zenophobic comment, one might not wonder 'whether there was not too little censorship and legal retribution'. For more general comment see F. S. Siebert (1956); T. Burden and M. Campbell (1985), 195; C. Bellenger *et al.* (eds.) (1969), 405; and G. Robertson and A. G. L. Nicol (1984), 65.

[26] J. S. Mill (1982 edn.), 75.

'good morals' and the 'right to property'. Magistrates and police were prepared to stretch the spirit of the legislation by instituting, through an inventive use of technical requirements, what was in effect a system of prior authorization.[27] Similar restraints existed also in France and in the late nineteenth century a series of new Acts were passed in an attempt to brake the development of pornographic papers and to muzzle the radical, particularly anarchist, press.[28]

By the turn of the century, the mainstream political papers throughout Europe were having to reappraise their position and prospects in a rapidly changing environment. With the extension of the franchise the 'democratic role' of the press began to be emphasized, no longer preaching solely to the party faithful but looking to a new readership and seeking new financial support. The press came to be considered first, and rather grandiosely, as a mechanism with which to check the failings and abuses of elected representatives in parliament,[29] and, secondly, as a means to 'educate' the newly enfranchised population to use their votes in a 'responsible' manner. This marked an important shift from the liberal and interactive view of the press as a vehicle for individual expression to an essentially uni-directional purveyor of objectively verifiable 'news'. Paternalism had found its way into the press long before Reith forged the outlines of his 'public service' philosophy for popular radio broadcasting.

But other 'educative forces' had an interest in the development of the press. De la Haye has suggested that by the late nineteenth century the French press was already being used as a tool of expanding capitalism, a useful support in the socialization of the growing urban classes to the rapid economic and technical changes of the industrial revolution.[30] 'Just as the school system was to be the instrument used to organize the social distribution of generations to come, information was to penetrate the pores and daily life of rural society, largely obscurantist and backward, so as to

[27] V. Castronovo (1979), 7.
[28] C. Bellenger *et al.* (eds.) (1969), 245 ff., though R. Barbrook (1995), 8, notes that the right to trial by jury rendered the 'potentially repressive parts of the 1881 law . . . largely unenforceable in practice'.
[29] S. Koss (1981), 31 ff., notes that in 1831 Jeremy Bentham had drawn up a prospectus for a newspaper, the 'Universalist', designed to act, through its coverage of parliamentary debates, as 'a mirror' in which the electorate could study 'the true effigies' of their representatives in the Commons. Koss draws parallels between the fight for an expanded franchise and the efforts made to abolish the continuing financial restraints on the printed press: realization of both these objectives was considered essential for the creation of an extensive and informed electorate.
[30] Y. De la Haye (1977), 201. See also P. O'Malley (1981) for similar developments in Britain, among them the establishment in 1826 of the Society for the Diffusion of Useful Knowledge. The 'recognition of the ideological importance of a large-scale press and its advantages for disseminating the entrepreneurial ideal, came to be of vital importance in influencing decisions about the granting of legislative concessions to the press' (75).

bring their consciousness into line with the dominant characteristics of the new emerging society, as it was seen by the bourgeoisie.'[31]

The potential offered by advertising revenue for new consumer goods, the fruits of advanced production techniques, and the homogenization of the news message to appeal to the widest possible readership cut the mass-circulation papers off from their overtly partisan past. Journalistic styles developed to meet the demands of the new paymasters: advertisers and the literate public. New forms of electronic communication heralded the displacement of lengthy articles of personal comment with 'exclusives' and raw reports of recent events. 'Independence' and 'impartiality', as opposed to political allegiance, became the new leitmotifs of the twentieth century; political involvement, no longer a necessary 'choice', was increasingly considered 'an irrelevance or, worse, a distinct liability'.[32] Moreover, although such journalistic concepts as 'impartiality' and 'honesty' are not without historical precedent they are, for the most part, quite recent constructs of a particular form of commercial press, seeking a mass circulation to fuel its advertising revenues, while rejecting the previous model of direct political tutelage and financial support.[33]

Nevertheless, the political masters, having lost control through the cheque book, were soon to employ more subtle, and for this reason possibly more effective, forms of press manipulation. The lobby system, for example, developed in Britain during the early part of the twentieth century, became an effective mechanism for standardizing news content and controlling sources. Politicians were quick to realize that journalists, flattered by their inclusion in a select and confidential circle, could be relied on to relay, for the most part uncritically, the unattributable material with which they were fed. Although certain journalists did voice their fears that the lobby system seriously compromised their 'independence', these fears were largely ignored. In consequence, Neville Chamberlain, the British prime minister, was able ruthlessly to manipulate the press in support of his policy of appeasement during the late 1930s.[34] It was a

---

[31] Y. De la Haye (1977), 202.

[32] S. Koss (1981), 5, rather contentiously notes that it was a 'self fulfilling prophesy of the "new journalism" . . . that the newspaper-reading public, as it expanded became proportionately less politically minded'.

[33] Early avowals of impartiality can indeed be found in the British and French press of the 18th century, though their practical import was often considerably reduced by *de facto* political allegiance or the cautious and largely uncontentious nature of the papers' content. Thus the French *Mercure* was able to vaunt in 1721 *le Mercure doit être toujours neutre. . . . L'impartialité sera le premier de nos devoirs* (The *Mercure* ought always to be neutral. . . . Impartiality will be the first of our duties): C. Bellenger *et al.* (eds.) (1969), 207.

[34] R. Cockett (1989) carefully charts how the closed, establishment networks of British society proved particularly amenable to the disguised manipulation of the press by influential politicians: a manipulation which went unchallenged, if not largely unnoticed, by the press

period which was seriously to tarnish the reputation of the British press, highlighting as it does the delicate nature of press 'independence' in a world in which information is rarely unconditionally available and where the nature of those conditions may be independence itself. Nor was the British press unique in its political subservience. In France, for example, during the 1920s and 1930s certain newspapers became dependent on 'editorial advertising' and bribes, particularly from fascist organizations, precipitating a concerted campaign against left-wing policies.[35]

The development of the commercial press also highlights an enduring feature of press freedom: the guarantees wrested from governments were essentially negative assurances that the state would not restrict or censor the written word. For these guarantees to have anything other than purely symbolic meaning for those individuals wishing to express themselves in print, access to the means of production and distribution was required. As Richard Barbrook notes in his study of the French media, the right to press freedom enshrined in the 1881 legislation depended on 'the natural right of the property ownership of printing presses'.[36] Moreover, the vagaries of distribution and literacy prevented many citizens from accessing the information which the press was now disseminating. The practical import of press freedom has always varied with the financial and educational resources, geographic location, and interests of the individual concerned.[37]

To conclude, the slogan 'freedom of the press', built as it was on a largely individualist and idealist concept of the role of the printed word in society, has all too frequently appeared to be merely a manifesto call for greater liberty, a call which outpaced the slow and faltering steps towards press emancipation from direct political control. The press has, throughout its history, been subject to both political and commercial constraints. The much-vaunted legal protection from prior restraint afforded French and Italian papers in the nineteenth century appeared all too often empty rhetoric, while restrictions on the printing of 'libellous', 'seditious', or 'blasphemous' texts posed a continuous threat to outspoken criticism of the established political or religious order. The emphasis on state intervention, on removing negative restrictions rather than introducing positive entitlements, meant that the 'individual right' to self expression proved for many an empty and irrelevant slogan.

---

itself. See also W. J. West (1987), 5, who discusses a similar 'conspiracy of silence' in the radio sector in the run up to the Second World War. Thus, although popular dissatisfaction with the press at the time may have led to greater recourse to radio news as a source of information, government pressures were equally at play in the new broadcast medium.

[35] R. Barbrook (1995), 21.
[36] R. Barbrook (1995), 17.   [37] J. Keane (1991), 42.

Financial independence undoubtedly enabled an expanding capitalist press to throw off the more compromising elements of political domination, but the price of this victory may have been the drastic containment of the radical press. In particular, the commercial mass-circulation papers reflected a different philosophy of press freedom: no longer did they pretend to be vehicles of individual thought or even instruments of party propaganda; rather they were self-confessed purveyors of 'objective' information for the newly expanded electorate. To depict a paper as 'independent' or as the outward manifestation of a brute property—as opposed to ideological—right may have made the transfer of power from the political to economic sphere less threatening to the political classes, yet the political classes were quick to develop secondary lines of control. These mechanisms, working behind the press's own assertions of independence, have enabled politicians to clothe selectively furnished information with the authority of the printed word. Questions of proprietorial control and the manipulation of sources by socially 'accredited' actors are as applicable to the press of the early twentieth century as they are to the radio and television services of today. It would therefore be mistaken, faced with the rapid changes currently shaking the established audiovisual media, to seek answers from the past in a simple model of 'press freedom': no such model was ever realized.

The pressure to deregulate audiovisual industries across Western Europe has, over the last fifteen years, grown apace. 'Light touch' regulatory regimes are advocated for both established and new audiovisual services, analogies are drawn with the 'print model', and reference is made to the historic struggle against state control. To evaluate these arguments we must, therefore, have some regard to the history from which they seek to draw succour. Who were and are the real beneficiaries of the marketplace of ideas and, if state power has diminished, has it been replaced with other, perhaps more insidious, forms of censorship and control? The above discussion indicates that media 'independence' is at best a relative, at worst a misleading, goal. It is rather through addressing and working with inherent problems of dependence and access to information, problems which have been present from the inception of the printed word, that solutions to present-day issues of individual access, ownership concentration, and the control of information sources may be developed.

3. THE PRESS: A VIABLE MODEL FOR RADIO?

If the printed press had by the turn of this century made some gains regarding its political independence, a new wave of repression was signalled with the development of totalitarian regimes in Germany and Italy. The rise of Fascism in Italy and the German occupation of France in 1940 spelled a definitive end to those advances which had so recently been made. Already by 1923 Mussolini had laid the groundwork for future control of the print media, and by the beginning of 1925 virtually all opposition papers had been closed down. Official directives were regularly sent to those papers which continued a precarious existence, seeking to ensure the uniform presentation of a successful, determined nation moving forward with a minimum of crime and disorder to fulfil its Fascist destiny. These directives became gradually more specific as war approached, extending to such matters as typographical style and the portrayal of women. Even the weather did not escape: M. Cesari dryly records the instruction to 'pay attention not to dedicate too much space or make too evident Italian bad weather and storms'.[38]

In Italy, therefore, just as radio was moving from its initial experimental phase the liberal ideals of the Risorgimento were being rejected in favour of centralized conformity. With the dissolution of opposition parties in 1926 the 'free press', along with free political debate, became concepts of the past for which there was no room in the *nuova Italia*. In consequence, any functioning paradigm capable of transfer from the 'old' medium of the press to the 'new' medium of radio was not that of limited state supervision but precisely that of intrusive governmental control. Initially, however, the Fascist government was more concerned to censor undesirable news than to control the entire broadcast output as a comprehensive tool in its propaganda battle. This may have been due in part to the slow development of radio in Italy: transmitter costs and licence fees remained prohibitively high, while certain rural areas still lacked electricity. Greater access to radio was nevertheless achieved through the activities of the Ente radio rurale, set up in 1933, to spread Mussolini's message to the peasant population and encourage efficient farming methods in the 'battle of the grain'. Over 14,000 radio receivers were distributed under this scheme for communal listening in schools and rural meeting points, though their impact has been debated: with its militant and patronizing tone the fascist propaganda all too often failed to understand the pre-occupations, the enduring web of superstitions and fears, which formed the enclosed culture of the peasant class.[39] By 1937, however, control over radio was on a par

---

[38] M. Cesari (1978), 35.
[39] For a sympathetic record of peasant indifference to the Fascist microphone see C. Levi (1983); G. Richeri (1980), 49; and F. Monteleone (1976), ch. 4: *La Radiodiffusione e la politica rurale del regime*. Monteleone recounts that despite being forced to listen to Mussolini from loudspeakers set up in the village squares, the peasants took part with sceptical indifference in 'a technological ritual the cultural significance of which they did not

with that over the press. Nor did the Italian cinema provide a precedent for a 'free radio' service. It, tóo, was subject to censorship, required to comply with certain moral and cultural norms, while foreign films were allowed only restricted access to Italian cinemas to protect the national film industry.

The French story displays a rather different combination of features, for here the press enjoyed a very real degree of freedom after the 1881 legislation. Competition existed also in the radio sector with private and state services offering their own programmes, and it was only with the occupation in 1940 that both press and radio became subject to comprehensive German or, in the south, Vichy government control. In Britain a further pattern is distinguishable: here we see a private, competitive press sector existing alongside a rapidly monopolized, ultimately public, radio broadcasting industry. The BBC was, however, afforded a degree of institutional protection from intrusive governmental control through the creation of an 'independent' board of governors capable, though not always so willing, of acting as a buffer between government and the broadcasting community. Nevertheless, broadcast output remained on the whole cautious, owing to the complex interweaving of social and political pressures, with a pervasive system of internal self-censorship.[40] No simple parallel between press and radio can consequently be drawn: in Italy by the early 1920s the press was already experiencing tight restrictions, while in France the broadcasting industry long held out against monopolization.

Sooner or later, however, the private press model, with all its explanatory limitations, was to be rejected in each of the three countries as a model for the new radio sector. We have seen that the legal recognition

understand' (47). The vast cultural and geographic diversity to be found in the Italian peninsula made the task of transmitting effective, unifying propaganda intensely difficult; there was no minimum national consensus which could serve as its basis. R. Williams (1974), 265, suggests that the introduction of an accepted public-service broadcasting institution in Britain was facilitated precisely by the fact that due to an effective communications network and small geographical land mass Britain had already, to an important extent, 'nationalized' its culture.

[40] One should be cautious, however, in dismissing BBC content, particularly in the early 1930s after the lifting of the ban on controversial issues, as simply entertainment or conformist comment. Although Paddy Scannell (1984) has highlighted the almost total absence of critical comment on major political developments during 1935–9, a silence imposed against considerable BBC resistance by the Foreign Office and government, he has also investigated the notable innovation which characterized the series on unemployment 'Time to Spare' in 1934: see P. Scannell (1986). This, together with its more conventional predecessor, 'SOS', caused considerable controversy, both series being used as tools in political debate and criticism. The uproar which surrounded these innovative products of the BBC's Talks Department ultimately led to greater caution in the coverage of politically sensitive issues across the whole field of broadcast documentary and comment.

of press guarantees and the abolition of stamp duties helped facilitate, in an increasingly industrialized society, the development of popular elements within the daily press. De la Haye has suggested that the removal of legal impediments to the press sanctioned 'the rise of the press-as-commodity', while aiding 'the decline of the press-as-correspondence'.[41] But technical developments enabling speedy mass production, growing literacy among the urban population, and an expanding advertiser market were also crucial factors in the growth of the popular press. Greater scope was given to entertaining stories, crime reports, sport, and 'light news': the cheap and sensationalist elements emerging in the American press were soon to find roots in many European counterparts.[42]

It should thus cause little suprise to find that in Britain, when radio's popular potential was just beginning to be grasped, political élites were very far from seeing the mass-circulation press—so recently a pliable tool, now proclaiming itself an 'independent' observer and requiring more sensitive mechanisms of control—as a model to be emulated. Both political and cultural considerations played their part in its rejection. In the eyes of influential sectors of society the press was guilty of having squandered its educative potential in a search for vulgar appeal and sensationalism. Moreover, as an independent force linked to public opinion there were fears within establishment circles that the press could subvert the accepted political order. It was precisely at this time that ' "freedom of the press", like other freedoms since, was beginning to shed its quality of absoluteness, and "freedom for what?" became an increasingly pertinent question'.[43]

Nor was the press the only 'role model' to be rejected. Tom Burns, in his penetrating study of the BBC, indicates that that other competitive,

---

[41] Y. De la Haye (1977), 202.

[42] One of the most well-known of the American newspaper barons, William Randolph Hearst, boosted the sales figures of the *Morning Journal*, which he bought in 1895, through the use of pictures, supplements, and scare headlines. His particular brand of sensationalist journalism became known as 'yellow journalism' from a comic strip entitled 'The Yellow Kid'. In Britain Alfred Harmsworth employed similar techniques to popularize his half-penny paper, the *Star*, and subsequently the *Evening News* and *Daily Mail*, subsidized through advertising revenue to keep down the cost. By the 1930s the *Daily Herald* was even employing free gifts to entice readers. The French daily papers displayed a similar development in style, though change took place at a somewhat slower rate. Greater use was made, for example, of catchy block-capital headlines, of illustrations, and even photographs. The Italian newspaper culture, however, proved more resistant to the lure of 'Americanization'. Dario Papa, editor of the *Corriere della Sera* from 1879 to 1881, visited the USA to study the American newspaper business. On his return he started, in 1883, a new paper entitled *L'Italia*. This attempt to translate into practice the lighter, less ponderous styles of the American papers lasted only a few years in the face of fierce critical censure and hostility from the papers' own council of administration. On this see, for America, M. L. De Fleur and S. Ball-Rokeach (1982), 37; for France, J. M. Auby and R. Ducos-Ader (1976), 45, 48; C. Bellenger *et al.* (eds.) (1969), iii, 277 ff.; and, for Italy, V. Castronovo *et al.* (1979), 101 ff.

[43] T. Burns (1977), 39.

entertainment medium in private hands, film, was equally thought to pander to popular tastes and was consequently held to be 'silly and vulgar and false'.[44] But the truth is, perhaps, rather more complicated, for the film industry was given little opportunity to be anything other than mere entertainment. As in Italy, British film was subjected to extensive censorship dating back to 1909 when local authorities construed the Cinematograph Act of that year to allow them to regulate film content. This construction was undoubtedly a forced one, the Act having been primarily concerned with the physical rather than moral safety of the viewing public. Local authorities, however, gradually relinquished their censorship activities and came to accept the certificates granted by the British Board of Film Censors, a trade body set up specifically to review films in 1913. The Board concerned itself not only with questions of sexual morality and violence but with 'the power of the cinema to affect the political outlook of uneducated people',[45] the city-dwelling, working classes which flocked to the picture houses in the 1930s. By 1937 Lord Tyrell, then president of the Board, was able to say that he could 'take pride in observing that there is not a single film showing in London today which deals with any of the burning questions of the day'.[46]

A powerful mix of disdain for the flippant and a strong sense of paternalism towards the working classes led many politicians to view film as displaying, just as the press was then thought to display, dangerous tendencies towards commercial irresponsibility. This paternalism in establishment enclaves was driven not merely by a firm belief in an ordained and correct social order but from a growing fear of the power of organized labour. The perils or possibilities of the 'fourth estate' in upsetting established hierarchies and side-tracking well-worn lines of communication were clearly evident to politicians, whether of a totalitarian or democratic bent, from the very inception of sound broadcasting.[47] If the telegraph provided an easy model for the new broadcasting technologies, for many, the private press and private film industries offered, on the contrary, more by way of warning than example.

---

[44] *Ibid.* 38.
[45] N. Pronay and J. Croft 'British Film Censorship and Propaganda Policy during the Second World War', quoted in J. Petley (1986), 44.
[46] J. Petley (1986), 44.
[47] As early as 1936 28 countries, including France and Britain, signed the 'International Convention Concerning the Use of Broadcasting In the Cause of Peace' which imposed on Treaty members the obligation to ensure that stations operating within their territories did not transmit programmes inciting war against other parties or 'acts likely to lead thereto'. For details see E. W. Ploman (1982), 168.

2

The Paradigm Established:
State Control and Monopoly

> Americans tend to say that the market must be relied on because no
> government can presume to decide what is in the best interests of a
> variegated public. But Europeans rejoin that they have pinned their
> faith on the possibility of getting a better wisdom than that of the
> marketplace.[1]

The First World War created a climate in which central planning and the
distribution of basic necessities came to be seen in many quarters as
desirable. The economic crisis and depression of the late 1920s and early
1930s revealed clear limits to capitalist provision and encouraged 'widespread dissatisfaction with the ad hoc nature of industrial competition'.[2]
Concern over the press and film industries was in part symptomatic of a
wider scepticism about the efficacy of a market economy in meeting public
'needs' as opposed to more vulgar 'wants'. Economic and social considerations were thought to militate in favour of state control over those key
services essential to industrial success and individual well-being. The
telegraphic industry did not stand alone as an example of a national
industry subject to state ownership; in Britain '[f]orestry, water, and
electricity were all important public corporations set up in the years before
the BBC was even thought of'.[3]

---

[1] R. S. Homet (1979), 98, quoted in S. W. Head (1985), 134.

[2] J. Curran and J. Seaton (1991), 135. For Britain see also R. Whish (1989), 11, 63. In the
French context J. M. Auby and R. Ducos-Ader (1979), 6, note that the intervention of the
state during the depression, which could have been withdrawn with the renewal of economic
activity, 'was maintained and even reinforced as a result of the war, the modern form of which
called for an absolute control by the state over the whole of the economy'.

[3] J. Curran and J. Seaton (1991), 134. Such moves were not, however, universal and when
state intervention did take place this varied considerably from one European country to
another: CEEP (ed.) (1995), 6–12. For example, in the early years of the Fascist government
economic policy in Italy was shaped by Alberto de Stefani, a firm believer in the capacity of
private initiative, freed from rigid state control, to further Italy's economic position. Fascist
economic doctrine was predominantly liberal in outlook: private initiative was given primacy,
with state intervention considered a secondary measure, brought into play to prop up failing
private industries or where sensitive state interests were at stake. Even where state
involvement was considered necessary this came to take the form, from the 1920s onwards, of
state shareholdings in private companies.

Greater economic efficiency was expected to result from the concentration of certain fragmented industries into larger units, under state regulation. Approval of state intervention, whether through public boards or industry-specific regulations, found in the Britain of the 1930s a considerable degree of cross-party support. The concentration of the railway industry under the 1921 Railway Act, which created four main-line railway companies from a plethora of 123 different companies, can be seen as a natural precursor to the creation of the British Broadcasting Company in 1922.[4] But not only did monopolization offer a solution to the often damaging effects of inter-company competition, in the broadcast sector it provided collateral support for the growing radio and electronic industries. Indeed, Tom Burns has seen in the creation of the BBC 'a blueprint for State financing of products and services which are either essential for, or favourable towards, profitable ventures by private enterprise'.[5] It should not, therefore, be surprising to find that the British creation of a public corporation and monopolization of the radio industry was not an isolated activity; it was part of a more generalized process seen in many European countries. K. R. M. Short has noted that 'of the 30 European national broadcasting systems in existence in 1938, 13 were state-owned and operated, 9 were government monopolies operated by autonomous public bodies or partially government controlled corporations, 4 were actually operated by government but only 3 were privately owned or run'.[6]

It is tempting to argue that the willingness to place radio under state control stemmed less from a desire to restrict or contain broadcast expression than from a simple failure to recognize radio's communicative possibilities. The very novelty of radio may have blinded some to the questions of power which are now considered so obviously to be at stake. In 1932 the writer Bertold Brecht was able to state 'some inventions are made and developed that afterwards still have to conquer a market, to demonstrate their raison d'être, in a word—inventions that have not been commissioned. . . . The public was not waiting for radio, radio was waiting for the public.'[7] The Crawford Committee of 1926, an official body of enquiry into British broadcasting, noted that the British Broadcasting Company of 1922 had been formed at a time when 'broadcasting was still embryonic—regarded by many as a toy, a fantasy, even a joke'.[8] Even in

---

[4] T. R. Gourish (1986): British railways were nationalized only after the Second World War in 1948, when the toll of war-time service and road-haulage competition finally began to bite. The tendency in Europe during the 1940s to nationalize key infrastructure industries was not matched in the USA where these industries were left in private hands under the supervision of industry-specific regulatory bodies. These bodies sought to control competition and create stability through the introduction of price and entry restrictions. See R. B. Horwitz (1989).   [5] T. Burns (1977), 11.   [6] K. R. M. Short (1983), 30.
[7] Quoted in M. Jenke (1984), 33.   [8] Crawford Report (1926).

America where free speech was afforded constitutional protection 'few people saw radio, in 1927, as an important source of news and opinion, or as part of the 'press' contemplated by the First Amendment'.[9]

Furthermore, in the early days of popular radio, broadcasting was first and foremost—as it continues to be today—an entertainment medium. Indeed, in the pioneering era 'entertainment' appears to have been derived more from the excitement of building and running a functioning radio set than from the quality of the messages received as the enthusiasts, equipped with the requisite headphones, sought to catch what signals they could from the air.[10] Early radio services undoubtedly offered a large proportion of music and light-entertainment programmes. In 1938 music accounted for 69 per cent of French national broadcast time, 72 per cent at the regional level, while in Italy music of all types accounted for something over half internal broadcasting hours by the end of the 1930s. It may be of some surprise to read that a similar musical predominance prevailed in Britain where, by 1934, the BBC was broadcasting 'more light music, comedy, and vaudeville than any other European station'.[11] Those arguments deployed to combat state censorship in the press context, emphasizing the benefits to be derived from a free exchange of political opinions, may consequently have seemed strangely inappropriate for a medium so firmly rooted in popular music and entertainment.

It is possible, then, that few strong negative reasons were considered to militate against state monopolization while a whole range of factors were recognized as pushing for its adoption. Thus monopolization appeased the suspicious military and postal lobbies, kept certain private actors—particularly the much-resented Marconi company—in check,[12] was argued to prevent the 'chaos of the airwaves', endemic to early American broadcasting,[13] and ensured a popular service which would boost the sales of,

---

[9] B. M. Owen (1975), 89. R. B. Horwitz (1989), 120, disputes the suggestion that scarcity was the real spur to broadcast regulation in the USA, arguing rather that it was the result of the commercial broadcasters' inability to 'establish workable arrangements for market behaviour'. The First Amendment was not considered a bar to this approach since 'radio, like motion pictures, was not really considered part of the press. In three associated cases in 1915, the Supreme Court upheld the right of states to engage in censorship of motion pictures.'

[10] L. Johnson (1981), R. Cathcart (1984), 2. On the Italian situation, F. Monteleone (1976), 39, notes that the 'interest in the technical aspects of radio clearly prevailed over the content of the programmes'.

[11] J. Curran and J. Seaton (1991), 139.

[12] Both the British government and the Post Office were suspicious of the Marconi company and its imperialist ambitions: opening the market to industry competition could have led to its domination by this one company. The risk was defused by ensuring that Marconi was just one of the 6 companies chosen to form the British Broadcasting Company in 1922. Similar suspicions existed in America and Italy.

[13] It should, however, be noted that this 'chaos' did not occur until mid-1926, prompted by the court decision in *US* v. *Zenith Radio Corporation*, 12 F 2d 614, on which see T. W.

preferably, national wireless sets. The British compromise also absolved the national government from direct responsibility for popular entertainment programming—not an activity with which it, or many other governments, would have wished to be closely associated in the early years of the century. For these reasons both listeners and the wireless industry tended to welcome regulation as in their own interests.

But the various preferences for monopolization, state control, and state ownership cannot be seen as altogether so benign and accommodating as the preceding discussion might lead one to believe. If, for the majority of the listening public, the introduction of a national service, sending a clear signal, free from competitive interference, was something to be welcomed without pondering unduly over any consequent loss of 'choice' or 'free speech rights', for the politicians the impact of radio was apparent from its inception. How else can we explain the strict controls over political programming which characterized the regulatory structures adopted in many European countries?[14] Radio was for the most part politically uncontentious simply because, just as for film, it was required to be so. Rex Cathcart, speaking of the early BBC radio service in Northern Ireland, argues that the broadcaster's primary purpose was to entertain: '[t]he programmes might attempt to improve the audience, they certainly were never meant to disturb it. Controversy and the controversial were strictly banned'.[15] The division between those who saw radio as a medium of political influence and those who saw it as a form of light entertainment thus separated those who *legislated for* or regulated the medium on the one hand from those who *listened to* the regulated product on the other.

The early regulation of British broadcasting displays considerable political anxiety over radio's persuasive potential. Indeed, Curran and Seaton go so far as to suggest that the BBC was founded on 'a rejection of politics'.[16] Until the General Strike of 1926, when it was forced to prepare its own reports on the national crisis, the BBC had relied on agency material for its news bulletins under pressure from a hostile press fearful of radio's competitive potential. In the same year the Postmaster General had given the BBC wide-ranging instructions not to 'broadcast on matters of

Hazlett (1990), 147. The questions of spectrum interference and spectrum allocation are, as Hazlett is at pains to point out, quite distinct. Just as central regulation and licence limitation were not strictly required in America, so monopoly was not necessitated in Europe to prevent signal interference. It was part of a wider political and industrial compromise.

[14] In the American context T. W. Hazlett (1990) skilfully argues that the 'private, legally-enforced rights option' was rejected by the political sphere, anxious to retain ultimate control through a regulatory system which extracted non-pecuniary public-interest rents. It should thus cause little suprise that these rents ultimately included 'the avoidance of broadcasting content offensive to the political party in power'.

[15] R. Cathcart (1984), 2.

[16] J. Curran and J. Seaton (1991), 136.

political, industrial or religious controversy'; furthermore it was to refrain from broadcasting 'any opinion of its own on matters of public policy'.[17] The ban on broadcasting on matters of controversy was finally lifted in 1928, presaging a period of greater experimentation, particularly by the BBC's Talks Department.[18]

Ironically, it was government involvement in broadcasting, precipitating calls from other political parties for air-time, which made the general perception of broadcasting as inherently insulated from politics increasingly implausible. An interesting, already touched-on, parallel may here be drawn between the British government's control of the press and its response to radio during the late 1920s and 1930s: just as the lobby system and 'old boy network' had been used to muzzle press criticism of international policy, so covert political pressure was used to keep radio coverage in check. Through a careful mix of flattery and threats the Foreign Office established the practice of vetting programmes before transmission and the BBC repeatedly showed itself unwilling to reveal to its audience the true nature of this control, preferring to explain away changed schedules by the 'delicacy of the international situation' or the 'undesirability' of the programme in point. W. J. West, in his excellent examination of early news coverage by the BBC, concludes that 'the BBC's alleged independence from Government supervision was a myth—widely propagated and, indeed, firmly believed in by many employees at all levels in the BBC from that day to this, but a myth none the less'.[19]

During the course of the 1930s it became increasingly impossible for politicians and public alike to ignore the political impact of broadcasting. Radio coverage of controversial political matters was certainly not unknown: as early as 1924 political parties in the United States had bought air-time and, in the presidential elections of 1928, the Republican and Democratic parties together spent over one million dollars on radio publicity. Radio's more sinister propaganda potential was also beginning to be revealed, as the medium increasingly came to be employed in precipitating unrest in a number of unstable European countries. In 1930 one of the first 'radio wars' broke out between Poland and Germany, and radio was used repeatedly to foment tensions during the Spanish Civil War. So serious a threat was radio considered to be that by the end of the Spanish Civil War a total ban on reception had been imposed. Aware of such manipulation, other governments moved to contain and control the

---

[17] T. Burns (1977), 16.

[18] D. Cardiff (1986), 233, 245; P. Scannell (1986), 214. On those occasions where social conditions were brought into question, broadcasters quickly retreated under political and social pressure to develop alternative formats and styles of reporting to protect them from further criticism.   [19] W. J. West (1987), 56.

new medium, action which came to be regarded as imperative with the cataclysmic slide into the Second World War.

If the moves towards monopolization of the broadcasting industry in the 1920s and 1930s were largely uni-directional, though somewhat piecemeal, the experiences of the Second World War consolidated the trend and confirmed for governments radio's potential as a powerful medium of mass communication. The desire to prevent radio from slipping into hostile hands led to close state supervision, while the techniques of white and black propaganda reached new levels of refinement, building on the comparatively crude experiments of the First World War.[20] Dr Goebbels, head of the German Ministry of Propaganda, was quick to see the potential of the new audiovisual media. Ahead of his time, he predicted that television might even supplant the then thriving film industry. Through the wide-scale introduction of cheap 'peoples' sets' and 'little radios' (designed to receive only local, 'official' broadcasts) and the imposition of draconian penalties for those who listened to foreign radio broadcasts or disseminated the messages contained therein (penalties ranging from penal servitude to death), Goebbels was able to cut the vast mass of German citizens off from foreign broadcasts, while ensuring continuous exposure to Nazi propaganda, carefully interspersed among more popular programming.

National governments, having seen the impact of radio in time of war, were reluctant to loosen their grip on such a useful instrument in time of peace. This reluctance could only have been confirmed by the daunting nature of the task of post-war reconstruction. Radio was an attractive tool to appropriate in the new battle, not only to reforge a sense of national pride, but to encourage citizens to work together to rebuild the structures of their broken cities and the very fabric of social relations, torn apart in the years of fear and collaboration. Within Europe the prestige and authority of the BBC ran high as a result of its war-time activities: Italians had listened clandestinely and in large numbers to 'Radio Londra',[21] while Général de Gaulle had spoken directly to the French people through a BBC microphone. Many regarded the British public-broadcasting monopoly, with its mission to 'inform, educate and entertain', a model to be emulated, thereby rejecting the system of American competitive broadcasting, centred on the sale of advertising time.[22]

Moreover, the scale of the destruction suffered by certain national radio networks was extensive. During the final stages of German resistance in Italy the majority of radio transmitters had been moved to the north and, by the time of their final retreat, the national network had been almost

---

[20] On this see, *inter alia*, A. Rhodes (1976); F. Monteleone (1976), 146 ff.; and D. S. A. Weidenfeld (1942), 272. [21] F. Monteleone (1976), 168 ff.

[22] R. Barberio and C. Macchitella (1989), 19, 23.

completely destroyed. In France, too, transmitters were methodically deactivated as the German forces retreated or were damaged in the fierce battles for their control. By the end of the war radio technicians could utilize only 6 per cent of the transmitter power previously available. Such devastation called for sizeable investment at a time of financial stringency, and a unified industrial approach, whether by private or state enterprise, probably seemed the only way to ensure the overall restoration of the radio infrastructure.

The widespread preference for the public option and consolidation of state monopolies was also encouraged by a general suspicion of private capital. In both France and Italy the parties of the left, particularly the Communist Party which found representation in the immediate post-war governments, were anxious to contain the influence of private capital. In particular, they sought to prevent the formation of powerful private monopolies or cartels, capable of using their financial influence to subvert the policies of parliament itself. In Italy the liberal movement, pressing for the careful containment of state intervention in the industrial sector, found itself ranged not only against the parties of the left but also against the Catholic Corporatists. The Corporatists, with their ambivalent, essentially functional, attitude to private capital, had been influenced by the Catholic Church's 'denunciation of monopolies, of "economic imperialism" and the trends towards "economic hegemony" '.[23] In France, private radio's history of collaboration with the Vichy regime led to early recission of all private licences, and it was generally felt that 'state supervision, far from being repressive, was the only way to guarantee freedom from the more dangerous control of commercial interests'.[24]

Given this history of governmental control of the audiovisual sector, it should cause little suprise that neither the French Constitution of 1946 nor the Italian Constitution of 1948 specifically places broadcasting in the protected domain afforded the printed press. This is in contrast to the direct reference to broadcasting and film contained in Article 5 of the post-war German constitution. In Germany the Allies sought to prevent any future appropriation of the mass media by political factions, establishing broadcast models structurally independent from the state. In addition a representative system, giving voice to many of the political and social groups found in German society, was built into the governing constitutions of the public-broadcasting organizations. This eagerness to ensure

---

[23] D. Sassoon (1986), 205. On this see also F. Galgano and S. Rodotà (1982), 34. P. Scoppola (1980), 78, suggests that the willingness of certain sectors of the Catholic community to work with the parties of the left was born out of a 'quite critical assessment of capitalism, inherited from the Catholic culture of the thirties and reinforced by the experiences of the war'.   [24] R. Thomas (1976), 5.

democratic representation and accountability in a defeated country contrasts rather starkly with the alacrity with which many European governments sought to control their own national broadcast media after the war.[25]

Stanley Ingber has suggested that the absence of a historical tradition of 'freedom' in the American audiovisual context led the Supreme Court to allow close regulation of the broadcast media by the Federal Communications Commission, while proscribing numerous restrictions on the press as unconstitutional: '[b]ecause electronic media are relatively young and have always been subject to some governmental control, there is no tradition of freedom to overcome and there is thus less appearance of illegitimate governmental action'.[26] Certainly such freedom is absent when we look to the history of Italian broadcasting. It may thus cause little suprise that the Italian Constituent Assembly, established in 1946 to draw up the terms of the new constitution, paid limited attention to television and the broadcasting media. On the contrary, it was the press, beaten into submission under Fascism and with at least some claims to prior 'freedom', which proved the focus of attention. A reading of Article 1 of the 1948 Constitution reveals that its primary concern is to provide specific guarantees for the protection of the printed press. For radio and cinema sensitivities seemed to pull, if anything, in the other direction, with calls for the introduction of specific *controls* for the protection of the public. It was argued that this was necessitated by the diverse technological bases of such media and their alleged capacity to 'impose' themselves on the passive public. This intrusive characteristic was contrasted with that of the press, whose message, so it was claimed, had to be actively sought out by the consequently better prepared consumer.[27] No such specific regime was established within the 1946 Constitution, however, and the audiovisual media consequently fall within the generalized protection offered by the first paragraph of Article 21, which provides that 'everyone has the right freely to manifest their own thoughts in words, writing and through *every other means of diffusion*'.

Fears of private monopolization of a still technically limited, but deemed politically influential, industry may have encouraged Catholic and Communist members of the Assembly to turn a blind eye to the constitutional position of radio. Moreover, at the institution of the Constituent Assembly in 1946, prior, that is, to the commencement of the Cold War in 1947 and the breakdown of the tri-partite government coalition, the future political make-up of the country remained uncertain. The Communist Party had gained widespread support for its courageous

---

[25] A. Williams (1976) and E. Etzioni-Halevy (1987).
[26] S. Ingber (1984), 60.   [27] R. Zaccaria (1977).

resistance during the Fascist regime, while Russia continued to enjoy an afterglow of appreciation for its heavy sacrifices in ensuring Germany's ultimate defeat. It was not beyond the bounds of all imagination that the political left could come to share in some of the spoils currently and assiduously being prepared by the Christian Democratic forces. Spoils which included the national broadcasting system, for, by the second half of 1946, the Christian Democrats had already gained control of the radio services. In November 1947 they facilitated political supervision by centralizing the organization of radio broadcasting at Rome, dismantling the system of decentralized stations set up by the instructively-named Allied Psychological Warfare Branch after the liberation.[28]

In consequence, at least one powerful faction within the Assembly had little reason to press for constitutional guarantees which might require alterations to the then politically unbalanced organization of the radio sector. After the war the government continued to enjoy a legal right of access to the national service of up to two hours daily to broadcast news of public interest, and it had at its disposal various mechanisms for controlling programme policy. The Minister of the Interior was, for example, empowered to alter for reasons of *ordine pubblico* the broadcast plan and timetable, previously submitted for approval by the chosen concessionary to a special postal commission. Such extensive powers led one liberal Assembly member to raise the issue of executive control when he complained that radio was effectively 'in the hands of the government', but his complaint fell on unreceptive, and consequently deaf, ears.

In the immediate post-war period the basic legal framework of radio broadcasting in Italy underwent little alteration. The name of the concessionary was changed from EIAR to Radio Audizioni Italia, with the new acronym RAI, but the old concession of 1927 was allowed to live out its time until 1952, and many of the old staff, journalists, and technicians stayed on with the company. The prior system of political direction continued virtually unchallenged from the dark days of Fascism. If the possibility of greater democratization had been signalled by the creation in 1947 of two new radio supervisory bodies (one of which, the Parliamentary Commission, was entrusted with the task of ensuring the political independence and objectivity of radio broadcasts) its realization remained distinctly distant given the restricted, solely advisory powers of the two bodies concerned.[29] The new concession of 1952 was to reconfirm the existing government hegemony in the broadcast sector, perpetuating its

[28] See F. Monteleone (1976), 230: 'the campaign in favour of monopoly which developed in the press and political circles was solely directed at the maintenance of the 'Christian Democratic monopoly' of radio information'.

[29] Decreto-Legge. C.P.S. 3 Apr. 1947, n. 428, in S. Fois and A. Vignudelli (1986), 1693.

right to air-time and to approve the three monthly programme plans, but went further to extend its powers of approval to the appointment not only of the president and managing director but also the director general. Public control over RAI was entrenched by the requirement, in Article 3 of the concession, that the majority of the company's shares be held exclusively by the state holding company, the Istituto Ricostruzione Industriale (IRI). This legislative picture was to continue until the mid-1970s when the activity of the Italian Constitutional Court rendered the status quo no longer a viable option.

In 1954 RAI commenced regular television broadcasts—the state monopoly expanding to embrace television—but the service was slow to take off, for, given the need for heavy post-war reconstruction, the emphasis was very much on the production of primary goods, while television was considered merely an expensive luxury for an élite few. Nor did the new medium immediately establish its own distinct style for, relying heavily on existing cultural forms, its programmes were frequently productions of famous plays or classical concerts. Gradually, however, television began to establish a unique voice, experimenting with popular adaptations of novels, with game and variety shows, consolidating as it did so a new audience and a new form of leisure activity.

Government interest was at first limited to the coverage of news and current affairs: Christian Democrat officials obtained extensive and favourable air-time, while the opposition were neither seen nor heard. News programmes reflected the government's own equation of both state and society with Christian Democracy; those trends which ran counter to Christian Democracy ran counter also to the state, and in consequence could find no place within the state broadcast service. Television was seen as an 'undertaking structured and directed to the attainment of political rather than economic profit, closed to the outside world and completely directed to bolstering the interests and needs of the government majority (or perhaps it would be more correct to say the party of relative majority)'.[30] For the most part, however, the government took little interest in the general content and nature of RAI schedules, though producers were careful to avoid offending the predominant Catholic morality.[31]

It was only with the advent of Ettore Bernabei, appointed Director General in 1961, that an attempt was made to orient the whole range of scheduled programmes to reflect Christian Democratic ideology. Bernabei

---

[30] R. Barberio and C. Macchitella (1989), 31.
[31] For an overview of the development of Italian television see: S. Balassone and A. Guglielmi (1983); C. de Gourney, *et al.* (1985); H. J. Kleinsteuber, *et al.* (1986), 171 ff.; F. Pinto (1980); D. Sassoon (1986); and L. Quartermaine (1987).

continued to believe in the legitimacy of employing the broadcast media for political profit, but a more sophisticated assessment of its capabilities led him to reject the blatant political appropriation of the past. Against considerable opposition from the established cadres, he opened television up to wider-ranging debate and discussion, allowing professional broadcasters greater personal autonomy. Nevertheless, Bernabei was careful to retain as the anchor to all discussion a bed-rock of Christian Democratic values, whose very centrality was endorsed even when exposed to searching examination.[32] Though Catholic hegemony was reaffirmed in a less obtrusive fashion, the dead weight of an ever expanding pay-roll, designed to silence criticism from the intellectual and professional classes, ultimately drained important resources away from production and devalued the service in the eyes of the public. It was this public dissatisfaction, coupled with the lure of advertising revenue, which encouraged the establishment of 'pirate' radio and television stations during the course of the 1970s and ultimately recourse to the Consitutional Court to challenge the state monopoly.

In Britain the BBC maintained its monopoly status until the mid-1950s in the television sector and the early 1970s in radio. The first commercial television channel was introduced in 1954 in the face of considerable opposition. There were widespread, and often strongly expressed, fears that recourse to advertising revenue would cheapen and trivialize a venerable social institution.[33] In part to win over this opposition, the new independent television service was subjected to many of the public-service obligations the BBC had traditionally sought to fulfil. Thus, although the British system has historically centred around one commercial and one public pole, it has in a very real sense been unified under a common set of aspirations and goals. The commercial sector did, however, run into criticism in the early years of its life, and the 1962 Pilkington Report lambasted ITV for failing 'to live up to its public responsibilities'.[34] Largely as a consequence of these criticisms the third television channel was awarded to the BBC and began transmission as BBC2 in 1964. This was intended to offer alternative and more demanding programming to that generally available on the existing channels, and as such proved the precursor to the highly innovative, though structurally disparate, fourth channel.

The television landscape remained for the most part unchanged until the early 1980s, although in the programme field the 1960s marked something of a renaissance for the BBC, under the director generalship of Hugh Greene. Greene fostered within the BBC a number of young, and at times

---

[32] P. Martini (1990), 8, 9; more generally see F. Pinto (1980).
[33] B. Sendall (1982), i.　　　　　　[34] Pilkington Report (1962).

anarchic, writers and actors, encouraging a fresh and challenging approach to broadcasting, particularly in current affairs. By the 1970s the cyclical re-examination of the existing order was once again under way, with a new committee, under the chairmanship of Noel Annan, called to examine the future of British broadcasting.[35] The committee's report, when it was published in 1977, marked a break with the paternalism of the past, in its advocation of a plural system free from the domination and preoccupations of an élite few. A call was made for greater attention to be paid to the cultural diversity within Britain, in that 'broadcasting should cater for the full range of groups and interests in society, rather than seek to offer moral leadership'. After considerable debate, both inside and outside Parliament, Channel 4 was finally inaugurated in 1982 with a remit to provide alternative programming 'not covered by the ITV network'.[36] The new channel was to receive financial assistance from the IBA, obtained through 'subscription' payments made by the ITV companies. The ITV companies were in turn to recoup at least a proportion of this loss through the sale of the channel's spot-advertising time, a system overhauled by the 1990 Broadcasting Act, which gave Channel 4 responsibility for the sale of its own advertising time. Channel 4 was set up to be structurally distinct in design from all previous British channels: as a commissioning, rather than production, company it has played an important role in stimulating the development of an independent production sector in Britain.

Channel 4 was not the only television child of the 1980s; also in evidence was the slow development of lightly-regulated cable services, heavily dependent on existing programming, and the introduction of direct-to-home satellite. The fierce and mutually debilitating competition between the Sky and BSB satellite services led to the merger of the two operations in the autumn of 1990 to form BSkyB. Britain has thus moved gradually, though at an ever-accelerating pace, towards a multi-medium, multi-channel environment. The 1990 Broadcasting Act was designed to increase competition and made provision for the introduction of a new commercial television channel, Channel Five, the franchise being awarded to Channel 5 Broadcasting in 1995. Many of the traditional public-service objectives received recognition in the 1990 Act, but their implementation is now monitored retroactively: primary responsibility for their realization rests with the licensed companies themselves. Provision for the introduction of digital terrestrial broadcasting was made in the 1996 Broadcasting Act.

In comparison to their Italian and French counterparts, British television stations have remained remarkably free from direct political interference and their claims to independence deserve recognition. Nevertheless, the discovery that BBC employees had been regularly vetted by MI5, the

[35] Annan Report (1977).   [36] D. Docherty *et al.* (1988).

British secret service, and the direct request by then Home Secretary, Leon Brittan, in 1985 to the BBC not to broadcast a documentary programme 'At the Edge of the Union' on Northern Ireland, indicate that this independence rests on shaky foundations. Moreover, British television stations have taken care to avoid direct confrontation with powerful political groups, air-time being balanced between the major parties and their representatives in interviews or debates. Factions within society which command little or no parliamentary representation have to date found it difficult to obtain coverage for their views. Increasing criticism from the political right during the 1980s over, for example, television coverage of the 1982 Falklands War, indicate that the political and broadcasting spheres do not see eye to eye on the boundaries of media independence.[37] From a more sinister perspective such criticism may be seen as a far-reaching and concerted attempt to 'chill out' controversial investigative reporting.

The development of broadcasting in post-war France is much closer to that of its Italian counterpart. No specific provision for the mass media was included in the preamble to the French Constitution of 1946, although a reference back was made to the 1789 Declaration of the Rights of Man, Article 11 of which affirms the freedom of the printed press and, more generally, speech. This may in part have been due to the pervasive, and what has proved to be enduring, view in French political circles that the broadcast media justifiably fall within the government's sphere of influence as direct representative, through the elective process, of 'the people'. There could be no gap between the 'public interest' and that of the government for the audiovisual media under government control served to convey to the public the authoritative 'voice of France'.[38] Further application of the same representative logic conveniently served to exclude all opposition comment.

Those on the French political left were slow to criticize the nature of the public monopoly—a monopoly which eventually extended to the programming and transmission of both radio and television services—hoping that they too would be able to enjoy similar spoils on being returned to power.[39] For this the wait was longer than they had anticipated, and by 1981, the year of the socialist victory, public expectations and technological possibilities had undergone a major metamorphosis. Thus François Mitterand who, in 1982, was to interpose an 'independent' regulatory

---

[37] P. Walters (1989).

[38] It was President Pompidou who in 1970 stated that the broadcast media represented the 'voice of France', noted in J. E. S. Hayward (1983), 164. The parallels between the approaches of the Italian and French governments are here obvious.

[39] R. Barberio and C. Macchitella (1989), 31.

agency between government and broadcasters had, as Minister of Information in the Cold War period of the Fourth Republic, attempted to purge French radio of its Communist staff. But his interest then extended well beyond the political matrix of broadcast employees: close political supervision was maintained over all news programmes through regular liaison between his *chef de cabinet* and the head of news broadcasting.[40]

The post-war French government, like its Italian counterpart, was quick to usurp control of the audiovisual sector, though the continual change of government which characterized the Fourth Republic hampered for a while the long-term incursion of any one party. It was only with the constitutional reforms of 1958, initiated by Général Charles de Gaulle, and the creation of a strong executive enjoying majority status that control shifted from 'negative' requests not to programme certain potentially contentious items to 'positive' governmental direction of the entire broadcast message. The introduction of specific constitutional guarantees for the broadcast media, whether in the 1946 or 1958 Constitutions, would thus have run counter both to widespread political aspirations and the concrete reality of government control.

French television, in the immediate aftermath of the war, was no exception in being widely considered an economic luxury, and its growth was slow. Regular broadcasts commenced in 1948, but it was only in 1958 that the number of people paying the television licence fee reached the one million mark. The mix of educational aspirations and governmental control encouraged many French people to tune in to alternative commercial radio stations such as Radio Luxembourg, broadcast into France from abroad. Gradually, however, these too came under governmental control as shares in the *radios périphériques* were bought up by nationalized French radio and advertising companies. The introduction of limited advertising in 1968 to supplement the licence fee encouraged transmission of more popular entertainment programmes, but political control remained unwavering during the presidency of Charles de Gaulle. In 1974 President Giscard d'Estaing attempted to create an element of internal competition within the state system by breaking up the national broadcasting organization, the Office de Radiodiffusion-Télévision Française (ORTF), into seven separate companies: the three television stations TF1, Antenne 2, and FR3 were now to compete against each other for audience share. State ownership was, however, to remain the dominant model for the French broadcasting media until the Socialist victory in the 1981 elections.

State appropriation of the broadcast media may also have been facilitated by a not uncommon attitude among intellectuals that television was, at best, a culturally moribund medium, at worst, a medium deeply

[40] J. E. S. Hayward (1983), 164.

destructive of other cultural forms and communications.[41] Critics of the
accepted social order looked to film and not television as their vehicle for
enlightenment, finding resonance in the films of the Italian neo-realists or
the British art cinema. Consequently those very people who might have
struggled to change television from within chose, for the most part, to
reject, if not vilify, its message from without. It was here that the
willingness of the Catholic Church and its political allies to attempt to
create not only a 'cinema for every belfry' but a channel for Christian
morality in every home through the humble television or radio receiver
gave them a distinctive advantage over their opponents. With such
effective voices as there were within the major broadcasting institutions
crushed or outnumbered, it was left to the commercial pirates and the
politically committed 'free radios' to point the way to a new broadcasting
order.

[41] J. Caughie, 'Broadcasting and Cinema. 1. Converging Histories', in C. Barr (1986), 189.
See also L. Quartermaine (1987), 9 ff.; R. Barberio and C. Macchitella (1989), 25.

3

The Paradigm Challenged: Regulatory Options for an Expanding Market

What we have charted so far is a half century in which first radio, then television, became dominated by the political and professional spheres: circumscribed by state control and shielded from commercial competition. Yet for a considerable period of time this division of spoils received remarkably little opposition from the vast mass of broadcasters or, indeed, from the consuming public. Why was this? Clearly, those employed within the public sector had a prudential interest in its survival and protection from destabilizing competition. Any critical impulse would have been tempered by the fear of losing one's job or stalled promotion prospects. For the audience, it is probable that initially many listeners were generally satisfied with what was available—the music, the entertainment, the sport—on the public channels, and for those who were not, commercial alternatives, such as Radio Luxembourg, broadcast from abroad, could be sought out.[1] But a central element underlying the widespread acceptance of state broadcasting monopolies in Western Europe after the Second World War was undoubtedly the concept of public-service broadcasting: a legitimating philosophy which the proponents of greater commercial competition have targeted tenaciously.

Although the term 'public-service broadcasting' has historically been linked to public ownership of domestic broadcast stations, it is increasingly used to refer to a distinct set of programming and technical standards rather than a particular system of media ownership. As dissatisfaction with government influence over the broadcast media hardened and commercial operators pressed ever more forcefully for access, both public ownership and public-service broadcasting objectives came to be challenged. Moreover, with satellite and cable technology offering a solution to the constraints imposed by spectrum shortage, the press model of a competitive, lightly regulated, market was put forward as a viable alternative to existing

---

[1] Radio Luxembourg was broadcast from one of the most powerful transmitters in Europe. Relying heavily on American advertising revenues, it proved during the 1930s a popular alternative to the non-commercial BBC. See E. Barnouw (1983), 192.

forms of radio and television regulation. It was consequently against a background of growing crisis in the public sector that European courts became drawn into the battle to open up established broadcasting systems to private enterprise.

The arguments for and against change, both within and outside the courts, have frequently been framed in terms of a choice between 'public-service' and 'free-market' models. Before we turn to examine the extent to which one or other of these models has received judicial endorsement it will be helpful to consider whether such a dichotomy is a useful one and the extent to which regulatory options have been affected by social and technological change. Such an exploration continues to be of relevance today, for, as additional audiovisual services are developed, decisions are having to be made about whether some or all of the established public-service requirements should be extended into these new areas or whether competition law, coupled with minimal regulation of such sensitive matters as obscenity and defamation, is sufficient.

1. PUBLIC-SERVICE BROADCASTING: VARIATIONS ON A THEME

The isolation of radio and then television from the field of commercial competition was quickly justified by the 'restricted' number of available frequencies. As we have seen, however, the consolidation of the broadcast media in the public sector went well beyond what was strictly necessitated by spectrum shortage and was in reality prompted by distinct industrial and political concerns. If state broadcasters were more blatantly employed for political profit by the governing parties in France and Italy than they were in Britain, the hierarchical command structure of the BBC has on occasion undoubtedly been used to shield the government of the day from adverse investigation or intemperate comment. Despite political concern at the power of the mass media to influence public opinion, the day-to-day running of radio and television stations was by and large left to a new professional cadre which sought legitimation for its position in the public-service ideal of informing, educating, and entertaining its audience. For these professionals broadcasting was definitely not a simple marketable product, to be left to the forces of demand and supply, it was instead a vehicle for public enlightenment, allied more to the world of state education or public libraries than to other forms of popular entertainment. The public-service model was thus an attractive regulatory option for the three main protagonists of the consumption triangle thereby created: the state was able to maintain a degree of control over a potentially threatening medium of communication, broadcasters were elevated from the level of mere commercial entertainers to professionals with a social mission, while the public gained access to new forms of information and entertainment.

The early development of the theory of public-service broadcasting in Britain owed much to the evangelical leadership of John Reith, managing director of the British Broadcasting Company and subsequently Director General of the British Broadcasting Corporation (the BBC) when it was formed in 1927. The son of a Scottish Calvinist minister, fired with a sense of moral purpose and an enduring religious conviction, Reith rejected the commercial models of the day to create a service which was 'moral in the broadest sense—intellectual and ethical; with determination that the greatest benefit possible would accrue from its output'.[2] Central to Reith's scheme was the 'brute force' of monopoly: only by limiting audience choice could Reith aspire to introduce the public to a range of ideas and musical types which were alien or even disturbing.[3] It was a paternalism encapsulated in the famous statement '[i]t is occasionally indicated to us that we are apparently setting out to give the public what we think they need and not what they want—but few know what they want and very few what they need'.[4]

The BBC philosophy was widely emulated by other broadcast services after the Second World War and has continued to find reflection in programme policies and regulatory aspirations, if not always regulatory realities, across Europe. But the concept of public-service broadcasting has not remained static, immune to the political and cultural changes of the last fifty years. The post-war increase in living standards and literacy led to a new spirit of individual advancement and optimism. The popular assertions of cultural diversity in the 1960s and early 1970s challenged the traditional arbiters of accepted taste to justify their position and found the answers wanting. If individuals were free to choose among the growing number of consumer goods which filled the shops, were free even to elect governments, should they not also be free to choose the radio or television programmes with which to occupy their expanding leisure hours? Indeed, the public were not slow to vote against the established radio channels by tuning in to popular music 'pirates' such as Radio Caroline, or the political stations which sprang up in France and Italy in defiance of the strict government controls over the audiovisual media. These alternative stations outflanked the established public-service channels, accustoming the public to an expanding choice of programmes. No longer could Reith's dream of an 'ethical' broadcast service be founded on the 'brute force of monopoly'.

---

[2] Quoted in A. Smith (1989), 10. See also F. Gillard (1989); S. Hood (1989); and R. Milner (1983).
[3] David Cardiff has argued that the development of 'middlebrow humour' was in part an attempt to assuage the anxieties caused by new and challenging programme types by debunking them: D. Cardiff (1988). [4] Quoted in T. Burns (1977), 6.

Attempts were made to defuse criticism by a reformulation of the public-service concept. In Britain the early paternalism gave way in the 1977 Annan Report to a new pluralist ethic, and Channel 4, the fourth national television station, was introduced in 1982 with a remit to provide alternative programming, not offered by the ITV network. This reflected a more general move across Europe to increase the number of public-service channels and widen the range of programmes on offer. But these changes did little to diminish the growing dissatisfaction with what were widely considered stuffy and out-of-touch institutions. It is instructive that the popular nickname coined for the BBC was 'Auntie', conjuring up the image of a benign but rather staid institution.

Despite the evolution of the public-service concept over time it is nevertheless possible to draw from the mass of regulatory provisions, government reports, and professional and academic pronouncements five constitutive elements which have found a wide measure of recognition:[5]

(a) The provision of broadcasting services on a *universal basis* within the national territory, receivable regardless of place of residence or social status.

(b) The fostering of *national, regional, and community identity*.

(c) *Editorial independence* from powerful vested interests, whether commercial or governmental.

(d) The provision of a *wide and diverse range of entertainment, educational, and informational programmes*, catering for minority as well as popular interests.

(e) *Accurate and responsible reporting* of the news and other information, a provision variously formulated to require either 'balanced' or 'objective' reporting.

Not every commentator would agree on all of these criteria and many would add further stipulations: a high quality of service measured in terms of technical excellence, creativity, and originality, for example, or patronage of the arts, and the commissioning or production of new broadcast works. Others, such as Paddy Scannell, prefer to emphasize only a couple of key characteristics: the provision of a mixed programme service on national channels available to all.[6] Nevertheless, the above criteria reflect the main elements which, over the last fifteen years, have been considered to characterize public-service broadcasting. It is important to note that these criteria are essentially concerned with setting normative

---

[5] There is an extensive literature on the public-service broadcasting concept, and the following texts have proved of considerable assistance: J. G. Blumler *et al.* (1986), 355; Broadcasting Research Unit (1988); J. C. Burgelman (1986), 199; J. Curran and J. Seaton (1991), 295; W. Hoffman-Riem (1986), 126; C. MacCabe and O. Stewart (eds.) (1986); V. Porter (1993); and P. Scannell (1989).   [6] P. Scannell (1989).

goals, and do not themselves mandate any particular ownership structure. The history of the British ITV network, composed of private companies broadcasting under tight regulatory supervision, indicates, for example, that a 'public service' on the lines set out above, can, in certain contexts, be provided by commercial companies operating for profit. To speak of *a* 'public-service model' is, therefore, misleading: not only may there be disagreement on the objectives to be attained, there may also be a number of different regulatory techniques or broadcast structures which can be deployed to realize those objectives which have been selected.

During the 1980s and early 1990s the public-broadcasting sector, like many other public services, came under increasing pressure. The attacks took two main forms. The first involved criticism of the public-service objectives themselves, considered by many to be outmoded, paternalistic, or simply misguided. How, for example, could the requirement to foster national identity be squared with the need to report objectively, and was it realistic to attempt to identify and then promote a sense of national identity in diverse western societies? The second criticized the regulatory strategies adopted to ensure realization of public-service objectives, particularly private broadcasters' limited access to the airwaves and the imposition of demanding content regulations. Even if certain objectives were considered worthwhile, it was unlikely, so it was argued, that they would be realized by existing public-service broadcasters. Was it possible, for example, for public broadcasters to remain editorially independent when they relied on the state for their licences and licence fees? Moreover, with the development of new cable and satellite outlets there no longer seemed the same need to dictate what could be offered to viewers or listeners: many argued that consumers rather than governments should decide on the available programme mix. The future of public broadcasting came, therefore, to appear increasingly bleak, with its objectives questioned and its supporting structures widely considered a barrier to greater consumer choice, a cause of inefficiency, and unsuited to an increasingly competitive environment.

The insecurity of the established public broadcasters was heightened by the fact that these criticisms came from a number of distinct quarters. The familiar, essentially negative, criticisms of the left, which sought to lay bare the failure of the public-broadcasting system to meet its own stated objectives of 'balance and impartiality', were both adopted and extended by the right in an all-embracing attack on the established system, its aspirations, and objectives.[7] On the one hand, liberal individualists challenged the paternalism and political manipulation they considered endemic to the old order. Competition was seen as an end in itself, a

---

[7] J. Curran (1990a).

mechanism for 'getting the state off the backs of the people'. On the other, free marketeers sought to lay bare what they considered the inefficiency and protectionism of the public system: not necessarily antagonistic to such traditional public-service goals as programme diversity and impartiality, they saw their realization through the play of competitive forces rather than regulatory fiat. Negative criticisms from the left thus incongruously dovetailed with liberal and free market critiques in a demoralizing onslaught on the public-broadcasting sector. These calls for a new regulatory settlement were, of course, fuelled by the development of cable and satellite technology, which underpinned predictions of a multi-channel, increasingly international, broadcasting environment. It was therefore against a background of ideological dissent and technological innovation that courts of law were first called to evaluate the established public-service model.

2. THE IDEOLOGICAL CHALLENGE

Negative evaluation of the public-service model has focused on two main issues. First, on its self-representation as a balanced and independent reporter of news, a 'fourth estate' challenging, on the public's behalf, those other repositories of power in modern democracy. Secondly, on its élitist approach to culture. Both have been exploited by those wishing to dismantle, or at least contain, the public-broadcasting sector.

Critical research in the first area has increased awareness of the political pressures to which even supposedly structurally independent public-services may be subject. Examples of governmental influence, familiar to French and Italian broadcasters, can also be furnished from British broadcasting history. During the Suez crisis, for instance, the government threatened to withhold financial support from the BBC's foreign radio services if it would not toe the government line. Additional transmissions to Rhodesia were also instituted at the British government's request after Rhodesia's unilateral declaration of independence from Britain in the mid-1960s. Recourse to the BBC was prompted by the government's belief that it 'was the best instrument available for the operation because of its reputation for objectivity and impartiality. Psychological warfare experience, it was said, had shown the importance of those qualities'.[8] Continued skirmishes between the BBC and the Conservative government during the 1980s, over coverage of the Falklands War and the 1985 American air-raid on Libya or the Zircon spy satellite episode of the

---

[8] G. Mansell (1982), 230 and 250.

'Secret Society' series, indicate an enduring tension between the political and professional view of broadcasters' responsibilities.[9]

But not only have the public sector's claims to impartiality been undermined by evidence of actual or potential political manipulation, the very notion of impartial reporting has itself been questioned. Studies by the Glasgow Media Group have sought to reveal that there is no politically neutral 'middle ground' which public broadcasters can claim as their own and which can simplistically be equated with impartiality.[10] Moreover, research into the control of information sources and the way in which news is 'created' has fostered a critical tradition which sees the audiovisual media as disproportionately reflecting the interests of dominant societal groups, able to influence, if not set, the news agenda. Although more extreme versions of this approach have recently been tempered—with renewed attention being given to the way in which different organizational structures and philosophies may alter the selection or presentation of material, to the potential diversity within 'dominant frames of reference' and to the adoption, in certain favourable conditions, by the mainstream media of stories carried in alternative outlets—there remains a continuing emphasis on the influence which particular individuals or groups, for example those who own the print or audiovisual media, are able to exert on the final message.[11] Nor has attention focused solely on the selection and packaging of information: passage of information from source to outlet to recipient is seen as a chain of highly complex transactions, and any suggestion that the mass media relay 'brute facts' to an uncritical, undifferentiated public would now be considered hopelessly simplistic.

Those seeking to open up the broadcasting market to competitive forces were quick to capitalize on the disorienting effect of this research to create a climate of mistrust in the established public-service order, an order which had founded its legitimation on the contested concepts of balance and impartiality. The public sector responded defensively to these critiques, even though many of the concerns raised, such as agenda-setting and political influence, require careful consideration in both public and private contexts—a point illustrated by criticism of the use recently made by Silvio Berlusconi of his private television stations to support his career in Italian politics.

The second element in this negative onslaught has been criticism of the

---

[9] P. Walters (1989); C. Horrie and S. Clarke (1994), 1–20, and see also R. Murdoch (1989), 9–10: '[p]ublic-service broadcasters in this country have paid a price for their state-sponsored privileges. That price has been their freedom.'

[10] Glasgow Media Group (1982).

[11] For a helpful overview of recent theoretical shifts see J. Curran (1990a). For more specific studies see J. Curran (1990b); R. Mathes and B. Pfetsch (1991); and P. Schlesinger (1990).

alleged élitism of many public-service programmes, criticism exemplified by Rupert Murdoch's suggestion that '[m]uch of what passes for quality on British television really is no more than a reflection of the values of the narrow élite which controls it and which has always thought that its tastes are synonymous with quality'.[12] Public broadcasters have undoubtedly often been slow to reflect popular tastes, incorporating light entertainment or music genres more as a bait to encourage 'highbrow' listening and viewing than as programming valuable in itself. Nevertheless, the picture painted of the public sector by its critics appears at times little more than a caricature, looking back to an already superseded model. Public broadcasters have for some time been careful to avoid the paternalistic stance of John Reith, officially acceptable in his day, but now replaced with a pluralist ethic which sees all tastes and interests as at least worthy of investigation. The pressure to maintain ratings in order to justify licence fees and advertising charges has also pushed the public sector into a more openly populist approach, so much so that in Italy many commentators consider the public and main private channels to be roughly comparable in terms of programming.[13]

The rejection of 'élitism' has, however, become linked with a more general denial of the existence of objective standards, laying the foundations for influential calls for 'consumer sovereignty': if the public-service professionals have been purveying a regressive, class-ridden view of society, who else in a modern democracy but the 'public' itself should be left as final arbiter of the broadcast message? The argument marginalizes the creative role of the broadcaster to a mere reflex of popular taste; the tyranny of the intellectual is replaced by the autonomy of the independent individual, we are all schedulers now. From this perspective individuals not only create the media message, they also, in the act of selection, give it æsthetic validation. Such cultural relativism undermines professional claims to determine quality through, for example, the allocation of international awards and prizes,[14] and it is little wonder that the ' "revisionists' " popular aesthetic has been incorporated into neo-liberal rhetoric to justify the destruction of public-service broadcasting in Europe'.[15] Such relativism slides into a bland commodification of the broadcast message, whose single and all-embracing role is to meet consumer demands. As such, it loses its elevated status as public informer/

---

[12] R. Murdoch (1989), 5.

[13] E. Andreatta and G. Pedde (1995), 8; A. Pace (1995), 254.

[14] Thus the compilers of the Peacock Report were 'alerted' to the need 'for careful examination of the different perceptions of broadcasters and of viewers and listeners as to what constitutes a satisfactory service': Peacock Report (1986) 41.

[15] J. Curran (1990a), 156.

educator, laying the ground for ultimate dismissal as 'spectacular illusion' or 'corrosive amusement'.[16]

The political right's growing attachment during the course of the 1980s to laissez-faire economic policy rendered the regulated broadcast sector a natural subject for critical scrutiny. The emphasis on individual autonomy and self-reliance rather than state provision made calls for greater audience choice and a lightening of the regulatory load particularly attractive. In Britain, the Conservative government of Mrs Thatcher moved a considerable way towards endorsing the consumer sovereignty thesis in its 1988 White Paper, illuminatingly entitled 'Broadcasting in the '90s: Competition, Choice and Quality'. The report held that the viewer and listener should be placed 'at the centre of broadcasting policy' and that 'viewer choice, rather than regulatory imposition, can and should increasingly be relied upon to secure the programmes which viewers want'.[17] In France, too, the 1986 electoral programme of the Right 'promised "the disengagement of the state" from all forms of broadcasting' and the government of Jacques Chirac subsequently took steps to realize this goal by privatizing the main public-service station, TF1.[18]

For those wishing to see a practical demonstration of a market moving towards minimal state intervention, there was always the United States. During the 1980s the Chairman of the Federal Communications Commission (FCC), Mark Fowler, set about introducing 'a marketplace approach' to American broadcast regulation, in which broadcasters were no longer to be seen as 'community trustees' but rather 'marketplace participants'.[19] During Fowler's chairmanship many of the established regulatory restrictions designed to ensure that broadcasters did act as community trustees were abrogated, on the basis that the market was likely to be more responsive to consumer demand than government regulation and would be less restrictive of the speech rights of broadcasters. Outside government, private broadcasters also pressed for market liberalization, reformulating the public-service concept in terms of 'a service which the public wants at a price it can afford'.[20] Though the equation of public-service and consumer choice may seem unduly simplistic, the powerful interweaving of egalitarian and populist themes gained widespread support for the consumer sovereignty thesis.

But not only was a free market system put forward as a mechanism for enhancing choice and individual autonomy, it was also considered essential for the innovative development of the high-technology goods and services

---

[16] P. Postman (1987).   [17] Home Office (1988), 1 and 5.
[18] R. Barbrook (1995), 131.   [19] M. S. Fowler and D. L. Brenner (1982), 209.
[20] R. Murdoch (1989), 4. For entertaining discussion of the criticisms levelled at the BBC see C. Horrie and S. Clarke (1994), 33–49.

required by our 'information society'.[21] Competition, it was also argued, would end the waste and inefficiency thought to characterize large government bureaucracies[22] and prevent the protectionism of agencies 'captured' by the industry they are supposed to regulate. Regulation may be attractive for established players as a mechanism through which competition can be contained, and there is evidence to suggest that regulatory agencies prefer to cling to the stability of the compromise they know, rather than upset the existing industrial balance through encouraging new entrants.[23] Although this critique has considerable cogency when applied to the American broadcasting sector, the FCC having sought over many years to protect established terrestrial broadcasters from cable competition, it seems less applicable to the industry-specific regulatory agencies in Europe. Here it is governments which have retained primary control, and it is they which, in the past, have significantly curtailed the growth of the audiovisual market, an approach which has facilitated political control and influence.

3. THE CHALLENGE POSED BY TECHNOLOGICAL DEVELOPMENT AND NATIONAL INDUSTRIAL POLICIES

Over the last decade broadcast policy across Europe has displayed two clear characteristics: the number of broadcasting outlets has increased and the regulatory load lightened, particularly on new entrants. If public-service broadcasting has been retained, it has survived as only one element in an increasingly complex and competitive audiovisual environment. Nor has change been simply a factor of ideology: the expansion in the audiovisual market owes as much to technological development and national trade rivalries as it does to the ideology of the right. Public ownership and state regulation were initially justified on 'spectrum scarcity' grounds: those priveledged with use of the limited number of frequencies made available for broadcasting could consequently be expected to provide a certain standard of programme service. These broadcasters held their licences in trust for the rest of the population which was excluded from the airwaves. With the growth of satellite and cable broadcasting the spectrum scarcity rationale ceased to be convincing.

---

[21] The cost of innovation in this field may, however, encourage co-ordination by market leaders. The audiovisual EUREKA project launched in Oct. 1990 under the auspices of the EEC is one example of attempts to improve European competitivity through shared research and development.

[22] See, e.g., consideration of BBC efficiency in Home Office (1986), 120, and British Government (1988), 7.   [23] R. B. Horwitz (1986), 190.

Moreover, as television stations have multiplied they have also become more specialized, offering channels dedicated to sport, films, news, or children's entertainment—radio, it may be noted, became specialized soon after its development as a mass medium. With the splintering of the schedules some commentators have questioned the continuing need for public-service regulations which require individual channels to shoulder the burden of a plural and unspecialized service.[24]

Looking at the development of state regulation in America, Robert Horwitz has shown that deregulatory policies have proved successful in only a precise area of the agency regulated field.[25] In the main, deregulation has hit the viable 'infrastructure' industries, where economic protection has been traded for cross-subsidization, rather than those regulated sectors dealing with the social 'externalities' of capitalism. It is in just these sectors that the possibility of undercutting the regulated industry through strict cost-based pricing or the deployment of new technology makes political pressure from would-be entrants most effective. Broadcasting undoubtedly falls within this broad category, in that public broadcasters, across Europe, have been required to cover the entire national territory, whatever the cost of transmission to individual subscribers, and to 'cross subsidize' those programmes which command only a limited audience. Nor is there a dearth of alternative transmission facilities: the new generation of medium- and high-powered satellites, multi-capacity optical-fibre cables, digital broadcasting, and signal compression techniques have opened the door to a truly multi-channel, multi-media environment.

As technology has facilitated competition, industry has lobbied hard for market expansion and governments have recently proved receptive to these arguments, seeing in the 'new technology' a way to break out from economic crisis and recession. Development of the hard- and software industries is one way to bring wealth and employment to ailing national economies. The British government, for example, considers that digital broadcasting will provide Britain's broadcasters and programme-makers with 'an opportunity . . . to move further ahead', as well as 'creating important new markets for manufacturers of receiving and transmission equipment', and has provided for the introduction of digital terrestrial broadcasting in its 1996 Broadcasting Act.[26] Similarly, government support for the commercial activities of the BBC is premised on its sustaining 'a United Kingdom presence in an international multi-media

---

[24] A. Cronauer (1994–5), 73.
[25] R. B. Horwitz (1989), 8, who argues that deregulation is the result of a 'mosaic of forces, of structures in interaction over time'.
[26] Dept. of National Heritage (1995b), 4.

world and increasing the United Kingdom's competitiveness'.[27] Industrial
policy has consequently underpinned the expansion of the audiovisual
market, with national rivalries accelerating this process further as countries
become fearful that they will be left behind in the new technological
revolution.

The European Commission is similarly enthusiastic about the introduction of digital technology and regards the resultant boom in information
and communication services 'a powerful factor for economic and social
cohesion: a factor for growth . . . a factor for development of new services
and hence a factor for job creation'.[28] Despite such powerful support the
'information society' has not been universally welcomed, some seeing
enhanced capabilities for social control or manipulation and a cause of
individual alienation from society. Others have emphasized the exacerbat-
ing effect technological development may have on social inequalities,
rendering the disadvantaged even less able to participate in the democratic
process.[29] Such concerns have, however, done little to dent the official
optimism over the benefits to be derived from the new electronic highways.

If technological developments have fuelled national competition they
have also served to undermine the predominantly national nature of
broadcasting policy. High-powered satellites can reach most of Western
Europe with their footprints and it is practically impossible for a country
which wishes to exclude such signals from its territory to do so.[30] Taken
together with the expansion in the co-production sector, the growing
importance of international sales for national broadcasters and steps taken
by the EC to create an open market for broadcasting goods and services,
the limits to national broadcasting policy are all too apparent. The
recognition that for the 'free flow' of television programmes across borders
to be acceptable basic ground rules must be established, has prompted
both the EC and Council of Europe to draw up new regulatory frameworks
for their Member States.[31] Such developments strike deeply at a traditional
cornerstone of the public-service ethic: that broadcasting is a *national*
service, a 'force for cultural integrity, helping society in all its parts to bind,

[27] Dept. of National Heritage (1994), 24.
[28] EC Commission (1994a), 17.
[29] P. Golding (1990). For further discussion of the 'information society' see P. Golding and
G. Murdoch (1986); M. Hepworth and K. Robins (1988); and I. Miles and J. Gershuny
(1986).
[30] J. G. Savage (1989) charts the variable effectiveness and enormous financial costs of
Soviet attempts to block Western radio broadcasts during the Cold War period.
[31] Dir. 89/552/EEC [1989] OJ L298/23 and European Convention on Transfrontier
Television, [1990] European Treaty Series no. 132. On the trends to internationalization see,
more generally, R. Negrine and S. Papathanassopoulos (1991) and K. Dyson and
P. Humphries (1988).

re-connect and commune with itself amidst all the fragmenting distractions'.[32] Henceforth, such communion can only be something less than total, with the internationalization of national broadcasting industries and growing public access to 'foreign' satellite channels fragmenting further this enclosed dialogue.

4. RE-EVALUATION OF THE PUBLIC SERVICE IDEAL

Recent years have been marked by a concerted effort on the part of many public-service broadcasters to adapt to changing circumstances while remaining true to key elements of their established remit. Despite its difficulties public-service broadcasting continues to enjoy a considerable measure of political support both at national and international levels. In Britain, for example, though the Conservative government now appears interested in the privatization of Channel 4, it has responded positively to the BBC's own plans for its future. In its 1994 White Paper the government concluded that the Corporation 'should continue to be the United Kingdom's main public-service broadcaster', 'should be able to evolve into an international multi-media enterprise', and 'should keep the licence fee as the main source of finance for its public-services for at least five years'.[33] The new Licensing Agreement entered into at the start of 1996 sets out in some detail a number of public-service obligations relating, for example, to balance, diversity, and impartiality, which were referred to only in very general terms, if at all, in the Board of Governors' Resolution annexed to the previous Licence.[34] Such political support for the public sector may stem from a desire to back domestic industry and a reluctance to lose complete control over an established domain. Privatization and the removal of licence-fee funding would also expose established private broadcasters to additional competition for limited advertising revenue, leading both public and private broadcasters to resist further change.

The BBC has won political support on the back of significant structural changes intended to address the familiar complaints of inefficiency and overmanning in the public sector. Although these developments severely rocked staff morale, they were considered essential by the BBC management to ensure competitiveness and render the BBC a credible vehicle for

---

[32] Blumler *et al.* (1986), 356.

[33] Dept. of National Heritage (1994), 1 and 3.

[34] Dept. of National Heritage (1995d), in particular at cl. 5. The imposition of a contractual obligation to ensure accurate and impartial reporting could, however, prove counter-productive were it to lead the BBC to avoid controversial programming which might trigger calls for 'reply programmes', much as the Fairness Doctrine was held to discourage controversial reporting in the USA.

political support. As well as cutting back on its workforce, the Corporation introduced an internal market system, known as 'Producer Choice', which allows BBC producers to choose whether to buy services from within or outside the Corporation. With internal services now costed, lighting, costume, and camera units all have to compete on price and quality with private companies. In addition, the BBC has moved to market its programme resources more aggressively, launching in 1995, for example, together with Pearson plc, two television satellite channels for Europe, and to expand its publishing activities. In terms of internal organization, employment practices, and commercial exploitation public broadcasters, even when publicly owned, may consequently appear little different from their private competitors.

At the international level, too, steps have been taken to endorse what is considered to be the positive contribution which public-service broadcasters make to the quality and reliability of the audiovisual sector. In December 1994 ministers of those European states participating in the fourth Council of Europe Ministerial Conference on Mass Media Policy in Prague adopted a resolution on 'The Future Of Public Service Broadcasting'. In this they affirmed 'their commitment to maintain and develop a strong public-service broadcasting system in an environment characterised by an increasingly competitive offer of programme services and rapid technological change'. There has also been considerable support for the principle of public-service broadcasting within the European Parliament, manifested most recently by its approval, in September 1996, of Carole Tongue MEP's motion for a resolution 'on the role of public-service television in a multi-media society'. The Resolution recognizes that public service broadcasting is 'a fundamental player in the public sphere' and calls on both the European Commission and Member States of the European Community to offer practical assistance to the public sector. From this perspective the remit of public broadcasters is expanded from reflecting simply national or regional concerns to providing a wider 'European dimension' in their programming. Considering the established position of many public-service broadcasters in Europe and the measure of political support which clearly remains, it seems probable that public broadcasting will prove a resilient part of the audiovisual landscape in Western Europe for some time to come.[35]

It is, however, not only in political, but also in academic, circles that public-service broadcasting continues to find a measure of support, support reflected in Paddy Scannell's classic declaration of faith: '[i]n my view equal access for all to a wide and varied range of common informational, entertainment and cultural services, carried on channels that can be

---

[35] J. Curran (1991), 108; D. McQuail (1990), 137.

received throughout the country, should be thought of as an important citizenship right in mass democratic societies.'[36] To criticize one system is not, by that very fact, to support another, and public-service broadcasting, with all its faults, may still provide a diversity and range of programmes which can be obtained from a lightly regulated private sector only at considerable cost for the individual consumer.[37] This, of course, should not be confused with unconditional support for the existing public-broadcasting systems in Europe. As we have noted these institutions have been attacked by both left and right for their susceptibility to government influence, their cautious reflection of alternative lifestyles and unconventional ideas, and for a lack of openness and accountability to the public they serve. Attempts to increase the commercial competitiveness of established public broadcasters, whether at home or at an international level, though responding to some of the organizational criticisms of the right, are unlikely to reassure the critics on the left.

Those who wish to see continued accommodation of public-service objectives within the audiovisual sector point to the important political and social functions performed by radio and television which, they argue, necessitate a degree of oversight to prevent distortion. For many, the mass media provide the only regular source of information on political and current affairs, information relied on by individuals when making important decisions about how they will lead their lives, vote at elections etc. Jürgen Habermas has argued that the mass media are capable of feeding into and nourishing a 'public sphere' which 'mediates between society and state, in which the public organizes itself as the bearer of public opinion'.[38] Building on a wide-ranging historical analysis, Habermas suggests that information relayed by the media is capable, in certain contexts, of facilitating critical debate within this distinct public sphere, leading ultimately to the supervision of public power. This informative role may, however, be subverted by commercial or state interests, manipulating public opinion for private ends.

Habermas' recognition of the role which the media can play in forming public opinion and facilitating rational political discourse is reflected in a number of recent academic works which seek to establish an enduring set

---

[36] P. Scannell (1989), 164, and, for more general comment, see T. Syvertsen (1991); Blumler *et al.* (1986); and A. Pragnell (1990).

[37] J.-P. Burgelman (1986), 177, suggests that certain traditional critics of the public-service model have now started 'to defend their former subject by idealizing it'.

[38] J. Habermas (1979 edn.), 198; J. Habermas (1992 edn.). Though Habermas' historical analysis has been questioned, see M. Schudson (1992), 142, and J. Curran (1991), 83, his normative delineation of a 'public sphere' has been used to promote a model of the media insulated from commercial and state influence, providing a locus for public debate and political evaluation: N. Garnham (1986).

of what can only be called 'public-service' objectives for the mass media, able to withstand technological and social change. Blumler and Gurevitch, for example, see the mass media as shoring up the democratic state, and compile a list of functions which include '[s]urveillance of the socio-political environment, reporting developments likely to impinge . . . on the welfare of citizens', setting meaningful agendas, providing a platform for espousing a variety of causes and facilitating dialogue between 'power holders . . . and mass publics', as well as holding officials to account.[39] Other commentators have emphasized the importance of the media, not merely for a closely defined political sphere but also as purveyors of entertainment. Nicholas Garnham, for example, notes that Habermas' theory of communicative action has been criticized for neglecting 'both the rhetorical and playful aspects' of communication, a neglect which leads to an overly rigid division between entertainment and information.[40]

Considering this wider role of the modern media, Denis McQuail has sought to establish the 'essential building blocks' for a modern and relevant 'social theory of the media'.[41] These building blocks comprise the values of freedom, equality, and order, which together point the way to the construction of a communicative system operating in the public interest. McQuail is careful to note, however, that these values are open to conflicting interpretations and must be evaluated in specific contexts on the basis of concrete evidence. Although open textured, these objectives may still serve as useful templates against which existing media systems may be measured. No longer associated simply with a particular, historical construct—the state-owned, monopolistic, public broadcaster—the idea of public-service, public interest, broadcasting clearly continues to resonate, and resonate quite strongly, within both political and academic spheres.

5. THE REGULATORY OPTIONS SURVEYED

The recent emphasis on reformulating objectives for the mass media rather than endorsing particular forms of ownership should warn against an analysis which posits a simplistic dichotomy between 'public-service' and 'free-market' models. The very reference to these 'models' may in fact lead to considerable confusion over means and ends. Moreover, by paying careful attention to the sort of communications system we wish to create we may prevent blind adherence to particular media structures, and ensure due regard for empirical evidence indicating that such structures are unsuited to attaining our desired ends.

[39] M. Gurevitch and J. G. Blumler (1990), 270.
[40] N. Garnham (1992), 359.   [41] D. McQuail (1991), 68.

The 'free-market' model may, for example, be based solely on the rejection of state intervention in the broadcasting arena, a model designed to prevent state censorship and ensure the autonomy of the individual in the face of political power. From this perspective evidence indicating that a deregulated, privately owned, television market may actually curtail consumer choice, and the meaningful transfer of information is irrelevant.[42] What is at stake is the ability of broadcasters to transmit such programmes as they wish free from state intervention: their interests are to be protected regardless of whether this best serves the audience.[43] Nor do 'market liberals' such as David Kelley and Roger Donway consider financial restrictions on individual access to the media to be problematic: the liberty of the individual is essentially a freedom to accumulate wealth and purchase goods in the marketplace. Although only very few among us can afford to own national television stations, other cheaper forms of expression are available in the form of local radio channels, pamphlets, or 'sound trucks'.[44]

Alternatively, the market may be seen, not as an end in itself, but as a means to realizing other goals. Such goals may be shared by those espousing public-service principles, for example, where the market is put forward as the best mechanism for ensuring diverse programming and reliable, informative reporting of current affairs.[45] Value judgements do not, of course, simply disappear where regulatory options are compared to determine which is more likely to realize a particular objective. Thus, Adrian Cronauer, in response to claims that the market may exclude certain opinions, argues that the market 'accommodates all viewpoints with enough proponents to warrant attention': he relies, that is, on the contestable assertion that there is no system of evaluation external to the market itself.[46] The way in which courts of law respond to the suggestion that either public-service or free-market 'models' should be developed in the audiovisual sector will consequently depend on whether their judgement is considered in any given case to turn on principle or the assessment of empirical evidence.

Polarizing the debate in this way may also lead to the assumption that 'a

[42] J. Keane (1991), 77, and J. Curran (1991), 94 and 96.

[43] See, e.g., M. S. Fowler and D. L. Brenner (1982), 242.

[44] D. Kelley and R. Donway (1990), 81. On this subject S. Ingber (1984), 38, notes '[n]o one today seriously would argue that picketing and leafleting are as effective communication devices as newspapers and broadcasting. Access to the mass media is crucial to anyone wishing to disseminate his views widely'.

[45] In America the proponents of deregulation frequently stressed the superior efficacy of the market for realizing public interest objectives over and above state regulation.

[46] A. Cronauer (1994–5), 74–5, who would include in the category of expendable broadcast speech the 'rantings of bizarre conspiracy theorists, paranoid delusionists, flat-earthers, anarchists, and others without any significant constituency'.

laissez-faire market regime is *prima facie* just', thereby imposing a heavy evidential burden on those who seek to restrict the freedom of market operators either through state regulation or public ownership.[47] In a recent work Cass Sunstein has argued that judges in the United States have tended to regard the distribution of goods through the mechanism of the market to be essentially neutral, entailing no exercise of state power.[48] Such 'status quo neutrality' is, he suggests, fundamentally mistaken, for the market is itself heavily underpinned by state support for private property through, for example, the laws of theft and trespass. The fact that the state has protected private property for many centuries makes it no less a form of intervention in social arrangements than the allocation of broadcasting licences. Sunstein's analysis erodes the familiar categorization of rights as either negative or positive, for such categorization turns in the end 'on assumptions about baselines—the natural or desirable functions of government'.[49] Thus, the argument that those who own broadcasting outlets should not be required to grant third parties access to their stations, that is, that broadcasters have a negative right to be free from state regulation, can be reformulated as a claim that the state should positively protect existing property rights from third-party intervention. A refusal to accept established ownership structures as given and immutable pushes one to consider creatively what role we now expect our courts and legislatures to play in regulating the mass media.

Such consideration indicates that our regulatory options are not limited to a broadcast environment dominated by the free market with a few pockets of 'public-service' provision. The market may indeed provide a service which fulfills many of the public-service objectives in an efficient and effective manner, but it may not meet them all. As John Keane has noted, the world of newspaper publishing reveals how 'Darwinian competition' can force 'publishers to gobble up their rivals—to expand in order to spread their bets and stabilize their revenues', leading to a high level of market concentration.[50] In an environment in which television output is influenced by the number of people prepared to watch a programme rather than the level of individual satisfaction it generates, particular preferences or viewpoints may also be lost in the process of viewer aggregation.[51] There is in fact considerable empirical evidence to the effect that competition for audiences among stations funded by

---

[47] M. J. Radin (1989), 166. [48] C. R. Sunstein (1993).
[49] C. R. Sunstein (1993), 70. [50] J. Keane (1991), 71.
[51] Although the proliferation of television channels in the USA has undoubtedly increased the choice of programmes available to individuals, these programmes appear to be located within a fairly restricted range of popular genres: see J. G. Blumler (1991), 208, and J. Curran (1991), 94.

advertising can lead to a reduction in the variety of programmes shown.[52] Moreover, viewers may wish to retain certain types of programmes which they themselves would not watch because they endorse the idea of a diverse service and wish to keep viewer options open in the future. Similarly, if one considers the media to perform a watchdog role, looking out for abuses by, and corruption within, not only government but also other powerful forces in society such as major corporations, then there may be good sense in insulating at least a part of the media from commercial pressures.

Nor is the choice facing our regulators limited to total adherence to either 'public-service' or 'free-market' principles. Media analysts such as James Curran now advocate a complex matrix of communication systems, each designed to pursue distinct ends and operate according to very different financial and regulatory imperatives. In Curran's matrix 'public-service television', comprising organizations which are either publicly owned or publicly regulated, is considered a core element, but a place is also afforded 'private enterprise', albeit on the periphery along with a 'civic sector', a 'social market sector', and a 'professional sector'.[53] Many would disagree with the relative positioning of these elements but the marked development across Western Europe of 'mixed' broadcasting systems, comprising operators subject to a variety of more or less demanding regulatory regimes, cannot be ignored.

It will be apparent from this discussion that there are two key issues which those who regulate our broadcasting media must address. First, what functions should our communication systems perform and which, if any, of the various public-service objectives should be retained in the broadcasting sector? Secondly, if some at least of the traditional public-service objectives continue to find endorsement, how best can they be realized? The regulatory means available to achieve a given end are, of course, considerable. Ownership criteria, sources of finance, and regulatory constraints can be assembled and reassembled in a kaleidoscopic display. Ian Hardin and Norman Lewis identify four such combinations, public and private ownership without state regulation and public and private ownership subject to such regulation.[54] Though helpful, such an analysis cannot begin to reflect the diversity of regulatory approaches which can be attempted in any specific economic sector. The various media may, for instance, be regulated differently depending on their territorial reach or means of relay. Initially, as we have seen, the print and audiovisual media were regulated as though they were discrete blocks: the 'press' was relatively lightly regulated, while radio and television were exposed to the

---

[52] B. Sturgess *et al.* (1995), 29.   [53] J. Curran (1991), 105.
[54] These distinctions are discussed in I. Hardin and N. Lewis (1983), 211.

full panopoly of public-service requirements. With the development of cable and satellite technology and consequent multiplication of available channels it became necessary to consider whether these new outlets should be regulated along press or broadcast lines. Given the specialized nature of many cable and satellite channels it is questionable whether it makes any sense to require compliance with such traditional public-service obligations as the provision of a wide-ranging mix of programmes. These issues are becoming increasingly pertinent as we move towards development of extremely flexible 'electronic highways', expected to offer a variety of facilities ranging from home shopping and banking to video on demand.[55]

A quick glance at the rapidly developing computer networks, of which the largest is the Internet, indicates how difficult it may be to fit new services into existing categories. For example, certain types of computer communications resemble traditional broadcasting, where information is left on a common bulletin board for any user to access, while others, such as the e-Mail facility, through which users can leave messages for specific individuals, seem more akin to the one-to-one exchange characteristic of telephone or postal services.[56] It is consequently no longer sufficient to look simply at the technological means of delivery, for any given delivery system may offer a variety of different services. Although some may see the introduction of these new services as inevitably leading to a lightening of the regulatory load across the whole audiovisual field, and this is the conclusion which Francesca Gitti draws from her examination of developments in the United States, it is possible that in the European context we will instead see a complex mix of regulatory regimes both within and across the various media.[57]

Reliance on private investment to fund new forms of information relay may also limit the regulatory authority of central governments. Although private enterprise undoubtedly values the security of a regulatory framework around which it can plan, it may no longer be willing to invest in new services if that framework imposes what it considers to be unjustified technological or content requirements. There is growing concern that the power to determine what is available on our television screens is now shifting from the state to a number of powerful 'gatekeeper' organizations, those organizations which control access to cable and satellite systems, and it seems probable that only the most basic 'public-service' requirements will be imposed on 'new' media services. It is also apparent that political decisions are increasingly being made not at the national but at the pan-national level, with the European Community playing an ever-growing role in regulating the audiovisual sector.

[55] Federal Trust (1995).   [56] D. K. McGraw (1995), 494.
[57] F. B. Gitti (1994), 4350.

Courts of law, when faced with questions of audiovisual regulation, have thus found themselves catapulted into not merely an ideological struggle of far-reaching implications but also an on-going technological revolution. In a very real sense the past offers limited guidance, for the problems posed reveal only too clearly that the nationally enclosed and circumscribed world of broadcast communications has now been superceded. It will be the burden of what follows to chart how certain courts have responded to, if not precipitated, recent developments in the broadcasting sector and to consider the extent to which they have been able—and willing—to draw upon the public-service traditions of the past in adding a legal dimension to the regulatory framework of today's fast-moving audiovisual world.

PART 2

A New Judicial Actor on the Scene?
The Parameters of Judicial Regulation
Considered

4

The Structural Framework for Judicial Intervention in the Audiovisual Domain

In Part 1 we tracked the social and political background to the development of state broadcasting monopolies, widely established in the aftermath of the Second World War. Protected by a philosophy of public service, simultaneously devalued by political appropriation and radical critique, these structures endured until technical advances, developments in marketing, and a change in popular aspirations made some form of accommodation inevitable. It should thus cause little surprise to find that the legitimacy of state monopolies was among the first and most central of the questions concerning audiovisual regulation to reach constitutional courts in Europe. The judicial response, in the three countries under examination, was far from uniform, owing to the very varied nature of the UK, French, and Italian constitutions. In order that courts may become meaningfully involved in challenging broadcast policy, it appears that at least three eventualities have to be realized:

First, *the disputed fact situation must be seen to raise legal issues*: the various arguments for or against a given position must be frameable in legally recognized terms. Those wishing to challenge a state broadcasting monopoly set up by legislation, for example, will need to have recourse to constitutionally recognized rights, such as freedom of speech or freedom of economic activity, which can be opposed to that legislation. The widespread appreciation of broadcasting as an activity qualitatively distinct from the print medium, a public service requiring careful regulation, undoubtedly played a part in retarding the move to frame questions of broadcasting policy in terms of recognized legal rights.

Secondly, *there must be a forum in which such disputes can be adjudicated*. As French history itself has shown, the protections afforded to citizens in bills of rights or other constitutional documents are often worthless when entrusted, not to an independent system of enforcement, but simply to the goodwill of the executive government. Thus, despite the proud pronouncement of freedom of the press and expression set out in Article 11 of the 1789 Declaration of the Rights of Man, the need for official authorization and payment of financial pledges to establish a newspaper or periodical in France was abolished only in 1881. Indeed, it has been suggested that those who framed the 1789 Declaration considered its primary purpose to be that of guiding future law, giving it additional authority, rather than restricting its sphere of concrete application.[1] Although solemn declarations of 'fundamental and civil rights' have all too often proved to be mere statements of aspiration, their symbolic, as opposed to strictly legal, importance within society should not be underestimated.

Thirdly, the heavy financial and temporal costs of pursuing legal remedies are such that only *when there appears a reasonable chance of success, and where the financial or moral rewards are commensurately great, will proceedings be brought or defended.* In this context the 'eldorado' of broadcast advertising, the 'licence to print money', has underpinned the tenacity and enterprise of many of the pirate broadcasters. But how might the probability of success be evaluated by an aspiring litigant? Clearly past judicial interpretations of constitutional and legislative provisions will be an important first guide, together with knowledge of the judicial make-up and background of the court in question. To be convincing, however, any such evaluation must go beyond the purely legal and look also to the changing political, social, and technical environment to which courts, particularly at the constitutional level, are sensitive. Strong political or social trends favouring a particular ideology at the time of an action may provide powerful support for those seeking to convince the court to adopt a precise interpretation of a constitutional or legislative norm.

The effectiveness of recourse to courts of law will thus crucially depend both on those background political and social attitudes which were examined in the previous section, and on the framework available for judicial challenge which is the subject of the present Chapter.

1. BRITAIN: JUDICIAL EXCLUSION FROM THE AUDIOVISUAL FIELD

In Britain judicial scrutiny of broadcasting regulation has been very limited. Although there has recently been a greater willingness to turn to the courts for review of administrative decisions, the general impression gained from consideration of past cases is one of restricted judicial impact on the day-to-day functioning of the audiovisual system. Two main factors have militated against a meaningful judicial role in the shaping and

---

[1] G. Bacot (1989).

monitoring of British broadcasting policy. The first is the absence of a written constitution establishing basic civil rights enforceable at law; the second is a political preference for allocating to specialized institutions the task of setting and overseeing broadcasting standards. Together these have isolated those in the broadcasting industry from judicial scrutiny, whether as regards the policies adopted or the procedures by which they have sought to put those policies into effect.

Before examining the constitutional position in more detail it is necessary to make an important point of substance and terminology. The terminological point is that where the term 'British' is employed, as in 'British broadcasting', it should be understood as a loose, but somewhat more euphonious, reference to the United Kingdom. The point of substance is that although the United Kingdom, as its name suggests, is a unitary state, it comprises three distinct legal systems, that of England and Wales, of Scotland, and Northern Ireland, each with its own legal profession and court structure. Since the majority of statutory provisions in the broadcasting field apply to the entire territory of the United Kingdom no distinction has generally been made between the various legal systems. Certain differences in both substance and procedure, for example in the field of English and Scottish administrative law, do exist and have been briefly noted, but my examination focuses primarily on the law applicable in England and Wales.

The British constitution is a motley collection of statutory provisions, political conventions, and common law principles, shaped over the years by the power struggles between Crown and Parliament. There is no one authoritative document, no written constitution, which seeks to establish the interweaving powers and duties of the main branches of the British state: legislature, executive, and judiciary. Certain of these powers and duties are established by statute, but many have evolved over time without direct legislative intervention. Nor is there a national charter of basic human rights comparable to the French Declaration of 1789: those rights which do find protection in the United Kingdom do so either through specific statutory enactment or through the legally recognized principle that certain basic freedoms of, for example, association and expression should be positively protected to the extent that they have not been directly restricted by statute or common law.

It is the 'distinctly English'[2] principle of 'parliamentary sovereignty'

---

[2] Lord President Cooper in *MacCormick* v. *The Lord Advocate*, 1953 SC 396, reserving the question whether, as regards matters of private right, UK statutes might be challenged in the courts of Scotland. In *Gibson* v. *The Lord Advocate* [1975] 1 CMLR 563, however, Lord Keith held (*obiter*) that Scottish courts could not determine the legality of a UK statute altering private rights on the basis that it was not for the 'evident utility' of the Scottish people

which currently prevents the judiciary from affording civil rights any entrenched or protected status. The principle is considered to have two main limbs: first, that statutory provisions override non-statutory provisions, for example those of the common law; and, secondly, that later statutes override earlier ones. Thus in *R.* v. *Jordan*, where the defendant applied for a writ of Habeas Corpus on the basis that his sentence of eighteen months' imprisonment under the Race Relations Act 1965 was an invalid curtailment of free speech, the court refused to evaluate the Act's compliance with the principle of freedom of speech, holding that it had no power to question the validity of an Act of Parliament.[3] It will therefore be apparent that the degree of concrete protection afforded to the 'residual' category of civil rights rests on the restraint and sensitivity assumed by courts and legislature alike, for, as Lord Wright said in *Liversidge* v. *Anderson* 'in the constitution of this country there are no guaranteed or absolute rights'.[4]

The principle of parliamentary sovereignty has now, however, to be read in the light of UK membership of the European Union and the provisions of the European Communities Act 1972. Whether or not the 1972 Act should be seen as a limitation on, or simply exercise of, parliamentary sovereignty, it is apparent that UK courts are prepared in the light of section 2 of that Act to 'override any rule of national law found to be in conflict with any directly enforceable rule of Community law', and they are prepared to do so even where the national legislation post-dates the 1972 Act.[5] Section 3 of the 1972 Act stipulates that, when applying Community law, UK judges are to treat as authoritative the decisions of the European Court of Justice. Although the Community has competence to legislate only in areas specifically set out in the EC Treaty, and the Treaty does not currently include a general statement of fundamental rights, the European Court of Justice has held that fundamental human rights form part of the general principles of law which are to be respected within the Community legal order. Thus, although the Community has no general remit to enforce fundamental rights, it is required to ensure that Community legislation and Treaty provisions are applied in such a way that fundamental human rights are not infringed. Consequently, fundamental rights come into play where Community measures or Treaty provisions have to be interpreted or

---

as required by Art. XVIII of the 1707 Act of Union. Additional doubts about the competence of the Scottish courts to challenge UK legislative enactments were raised in *Sillars* v. *Smith*, 1982 SLT (notes) 539. The matter is, however, far from conclusively determined and, for discussion of more recent cases, see M. Allen, B. Thompson and B. Walsh (1994), 75–7.

[3] [1967] *Crim. LR.* 483.
[4] [1942] AC 206, 261.
[5] *R.* v. *Sec. of State for Transport, ex p. Factortame Ltd and others (No 2)* [1991] 1 AC 603, 659.

implemented by Community institutions or Members States, and the European Court of Justice has also held that Member States must respect fundamental rights when they derogate from basic Community freedoms.[6] In those areas which remain outside the sphere of Community competence, fundamental human rights, as interpreted by the European Court of Justice, will not be directly binding on UK courts. Despite their restricted field of application, fundamental human rights have thus acquired an important toe-hold in the United Kingdom through the application of European Community law.

In establishing those fundamental rights which find recognition in Community law the European Court of Justice has drawn not only on the constitutional traditions of the various Member States but also on international human rights treaties on which the various Member States have collaborated or which they have signed.[7] Principal among such treaties is, of course, the European Convention on Human Rights. Apart from its impact through Community law the Convention, as an international treaty, is not itself a direct source of individual rights within the United Kingdom. Outside the Community context, the Convention provisions require statutory enactment to become effective in UK law, though they have been considered by the English courts when developing the common law and are interpretative aids when construing ambiguous legislation.[8] There are, however, limits to this rule of construction and in *R.* v. *Secretary of State for the Home Department, ex parte Brind* the Law Lords held that they were not bound to construe widely drafted provisions, affording general regulatory powers to the executive, so as to conform with the Convention.[9] Generality was not, in their Lordships' view, to be treated in the same way as ambiguity. In Scotland the courts have been unwilling to use the Convention as an interpretative tool even when a statute is ambiguous, though in the recent case of *T, Petitioner* it was held that the distinction between the two jurisdictions could no longer be justified, thereby pointing to a similar use of the Convention in Scotland.[10]

Although UK accession to the European Community created new possibilities for contesting primary legislation, legal action in the broadcasting field has concentrated around challenges to the exercise of statutory or devolved powers by regulators or broadcasters. Indeed, the idea that fundamental rights may impose restrictions upon the formation or

---

[6] P. Craig and G. de Búrca, (1995), 310–24; T. C. Hartley (1994), 148.
[7] Case 4/73, *Nold* v. *Commission* [1974] ECR 491.
[8] See, e.g. *Waddington* v. *Miah* [1974] 1 WLR 683.
[9] *R.* v. *Sec. of State for the Home Department, ex p. Brind* [1991] 1 All ER 721.
[10] *T, Petitioner* [1996] *The Times* Scots Law Report, Aug. 20, disagreeing with the approach taken in *Kaur* v. *Lord Advocate*, 1981 SLT 322.

content of broadcasting policy at the legislative level has received minimal attention in establishment circles. As we have already seen, the initial creation of the British Broadcasting Company in 1922 as a consortium of six companies had very little, if anything, to do with freedom of speech—the objectives were too blatantly factional and commercial for that—while the preference for a monopolistic rather than a competitive industry helped to exclude the UK courts from the very start. The introduction of this closed cartel, subsequently to be replaced by a monolithic public corporation, prevented them from assuming their classic role of allocating and protecting private rights in a competitive environment.

If there had remained any scope for judicial intervention in programming decisions on, for example, religious or moral grounds this was quickly minimized by the rapid development of the pronounced public-service ethic established by John Reith. Almost from its inception British broadcasting has been seen as a one-way conduit, a service for public advancement, in which 'free speech' has an important place but does not constitute the underlying objective of the enterprise, more a means than a distinct end. This emphasis on 'public service' has tended both to pre-empt (through a growing recognition of the need for a diversity of programme types and opinions expressed within them) and at times to shroud legitimate questions of freedom of speech and pluralism.

As will be apparent, the discussion of rights and standards in British broadcasting has seldom taken place in a courtroom context. Instead, there has been an enduring attachment to the use of specific regulatory bodies to set standards and oversee conformity with them. Over time a whole series of regulatory bodies have been established to run the broadcast sector, bodies ranging from the self-regulating BBC to the Independent Television Commission (ITC) and Radio Authority (RA). These bodies have traditionally drawn up extensive guidelines covering all aspects of programme policy. More particularly, they establish the parameters for individual decision-making and ensure that contentious material, potentially open to judicial scrutiny, is either deleted or officially legitimized through a powerful system of 'reference up' the relevant broadcast hierarchy. Although the ITC now plays an essentially reactive rather than proactive regulatory role it is to be envisaged that British broadcasting will continue to be very much a self-contained and self-regulating medium.

What happens, however, when this internal safety net fails to function and broadcasters find themselves at odds with prevailing political or social norms? Public disquiet and questions of accountability come to the fore where there have been invasions of individual privacy or where common standards of taste and decency have been transgressed. Here again, the preferred remedy has not been to stimulate judicial accountability but to create two industry-specific 'watchdog' bodies, the Broadcasting

Complaints Commission and the Broadcasting Standards Council, recently merged to create the Broadcasting Standards Commission by the 1996 Broadcasting Act (Part V). Nicol and Robertson, two leading comment-ators on the British media, suggest that a number of reasons underlie this preference for specific regulatory bodies. They point to what they consider the law's inability to take account of the 'means of visual presentation', the British government's desire to encourage big-business investment in the media field—deterred by the prospect of legal action—together with the potential for surreptitious governmental 'guidance' where institutions are run by selected appointees.[11]

Recently, however, there have been indications of a greater political willingness to allow judicial checks to penetrate the professional world of the broadcaster. Section 162 of the 1990 Broadcasting Act, for example, extended the provisions of the 1959 Obscene Publications Act to television, while the BBC's new operating Agreement with the government includes for the first time detailed programme standards which may facilitate judicial review.[12] The system of ITC licence awards, introduced by the 1990 Act, in which administrative discretion was reduced as the weight given to the size of the financial bid increased, led to a series of applications for judicial review of the ITC's initial allocation of franchises.[13] The award by the ITC in October 1995 of the ten-year licence to run a fifth terrestrial television channel to Channel 5 Broadcasting similarly led disappointed applicants to seek judicial review. Both Virgin Television, which matched the Channel 5 bid, and UKTV, which offered an additional 14.6 million pounds, unsuccessfully challenged the ITC's decision, which had been based on the determination that neither company reached the set quality threshold. Were all applicants to have crossed the quality threshold, the 1990 Act would have required the ITC, absent exceptional circumstances, automatically to award the licence to the highest bidder.[14]

The complexity and cost of judicial action undoubtedly deter litigation and, until relatively recently, English standing requirements were a potential minefield for applicants, varying with the remedy sought.[15] The

---

[11] G. Robertson and A. G. L. Nicol (1984), 363 ff. See also P. Walters (1988), 393–4, for a discussion of the impact of appointments under the Thatcher government to the BBC Board of Governors on public and professional perceptions of BBC impartiality.

[12] Dept. of National Heritage (1996b); see, in particular, cl. 5.

[13] T. H. Jones (1992).

[14] *R. v. ITC, ex p. Virgin Television Ltd*, *The Times*, 17 Feb. 1996.

[15] P. P. Craig (1994), 479–89. It should be noted that there are both substantive and procedural differences in the approach to public-law issues in Scotland and England. A special procedure for judicial review was introduced in Scotland in 1985 with similar grounds for review to those employed in English courts, although there are differences in the criteria applied to determine which bodies are subject to review. For a brief overview see T. Prosser and T. Mullen (1995) and E. C. S. Wade and A. W. Bradley (1993), 609, 727.

unified procedure for applications for judicial review introduced in 1978 through revision to Order 53 of the Rules of the Supreme Court now requires applicants to satisfy the court that they have a 'sufficient interest' in the matter to which the application relates. In determining whether or not the applicant has sufficient interest the court considers not only the statutory terms, the applicant's interest in the issues raised, and its representative nature and expertise in the field, but also the subject matter or merits of the claim.[16] Recently the courts have adopted a relatively liberal approach to standing, allowing charities and pressure groups to challenge administrative decisions on the public's behalf.[17] Nevertheless, it is possible to point to fairly recent decisions in which pressure groups or individuals have been denied standing on the basis that they have no special interest in the challenged action: in the 1987 case of *Holmes* v. *Checkland*, an individual opposed to smoking was refused standing to challenge transmission by the BBC of a snooker championship sponsored by a tobacco company on the ground that he was no more affected than anyone else.[18] This may be contrasted with the earlier case of *R.* v. *IBA, ex parte Whitehouse*, in which the holder of a television licence was held to have sufficient standing to bring an action for judicial review of IBA programming policy.[19]

The question of who is competent to seek review of the BBC's programming decisions was again raised in a case brought in April 1995. Here candidates in Scottish local elections sought an inderdict to prevent transmission by the BBC of an extended interview with the Prime Minister in the same week as those elections. The BBC argued that its duty of impartiality was owed solely to the Queen in Parliament and consequently could not be enforced by election candidates or political parties. The 'duty' to treat controversial topics impartially was not specifically set out in the 1981 BBC Charter or Licence and Agreement but was instead included in a resolution by the BBC's Board of Governors annexed to the Licence and Agreement. Whether compliance with such a self-imposed obligation could in fact be enforced by third parties was not, however, finally resolved in the Scottish appeal, although an interim interdict was granted prohibiting transmission of the interview.[20]

The new Agreement entered into by the government and the BBC at the

---

[16] *R.* v. *Inland Revenue Commissioners, ex p. National Federation of Self-Employed and Small Businesses Ltd* [1982] AC 617; *R* v. *Sec. of State for Employment, ex p. Equal Opportunities Commission* [1994] 1 All ER 910.

[17] *R.* v. *Secretary of State for Foreign Affairs, ex p. World Development Movement* [1995] 1 All ER 611, *R.* v. *Insp. of Pollution, ex p. Greenpeace (No 2)* [1994] 4 All ER 329.

[18] *Holmes* v. *Checkland, The Times*, 15 Apr. 1987, discussed in H. W. R. Wade and C. F. Forsyth (1994), 715.   [19] *The Times*, 14 Apr. 1984.

[20] *Houston* v. *BBC* [1995] SLT 1305.

beginning of 1996 specifically sets out, unlike its predecessor, legal requirements concerning programme content and standards. It might be argued that the relationship between the BBC and the Secretary of State for National Heritage under this Agreement is a purely private, contractual one, so that only the parties are entitled to bring an action to enforce its terms. The fact that the Agreement establishes the terms on which the BBC is to provide a public-broadcasting service does, however, indicate that there is an important public aspect to the contract, and for this reason it is possible that a suitably interested individual or body, not merely the contracting parties, would be permitted to seek review of the BBC's performance. This would place the BBC on the same footing as the ITC, which is clearly subject to judicial review of the exercise of its statutory powers and duties.[21] Further support for this view may also be derived from *ex parte Brind* where the exercise by the Secretary of State of contractual powers set out in the 1981 Licence and Agreement was judicially reviewed in an application brought by individual radio and television journalists.[22]

In England an interested party may apply for judicial review in three main circumstances: first, where the public body, or body carrying out a public function, acts outside its established remit; secondly, where it carries out its duties in an irrational or unreasonable fashion; and, thirdly, where there has been some procedural impropriety.[23] The importance of respecting human rights will be taken into account when determining the reasonableness of an administrative action.[24] It may be noted that English courts have not established with anything like the clarity of administrative courts in certain civil law jurisdictions such as France specific substantive requirements which bodies providing essential public services must meet, such as continuity of service, neutral provision, and universal access. Nevertheless, it is possible to point to a number of English cases in which the final decision has clearly been influenced by such concerns.[25]

When called to review decisions taken by specialized regulatory bodies English judges frequently express their concern not to cross the border from review to appeal. Particularly in the programming field, where

---

[21] See, e.g., *R.* v. *ITC, ex p. Virgin Television Ltd, The Times*, 17 Feb. 1996.

[22] *R.* v. *Sec. of State for the Home Department, ex p. Brind* [1991] 1 All ER 721.

[23] A tri-partite distinction adopted by Lord Diplock in *CCSU* v. *Minister for Civil Service* [1985] AC 374, 410. For brief details on Scottish procedure see T. Prosser and T. Mullen (1995).

[24] *R.* v. *Ministry of Defence, ex p. Smith and other appeals* [1996] 1 All ER 257.

[25] See, e.g., *Wheeler* v. *Leicester City Council* [1985] AC 1054, where Lord Templeman held that the City Council could not exclude a rugby club from using its recreation ground where the club had committed no wrong, simply because it failed to display sufficient 'zeal in the pursuit of an objective' sought by the Council.

complex policy decisions have to be taken, the courts are wary of intervention. In *McAliskey* v. *BBC* the court refused to overrule the BBC's allocation of air time to the thirteen candidates in a Northern Ireland European Assembly election.[26] Eight of the candidates had been allocated one and a half minutes to state their case, while the remaining five were to take part in a thirty-minute discussion. Murray J held that '[t]he BBC has a difficult task in dealing with 13 candidates in one large constituency in one programme. It takes the view that a 13 member panel is out of the question, and I would not be prepared to hold that this is a view which could not reasonably be held'.[27]

Furthermore, many of the duties imposed on the broadcasting authorities are of an 'open-ended' nature, which affords them considerable discretion to shape their services as they see fit. The obligation to provide certain categories of programmes or maintain given standards is often framed in nebulous and non-binding terms—to 'satisfy themselves' or 'do all they can to ensure'—which serves to deter meaningful judicial scrutiny.[28] If some consideration has been given to the relevant statutory objective by the body in question the courts will be reluctant to hold its decision to be one which they could not reasonably have reached. Only where the body has failed to give any consideration to the specified statutory objectives does it become likely that its decision will be quashed. In *Attorney-General, ex.rel. McWhirter* v. *Independent Broadcasting Authority* the three members of the Court of Appeal were clearly reluctant to classify as unreasonable the decision of the IBA, the regulatory body then responsible for independent television, to screen a contentious documentary on the painter Andy Warhol, even though they personally found the programme dull or indecent:

[B]efore this court could adjudge that the authority had made a perverse decision there would have to be very strong evidence indeed . . . In the realm of good taste and decency, whose frontiers are ill-defined, I find it impossible to say that the authority have crossed from the permissible into the unlawful.[29]

There are, of course, exceptional cases where a broadcasting body has clearly misinterpreted or failed to perform its statutory or contractually imposed duty. In *Wilson* v. *IBA* the IBA had planned four party-political broadcasts prior to the 1979 referendum on the 1978 Scotland Act.[30] The

---

[26]   1980 NI 44.

[27]   *Ibid*. 53. See also *R.* v. *Radio Authority, ex p. Bull and Another* [1995] 4 All ER 427.

[28]   See, e.g., s. 17(3) of the Broadcasting Act 1990, which enables the ITC to award a broadcasting licence to an applicant who has not submitted the highest bid 'if it appears to them' that there are justifying exceptional circumstances.

[29]   [1973] 1 QB 629. The quotation is taken from the judgment of Lawton LJ at 659.

[30]   1979 SC 351.

broadcasts had been allocated in such a way that three were on behalf of parties favouring a 'yes' vote while only one was on behalf of those advocating a 'no' vote. Members of the 'Labour Vote No Campaign Committee' petitioned the Scottish Court of Session for an interdict to prevent transmission of the programmes, arguing that if they were transmitted the IBA would be in breach of its statutory duty to ensure programme balance. The court held that, since three of the programmes were in favour of a 'yes' vote and only one against, there was a *prima facie* failure to maintain a proper balance.

If, however, one moves beyond the question of single-issue referenda and party-political or election broadcasts to documentary programmes and the more 'open', personal-view genres represented by single plays or drama series then judicial intervention appears increasingly unlikely. Assessing whether a programme, or indeed a series of programmes, has failed to be suitably impartial inevitably involves the courts substituting their own appreciation of fairness or balance for that of the producer, a step which they have been reluctant to take. Regulatory decisions will thus be left virtually untouched, even where these lead to the exclusion from air-time of political parties with a small parliamentary presence or which do not in fact seek parliamentary representation at all.[31] An application for judicial review is thus a limited mechanism for challenging the decisions of special regulatory bodies, especially where a particular programme has passed through the net of professional self-censorship and the usual 'reference up' to the higher levels of management. A considerably more effective and well-publicized form of redress is likely to be obtained from media coverage of the grievance itself. Indeed the criticisms voiced by certain members of the Conservative government over television coverage of the American bombing of Libya and the shooting of suspected IRA terrorists in Gibralta were adjudicated not in the courts of law but in the possibly more damaging public forum offered by the printed press, seldom unwilling to attack the standards of what may be considered its natural competitor.

What conclusions can we draw from the above discussion? First, little, if any, accommodation for judicial scrutiny was made when broadcast structures were worked out in the course of the 1920s, and from that time neither government, for which informal means of control have seemed an attractive goal, removed from the stigma of overt censorship or the restraints of due process, nor industry, anxious to preserve its own field of 'professional competence' and avoid head-on conflict with the political masters, has had little reason to support judicial involvement in the broadcast sector. Nor have the courts appeared an attractive forum for the

---

[31] A. E. Boyle (1986), 578.

viewing public: heavy costs and limited grounds of review have, for the most part, deterred complaints, so that the only available remedy has all too often been recourse to the offending institution itself, backed, where possible, by public pressure.

There are, however, some indications of a sea change in the level of judicial involvement in broadcast matters. In an increasingly competitive environment, with the media interests of major multinational companies spanning the globe, legal challenge to regulatory restrictions has become just another tool in the battle to survive. Within the United Kingdom there has been a greater readiness to turn to the courts to challenge administrative decisions made by the broadcasting authorities, particularly, as the recent Channel 5 television award illustrates, in the field of licence allocations. Moreover, pressure groups, big business, and politicians may be encouraged by the recent Scottish decision suspending the BBC's interview with the Prime Minister prior to local elections to test out the willingness of the courts to ensure compliance with stipulated technical and programme standards.[32] With heightened financial stakes, broadcasters and business interests may also consider rather more closely the extent to which judicial scrutiny of regulatory practices may assist their position.[33] The development of European Community regulation in the audiovisual field and direct effect of many of the Community competition rules also offer scope for judicial challenge to statutory provision and administrative action alike.[34] Despite technical limitations and a slow start British litigants could soon be making up for lost time.

2. ITALY: JUDICIAL ACTIVISM AND POLITICAL PROCRASTINATION

The roles played by the Italian and British judiciaries in the broadcasting sector could not be more different, and this disparity owes much to the diverse constitutional traditions of the two countries. Most noticeably, the powers of the various governing organs of the Italian state are set out in the Italian Constitution of 1948, a document which, in contrast to its predecessor, the Statuto Albertino of 1848, establishes a Constitutional Court, la Corte costituzionale.[35] The Constitutional Court is empowered

---

[32] R. Clancy, J. Thynne and G. Jones, *Daily Telegraph*, 5 Apr. 1995, 5.

[33] The ITV companies, for example, indicated that they would like a judicial ruling on the powers of the ITC to require them to conform to certain scheduling policies, a move precipitated by the ITC's opposition to the proposal that News At Ten be rescheduled to the early evening to allow uninterrupted transmission of films during prime time.

[34] As the Red Hot television litigation illustrates: *R. v. Secretary of State for National Heritage, ex parte Continental Television BVio and Others* [1993] 3 CMLR 387.

[35] The role of the Constitutional Court is discussed by C. Rodotà (1986) and G. L. Certoma (1985), 155–7.

to review legislation for conformity with the Constitution and, where a legislative provision is held to contravene the Constitution, it is rendered unenforceable. The Court is not limited simply to granting or rejecting the reference; in many instances it will give what is referred to as an 'interpretative judgment' in which it rejects the reference, but only on the basis that the legislative provision is interpreted in a particular way. On other occasions it has held provisions to be constitutional, but only on a temporary basis, pending further legislation. Individuals do not have direct recourse to the Constitutional Court, but they may raise the issue of constitutionality in proceedings before one of the ordinary or administrative courts. These courts do not themselves have jurisdiction to determine the constitutionality of a legislative provision, but where the judge considers that such an issue has been made out by a party the case will be stayed and a reference made to the Constitutional Court. Alternatively, the judge may raise the matter with the Court of his own motion. The reference will determine the issues to be considered by the Constitutional Court, which is limited to its terms. Only the State and Regional governments and the Provinces of Trento and Bolzano can make a direct reference to the Court outside the context of a specific legal dispute. The existence of a written constitution, guaranteeing important social and political rights, and a system of judicial review of primary legislation clearly, therefore, marks out the Italian constitution from its UK counterpart.

Though the blueprint for the Constitutional Court was laid out in 1948, it was many years before the Court came to play a central role in the Italian constitutional system. In fact the crisis of the liberal state and the rise of Fascism in the 1920s had already led to calls for the institution of an external check on political power, possibly along the judicial lines mapped out by the American Supreme Court, but no such action was then taken.[36] Whether the introduction of such a body at that time could indeed have stopped the ultimate slide into totalitarianism, it was widely seen in the dismembered aftermath of the Second World War as a central guarantee of a new, resolutely democratic and legal, order. The establishment of a constitutional court enjoying wide powers of legislative review was not, however, an inevitable development: not all the political factions represented in the Constituent Assembly, elected in 1946 to draw up the new constitution, favoured a judicial solution.

The 1948 Constitution was very much a compromise between the Christian Democratic and Communist parties, which dominated in the immediate post-war period. Of these, the Christian Democratic forces tended to welcome the introduction of a constitutional court, while the

---

[36] For a general examination of the origins of the Italian Constitutional Court see: C. Rodotà (1986); G. D'Orazio (1981); and G. Zagrebelsky (1977).

Communists expressed reservations at the introduction of a judicial, largely unaccountable body, acting outside the established democratic system. Prior to the parliamentary elections of 1948 the ultimate balance of Italian political power had not yet been set, and it has been suggested that the Christian Democrats then considered the constitutional court a last-ditch defence against the possible 'excesses' of a popularly elected government of the left.[37] Furthermore, a constitutional court was considered a potential forum for the articulation of 'natural-law' principles, the subject of renewed interest in Catholic circles. The corporatist leanings of many in the Catholic Church also led to a devaluation of the role of central government, preference was instead given to a decentralized network of representative economic councils and professional bodies through which existing social problems could be solved. The checks which a constitutional court would place upon the elected government appeared to pose little threat to this separate and diffuse power base.

Inevitably, the Communist and Socialist members expressed greater diffidence, fearing that a constitutional court could be used to block essential post-war redistributive measures. These fears were fuelled by the traditionally conservative nature of the Italian judiciary, a body which had shown little resistance to the legislative and procedural changes introduced under the Fascist regime. This mistrust of judicial power seemed also justified by events in America during the 1930s, where that early role model, the Supreme Court, had opposed a number of the 'New Deal' policies introduced by President Roosevelt to help alleviate the worst manifestations of the depression. Although the American judicial–political confrontation had been settled by the end of the decade—through the popular endorsement of Roosevelt's policies in the 1936 election and by his use of the presidential power of judicial appointment gradually to tip the balance of the Supreme Court in favour of those sympathetic to his cause—its memory lived on in the minds of those Italian politicians anxious to rebuild their country materially and socially after the devastation of the war. The Left's resistance to the establishment of a constitutional court was, however, a restrained one, and it is significant that at the end of the day both Socialists and Communists voted for its introduction.

If the Left had, at first, been resistant to and the Christian Democrats broadly supportive of the court, allegiances were to undergo a dramatic reversal after the 1948 elections in which the Christian Democrats secured an outright parliamentary majority. The Christian Democrats, once

---

[37] This was indeed an appraisal shared by Palmiro Togliatti, then general secretary of the Communist Party, who believed CD support for the constitutional court to stem from fears of a left-wing parliamentary majority seeking profound changes to the political structure: see C. Rodotà (1986), 14.

established in government, came to regard those very checks and balances they had pressed to have accepted in the 1948 Constitution as leaving open pockets of influence for colonization by the 'undemocratic' forces of the Left—their new-found ideological adversaries after the dissolution of the post-war tri-partite coalition and the insidious advance of Cold War hostilities. Among those checks on governmental authority was, of course, the Constitutional Court, the governing principles and composition of which had been left, under the terms of the 1948 Constitution, to be subsequently established by Parliament. It was to be eight more years before such consideration was grudgingly facilitated by the Christian Democrats, seemingly content to enjoy the continuing protection offered by the repressive police and information laws established under the Fascist regime.

In contrast, the parties of the left now championed the Constitutional Court as a newly legitimate tool to break the enduring dominance of an old and discredited social order. It was only in 1956 that the Court became fully functional, with its own specific procedures and personnel, but in its very first judgment it indicated a willingness to carve out for itself a significant role in the development of post-war Italian society. Not only did the Court adopt a wide interpretation of its powers of review, holding these to permit scrutiny of legislation passed before as well as after the 1948 Constitution, but it also refused to limit its jurisdiction by adopting a distinction between 'programmatic' and 'directly enforceable' constitutional norms which had become established in the ordinary courts. It had become judicial practice to enforce only the more specific constitutional provisions, holding that the general and wide-ranging nature of the programmatic or policy provisions in the text rendered them poorly suited for application by a court of law: effect could be given to these norms, which made up a significant proportion of the 1948 Constitution, only after more precise formulation in subsequent legislation.

In its willingness to uphold even the most open-ended of the Articles set out in the 1948 Constitution the Court left a wide margin for future action. The members of the Constituent Assembly had been concerned not merely to establish the basic structure and balance of powers among the governing organs of the Italian state, but also to determine a framework of rights and obligations for all citizens. Thus the first part of the Constitution, bearing the marks of the delicate compromise reached by the various factions present in the Assembly, sets out a wide range of civil, social, economic, and political entitlements and duties, among them freedom of the press and expression.[38] As will be readily apparent the scope and open texture of these provisions, the power to combine or play one Article off against

---

[38] Art. 21.

another, affords the Constitutional Court a virtually unlimited field of review.

Nevertheless, this very power poses serious practical problems for the Court within the context of the Italian political system. The government, often for its own vested interests, but at times because of the fragile matrix of alliances on which its power tends to rest, frequently responds slowly to judgments of the Court, if it responds at all. When deciding to overrule a piece of existing legislation the constitutional judges are thus forced to take into account the probability that there will be no legislative initiative to fill the void created by their decision. At times the void has seemed worse than the law itself, and the judges, with their *horror vacui*, have preferred to leave the law standing while minimizing, where possible, its unconstitutional elements through a creative system of legal interpretation and directions for action to the legislature.

During the first two decades of its existence the Court faced only marginal political opposition, the bulk of its work being to evaluate the pre-war legislation of the Fascist regime. This caused only limited institutional conflict and won the Court considerable prestige in the latter part of the 1960s. By the 1970s, however, much of this legislation had been cleared out of the way, and the Court was increasingly called upon to evaluate post-war legislation, almost without exception the result of exhaustive political negotiation and compromise. The legitimacy of the existing system of state broadcasting first came before the courts in 1960, and since then the Constitutional Court has been used repeatedly as a forum in which Italian audiovisual regulations can be evaluated. Any analysis of the Court's role must take into account not only its potentially far-reaching powers of review but also the existence of an influential and expanding private sector and a largely inert legislature, paralysed by the manœuvering of party factions and vested interests.

Although the ensuing discussion focuses on the role of the Constitutional Court, a key player in establishing general guidelines for the audiovisual sector, the ordinary civil and administrative courts have also taken an active role in regulating the broadcasting media. Not only have they been called upon to work out the practical implications of the Constitutional Court's decisions and the often unsatisfactory legislative provisions in force, they have also sought to address the immediate and very real problems which stemmed from the regulatory void during the late 1970s and 1980s by imposing some order on the use of frequencies pending further legislative enactment. Both the ordinary[39] and the separate

---

[39] The competence of the civil courts of first instance, the Conciliatori, Preture, and Tribunali, is determined by the value and nature of the issues in dispute. From these courts appeal is to the Preture, Tribunale, and Corte d'appello respectively. The final court of appeal on questions of law is the Corte suprema di cassazione: G. L. Certoma (1985), 189.

administrative[40] courts have jurisdiction to review administrative decisions. Which court the dispute ends up in will depend on the nature of the individual interest considered to be at stake. Italian law draws a distinction between individual rights, the *diritto soggettivo*, and legitimate interests, *l'interesse legittimo*. Where an individual has a *diritto soggettivo* he or she will enjoy a right of ownership over property, or control over the actions of third parties, which the state will support and protect. The holder of an *interesse legittimo* has an interest in the proper exercise of administrative power, according to legal requirements, where he or she stands to benefit from either the removal of an impediment or the grant of a particular status or advantage.[41] Administrative disputes relating to individual rights are heard in the ordinary courts which, in accordance with the Italian concept of the separation of powers, do not have jurisdiction to overrule or amend the administrative measure. Instead, they have power merely to disapply the provision in the case at hand and award damages against the public body. Disputes relating to legitimate interests are heard in the administrative courts, which are empowered to quash the administrative measure.[42]

This distinction is of considerable importance in the audiovisual sector because of the role which the administration plays in granting broadcast licences and overseeing compliance with their terms. In 1976 the Constitutional Court held the prohibition of private broadcasting at the local (terrestrial) level to be unconstitutional, leading certain broadcasters to assert that they had an individual right, in the absence of applicable legislation, to establish their own local radio and television stations.[43] Only after some considerable time did the Constitutional Court reject this interpretation, confirming in 1990 that individuals do not have a right to set up and run a broadcast station, but only a legitimate interest in the proper management of the radio frequencies.[44] In consequence, disputes concerning the allocation or withdrawal of broadcast licences are considered in the administrative and not ordinary courts.

If we turn to examine the enforcement of international treaties in domestic law, it may be noted that Article 11 of the Italian Constitution provides that it is possible for the State to limit its sovereignty, on condition that this is done on the basis of reciprocal undertakings entered into by other states and that the agreed provisions are necessary to ensure

[40] The Tribunali amministrativi regionali deal with administrative law issues at first instance from which appeals are made to the Consiglio di Stato.
[41] These relationships are explained in more detail in G. L. Certoma (1985), 20–3.
[42] This distinction has, however, become less clear-cut in recent years as administrative courts have extended their jurisdiction into specific areas where individual rights may be affected: L. N. Brown and J. S. Bell (1993), 257.
[43] Dec. 202/1976 [1976] Giur. cost. 1267.
[44] Dec. 102/1990 [1990] Giur. cost. 610.

peace and justice among nations. Italy ratified the European Convention on Human Rights in 1955, but the status of the Convention in domestic law has been subject to considerable jurisprudential debate and uncertainty. Some clarification was provided by a decision of the Corte di cassazione in 1988 which held those Convention provisions capable of direct application in Italy to have the status of domestic law.[45] Nevertheless, it remains debatable which provisions are capable of direct incorporation into the domestic system and, even for those provisions which are held to be internally applicable, their status is that of ordinary, not constitutional, law, leaving open the possibility that they may be overruled by subsequent legislation. Italy is also a member of the European Community and the Italian courts have for the most part accepted the supremacy of Community over national law. The Constitutional Court has, however, indicated that, were a Community measure to contravene one of the guarantees of human rights established in the Italian Constitution, then Italian and not Community law would be applied.[46]

3. FRANCE: A DECADE OF POLITICAL AND JUDICIAL SYMBIOSIS

The involvement of the Italian Constitutional Court in broadcasting matters predates that of the Conseil constitutionnel by two decades. Meaningful intervention by the French Conseil constitutionnel commenced only in the 1980s, a delay which finds its roots in the restricted role afforded constitutional review within the French political system. France, unlike Britain, may boast both a charter of individual rights, the *Déclaration des droits de l'homme et du citoyen* ('the 1789 Declaration'), and a formal, written constitution adopted in 1958. The 1958 Constitution was primarily designed to establish a new balance of power between the government and Parliament, a balance which favoured the executive and was prompted by the years of government instability under the post-war Fourth Republic. The 1958 Constitution does not itself enumerate an exhaustive list of guaranteed individual rights, along Italian lines, but it was this document which finally instituted, after years of debate, promises, and half measures, the present French Constitutional Court, the Conseil constitutionnel.

The Conseil constitutionnel is empowered to oversee the conformity of parliamentary legislation with the Constitution prior to its promulgation. Under the 1958 Constitution the French Parliament has power to legislate only within a carefully defined area, principally that set out in Article 34. Unlike the UK or Italian Parliaments, therefore, the French Parliament

---

[45] G. E. Longo (1992).   [46] P. Craig and G. de Búrca (1995), 263–7.

can enact statutes, or *lois*, only if they fall within a delimited field of competence. Residual legislative capacity rests with the government, which passes legislation in the form of *règlements*. Under Article 34 rules relating to civic rights, civil liberties, property rights, and commercial obligations are to be established by statute, and the key legislative texts governing the organization of the mass media have consequently been established by *lois*, although executive decrees have been passed in certain areas to fill in detailed regulations. It has thus been possible to subject the major legislative initiatives of the 1908s in the broadcasting field to the scrutiny of the Conseil constitutionnel.

If the establishment of the Conseil constitutionnel was a necessary step in protecting constitutionally recognized rights it was by no means a sufficient one. Although the Conseil constitutionnel today enjoys a high level of public recognition as an important protagonist in the current French legislative process, this has not always been so. Initially, the Conseil constitutionnel adopted a restrictive evaluation of its own role, limiting itself, for the most part, to ensuring that Parliament did not overstep its powers by moving into the strengthened regulatory domain carefully reserved for the French government under the 1958 Constitution. This, indeed, was exactly the role which those who had drafted the constitution had envisaged for it: a *chien de garde de la suprématie de l'exécutif.*[47]

This early reserve on the part of the Conseil was undoubtedly also a reaction to the hostility to judicial control of legislative action within French political doctrine.[48] Although in the immediate post-war period the introduction of judicially protected fundamental rights found a receptive home in West Germany, France still clung to its Republican vision, in which neither church, nor monarchy, nor the judiciary itself could be allowed to intervene in the workings of the elected representatives of the people. If the French were prepared to make solemn declarations of right in the preamble to the 1946 Constitution, they were not yet ready to place the enforcement of such rights outside the hands of the legislature and the existing civil-service administration. Moreover, the parties of the left in France, like their Italian counterparts, were suspicious of a judicial solution to what were considered political problems, fearing resistance to any alteration in established economic or property interests. Here, too, the lesson of the American Supreme Court's opposition to the government's 'New Deal' policies of the 1930s, had not been forgotten.

In consequence, when the Conseil constitutionnel was finally established its powers and ordained role were carefully contained. As initially adopted the 1958 Constitution provided that only the President of the Republic, the

[47] J. T. S. Keeler (1985).   [48] J. Bell (1992), 20–7.

Prime Minister, or the presidents of the two Assemblies could challenge the constitutionality of proposed legislation: no standing was afforded to individual citizens. Furthermore, allegations of unconstitutionality could only be raised prior to the final adoption of legislation; review of extant legislation was therefore precluded. The Conseil's initial reticence was thus both a tactical response to the continuing hostility to its role and an inherent consequence of the structural limitations set out in the 1958 Constitution. It should come as little suprise to read that from 1960 to 1974 there were only nine applications under the Article 61.2 procedure, authorizing the submission of a bill to the Conseil constitutionnel for review.[49] If, however, we look to the period from June 1981 to December 1984, a quantum leap in the number of such applications can be detected, sixty-five in all, and the French Court had at last embarked on its analysis of the constitutional imperatives for the audiovisual sector. What stimulated this expanded jurisdiction?

Two crucial events served to move the Conseil constitutionnel to the centre of the political stage. The first, instituted in 1974 under the presidency of Giscard d'Estaing, was an enlargement of the rights of standing: this permitted sixty deputies or sixty senators to refer pending legislation to the court for review. At a stroke opposition parties gained access to a potent weapon of last resort which could be set against the extensive powers of an incumbent government. A weapon which, as the figures illustrate, was widely used during the swings in political fortunes of the 1980s.

The second stimulus to recourse to the Conseil constitutionnel stems from the development of the Conseil's own case law. Over the course of the last two decades the Conseil has been prepared to look beyond the operative Articles of the 1958 Constitution to its preamble and to the additional documents thereby 'incorporated' as part of a widened 'block' of constitutional imperatives. This has opened a Pandora's box of potentially far-reaching, fundamental, and necessarily abstract principles, encouraging greater recourse to the Article 61.2 review procedure. In the early years of the Conseil's activities there had been considerable debate over whether the preamble to the 1958 Constitution could correctly be afforded constitutional status. The powers of the Conseil constitutionnel's precursor, the Comité constitutionnel, had been expressly curtailed to exclude recourse to the 1946 preamble and related texts. The 1958 Constitution, however, was tantalizingly silent on the status of *its* preamble. Some argued that the intention to impose a similar restraint could be read from this silence, others that the failure to make an express exclusion indicated a

---

[49] J. T. S. Keeler (1985), 136.

willingness to include the texts in question within the accepted 'block' of constitutionality, opening them up to use by the Conseil.

It was the latter view which the Conseil constitutionnel itself finally adopted in its central decision 71–44 DC of 16 July 1971.[50] The Conseil, in holding unconstitutional the requirement that political groups attain prior administrative authorization, recognized not only that the preamble to the 1958 Constitution had similar force to its other 'operative' provisions but that the therein-stated 'attachment' of the French people to the rights of man and the principles of national sovereignty set out in the 1789 Declaration, as completed by the preamble to the 1946 Constitution, served also to imbue the provisions of these two documents with constitutional status. If the Conseil constitutionnel had until this decision been faced with a paucity of principles establishing the rights and duties of French citizens, it was henceforth to have at its fingertips a powerful panoply of inter-relating guarantees.

The resulting 'practically unlimited possibility of invoking a rule or principle as a superior norm, the freedom left to the judge in the interpretation and definition of this rule'[51] caused considerable unease, if not alarm, in those quarters, essentially to the left of the political spectrum, opposed in principle to the concept of judicial review of legislation. Despite such reservations, recourse to the Conseil has mushroomed, with both right and left making use of the new possibilities for legislative scrutiny and also perhaps political delay.

The relatively late arrival of the Conseil constitutionnel into the broadcasting field was therefore a product of its carefully contained position within the French balance of powers, and, despite its more recent activism, the Conseil continues to be restrained by a number of important limitations to its jurisdiction. Perhaps the most far-reaching of these is the Conseil's inability directly to evaluate legislation which has already reached the statute book. It is sometimes said that French legislative review is of an *a priori* nature to distinguish it from the wider-ranging forms of *a posteriori* review found in the American and Italian constitutional systems. Referrals to the Conseil in any given field are thus bunched around the passage of new legislation through Parliament, being tied in to, even an integral part of, the legislative process itself. Consequently, the first meaningful opportunity for the Conseil to review government audiovisual policy—after the liberalization of standing in 1974 and the expansion in the range of constitutional principles heralded by the 1971 case—came only with the legislative changes ushered in by the new Socialist government in 1981 and 1982.

The second limitation stems from the mechanism by which questions of

---

[50] [1971] Rec. Cons. constitut. 29.   [51] Quoted in L. Hamon (1987), 166.

constitutionality are referred to the Conseil. We have already seen that there is no scope for an individual member of the public to challenge proposed legislation where the parliamentary delegates for whatever reason are prepared to let the statute through. The determination of which parts of which statutes to refer to the Conseil constitutionnel is very much a parliamentary affair, with all the scope that may leave for political compromise and negotiation. It may be noted, however, that the Conseil is not completely tied to the terms of complaint drawn up by the referring deputies or senators for, although Article 61.2 does not clearly specify the Conseil's powers of scrutiny regarding ordinary laws, the Conseil, after some initial reticence, is now prepared to consider in certain instances the entirety of the statutory text before it, not just the particular clauses brought specifically to its attention in the *saisines*.[52]

It will thus be apparent that the Conseil constitutionnel can, despite the recent willingness to expand the sphere of its scrutiny, play only a comparatively restricted role in ensuring that new legislation complies with the various constitutional imperatives. The Conseil is deeply tied into and circumscribed by the parliamentary process, increasingly a last resort for opposition challenge to controversial legislation. Consequently it would be a considerable oversimplification to view the Conseil constitutionnel as having been in some way dilatory in comparison with its Italian counterpart: the formal position of the two courts is currently very different. Despite these limitations, however, the Conseil constitutionnel has been considered a central actor in the development of the present system of audiovisual regulation in France. Indeed, Pepy and Whal have even suggested that the *'institution d'une législation multimedia dans notre pays . . . résulte directement d'une jurisprudence constitutionnelle audacieuse et novatrice'*,[53] and although other authors have proved more cautious in their estimation, fearing that the Conseil may not yet have got to grips with the intricacies of the intermeshing economic and cultural forces at play in the broadcast sector,[54] a proper understanding of this field could not be reached without examining the role played by the Conseil constitutionnel in the course of the 1980s.

As in Italy, the French administrative courts have also played a role in overseeing the activities of the various regulatory bodies set up to supervise the broadcasting sector. The French administrative courts are separate from the ordinary civil and criminal courts and have at their head the Conseil d'Etat. Below the Conseil d'Etat are the regional Cours administratives d'appel and the Tribunaux administratifs.[55] The Conseil supérieur de l'audiovisuel (CSA) currently regulates the audiovisual sector, an

---

[52] B. Genevois (1988), 48.   [53] G. Pepy and P. Whal (1987), 47.
[54] V. Porter (1989), 25.   [55] L. N. Brown and J. S. Bell (1993).

independent authority introduced to replace the Commission nationale de la communication et des libertés (CNCL) in 1989, which was itself a substitution for the Haute Autorité set up in 1982. The CSA has power to grant operating contracts to private broadcasters and ensure compliance with their terms, through its ability to impose a variety of sanctions including significant fines. In certain areas, such as advertising and sponsorship, primary legislation has made provision for operating rules to be established by decree and in such fields the CSA cannot itself regulate. Private broadcasters have not been slow to turn to the Conseil d'Etat to contest enforcement measures taken by the CSA on the basis that it has either gone beyond its legislative powers or has developed, rather than simply interpreted, the specific regulations established by decree.[56]

French administrative courts have wide powers to ensure the legality of administrative action, the ambit of which was traditionally determined by the twin requirements that the activity under review be of a public-service nature, carried out by a public body.[57] Though the concept of public service continues to exert a strong influence in French administrative law, it has for some time been apparent that the existence of a public-law body is no longer essential provided the body concerned participates in the functioning of a public service. The scope of administrative law extends beyond establishing that public bodies are acting within their specified powers and following proper procedures to monitoring compliance with certain substantive principles. Public bodies are expected to conform to the Constitution, international treaties, and parliamentary statutes, as well as to certain 'general principles of law' which have been derived by the administrative courts from the various constitutional texts and preambles. The category of general principles is a wide one, including important civil liberties and principles, such as equality of access and continuity of service, which have been applied when reviewing the activities of key public services. Even government regulations may be invalidated if they fail to conform to these principles. The Conseil constitutionnel has also recognized the importance of these general principles and has afforded certain of them constitutional status, using them to scrutinize parliamentary legislation prior to its promulgation. In addition the Conseil has distinguished a number of 'objectives of constitutional value' capable of imposing restrictions on the freedoms recognized by the Constitution; among these objectives is that of pluralism which has assumed considerable importance in the broadcasting field.[58]

---

[56] For general discussion of the administrative status of the CSA see B. Cousin and B. Delcros (1990), 64–5.
[57] For a helpful overview see L. N. Brown and J. S. Bell (1993), 125–31.
[58] R. Badinter and B. Genevois (1990), 321.

France has ratified the European Convention on Human Rights (1975) and is also a founder member of the European Community. By virtue of Article 55 of the Constitution, which provides that duly ratified treaties have, subject to reciprocal implementation by other parties, a higher authority than statute, the fundamental rights established in the European Convention are directly applicable within the domestic legal system and take precedence over both prior and subsequent legislation. The task of ensuring conformity falls to the ordinary judge. The Conseil constitutionnel views its role as limited to establishing the constitutionality of a law, and will not itself check the compatibility of a proposed law with a treaty.[59] Despite initial resistance, particularly by the Conseil d'Etat, all courts now recognize the supremacy of Community law over domestic law.[60]

4. THE EUROPEAN COURT OF HUMAN RIGHTS AND THE EUROPEAN COURT OF JUSTICE: GROWING IMPORTANCE OF THE PAN-EUROPEAN COURTS

Broadcast signals show no respect for national boundaries, and the implications of transfrontier broadcasting raised international concerns well before radio became established as a key propaganda tool in the Second World War. For those frustrated by the monitored content of domestic broadcasting, or wishing to establish commercial broadcasting stations of their own, there has been a growing temptation to look beyond national courts to international fora where their arguments may find a more receptive hearing. Domestic courts have not, therefore, stood alone in considering the legal parameters to government broadcast policy: the European Commission and Court of Human Rights as well as the European Court of Justice have handed down a number of decisions with important implications for the way in which the audiovisual media are regulated.

The European Commission and Court of Human Rights were established under the European Convention on Human Rights and Fundamental Freedoms which came into force on 3 September 1953. The Commission and Court share responsibility for monitoring state compliance with the guarantees set out in the Convention. The introduction of an independent monitoring body constituted a novel qualification to existing notions of state sovereignty and was strongly criticized by certain states as likely to lead to abusive and unfounded claims. Some provision was made for these concerns by restricting the availability of individual petition to those countries which had expressly recognized such a right and holding back

---

[59] *Ibid.* 328 and J. Bell (1992), 31.
[60] P. Craig and G. de Búrca (1995), 252–5.

establishment of the European Court of Human Rights until eight Member States had accepted its compulsory jurisdiction. It was not until September 1958 that the eight acceptances had been given and the Court was finally constituted in January 1959.

The original system established by the Convention, and which currrently remains in force, permits an individual to refer his or her complaint to the Commission only after having exhausted all domestic remedies. Applications must be made within six months of the date of the final decision in the national forum. The Commission seeks to obtain a 'friendly settlement' but, failing this, will draw up a report specifying whether it considers on the given facts that the state has acted in breach of the Convention. This report is transmitted to the Committee of Ministers and the Commission or one of the states involved can then refer the matter on to the Court. At present, therefore, individuals do not have direct recourse to the Court.

The recent addition of Protocol 11 to the European Convention has, however, set the stage for the establishment of a new European Court.[61] Protocol 11 was introduced in order to speed up the consideration of cases, which can currently take five or six years. Under Protocol 11 individuals will be able to apply directly to the Court, which will take over the role of the Commission in determining the initial admissibility of a complaint. Most cases will be decided in Chambers consisting of seven judges, although particularly important cases may be referred to, or re-heard by, a Grand Chamber of seventeen judges. These new arrangements will come into effect one year after all the Member States have ratified the Protocol, and it is possible that the Court could be functioning in 1998. For the moment, however, the original procedures continue in operation. As we have seen from the preceding sections, although the United Kingdom, Italy, and France have all ratified the Convention and recognize an individual right of petition, the impact of the Convention differs markedly from one state to another.[62]

Although the European Convention has had a relatively limited impact on the domestic broadcasting policies of the three countries under consideration, the same cannot be said of the EC Treaty. The direct effect of much Community law and the scope this offers for individuals to enforce Community rights against the state or its organs through the domestic courts render it impossible to consider national rules and regulations in isolation from the wider Community context. The Community emphasis in the run-up to completion of the Internal Market in 1993 on the removal of national barriers to trade and free-market competition played an important

---

[61] A. R. Mowbray (1994), 540.
[62] For further details see J. E. S. Fawcett (1987).

part in the realignment of the audiovisual media with the world of industry and business, away from the purely political or cultural domains.

The Treaty establishing the European Economic Community of 1957 ('the EEC Treaty') was primarily designed to further the economic integration of its Member States, though certain countries undoubtedly hoped this would prove merely the prelude to greater political integration, a hope reflected in the reference in the preamble to an 'ever closer union among the peoples of Europe'. The four basic freedoms established in the Treaty, namely the free movement of goods, services, persons, and capital among the constituent Member States, were presented as essentially economic concerns, and there was no attempt to include a more far-reaching charter of human rights. It was left to the European Court of Justice to seek to allay the unease expressed by certain domestic courts over potential conflicts between Community law and national constitutional rights by holding that the Community would itself be required to conform to fundamental rights.[63] Fundamental human rights consequently represent a constraining framework for Community action but, as noted in more detail in section 1 above, they are not a direct source of rights under Community law.

Although the EEC Treaty of 1957 did not expressly refer to the cultural field, it soon became apparent that the commercial nature of many cultural activities meant that they were subject to Community competition and free-movement rules. Given that no simple line can be drawn between cultural and economic activities, the Community began to give further thought to what role it should play in the cultural field, and in 1977 the Commission published its first communication on Community action in the cultural sector.[64] In May 1988 the Culture Ministers isolated four priority sectors for Community action, among them the audiovisual sector, and in October 1989 the important 'Television Without Frontiers' Directive (the '1989 Television Directive') was agreed, which sought to lay the foundations for a pan-European market in television services.[65] In 1992 the Commission published a wide-ranging document entitled 'New Prospects For Community Cultural Action' which emphasized the role of the Community in promoting cultural expression both at the regional and national, as well as at the European, level.[66] In addition, it called for cultural aspects to be taken into account in the development of all

---

[63] J. H. H. Weiler (1991).
[64] 'Community Action in the Cultural Sector', 22 Nov. 1977, *Bull. EC*, supplement 6/77. For a more comprehensive study of the evolution of Community involvement in the audiovisual sector see R. Collins (1994), 20–40.
[65] Dir. 89/552/EEC, [1989] OJ L298/23.
[66] COM(92)149 final, 29 Apr. 1992.

Community policies, in particular in the audiovisual field, a requirement now explicitly set out in Article 128(4) of the Treaty in its revised form.

The Treaty on European Union, which entered into force in November 1993, renamed the European Economic Community the 'European Community' and added new areas of Community competence to the 1957 Treaty (referred to in its amended form as the 'EC Treaty'). In particular, it specifically recognized the legitimacy of Community action in the cultural field. Article 3(p) of the EC Treaty now provides for Community action which will contribute to the provision of 'education and training of quality and to the flowering of the cultures of the Member States', while a new Title IX dealing with cultural matters has also been added. These provisions do not, however, create directly enforceable individual rights, and the essentially supportive role to be played by the Community in assisting Member States in this field is emphasized in Article 128 of Title IX. Specific recognition of cultural concerns can also be found in paragraph 3(d) of Article 92, also added by the Treaty on European Union. This provides that state aid, treated as suspect under the EC Treaty as a distortion of competition, may, where it promotes culture and heritage conservation, be compatible with the Treaty provided 'such aid does not affect trading conditions and competition in the Community to an extent that is contrary to the common interest'. Despite its initial emphasis on economic relations the European Community has consequently become closely involved in cultural matters and has developed its own cultural agenda.[67]

The scene was set for Community involvement in the broadcasting sector in 1974 when the European Court of Justice held that the transmission of television broadcasts fell within the provisions relating to the supply of services in the EC Treaty, while the sale of sound and video tapes were covered by the rules relating to the free movement of goods.[68] As the economic importance of the broadcast sector has become ever more apparent, so Community intervention in the field has expanded, with initiatives tending to take one of three forms. In the first instance, the Community has sought to open up national markets to foreign competition, encouraging operators to expand and reap the benefits of economies of scale. The 1989 Television Directive, which limits the ability of Member States to require that foreign broadcasting services comply with domestic programme requirements, is the central plank of this initiative. Secondly, the Community has sought to ensure that there is a 'level playing field' and that no operator, whether public or private, acts in contravention of the Treaty competition rules. Thirdly, the Community has encouraged the

---

[67] For more detailed consideration of these trends see B. de Witte (1995).
[68] Case 155/73, *Italy* v. *Sacchi* [1974] 2 CMLR 177.

development of the European audiovisual market by injecting financial support at certain key points in the production and exploitation chain, usually on terms requiring a degree of co-operation between operators from different EU countries. Underlying such initiatives there is, as Richard Collins notes, an inevitable tension between liberal and interventionist philosophies.[69]

The European Court of Justice has, throughout, been an important focus for Community scrutiny, primarily as a result of the reference procedure established in Article 177 of the EC Treaty. Under Article 177 national courts and tribunals may refer questions relating to the interpretation of the EC Treaty or Community measures, for example directives and regulations, to the European Court of Justice and, where there is no right of appeal from the national court or tribunal, that body may be required to make such a reference. The Commission has also used Article 169 to refer potential infringements of Community law by the Member States to the European Court of Justice, while the propriety of actions taken by the Community institutions may itself be challenged by Member States and other Community institutions under Article 173. The Court of First Instance, which was set up in 1988 to relieve the European Court of Justice of some of its workload, has jurisdiction to hear all actions brought by individuals against Community institutions.[70] Together, the European Court of Justice and Court of First Instance have come to establish key principles governing Community involvement in the audiovisual sector. In particular, the European Court of Justice, by demarcating the line between state and Community competence, has often pointed the way to Community initiatives designed to set standards and liberalize trade in audiovisual goods and services throughout the Common Market.

[69] R. Collins (1994), ch. 2.
[70] For details on both the ECJ and CFI see P. Craig and G. de Búrca (1995), 70–88.

5

The Constitutional Tools
of the Trade

In their search for legal assistance private operators have taken full advantage of the fact that constitutional charters tend not to speak with one, unified voice as to the legal requirements for the audiovisual sector, but rather pose a number of potentially conflicting ways of looking at the broadcast media. As a general rule the national constitutions of European states do not set out detailed provisions governing the regulation of radio and television services as they frequently do for the printed press.[1] Only very exceptionally does one find a specific provision of the type contained in Article 38 of the 1989 Portuguese Constitution which stipulates that the state is to ensure that there is a functioning public radio and television service. The absence of any direct reference to broadcasting in the various French and Italian constitutional texts is thus not at all unusual, but the resulting indeterminacy has forced judges to make creative use of a number of generalized provisions applicable to a wide spectrum of activities, provisions developed at a time when radio and television services were simply non-existent or enjoyed a social and cultural status very different from that of today.

It is possible to isolate four main categories of constitutional guarantees which have a potential bearing on the organization of the audiovisual media:[2]

(i) Those setting out a *right to property* and the closely allied provisions guaranteeing a *right to free economic initiative* (Articles 41 to 44 of the 1948 Italian Constitution (the 'Italian Constitution'), Articles 2 and 17 of the 1789 French Declaration of the Rights of Man and the Citizen (the '1789 Declaration'), and the First Protocol to the 1950 European Convention for the Protection of Human Rights and Fundamental Freedoms (the 'European Convention')). The provisions of the EC Treaty guaranteeing free movement of goods and services, and freedom of establishment within the European Union, also serve to protect economic activity with an inter-state dimension from national restraint (Articles 30–37, 52–58, and 59–66). Drawing

---

[1] See, e.g., Art. 21 of the 1948 Italian Constitution.
[2] The principal constitutional Arts. considered in this book are set out in the App.

on the constitutions of the EU Member States, the European Court of Justice has included rights to property and to trade within the category of fundamental human rights to be respected in European Community law.[3]

(ii)   Those guaranteeing *freedom of speech and expression*. These may be more or less detailed in their exposition. They range in scope from the relatively perfunctory Article 11 of the 1789 Declaration and Article 21 of the Italian Constitution,[4] which *prima facie* focus on the individual's right to *express* and *communicate* his or her thoughts or opinions, to the rather more expansive provisions of Article 10 of the European Convention, which refers in its first paragraph to the freedom to 'hold opinions and to *receive* and *impart* information and ideas without interference by public authority and regardless of frontiers'. Additionally, Article 19(2) of the 1966 International Covenant on Civil and Political Rights establishes a right to *seek* information. Freedom of expression within the terms set out in Article 10 of the European Convention has also been recognized as a fundamental human right by the European Court of Justice.[5]

(iii)   Those providing for *equality* among citizens in the enjoyment of their rights and freedoms. Many provisions outlaw quite specific forms of discrimination, on the basis, for example, of sex, nationality, religion, or race. A number of articles, such as Article 3 of the Italian Constitution, Articles 1 and 6 of the 1789 Declaration, Articles 1 and 2 of the 1958 French Constitution, and Article 14 of the European Convention, are, however, expressed in wide-ranging terms. Although the EC Treaty targets only specific forms of discrimination, the European Court of Justice has held equality to be one of the general principles of law recognized by the Community legal order.[6] The principle of equality imposes upon the legislative body a duty to ensure that statutory provisions do not draw arbitrary or unreasonable distinctions between individuals or groups. Constitutional guarantees of equality have been used to challenge the adoption of differing regulatory regimes for the press and broadcasting, as well as the establishment of disparate rules for television operators depending on their means of transmission—cable, satellite etc.[7]

The principle of equality is closely linked to that of *proportionality*,

[3] Case 44/79, *Hauer* v. *Land Rheinland-Pfalz* [1979] ECR 3727.
[4] Though the provisions relating to the press are here quite specific.
[5] Case C–260/89, *Elliniki Radiophonia Tileorassi AE* v. *Dimotiki Etairia Pliroforissis and Sotirios Kouvelas* [1991] ECR I–2925.   [6] T. C. Hartley (1994), 157.
[7] See, e.g., the Italian Dec. 202/76 [1976] Giur. cost. 1267, where distinctions between cable and terrestrial transmissions, at least at the local level, were held to infringe the guarantee of equality enshrined in Art. 3 of the Italian Constitution.

a principle generally understood to require that restraints on individual action be suitably tailored to achieve their objective and not be excessive. Proportionality consequently mandates a reasonable relationship between means and ends. The link between the two principles is very apparent in the Italian legal order where proportionality, which receives no separate constitutional recognition, is considered an aspect of equality.[8] In France, the Conseil constitutionnel ensures respect for the principle of proportionality when this is specifically stipulated in a constitutional provision, and, on a number of occasions, has recognized the need for proportionality in contexts where there is no such express requirement.[9] Nevertheless, proportionality is not considered by the Conseil to be a generally applicable constitutional principle. A proportionality test is incorporated in those provisions of the European Convention which establish permissible derogations from fundamental rights: only restrictions which are 'necessary in a democratic society' will be accepted. The European Court of Human Rights, when faced, for example, with a restriction on freedom of expression under Article 10, will require the relevant state to provide 'convincing justification' for its introduction. The European Court of Justice considers proportionality to be a general principle of Community law and the principle is now embodied in Article 3b of the EC Treaty which provides that '[a]ny action by the Community shall not go beyond what is necessary to achieve the objects of this Treaty.' Where a Member State seeks to derogate from Community freedoms the European Court of Justice applies a demanding proportionality test under which it must be shown that there was no alternative way of achieving the Member State's objective which was less restrictive of Community rights.

(iv) Finally, reference should be made to a hotchpotch of provisions which seek to ensure that individuals have *access to the basic skills necessary for effective social and political participation* in the world around them. One of the clearest expressions of such an objective can be found in the second paragraph of Article 3 of the Italian Constitution and, from a French perspective, similar concerns are apparent in paragraph 13 of the 1946 Preamble. It is worth noting that the EC Treaty as amended now provides in Article 3(p) that the activities of the Community are to include 'a contribution to education and training of quality and to the flowering of the cultures of the Member States'. This commitment to European culture and education should not, however, be read as creating directly enforceable individual rights. Instead, it envisages the development by the

[8] A. Pace (1994), 228.　　　[9] M. Fromont (1994), 106.

Community of policies designed merely to 'support and supplement' Member State action in these fields (Articles 126 and 128).

This, of course, is not an exhaustive list, and it is possible to point to a number of other provisions—the protection afforded to artistic endeavour in Article 33 of the Italian Constitution, or the guarantee of privacy in Article 8 of the European Convention, which are undoubtedly of relevance for the mass media. The provisions mentioned above are, however, those which have featured most prominently in the legal debates about the structure of the broadcasting industry and are the main subject of discussion in the following chapters. It is also important to bear in mind that although there is no charter of fundamental rights in the United Kingdom, domestic courts have nevertheless recognized a number of key interests, among them freedom of expression, which they will endeavour to protect when interpreting legislation or applying the common law.

It will be immediately apparent that these constitutional provisions, for the most part phrased in very general terms, leave ample scope for judicial interpretation and the construction of quite divergent regulatory frameworks for the broadcast media. A focus on the protection afforded to property rights and entrepreneurial freedom, identified in paragraph (i) above, would lead one, for example, to emphasize the economic aspects of broadcasting and the creation of a competitive market in broadcast goods and services. If, however, one turns instead to focus on those provisions which look to the individual's need for social and political participation, identified in paragraph (iv) above, then the role of the mass media in conveying information, education, and entertainment to all members of society becomes a central consideration. From this perspective the media are not simply commodities like any other, but rather key social institutions which, like the right to vote, cannot satisfactorily be allocated on the basis of financial means. Attempts to construct an audiovisual system around one only of these diverse concerns would undoubtedly yield a very different blueprint from that centring on another aspect. But consideration must be given to each of the various functions played by the mass media in society, for broadcasting is at one and the same time an economic and a cultural endeavour. Any sensitive appreciation of the subject must therefore seek to accommodate both these elements. This lies at the root of the considerable judicial challenge, for economic and cultural needs may be at variance: as Nicholas Garnham has noted, 'there is a fundamental contradiction between the economic and the political at the level of their value systems and of the social relations which these value systems require and support'.[10]

The constitutional texts seem, then, to draw attention to rather than

[10] N. Garnham (1986), 31.

resolve the tension between individual freedom and social needs. This is illustrated by a comparison of the French Declaration of 1789 with the Preamble to the 1946 Constitution. The former is widely regarded a resounding vindication of individual rights in the face of arbitrary and corrupt monarchic power,[11] while the latter focuses firmly on the social and collective needs of a country devastated by two world wars. But not only do the constitutional texts bring into stark relief the conflict between *individual* and *social* demands—as, for example, the conflict between an owner's claim to use his broadcasting station as he sees fit by transmitting only programmes propounding a particular religious faith, with his audience's 'right' to have access to information fitting its members for life in a multi-racial, multi-faith democracy—they also lay bare conflicts between *competing individual* rights—an individual's right, for example, to express her Jewish faith on a Buddhist channel owned by another. The assertion, that is, of an individual right to expression, may collide with what many consider to be the property right of station owners to transmit what they wish over their radio or television channels.

Nor does textual uncertainty stop there, for tensions can be seen to exist not only *between* the various constitutional guarantees but also *within* them. This is particularly marked if we turn to consider the key constitutional provision for the audiovisual media, the guarantee of freedom of expression. 'Freedom of expression' has become a shorthand term for a varied bundle of rights and interests, interpreted as more or less extensive in scope depending on the objectives the interpreter seeks to realize. At one extreme it is seen as simply protecting from government censorship those who wish to express themselves, guaranteeing, that is, 'negative' liberty rights. At the other, freedom of expression is thought to necessitate 'positive' state intervention in order to shape a broadcasting industry which, though limiting the capacity of some to speak, gives greater numbers of citizens access to the media.[12] Such intervention may go

---

[11] J.-P. Costa (1986), 21, notes the absence of all reference in the Declaration to '*groupes, associations coalitions . . ., non plus qu'à la famille ou au corps intermédiaires.*' For further examination of Costa's suggestion that the 1789 Declaration was an essentially 'bourgeois' document see W. Doyle (1981) and F. Furet (1988). Yet the argument that the 1789 Declaration was primarily designed to ensure individual emancipation from state control may lead one to overlook those aspects of the text which recognize that individual freedoms are not exercised in social isolation and, for the common good, may have to be curtailed. A more wide-ranging criticism of the characterization of the freedoms espoused by classical liberals as exclusively 'negative', designed to wall off 'a private sphere beyond the competence of public officials', can be found in S. Holmes (1990), 23: 'Lockean rights are not merely shields against governmental involvement; they include explicit *entitlements to affirmative state action* to protect individuals from harm by third parties.'

[12] For what has become, perhaps, the seminal exposition of 'positive' and 'negative' freedom see I. Berlin (1969). Although useful conceptually, it is questionable to what extent this distinction offers us concrete answers to the type of value conflicts indicated above, at

beyond mandating third-party access to require the transmission of particular programmes, for example news and current affairs, and in this formulation freedom of expression can be seen to embrace a right on the part of the public to information.[13]

Faced with a conflict between a station owner's wish to broadcast exactly what he or she wishes and the public's interest in obtaining access to additional or alternative information, how should a judge decide? The constitutional texts under consideration provide, on their face, no simple solution: for example, the right to free expression is held by Article 10 of the European Convention to embrace *both* the right to speak and the right to hear. On one view the right to hear is no more than a reflex of the right to speak; it merely prohibits intervention with reception, for without an audience the capacity to speak has limited importance, speech being an essentially communicative activity. A more expansive interpretation would regard the right to hear as necessitating access to such information as individuals may require in order to make informed social and political choices.

It is possible to conclude from the preceding discussion that for courts of law, called to establish legal guidelines for the regulation of the audiovisual media, there have been two key and overlapping issues:

(i)   Which of the various rights and freedoms are applicable in the broadcasting field? Do different principles apply to different media?
(ii) How should the various rights be interpreted in this context? Does freedom of expression, for example, serve merely to 'protect' broadcasters from state intervention or does it guarantee the public a right to diverse and varied information?

Given that the answers to these questions cannot simply be 'read off' the legal texts, it has been necessary for judges to consider what sort of communications system would be compatible with the democratic and social traditions found in Western Europe. Before them have been parties eager to recreate, at the level of constitutional rights, the battle for free-market or public-service models discussed in Chapter 4. Those who seek to prevent the 'appropriation of legal rights and democratic processes for private or partial ends'[14] have found themselves confronting others who consider legal rights to have been designed to further exactly these ends.

---

least if we reject, as does Berlin himself, any simple hierarchization of the two types of liberty: 'I should like to say once again to my critics that the issue is not one between negative freedom as an absolute value and other, inferior values. It is more complex and more painful. One freedom may abort another . . . positive and negative freedom may collide; the freedom of the individual or the group may not be fully compatible with a full degree of participation in a common life, with its demands for co-operation, solidarity, fraternity': *ibid.*, at lvi.

[13] See E. Barendt (1985), 81–6, for discussion of the political arguments concerning claim rights to free speech.   [14] *Ibid.*

The textual openness of constitutional guarantees has consequently left judicial decisions vulnerable to political criticism, a factor which may explain the initial caution of the Italian Constitutional Court and the European Commission of Human Rights when considering the legitimacy of existing broadcasting structures. Concern over the 'unaccountable' role played by constitutional judges in a democratic state may lead to the search for some 'automatic', discretion-free, system of adjudication. As we have seen, however, at least one proposed method—looking to the intentions of those who framed the constitutional texts—will often be vitiated by the fact that those intentions evolved, indeed changed, over time: the men who framed the French 1789 Declaration held a very different view of social relations from that espoused by the men and women who gathered together in the aftermath of the Second World War to frame the 1946 Constitution. Indeed it has been noted that these are *deux documents dont il faut bien reconnaître qu'ils sont assez sensiblement contradictoires*.[15] Moreover, such documents are the fruit of often long and acrimonious negotiation: ambiguity may deliberately be introduced to facilitate agreement. In such circumstances all attempts to ascertain a unified, underlying intention are doomed to failure. But even if one were to be dealing with a single text, framed by a homogeneous body of drafters whose intentions have been well-documented, there must be other, deep-rooted anxieties about the desirability of adopting such an approach. For an attempt to shackle the development of constitutional principles in the audiovisual sector to principles, however nebulous, established in the eighteenth and early nineteenth centuries, when radio and television had hardly been dreamed of, displays a fear of judicial innovation verging on the pathological.

Other attempts to delineate a 'judge-neutral' method of adjudication seem equally problematic.[16] Judge Richard Posner has suggested, for example, that a form of economic 'cost-benefit' analysis may be employed to determine entitlements when human rights come under legal scrutiny.[17] But though such an approach may assist in isolating the various interests or issues at stake, economics may ultimately prove not to be that helpful 'in the inherently subjective process of weighing and quantifying competing concerns'.[18] For the cost-benefit equation to be a useful guide to action some comparable unit of measurement must be attributable to its various constituent elements, but all too often this appears an impossible attempt

---

[15] Jean Foyer, quoted in L. Hamon (1987), 178 ('two documents which it is necessary to recognise as being quite noticeably contradictory'). For a thoroughgoing critique of the American New Right's call for constitutional provisions to be interpreted in the light of the framers' 'intentions' see S. Macedo (1991), 164–7.   [16] T. Mullen (1986), 24.
[17] R. A. Posner (1986).   [18] P. J. Hammer (1988), 499.

to quantify the unquantifiable, as indeed Posner himself recognizes.[19] The danger that the selection and weighing of variables may ultimately prove a subjective enterprise is itself illustrated by Posner's deployment 'of the size of actual and potential audience as a simple proxy for the value of speech',[20] an equation which may be challenged as discounting the spectrum of values which the individual audience members would themselves ascribe to the speech in question. Although it would not be impossible to build into the cost-benefit equation some weighting for audience appreciation, the approach adopted by Posner gives credence to Peter Hammer's observation that '[m]arket analysis shifts attention away from the individual and towards socially aggregated sums where the individual can become an expendable victim of marginal analysis'.[21] Thus Posner's formulation, despite its obvious attractions for those free marketeers who seek to justify their services on the basis of audience ratings, is likely to prove anathema to those in the broadcasting industry who regard the question of 'value' to be infinitely more complex than whether a certain number of viewers are prepared to switch on or off their television sets for any given programme. If cost-benefit analysis may usefully help us to clarify certain of the issues at stake in cases involving constitutional rights, it is far from rendering our judges simple arithmeticians or neutral brokers in a world of quantifiable values.

Opinions about the acceptability of judicial discretion in applying constitutional principles are inevitably divided. On the one hand there is the view that central policy decisions are better taken by a democratically elected legislature. The choice between a public sector and a 'free' market in broadcast services is considered by many, and particularly those brought up in the British constitutional tradition, essentially a matter for elected parliaments rather than unelected judges. On the other, it is argued that it is necessary to adopt a charter of individual rights to serve as a deliberate brake on the potential tyranny of majoritarian rule.[22] Seen in this light, what is at issue is not so much democracy but judicial accountability: has the constitutional settlement itself established adequate and justifiable parameters to judicial action? Concern, particularly by those on the left, that judges have in the past all too often sought to protect established property rights from the full impact of reallocative measures may lead to the conclusion that the parameters of these rights are frequently too

---

[19] 'To try to measure the value of particular speeches (or writings) would often—though, not always, as we shall see—involve intractable, subjective, and arbitrary inquiries, implying that E (error costs) would be very high': R. A. Posner (1986), 9.

[20] R. A. Posner (1986), 54.

[21] P. J. Hammer (1988), 522.

[22] For an examination of these issues see S. Macedo (1991), particularly at ch. 5.

sketchily drawn.[23] Faced with a choice between the individual property and speech rights of broadcasters and a general social right to information the judicial answer may seem a foregone conclusion.

It is, however, possible to argue that the very generality of these constitutional provisions represents a reasonable response to the complexities of everyday life: those who frame such documents wish them to be expansive in reach and enduring in time. As Judge Posner has noted with regard to the American Constitution: '[i]n default of scholarly consensus, the best assumption may be that the framers deliberately chose a rather indefinite and non-committal formulation and left to the future the task of giving it precise content.'[24] Indeed, it would be surprising if such provisions, establishing as they do the bare bones of a nation's constitutional rights, did not leave ample scope for evolution. Without this openness provisions such as Article 11 of the 1789 Declaration could not be applied to today's audiovisual media, tied as they would be to the technology of the time. Where legislation crosses over into the area covered by constitutional guarantees judges may, however, exercise a degree of circumspection in deciding whether or not to strike it down. The existence, within a constitutional system, of a higher order of fundamental rights does not inevitably entail wholesale judicial intervention in the legislative process, and there are strong arguments against any such role.[25] In framing legislation, governments are not tied to the limited perspective of a particular court action, are ultimately accountable to the public through the election process, and, unlike courts of law, have extensive powers of consultation and deliberation. Nevertheless, the particular allegiances of political parties and the influence of wealthy interest groups may lead to constitutionally recognized interests being disregarded in the political process: in such circumstances judicial intervention may seem both desirable and legitimate.

If judges when applying constitutional provisions cannot be outcome-neutral they are not simply thrown back onto unbounded discretion. Constitutional settlements establish their own systems of checks and balances, of opportunities and areas delimited 'off limits' not only for the executive and legislative branches of government but for the judicial branch as well. Law, as Felix Cohen has colourfully argued, 'is not a mass of unrelated decisions nor a product of judicial bellyaches' and judges in adjudicating a case face both internal and external restraints on their discretion.[26] Internally, they must pay due attention to constitutional and

---

[23] See, e.g., the discussion of the US Supreme Court's resistance to racial equality in the 'social sphere' and minimum wage and maximum employment hours legislation during the early decades of this century, in C. R. Sunstein (1994), 40–51.

[24] R. A. Posner (1986), 5.   [25] C. R. Sunstein (1993), 149.

[26] F. S. Cohen (1935), 843.

legislative provisions, to the system of precedent as it is recognized in their country and the collective history of past decisions. Moreover, on grounds of legitimacy and fairness, judges strive to present their decisions as generally consistent and coherent. Externally, judges are required to take into account not only changing social practices and the march of technological development but also the realities of political power. Courts act against a background of legislative action or inaction and the nature of this background may influence the options for judicial action. Nowhere has the influence of political inactivity on the courts' development of an audiovisual jurisprudence been more marked than in Italy.

Tom Mullen has suggested that we may help to allay fears of unchecked judicial activism by creating in the judicial context the 'best possible conditions for agreeing on moral truth'.[27] These conditions may be fostered by an attempt to achieve 'wide reflective equilibrium' which requires optimum 'order and coherence amongst particular judgements, principles and background theories'. But Mullen's call is not merely for procedural propriety; it is also a call for meticulous openness in the exposition of background theories: only through overt and rigorous moral reasoning can doctrinal coherence be achieved. This openness necessitates, when considering human rights, a careful examination of their underlying objectives, for '[i]ncoherent doctrine is partly the product of failure to attend to the question of what the purpose of a right is, or of failure to identify the purpose of a right correctly'.[28]

With these observations in mind we may now ask whether the various judicial bodies under consideration have come up to such exacting standards, or whether they have excercised their powers of interpretation to advance in an unquestioning way those interests traditionally favoured by the judiciary. To what extent have they deployed the legal principles to hand to produce a compelling and coherent constitutional theory of modern broadcasting? To start to provide answers to these questions we must look back to the initial cases of the late 1950s and 1960s which, spurred on by the commercial opportunities of economic recovery, began to find their way before courts of law. In particular, the early Italian cases reveal a judicial willingness critically to examine established structures and practices in the broadcasting industry, pointing the way to the more far-reaching appraisal which was to characterize the French and Italian Constitutional Court decisions of the 1980s.

---

[27] T. Mullen (1986), 28. Mullen's call for openness and coherence finds reflection in Stephen Macedo's categorization of constitutional interpretation as 'a moral enterprise': '[t]he best way of affirming the Constitution's supremacy is self-consciously, self-critically, and on the basis of reasons that can be publicly articulated and widely seen to support the contention that this Constitution really is a good way of setting in motion a government capable of pursuing ends that governments ought to pursue': S. Macedo (1991), 172.

[28] T. Mullen (1986), 31.

PART 3

The Judicial Role Established?
A Comparative Study of the Courts and the Audiovisual Media

6

The Legal Debate Begins:
Public Monopoly and Private
Ownership

Non è facile, ragionando in astratto, cioè in termini sganciati da una ben determinata realtà politico-istituzionale, esprimere un'opzione precisa a favore del sistema pubblico o del sistema privato. È più facile dire che l'uno e l'altro vantano pregi e difetti in misura proporzionale.[1]

La réduction du service public à une conception matérielle, indépendante de la nature publique ou privée des organismes gestionnaires, peut constituer—et constitue, de fait, aujourd'hui—une première étape dans un processus de rejet de l'État.[2]

It will be clear from the foregoing discussion that the time-lag which occurred between the general availability of radio and television services and judicial scrutiny of national broadcasting policies had a number of causal roots both social and organizational in nature. First, widespread government appropriation of the audiovisual media, coupled with deployment of an internationally recognized licensing system, tended to hide issues of individual rights behind a wall of patronage and regulatory fiat. Secondly, the post-war search for cohesion in fractured and radically altered societies helped to legitimate the pre-existing 'public-service' ethos of the audiovisual media: broadcasting was provided *for* the citizens, it was certainly not to be provided *by* them. Nor, indeed, was broadcasting generally considered the material of which human rights are made. Thirdly, for those who did see important issues of individual liberties to be at stake, access to judicial intervention was in many instances hampered by the incremental growth both in confidence and powers of constitutional courts. The initially high level of government control of the broadcast

---

[1] P. Caretti, *et al.* (1981), 503: 'It is not easy, reasoning in the abstract, that is in terms cut off from a given political/institutional reality, to express a precise preference for a public or private system. It is easier to say that each displays values and defects in equal measure.'

[2] S. Regourd (1987), 31: 'The reduction of the public service into a material concept, independent of the public or private nature of the body providing it, can constitute—and in fact today constitutes—a first stage in a process of rejection of the state.'

media present in many European countries made judicial intervention a high risk and politically unattractive option for these fledgeling courts. Finally, the toll of European economic reconstruction and restrictive state ownership kept the lid on an infant audiovisual advertising sector, thereby postponing direct challenge by the private sector to the status quo.

Thus, by the time courts of law were called upon to evaluate the legitimacy of national broadcasting policies, the shape of radio and television broadcasting was already well established. If, in the early days of popular broadcasting, direct analogy with the printed press may have seemed possible, by the 1960s the audiovisual media were already set on their own distinct regulatory path and it would have taken a brave court indeed to challenge the basic tenets of the established order. This late entry into the field posed judges difficult questions of legal coherence: how could the existing political hegemony be reconciled with traditional liberal theories of the free press and their rejection of state intervention? Initial attacks on the established post-war broadcasting order took essentially two forms. At one level they were political and parliamentary in origin, as opposition parties sought to break the government stranglehold over the public channels. At another, they originated from the 'private' sector, from social or political groups seeking autonomy from, not access to, the public stations, and from commercial operators, lured by the commercial promise of an underdeveloped advertising market.

The first line of attack—that coming from within established political forces—did not directly confront the basic tenets of the public service order. The old system was not to be disbanded; far from it, all that was required was enhanced access time for the parliamentary opposition and a more democratically accountable system of management. If the need to apportion political spoils more fairly among the people's representatives became ever more apparent, this was not deemed to require a further dilution of political power by letting in private, commercial operators. The second line of attack, which advocated exactly this, posed a direct challenge to the political appropriation of the audiovisual sector. Put bluntly, one approach brought into question the current practice of state ownership, the other its existence. Both of these challenges were mounted roughly concurrently, and it will be seen that there was an initial tendency for certain courts to respond to claims made by the *private sector*, with calls not for the development of a private market but merely for *public-sector* reform. One claim was to find its answer in the other, and a judicial solution was posed which, though unattractive from a governmental perspective, was unlikely to alienate overall parliamentary support.

The central regulatory issues in the field of radio and television may conveniently be specified as: *who* should be allowed to hold *how much* of *which market* and on *what terms*? Given the structure of the audiovisual media after the Second World War it was to be expected that the primary question which would begin to exercise the judicial mind was the legitimacy of state ownership and, more particularly, state monopoly. As state, if not government, control was central to many European broadcasting orders, calls for meaningful change inevitably challenged that domination. For the first time courts were being directly asked to develop a constitutional theory of the role of the audiovisual media in society and the role of the state within that sensitive sector. Was there, or was there not, a legal response to the increasingly insistent calls for deregulation and market expansion? It is thus with the 'who' question that we begin this examination of judicial intervention in the broadcast media.

An initial element of clarification is necessitated by the need to establish what exactly is meant by the phrase 'broadcasting monopoly'. Broadcasting is a complex industry and markets may be delimited by applying a number of distinct criteria, a consideration which poses no small problem for those charged with overseeing its competitiveness. It is possible, for example, to draw distinctions along *technical* lines by looking at the form of signal relay and reception, treating cable and satellite services as distinct from traditional 'terrestrial' radio and television channels. Alternatively, one can divide the broadcasting cake still further by employing *territorial* criteria: distinguishing community, local, or regional services from national or international ones. Finally, it is possible to separate out the *various operations* which underlie the creation of the finished programmes we hear and see on our radio and television sets: the physical production of those programmes; programming, that is the construction of a programme schedule; the technical process of transmission already mentioned above; and the financing of the service, whether by advertising, sponsorship, subscription payments, licence fees, or government subvention. A broadcast, as the Commission of the European Communities has noted, 'is not a material, tangible asset but a set of activities' and any discussion of state monopolies must consequently endeavour to clarify which aspects of this composite activity are under scrutiny.[3]

As the television industry took shape in the late 1940s and 1950s state broadcasters were commonly granted a monopoly over the use of available broadcasting frequencies and licence-fee receipts, together with sole diffusion rights. They also enjoyed a monopoly over programming which, in its turn, afforded organizations such as RAI, RTF, and the BBC something of a *de facto*, if not *de jure*, monopoly over production.[4]

---

[3] EC Commission (1984), 105.
[4] See P. Caretti, *et al.* (1981), 494, for an overview of these trends. The authors focus particularly on the Italian situation, but include a salutary reminder of alternative European models such as the Dutch 'pillar' system. For a summary of the French position see F. Balle and C. Leteinturier (1987), 94, and B. Cousin and B. Delcros (1990), 138.

Consequently, the monoply enjoyed by state or public broadcasters extended in many instances to most of the areas identified above. The would-be private operators who sought to challenge this entrenched position were initially restrained in their demands, a restraint born of a sense of practical and financial realism. In the main they did not seek to denude the public broadcasters of pre-existing capabilities; rather they claimed the right to work alongside them in the space made available at the periphery through new technology and the economic potential offered by advertising. Prime targets for expansion were consequently new radio channels or local television and cable stations, able to fill the all-too-apparent gaps in the programme provision of the public-service stations. In seeking to protect themselves from the draconian penalties of closure, confiscation of equipment, fines, and even prison sentences the new broadcasting entrepreneurs began to look to the courts for assistance rather than restraint.

1. THE ROAD TO REFORM

For anyone wishing to challenge the established order the most obvious departure point was, as we have noted, the legitimacy of state ownership: ownership which could be seen to raise not only the questions of 'who' and 'how much' but also, with the arrival of new forms of technical relay, the important question which of the various market sectors—terrestrial, satellite, cable, etc.—could legitimately be publicly owned. Were state broadcasting monopolies unconstitutional, merely permissible, or, on the contrary, legally required? And if state monopoly was unconstitutional to what extent was *any* form of public ownership acceptable: how then was the broadcast cake to be divided? It was with these difficult questions that a number of European courts were asked to grapple, and their initial response tended on the whole to be conservative. State monopolies seemed to be just too well established, too politically sensitive, to dismantle head on. But a careful reading of these cases reveals that the status quo was afforded less than unconditional acceptance: not all was well, warned the courts, with current practice and changing broadcast capabilities could undermine the legal foundations of the existing order.

(i) Italy

One of the earliest cases at the national level to consider state control of the audiovisual sector was the 1960 decision of the Italian Constitutional Court in the matter of the broadcasting company 'Il Tempo TV'.[5] In 1956

---

[5] Dec. 59/1960 [1960] Giur. cost. 759.

Tempo TV had requested from the Minister for Posts and Telecommunications the right to utilize six UHF frequencies to provide a commercial television service for the Lazio, Campania, and Toscana regions. Permission had been refused by the Minister on the basis that RAI had, from 1952 onwards, been granted sole rights to broadcast radio and television services for Italy. Tempo TV was not, however, willing to let the matter rest there and challenged the Minister's decision on the basis that the state monopoly was itself contrary to Articles 21 (freedom of speech), 33 (freedom for art and science), and 41 (freedom for private economic initiative) of the 1948 Constitution.[6] It was suggested that Article 21 guaranteed to each individual not only the freedom to express his or her opinion but also the freedom to use every means of expression in order to do so, means which in the twentieth century must also be taken to include television. The limited number of available broadcasting frequencies could not justify the introduction of a state monopoly with all the dangers that posed of qualitative or quantitative restrictions on expression, and attention was drawn to the not insignificant number of broadcasting frequencies which, having been made available by international agreement to the Italian government for allocation, still remained unused.

RAI tried to counter this wide-ranging threat to its position by suggesting that Articles 21 and 33 simply did not apply to the type of commercial channel Tempo TV was proposing. At stake might indeed be the company's right to *economic enterprise*, but not its right to *free speech*: private channels were interested in money, not individual expression. This has proved a particularly resilient argument, reappearing in discussions over the regulation of cable and satellite television and the legitimacy of restrictions on broadcast advertising.[7] The attraction presented by this unconvincing splintering of the broadcasting enterprise to focus on one only of its many component elements was the possibility of side-stepping Article 21, with its prima facie concern for individual expression, and to focus instead on Article 43, with its emphasis on the collective needs of the community.

Article 43 enables the state to place in public hands, for the general benefit, enterprises providing either an essential public service or having a tendency to monopoly and which are of important general interest.[8] It is the Italian exemplar of a widespread constitutional provision enabling state appropriation of private property for public ends. Even in the United States, where the protection of private property and free enterprise has

---

[6] See App.
[7] See, e.g., the government submissions in *Autronic AG* v. *Switzerland* (1990) 12 EHRR 485, 489, and the concurring opinion of Judge Valticos in *Groppera Radio AG* v. *Switzerland* (1990) 12 EHRR 321.   [8] For the full text see the App.

become a central tenet of belief, the Constitution's Fifth Amendment envisages state appropriation for 'public use' on the basis of 'just compensation'. Such clauses are a recognition that, although a system of private property rights may, when backed by adequate mechanisms for transfer and exclusive enjoyment, prove more efficient in economic terms than public ownership,[9] in certain circumstances, where either the market fails to operate effectively or where competing welfare considerations are valued highly, public ownership may prove a preferable regulatory option.

Market failure may stem from the nature of the goods themselves, where they are classifiable as 'public goods' (goods which exhibit the characteristics of non-excludability and non-subtractability), from economies of scale leading to monopolization, or from an individual's refusal to act as a rational wealth maximizer. A central problem with the 'market failure' approach, however, is determining the point at which market failure becomes so great that state intervention is necessitated. For many goods externalities at the production or consumption stage may be identified and the range of true 'public goods' appears fairly restricted—non-excludability is more often a function of cost than technical impossibility—and even a monopolist may be restrained by the threat, as opposed to the concrete reality, of market intervention. Such considerations have led J. E. Lane to observe that we need an 'independent criterion to tell us which externality is to be the target of public policy'.[10] Market failure is rarely, therefore, a value-neutral determinant for ascertaining the scale of the public sector.

Moreover, controlling ownership is just one among a number of regulatory techniques: where market failure seems inevitable, or non-market considerations paramount, state regulation of private industry may be as effective a remedy as public ownership. As Michael Botein has noted '[r]egulation and public ownership thus are just polar opposite approaches to achieving basically the same goals.'[11] Which approach is adopted will depend on such factors as the level of preoccupation with the cost of public bureaucracy or political intervention in the public sector, or on the perceived unresponsiveness of even the most carefully regulated private industry to public needs. Initial assessment of whether public ownership in

---

[9] By encouraging long-term investment in the property and avoiding a situation known as the 'tragedy of the commons' where uncontrolled (unregulated) depletion of 'common' resources, for example fish stocks, leads to exhaustion. For discussions of the various arguments which can be used to support the adoption of a public or private property regime see: F. H. Stephen (1988); R. Cooter and T. Ulen (1997); J. E. Lane (ed.) (1985) and R. A. Epstein (1987).

[10] J. E. Lane (1985).

[11] M. Botein (1988), 1. The American 'public utility' doctrine which enables price controls to be imposed on certain public services provided by public entities can thus be seen as a counterpart to the doctrine of 'eminent domain' facilitating state 'takings' under the Fifth Amendment.

any given sector will be for the 'general utility' is left, under Article 43, to Parliament.

Given the complex interweaving of economic and policy issues underlying any such assessment it is not surprising to find that the Italian Constitutional Court was initially unwilling to challenge the assumptions on which the state broadcasting monopoly had been built. In Decision 59 of 1960 the Court held that the institution of a state broadcasting monopoly was not *ipso facto* unconstitutional: it accepted the argument that the limited number of frequencies available for hertzian television justified the creation of a state broadcasting monopoly under Article 43.[12] But the Court was not prepared to leave the public sector free from all constitutional scrutiny, and refused to follow the line of argument that Article 21, guaranteeing freedom of expression, was simply inapplicable to 'off-air' television. Articles 43 and 21 were not mutually exclusive, and the state monopoly created under Article 43 would still have to be scrutinized for compliance with Article 21. In the case in point the Court held that there was no infringement of Article 21, since it considered that spectrum shortage would deliver television, if not placed under state control, into the unrepresentative hands of a few powerful individuals. Public ownership in such circumstances was best able to assure access under conditions of 'impartiality' and 'objectivity' to those who wished a mass-media platform.

Although the creation of the RAI monopoly was found to be constitutionally acceptable, the Court made plain that its system of management and operation would also have to be scrutinized for compliance with Article 21. In particular, regulation was required to ensure that individual expression was catered for through a system of access entitlements. Such provision might, however, be legitimately curtailed owing to technical limitations and the need to accommodate certain other interests 'worthy of protection'. These interests were specifically held to include the variety and propriety of programmes.[13] The Court therefore endorsed a level of public regulation which went beyond protection of the individual right to self-expression, generally considered to lie at the heart of Article 21, and accepted the imposition of restrictions designed to ensure the provision of a diverse and varied programming schedule, even where this might curtail the scope for individual expression.

The Court in its 1960 decision was not prepared to unsettle existing patterns of ownership, but it nevertheless established a bipolar public–private divide which would reverberate throughout its subsequent rulings. The requirement that public ownership be justified mirrored the constitution in affording private ownership primacy: it was *because* a competitive private market could not be instituted that the 'reversion' to public

---

[12] Dec. 59/1960 [1960] Giur. cost. 759.   [13] *Ibid.* 783.

ownership became acceptable. Once in the domain covered by Article 43 the Court was prepared to endorse the government's rejection of that other regulatory option—public regulation of private property, left open by Article 41.[14] It was not arbitrary for the state to conclude in these circumstances that the public rather than the private sector would be more likely to act objectively and impartially, serving the whole national territory. Thus although the Court clearly recognized the dangers inherent in *both* private and public power it preferred to leave the response to the threat of private power in government hands and held back from setting guidelines for a new, albeit competitively limited, private sector.

The Court's willingness to consider public monopoly a reasonable response to market failure may seem perplexing at a time when other regulatory patterns were in evidence: public regulation of private broadcasting was, for example, already proving itself in the popular British independent television service. The answer may again lie in the political, social, and legal circumstances surrounding these early decisions. In the first place, although alternatives to public monopoly did exist, they were not so common or well enough established to appear imperatives. Secondly, the appropriation of Italian broadcasting by the political system, with control of RAI considered by the governing Christian Democratic Party to be an important spoil of office, could only have deterred direct judicial confrontation. Moreover, the Court was being asked to determine the legitimacy of not just a peripheral part of the then existing broadcasting order but its central structure, and the Court would have been only too aware that to hold the state monopoly unconstitutional in its entirety would have created a regulatory void of enormous proportions. Such action would have unleashed an anarchic battle among private broadcasters, eager to capitalize on a market environment devoid of any established antitrust legislation.[15]

The Court, in its initial 1960 decision, thus preferred to concentrate its efforts on making what was already in existence more politically accountable. For this it was enough to embrace the public monopoly on the basis of spectrum shortage, via Article 43, yet keep the threat of unconstitutionality alive by reference to Article 21, which, as we have seen, the Court held could only be accommodated by generous access facilities. This raises the question why the Court did not take what would,

---

[14] It could be objected that this fails to take account of the fact that RAI was technically a *private* company, acting under government concession, the very combination I consider to have been discounted. Until the 1995 referendum, however, shares in any company awarded a public broadcasting concession had to be publicly owned.

[15] General antitrust regulation was enacted only in 1990 (Law 287/1990), though specific legislation for the press was passed in 1981 (Law 416/1981, amended by legge 67/1987).

on its own reasoning, have been the perfectly logical step of converting the state monopoly into a common carrier, thereby splintering control of transmission and programming. Indeed, where a content-neutral method of allocating programme time to interested parties is adopted, such as 'first come, first served', it is by no means clear why the state should be regarded a constitutionally more desirable carrier than private operators. But such a move, though consistent with the Court's principles, would have struck just as deeply at government control as a direct finding that state ownership was unconstitutional. Perhaps, after all, the rhetoric of individual access was always meant to go further than the reality of the public television service. Moreover, it is important to remember that the Court in its 1960 decision referred, as we have noted, to 'other interests worthy of protection', namely the variety and propriety of programmes: in the field of community interests mapped out by Article 43, therefore, the individual interest in self-expression protected by Article 21 was to be carefully 'contained'.

If the state had temporarily won the battle, the Court had made it quite clear that it might still lose the war. Was, for example, the state monopoly as then constituted really open to those who wished to find a television voice: the parliamentary opposition and large segments of society clearly thought not. Was perhaps the structure of Italian public broadcasting, after all, unconstitutional? Although the Court specifically refrained from determining the acceptability of the present order its decision pointed to radical reform within the existing system. The Court's price for refraining from a wholesale revision of the public–private divide was to be greater political and public accountability. This initial endorsement of an albeit reformed public sector was not unique to Italy: the West German Constitutional Court, for example, held a year later in 1961 that public ownership of the broadcasting sector was legitimated, at least for the time being, by the limited number of available broadcasting frequencies,[16] and six years after this the European Commission of Human Rights, having noted the widespread existence of state broadcasting monopolies across Europe, determined in *X* v. *Sweden* that the introduction of such a monopoly fell within the latitude afforded contracting states by the licensing clause of Article 10(1)(3) of the European Convention on Human Rights.[17]

It was not to be long before the Italian Constitutional Court itself returned to the audiovisual arena, its 1960 pronouncements on broadcasting objectivity and completeness having failed to precipitate any concrete

---

[16] For a thorough overview of the decisions of the West German Constitutional Court relating to the structure of the broadcast media see E. Barendt (1991), 98 ff., and, more generally, V. Porter (1989) and C. Holtz-Bacha (1991).

[17] App. No 3071/67, *X* v. *Sweden*, 26 Coll. 71.

legislative response. In two co-terminous cases in 1974 the Court was to both reiterate its reformist requirements for the public sector and indicate that reform might no longer be an entirely satisfactory response to developments in the audiovisual sector.[18] Public ownership was still regarded as a viable option, but notice was given that it would not be allowed to expand uncontrollably. In Decision 225 of 1974 the Court confirmed that spectrum scarcity continued to justify the state 'off-air' radio and television monopoly, but went further in setting out 'seven commandments' which detailed, with some precision, what the Constitution required of a state system.[19] Among other things a model system would not be under the control of the government, would be subject to an effective system of parliamentary scrutiny and would give access impartially to those political, religious, and cultural groups which represented the matrix of beliefs and opinions at play in society. In this case, therefore, the Court's central focus continued to be on the danger of unchecked, partisan political power within the public radio and television system: dilution of this power was to be effected through grafting onto the public system internal mechanisms of accountability and access facilities. Individual access was still primarily seen as access to time on the public radio and television channels, not private access to the airwaves themselves.

Nevertheless, the Court could not have ignored the fact that, in continuing to tie the viability of the public broadcasting sector to spectrum scarcity, it was subjecting its own decision-making to a technological criterion beyond its control. Scarcity of frequencies has always been a shaky basis for public monopoly in the broadcasting field for, as Fowler and Brenner point out, many goods are in short supply, yet we leave it to market bidding to determine what we hope will ensure their efficient allocation.[20] There is no *technical* barrier to imposing a market system on the audiovisual sector: frequencies may be bought and sold, as the auction in 1990 of private television franchises in Britain illustrates. Moreover, the number of frequencies made available by states for broadcasting purposes has proved more restricted than that actually permitted by the technical state of the art, a point repeatedly made by Italian litigants. Across Europe the public television sector remained for many years limited to one, or at most two, channels, despite a technical capability of four, if not five, national services. In addition, a considerable proportion of available frequencies were and remain allocated by governments for alternative uses, such as emergency and defence services.

By the mid-1970s the possibilities presented by cable and satellite and the realities of pirate radio clearly indicated that rather more voices could

---

[18] Dec. 225/1974 [1974] Giur. cost. 1775 and 226/1974 [1974] Guir. cost. 1791.
[19] Dec. 225/1974 [1974] Giur. cost. 1775.
[20] M. S. Fowler and D. L. Brenner (1982), 221 ff.

be accommodated than had previously been thought possible, and these voices were noticeably adding to the range of opinions expressed on the established state channels. Even for those who regarded the national, off-air television sector to be a discrete market, it was apparent that steps could be taken to enhance access, where that was the central concern, by, for example, adopting a common-carrier model of provision, or where concern was over the dangers posed by a concentration in ownership, by breaking down permissible shareholdings into relatively small units—an approach subsequently adopted, not entirely successfully, in the French private television sector. Thus monopoly, even at the national level, appeared increasingly a political or economic rather than strictly technical affair.

It is tempting to conclude that some recognition of these developments and the threat they posed to even a judicially-reformed public sector underpinned the Italian Constitutional Court's finding that the state broadcasting monopoly could also be justified as an 'essential public service' under a different head of the same Article 43. In bringing into play this considerably more malleable 'public service' concept the Court could indeed have left open the possibility that a sector of the broadcasting market might be 'walled off' from private ownership, even where technical or economic circumstances rendered a competitive private market perfectly functional. Contrary to the approach adopted in its 1960 decision, the Court could consequently have categorized broadcasting, like the right to vote, as an activity where adherence to a doctrine of market primacy, albeit to ensure maximum freedom of individual expression, would be inappropriate. But the Court did not in fact leave itself this element of discretion, for it went on to conclude that it was the importance of keeping radio and television services out of the hands of a few individuals which fulfilled the additional 'general interest' requirement of Article 43. If questions of market concentration were by-passed at one level, public service, they were brought in at another, general interest. A competitive market was still constitutionally preferable to even a 'public-service' state monopoly.

If we stand back from the Italian cases considered so far it is possible to conclude that although initially willing to validate the RAI monopoly, albeit after a number of critical internal reforms, the Court in fact opened the way to disestablishment by opposing the collective interests reflected in Article 43 with a paradigm of free market competition, backed by Article 21. The political implications of judicial divestiture, however, and an awareness of the dangers posed by unregulated private power undoubtedly discouraged the Court from moving too rapidly towards privatization. Nevertheless, the principles were firmly in place for the Italian Constitutional Court to step well beyond reform of the existing state structure and open the way to development of a new broadcasting order combining both public and private operators.

(ii) France

In France judicial developments were held back by a constitutional order which, as we have seen, centres review round the passage of new legislation. This afforded the government a degree of protection from legal scrutiny during the unrest of the late 1960s, when striking broadcasting professionals mirrored widespread public dissatisfaction with the existing social settlement. In consequence, when the status of the public monopoly was directly raised before the Conseil Constitutionnel in 1978, with new legislation establishing heavy penalties for radio piracy, the Conseil was compelled to hold that since the state monopoly had been well established in prior legislation it had no competence to determine its constitutional legitimacy.[21] Jean-Paul Costa has contrasted the approach taken by the French Conseil with the activism of its Italian counterpart well over a decade earlier, but the comparison is not an entirely fair one.[22] The situation of savage and largely unregulated competition among private Italian broadcasters, precipitated by the decisions of the Italian Constitutional Court in the mid-1970s, was well known to French political leaders of the time, and Giscard d'Estaing had cited this Italian 'chaos' to justify his draconian proposals for the burgeoning number of radio pirates. Moreover, the restricted focus of the legislation sent for the Conseil's perusal—containment of pirate radio stations—made meaningful reform virtually impossible. To have declared the state monopoly unconstitutional would have created exactly that type of legislative void which the French system has been designed to prevent. It is also probable that the political implications of confronting head on the established broadcasting order at a time when the President was increasingly on the defensive were not lost on the Conseil. Consequently, it was only with the major reforms initiated by the Socialists after their election victory in 1981 and the return to power of the right in 1986 that the Conseil Constitutionnel was able to come into its own and develop far-reaching guidelines for the French audiovisual media.

---

[21] Dec. 78–96–DC of 27 July 1978 [1978] Rec. Cons. constit. 29. The legal position was not, however, quite as inevitable as this decision indicates. Only months before a court in Montpellier, admittedly at first instance, held, at the recourse of the Republican pirate radio station, Radio Fil Bleu, that the state broadcasting monopoly was contrary to the guarantee of liberty of expression in the 1789 Declaration and Art. 10 of the European Convention which France had recently ratified. This decision was, however, overturned on appeal, and for details see R. Barbrook (1995), 132, and *The Times*, 6 Dec. 1977, 4.
[22] J.-P. Costa (1986).

2. BEYOND REFORM TO A 'MIXED' BROADCASTING SYSTEM

(i) Italy

It seems that the Italian Constitutional Court lost faith in public-sector reform for, although a new law, legge 103, was passed in 1975 which shifted the balance of power in overseeing RAI from the executive to Parliament, the public sector remained discredited by the ensuing political scramble to divide up the broadcasting cake. It has also been suggested that the success of the Communists in the 1976 elections and the consequent potential for shared Communist–Christian Democrat control over the information transmitted by RAI, led the Court to favour an opening of the broadcasting sector to private initiative.[23] What is certainly apparent, starting in the mid-1970s, is a shift in emphasis as the Court moved to declare particular radio and television services off-limits for public appropriation: if the public sector was to remain a political football, albeit kicked by a wider range of partisan feet, the Court could prevent its expansion into areas as yet poorly developed.

The Court's focus on those areas of the audiovisual industry which had not yet received much government attention represented something of a compromise. On the one hand it opened up the audiovisual arena to at least some of the voices which had been consistently excluded from the state channels. On the other, by carefully restricting private development to the local level, it left the established, highly politicized, national channels untouched. This was clearly less threatening for the ruling Christian Democrats than a holding that existing services were unconstitutional, and the development of this more limited private sector found favour in certain political spheres as a pliable resource for personal advertisement.[24] Thus, although judicial reference to the 'public service' head of Article 43 appeared at first sight designed to facilitate government appropriation of new media outlets, the Court instead rejected such an approach and moved quickly to contain the public sector.

The first stage of this judicial 'paring' took place prior to the 1975 legislation in Decisions 225 and 226 of 1974, previously discussed.[25] Decision 225 held the state monopoly over the relay in Italy of foreign channels to be unconstitutional. This was logically in line with the Court's earlier spectrum-shortage reasoning, though based on erroneous premises, since the Court mistakenly believed that Italian broadcasting stations relaying Swiss and Yugoslavian television signals utilized frequencies other than those allocated to Italy by international agreement. The belief that

---

[23] A. Pace (1995), 247.   [24] G. Rao (1988), 47.
[25] Dec. 225/1974 [1974] Giur. cost. 1775 and 226/1974 [1974] Guir. cost. 1791.

the relay activities did not eat into the limited Italian frequencies led them to be considered additions to, not detractors from, the available national channels. In consequence, the Court determined that the state monopoly in this context served merely to hamper the free flow of ideas and created a form of 'national autarchy' where there was no countervailing constitutional justification. Nevertheless, the Court indicated that the institution of broadcasting relay stations was not a matter to be left entirely to individual initiative; their establishment could be controlled, in the public interest, through the award of authorizations.

More radical containment took place in the coterminous Decision 226, where the challenge this time was directed at the state cable monopoly. As with foreign relay, spectrum shortage, of the type considered in the Court's 1960 decision, did not appear to be an issue: cable relay did not eat into the Italian 'off-air' frequencies, and not only could each cable system transmit a considerable number of radio and television channels, but competing cable services provided by different operators were, at least technically, perfectly feasible. In Decision 226, however, the Court noted that the *economics* of a particular market could lead to an unconstitutional concentration of private power, even where there were no *technical* constraints on market entry. The costs of establishing a national cable network were such that ownership would be withheld from all but a few of the wealthiest individuals or firms, and for this reason retention in the public sector could be justified under Article 43. At the local level, however, where the costs were thought manageable for a wide range of individual operators, the Court held that this could not be withheld from private enterprise. Decision 226 thus reveals a continuing adherence to the philosophy of market primacy: where the risk of private monopoly or oligopoly threatened market viability public ownership was considered a constitutionally legitimate response, but where there was extensive opportunity for market entry private ownership was necessitated.

This division of the market into national (public-sector) and local (private-sector) was carried over, two years later, into the mainstream field of 'off-air' broadcasting. In Decision 202 of 1976 the Constitutional Court held that although local broadcast frequencies were not infinite, there were sufficient frequencies to make a plural broadcasting sector a reality, given what was considered the not unreasonable cost of establishing a local broadcasting station.[26] As with cable, however, the Court held that the private local broadcasting sector would require careful regulation, necessitating the introduction of a licensing system, antitrust provisions, and controls over advertising time. Five years later, in Decision 148 of 1981, the Court was called to re-examine the propriety of the national radio and

---

[26] Dec. 202/1976 [1976] Giur. cost. 1267.

television monopoly, it being argued that technological developments had at last undermined the 'spectrum scarcity' and 'elevated cost' rationales.[27] Once again the Court was prepared to protect the national broadcasting monopoly, holding, in line with Decision 202 of 76, that it was an essential public service, but the Court also made reference to the 'general utility' test of Article 43: public ownership could be justified under this Article, even where the activity was clearly of a public-service nature, only if there was *also* the risk of private monopoly or oligopoly.[28] The novelty of the case lay in its recognition that individuals could still gain excessive power, regardless of spectrum shortage or exorbitant start-up costs, through linking local stations to form national networks. The need to prevent such unchecked private influence at the national level was sufficient to justify public ownership both under the 'general utility' head of Article 43, here specifically brought into operation, and, it seems, under Article 21, the power of network owners being considered sufficient to limit the capacity of other willing speakers to express themselves.

In choosing to compartmentalize national and local markets as discrete sectors, so that diversity at the local level did not undermine public ownership at the national level, the Court rendered effective challenge to RAI's status as a national broadcaster exceedingly difficult. If the principle of 'public service' has not been used by the Court as a definitive tool for regulating the entry of private operators, market definition undoubtedly has. If one discounts satellite and cable provision, poorly developed in Italy, then the number of national 'off-air' television channels would have appeared, at least during the 1970s and early 1980s, likely to remain limited to a handful of stations owing to international frequency restrictions and the high cost of provision.[29] Unless the ownership of these channels could be splintered by, say, provision for time-sharing, the introduction of some form of common-carrier system, or through limiting individual share-holdings in national broadcasting companies, it is not clear how oligopoly, and thus state monopoly under Article 43, could be avoided. It is therefore interesting that the Court did in fact acknowledge that it might feel able to reach different conclusions were the legislator to introduce comprehensive regulation for the audiovisual sector: regulation designed to prevent monopolistic or oligopolistic concentrations, whether through network

[27] Dec. 148/1981 [1981] Giur. cost. 1379.
[28] In taking this approach the court was in fact confirming the position it established 7 years earlier in Dec. 225/1974 [1974] Giur. cost. 1775.
[29] Prior, that is, to the development of digitial relay and signal compression technologies. In the review of Italian broadcasting carried out for the Constitutional Court in Case 826/1988 [1988] Foro it. 2477, it was established that 4 private television networks had been established of near national reach, which, together with the 3 RAI stations, amounted in total to 7. 5 additional stations covered about half the Italian peninsular.

arrangements or multi-media ownership. Did the Court, therefore, imagine that a satisfactory regulatory scheme could be introduced to prevent concentration at the national level, opening the way at last to private enterprise?

Despite this rather oblique indication to the contrary, the 1981 case, through its chosen method of market division, came very close to finding public ownership at the national level not merely contingent but necessitated. The importance of the public broadcasting sector was further underlined by the Court's emphasis on the dangers which it believed private national channels posed to a democratic state as a result of their ability to influence an entire population. Although the Court was here relying on a hotly contested theory of media effects, the long history of governmental intervention in the broadcast media in Italy had been premissed on their capacity to manipulate public opinion. The possibility that private power might be concentrated in a few unaccountable hands was supported by developments surrounding the 1981 case itself: in the absence of effective antitrust legislation, private broadcasting was being carved up among a few industrial giants, with the publishing firm Rizzoli linking local transmitters to form a *de facto* national service. The public sector, for all its manifest shortcomings, might still have been thought to offer a degree of political equilibrium which private operators could reject in return for political favours. Certainly, the introduction in 1979 of a third 'regional' RAI network in the hands of the Communists had increased the range of political representation in the public sector, the two other RAI television stations being under Christian Democrat and Socialist control.

The public–private balance thus far developed received little amendment by the Italian Constitutional Court as it waited, with increasing impatience, for the legislature to bring an end to the anarchy of the private sector by introducing comprehensive broadcasting legislation. In 1984 judges in Rome, Turin, and Pescara ordered the deactivation of a number of extensive private networks, created through the distribution and simul-taneous transmission of video cassettes by 'local' stations, co-ordinating their activities. The rulings led the owners of these stations to 'black out' all their programmes, though suspension of all services was not strictly required, since private broadcasters were prohibited from providing only national and not local services. The sudden withdrawal of popular broadcasting stations resulted in a well-orchestrated public outcry, facilitating the government's rapid endorsement of the private networks. By now there was considerable political momentum in favour of a 'mixed' broadcasting system: the Christian Democrats were willing to tolerate growth in the private sector in return for a strengthened position within RAI, while the Socialists saw political gain to lie in a private sector increasingly dominated by the Fininvest channels owned by Silvio

Berlusconi, a personal friend of the then Socialist leader and Prime Minister, Bettino Craxi.

Reacting quickly to this judicial challenge to the private networks, legislative decrees were hastily passed by the Craxi government, authorizing those broadcasters already operating on 1 October 1984 to continue their activities pending passage of a comprehensive audiovisual Act. This approach was confirmed by legge 10 of 1985 which had the remarkable effect of protecting from further competition precisely those companies which had been broadcasting illegally, enabling them to consolidate their position right up to the passage of new legislation in 1990.[30] Moreover, Article 1 of the statute, while endorsing the legitimacy of state ownership at the national level, also made specific reference to a 'mixed' broadcasting system. The question was thus clearly posed: how could a mixed, but numerically limited, national broadcasting system (with ownership in the private sector concentrated in the hands of the Fininvest company) be squared with the Constitutional Court's well-established allegiance to competitive market principles? Where a private 'market' was possible, with proper provision to prevent undue concentration, there seemed no scope for state ownership but, where there remained the prospect of oligopolistic control, the Court had stood firm in its defence of public ownership.

Before these issues were directly addressed in 1988, the Constitutional Court was further to erode what remained of the public monopoly in its Decision 153 of 1987.[31] The Court held that the 'public-service' characteristics of national 'off-air' broadcasting—increased participation by citizens in the broadcast system and assistance given towards the social and cultural development of the country—were not applicable to the services transmitted abroad from Italian stations. The Italian state, held the Court, had no obligation to keep the citizens of other states informed, signalling an appreciation of 'public service' as an essentially nation-oriented concept. The state monopoly over foreign broadcasts was thus declared unconstitutional. The case is interesting for the Court's failure to consider, contrary to previous practice, the likelihood of private foreign broadcasting from Italian soil becoming monopolized. This omission may be explained by the extraterritorial nature of the stations under consideration, and the Court's own willingness to permit the administration to select licensees because of the potentially sensitive nature of international broadcasting. It is apparent that, in this context at least, regulation of the private sector, not merely on technical matters, was considered acceptable by the Court. Such regulation was to be guided by the principle of 'pluralism', acknowledged to be the most important constitutional value in the field of radio and television.

[30] A. Pace (1995), 248.   [31] Dec. 153/1987 [1987] Giur. cost. 1141.

Finally, in Decision 826 of 1988, the constitutional status of the private networks was called directly into question, and it is in this judgment that the Court, despite some pretence at continuity, broke decisively with the past.[32] In the words of one observer 'la *demise* del progetto di un tempo— emittenza nazionale riservato allo Stato, stazioni locali in libero concorrenza tra loro—non potrebbe esser più netta'.[33] The case is illustrative of the way in which established judicial theory may have to be modified in the face of social, technological, and, most importantly, political change. By 1988 private national broadcasting was becoming a well-established European phenomenon. The Court would undoubtedly have been aware that in France two new national television channels, TV6 (from 1987 M6) and la Cinq, had been placed in private hands, and that the French Constitutional Court had, in 1986, sanctioned the privatization of the main public station, TF1. In Britain an additional commercial station, Channel Four, had been in operation since the early 1980s. Moreover, in Italy itself, many among the Christian Democrats and Socialists supported the *de facto* mixed system, evidenced by their passing legge 10 of 1985, though there was little incentive for them to fight their way through the inevitable maze of compromise and barter which permanent legislation would entail. By continuing to protect the public sector at the national level the Court could no longer be seen as simply upholding the will of Parliament against the incursions of private enterprise; such protection now ran directly counter to the wishes of important factions within the governing political parties.

This reality found accommodation in the 1988 judgment: if the government chose not to utilize its power of appropriation under Article 43 of the Constitution, the Court indicated that it was not in principle prepared to stand in its way. General utility, it seemed, no longer required that all the national television channels be state-owned, even though their potential number remained strictly limited. To bring about this change in direction the Court returned to its Decision 148 of 1981, in which it had held that national broadcasting, acknowledged to be an essential public service, could be reserved to the state in order to prevent the development of a private broadcasting monopoly or oligopoly.[34] The Court effectively 'reinvented' this passage to envisage 'the possibility of the abandonment of the state broadcasting monopoly at the national level, on condition that the legislature establishes an effective system of guarantees designed to realise the fundamental principle of pluralism'.[35] By replacing the requirement,

[32] Dec. 826/1988 [1988] Foro it. 2477.
[33] R. Pardolesi (1988), 2479: 'the demise of the previous project—national stations reserved to the state, local stations in competition between themselves—could not be more clear'.   [34] Dec. 148/1981 [1981] Giur. cost. 1379, 1406.
[35] Dec. 826/1988 [1988] Foro it. 2477, 2495. The term 'reinvention' is that of R. Pardolesi (1988), 2479.

specified in its 1981 decision, that controls be introduced to prevent *monopoly or oligopoly* with the rather more pliable requirement that there be guarantees of '*pluralism*' the Court indicated that it might yet endorse a numerically restricted private broadcasting sector at the national level. Market primacy as the key objective had unequivocally been supplanted by the notion of pluralism, a concept now firmly at the centre of the Court's case law.

Under this guiding principle the Court at last felt able to endorse a 'mixed' national system of public and private broadcasters: public and private domains were no longer mutually exclusive. Nor was the public sector seen simply as an unfortunate reflex to the perils of private power: it was now a separate element, fulfilling its own distinct role, alongside its private counterpart. The Court's emphasis on the public sector's particular contribution to the broadcasting landscape, its calls on the legislature to ensure that it had at its disposal adequate finances and frequencies to fulfil its allotted role, moved it from a state of permanent contingency to an admittedly contained imperative. By 1988, therefore, the Court not only had opened the door to private broadcasting at the local level but had acknowledged its inevitability also at the national level. The public sector was to be governed by the principles of 'internal pluralism'—ensuring through a complete, objective, impartial, and balanced service the expression of as many social, political, and cultural opinions as possible— while the private sector was to be run in such a way as to maximize 'external pluralism', satisfying the citizens' constitutional right to information, through the competition of many individual operators.[36]

Endorsement of a mixed national system undoubtedly left the Court in some difficulty over the ownership of all three non-state national television stations by Silvio Berlusconi's Fininvest company. Indeed, it had been the prospect of exactly such a concentration of power which had led it to hold out against private ownership at the national level. In one of the Court's few specific guidelines for the new legislation it indicated that the constitutional requirement of pluralism would not be fulfilled at the national level by the creation of one public and one private pole in the hands of a single subject. The requirements indicated by the Constitutional Court were studiously ignored when legislation was finally passed in 1990. Legge 223 facilitated a division of spoils along existing lines, permitting a single entity to hold licences for up to three national television channels, on condition that it divested itself of any interests in the daily press. That possibility became reality when the broadcasting licenses were finally awarded on 13 August 1992: out of the twelve national licences awarded, RAI retained the three public channels and the Fininvest company of

---

[36] Dec. 826/1988 [1988] Foro it. 2477, 2499.

Silvio Berlusconi remained in control of its three commercial networks: Canale 5, Italia 1, and Retequattro. The dominance of these two operators is underlined by the fact that together RAI and Fininvest obtain nearly 90 per cent of the television audience and a similarly high percentage of television advertising revenues.

Legislative endorsement of the polarized RAI–Fininvest broadcasting system illustrates some of the advantages and disadvantages inherent in the French and Italian constitutional systems. On the one hand, the 1990 Italian media legislation was drafted with an awareness of, but ultimate disregard for, the indications given by the Constitutional Court in its 1988 ruling. If a system similar to the pre-legislative review found in France had been operative in Italy it is possible that those on the left wing of the Christian Democratic Party and Communists who considered the provisions unduly favourable to the Fininvest company could successfully have challenged the antitrust regulations prior to their enactment. On the other, under the Italian system, the Constitutional Court can review legislation at any time after its enactment, given, of course, a suitable reference from a lower court, and such references were certainly forthcoming with regard to the 1990 statute.[37] Indeed, the manifest failings of the 1990 legislation, in attempting little more than endorsement of the existing status quo, led to its close scrutiny in opposition quarters: the hunt to lay bare the unconstitutional nature of its provisions became 'something of a national sport among media theorists and lawyers'.[38]

At the end of 1993 the Lazio administrative court (TAR) referred to the Constitutional Court a number of issues relating not only to the 1990 statute but also to subsequent legislation passed in 1993.[39] Legge 422 of 1993 had been precipitated by criticisms of the original frequency plan, provided for in the 1990 legislation, and a criminal investigation was initiated into the practices of those who had drawn up the plan. Uncertainty over the frequency plan inevitably called into question the concessions which had been based upon it. As a result legge 422 made provision for a new frequency plan and specified, as a temporary measure, that those private broadcasters which had been in operation when the 1990 statute came into force, and benefited from *its* provisional measures, could continue to broadcast, using only the equipment at their disposal in 1990, until the passage of new legislation or, at the outside, for a further three years. The position of Fininvest's three national channels consequently looked assured until August 1996.

The Lazio reference to the Constitutional Court questioned the

---

[37] See, e.g., the issues raised in Dec. 112/1993 [1993] Foro it. 1339 and Dec. 420/1994 [1995] Giur. it. 129.   [38] F. Caringella (1993), 1340.

[39] Dec. 420/1994 [1995] Giur. it. 129.

legitimacy of both Article 15(4) of the 1990 legislation, which restricted individual ownership of national television and radio stations to 25 per cent of their total number, with a maximum limit of three, and the temporary amnesty for existing broadcasters contained in Article 1(1) and (3) of legge 442 of 1993. The Court struck down Article 15(4) as contrary to Articles 3, 21, 41, and 43 of the 1948 Constitution, and again affirmed its vision of a 'mixed' broadcasting environment, with public broadcasters governed by the principles of 'internal pluralism' and private broadcasters subject to a regime of 'external pluralism', designed to provide a multiplicity of voices. The distinct status of the public and private sectors was confirmed by the Court's willingness to examine concentration of ownership solely in the context of the private sector: the three RAI stations were left out of the equation. Lack of diversity in the private sector could not be remedied by the existence of innovative and varied public channels. The provisions of the 1993 statute were, however, upheld, even though they enabled the three Fininvest channels to continue in operation, because of their temporary nature and because they enabled all stations which had been broadcasting at the time of the 1990 legislation to continue, rather than only those awarded concessions under the terms of that statute.

Although the Italian Constitutional Court has now moved to afford the public-broadcasting sector a protected position, it is apparent that the Court does not envisage the distinction between public and private sectors to turn on ownership, but rather on the applicable regulatory regime. Identifying features of the public sector noted by the Court in Decision 112 of 1993 are the existence of operators legally categorized as 'companies of national interest', of special mechanisms of control and direction to which such operators are subject, for example, through the Parliamentary Commission, of the provision to them of licence-fee revenues, and their subjection to exacting programme obligations, designed to ensure diversity and the transmission of different views and opinions. By contrast, the private sector is free from many of these requirements, the principal regulations being designed to prevent undue concentrations of ownership, and private operators do not share in licence-fee revenues.[40]

That the public and private sectors, recognized as distinct and mutually complementary by the Constitutional Court, do not follow lines drawn simply on the basis of public or private participation finds confirmation in the Court's recent ruling that the public sector need not be publicly owned. In 1995 a number of important referenda were held in Italy, four of which related to broadcasting.[41] Prior to being put to the vote, their constitutional

---

[40] Dec. no 112/1993 [1993] Foro it. 1339, 1351.

[41] The issues raised were whether individuals should be able to own only one national television station; whether advertising should be prohibited during distinct parts or acts of

legitimacy was considered by the Court which, when examining the proposals seeking abolition of the requirements that public-service concessions be restricted to entirely state-owned companies[42] and that RAI's shares be open only to state ownership, held that private ownership need not undermine the public nature of the service provided by RAI or its categorization as a company of national interest: this was dependant not on a particular form of ownership but rather on the legal regime to which the company was subject. The results of the referendum favoured the removal of the restrictions on private ownership, and legislative proposals now point to the partial privatization of a restructured RAI.

In reaching these key decisions during the late 1980s and early 1990s the Italian Constitutional Court would undoubtedly have been aware of the broadcasting rulings of courts in other European countries, in particular those of the German Consititutional Court. The German Court in its 'fourth television case' of 1986 also considered the public and private broadcasting sectors to perform complementary activities, although its emphasis was here quite distinct, in that the public sector was put firmly at the heart of the broadcasting order.[43] It was only where the public sector was able to fulfil its 'basic', informational role that private broadcasting could be countenanced. If the Italian Court had commenced its audiovisual analysis with a faith in market primacy, the German Court, recognizing that competition for advertising finance could push minority programming from the schedules, had instead placed the public sector at the centre of its constitutional case law.

(ii) France

Though the constitutional position of the Conseil constitutionnel restricted its involvement in audiovisual matters during the 1960s and 1970s, the outburst of legislative activity concerning the mass media during the 1980s enabled it to move from mere bystander to a central actor in shaping French broadcasting regulation. What serves to distinguish the French and Italian situations is that the French Conseil, unlike its Italian counterpart, acted alongside governments anxious to put their own distinctive stamp on the national broadcasting system. Many of the Italian Court's 'innovations', the introduction of private local radio for example, were, in the French context, the direct result of legislation. But, although the Conseil has been consigned to play an essentially 'reactive' rather than 'pro-active' role, this,

---

films, plays, or musical works; whether companies should be prevented from placing advertising for 3 national television channels, including those they control; and whether private companies should be allowed to hold RAI shares.

[42] Established in Art. 2(2) of the 1990 statute.

[43] For commentary on the German broadcasting cases see E. Barendt (1991) and W. Hoffmann-Riem (1990).

in the audiovisual field, has proved to be by no means negligible, for, in the words of one commentator, *'il Conseil constitutionnel ha giuocato un ruolo essenziale nella definizione e nella protezione della libertà di comunicazione'.*[44]

A similar process to that noted in the Italian context, by which calls for public-sector reform gave way to support for private broadcasting, can also be charted in France.[45] As we have seen, political control has dominated French broadcasting history, and political parties, once in power, have proved stubbornly attached to the view that the audiovisual media are legitimate spoils of governmental office. The transition from a 'state' to a 'public-service' broadcasting ethos was a continuous process spanning ten to fifteen years. Direct political control began to appear increasingly anachronistic and a move to more covert forms of manipulation was concrete recognition of the fact that such practices were now likely to expose the government to negative press coverage.[46] Attempts during the course of the 1980s to enhance the independent status of the audiovisual media through the creation of specialized regulatory bodies at one remove from the executive were the result of legislative, rather than judicial, innovation.[47]

Similarly, the move to 'privatize' French radio and television was a legislative initiative, with the Conseil constitutionnel being called to respond to a privatization programme already under way. The term 'privatization' is here frequently taken to mean the development of privately-owned broadcasting stations, subject to a reduced burden of state intervention and oversight. But privatization of the French broadcasting media has been an incremental process, pre-dating even the legislative endorsement of private broadcasters in the above sense. Serge Regourd has charted the way in which the public sector was itself gradually 'privatized' from within: from 1959, for example, RTF took the form of an 'industrial and commercial' organization, a structure also adopted for its successor, ORTF, in 1964, which indicated a degree of comparability with private commercial companies. The separate television and radio stations TF1, Antenne 2, FR3, and Radio-France, created in 1974 when ORTF was broken up, took the form of private companies and were expected to compete with each other for audiences and advertisers, advertising having been introduced in 1968. Although the public sector in terms of structure

---

[44] A. Roux (1987), 373. [45] R. Barbrook (1995), 85–9, 115–46.
[46] C. Sorbets and M. Palmer (1986), 92.
[47] Though political influence remained apparent: the decisions made by the Haute Autorité, the independent regulatory body set up in 1982, and its 1986 successor the CNCL, were heavily criticized for reflecting the interests of their political paymasters: see C. Chevallier (1989), 60.

and outlook came to look increasingly commercial, it still exhibited features which were decidely more public than private: for example, the separate television and radio operating companies created in 1974 were entirely state-owned, they benefited from licence-fee revenues, and continued to be subject to exacting programme standards.

It was the Socialists who ultimately opened the way to establishment of a truly private sector operating alongside the established public stations. Critical of continuing government influence over the audiovisual media, the Socialists, while in opposition, had openly supported the free radio movement, not least through the creation of their own radio station, 'Radio Riposte'. On gaining power they were quick to ease private radio's outlawed status with loi 81–994 of 9 November 1981, confirmed by more far-reaching broadcasting legislation in 1982.[48] Although this was an important step towards the creation of a private-broadcasting sector, private radio stations remained subject to considerable restraints on their freedom: they were required to obtain an operating licence and could broadcast only within certain geographical limits; multiple ownership was prohibited; and recourse to advertising revenue outlawed. These restrictions were widely ignored, and the ban on advertising was lifted in 1984.

The 1982 legislation also made provision for the future development of private television channels, operating under public-service concessions, and in 1985 and 1986 two such concessions were granted to La Cinq and M6.[49] The fifth channel, awarded in the run-up to the 1986 elections, was granted to a consortium led by supporters of President Mitterand and, though both stations were technically classed as public-service enterprises, their conditions of operation were unusually favourable and undemanding. The concessions were referred for consideration to the Conseil d'Etat which concluded that they were indeed concessions of a public-service nature, despite the clearly commercial outlook of the successful applicants. In granting public-service concessions the Government enjoyed considerable freedom to determine how it would choose the operating companies and the terms on which they could operate, and the Conseil d'Etat refused to intervene in the exercise of this discretion absent evidence of manifest errors.[50] Despite endorsement by the Conseil d'Etat, the government was clearly seen to have been acting for its own partisan interests, and the concessions were withdrawn and reallocated when the Right was returned to power in the 1986 elections. This debacle meant that although the

---

[48] Loi 82–652 of 29 July 1982.

[49] *Ibid.*, Art. 79. An examination of the turbulent history of these two channels can be found in J.-P. Dubois (1987).

[50] [1986] Rec. déc. Cons. D'Etat 692; P. Devolvé (1987); and N. B. Brown and J. S. Bell (1993), 194.

Socialist Party continued to voice its support for the public sector, holding that it was only *'dans et à travers le service public, que la liberté de communication peut se concevoir'*, when it came to oppose the privatization of the key public channel, TF1, in 1986 it had cut the moral ground from under its own feet.

The public/private distinction in the French audiovisual sector has consequently become increasingly blurred over time: early attempts to categorize the public service as (i) an activity in the general interest, (ii) provided by a public body, no longer reflect the complexity of the modern audiovisual environment.[51] Moreover, the disparate use to which legislatures have put the term 'public service' has led some commentators to question whether it has any clear functional meaning at all. Is it, as Didier Truchet suggests, essentially a label, an *ex post facto* rationalization of policy choices already taken?[52] The 'public-service' concept undoubtedly received far from consistent support in the French broadcasting legislation of the 1980s. The loi of 1982, though recognizing that *'[l]a communication audiovisuelle est libre'*, clung to the conventional view that this freedom could only be guaranteed through a public-service system (Article 4).[53] In the loi of 1986, however, references to 'public service' were carefully replaced with the term 'public sector', and the public service was listed, in Article 1, as a potential restriction on the freedom to install and exploit broadcast services.[54] Finally, in 1989, the Socialists argued that their new loi was not a statute 'of' public service, but was rather 'inspired by' the spirit of public service.[55] Public service had clearly changed from being a concrete imperative for the broadcasting sector to a mere source of inspiration.

The uncertainties surrounding the meaning of 'public service' and the fluctuating fortunes of the 'public sector' provided an important backdrop to the decisions of the Conseil constitutionnel on the mass media. It may, indeed, explain why the Conseil has appeared relatively indifferent to these concepts, developing instead a specific set of constitutional imperatives for the broadcasting sector, whether in public or private ownership. It was respect for these imperatives, rather than for any particular broadcasting structure, which the Conseil considered to be of paramount importance. In 1981 it faced legislative changes which were already moving the broadcasting media towards a mixed system, whereas in Italy such changes were the result, at least in part, of judicial innovation. It is not perhaps so surprising, therefore, that the Conseil, unlike the Italian Constitutional Court, did not express a preference for market primacy

[51] S. Regourd (1987), 16; N. B. Brown and J. S. Bell (1993), 126; and P. Jourdan (1987).
[52] D. Truchet (1987); and see also S. Regourd (1987).
[53] Loi 82–652 of 29 July 1982.   [54] Loi 86–1067 of 30 Sept. 1986.
[55] Loi 89–25 of 17 Jan. 1989.

based on constitutional guarantees of free speech: in France, a private sector was already being grafted on through legislation.

On being called to examine the provisions of what was to become loi 81–994 of 1981 the Conseil constitutionnel held that it was for the legislator to define the conditions under which derogations could be made to the state monopoly, provided, of course, that the principles and rules of consitutional value were respected.[56] Moreover, the Conseil concluded that this margin of appreciation was sufficiently wide to allow the legislator to impose on the private radio sector a system of prior administrative authorization and to institute a total ban on recourse to advertising revenue. The Conseil seemed willing to perpetuate the traditional distinction between print and broadcasting regulation, allowing restrictions to be imposed on the broadcast media which would be held unconstitutional if applied to the press. Indeed, three years later, when examining legislation designed to limit concentration of ownership in the press, the Conseil expressly noted that the introduction of a prior licensing regime would, in this context, be contrary to Article 11 of the 1789 Declaration.[57]

Calls to bring the audiovisual media into line with the press were in fact made at the time of the 1982 legislation: certain parliamentary deputies had argued that, with the abrogation of the state monopoly, only restrictions justifiable on 'law and order' grounds could legitimately be imposed on private broadcasters. Restrictions of the kind contained in the statute—requiring, for example, television operators to obtain prior concessions and operate under terms set out in *cahiers des charges*—would thus conflict, as they would in the field of the printed press, with the right to individual expression in Article 11. As we have seen, however, the Conseil held that the legislature enjoyed a wide margin of discretion in regulating radio and television: it was for the legislator to reconcile, under current technical conditions, the freedom to communicate with, on the one hand, the technical constraints inherent in the audiovisual media and, on the other, those objectives recognized to be of a constitutional nature.[58] These objectives were specified to be the safeguarding of public order, respect for the freedom of others, and preservation of the pluralist character of the socio-cultural currents of thought in society. Such pluralism, held the Conseil, could be threatened by the considerable influence and power of the audiovisual media.

Just as the Conseil constitutionnel had refrained from censoring the carefully controlled introduction of private actors under the Socialist

---

[56] Dec. 81–129 of 30/31 Oct. 1981 [1981] Rec. Cons. constit. 35.
[57] Dec. 84–181 of 10/11 Oct. 1984 [1984] JO 3200.
[58] Dec. 82–141 of 27 July 1982 [1982] JO 2422.

government, so it was prepared to accept privatization of the key public-sector television channel, TF1, by the Government of Jacques Chirac. There exists in the preamble to the French Constitution of 1946 a provision very similar to Article 43 of the 1948 Italian Constitution: paragraph nine provides that industries which have acquired the characteristics of a national public service or which are *de facto* monopolies must pass into public ownership. In contrast to the repeated use of Article 43 in the Italian context, paragraph nine has hardly been deployed to challenge French audiovisual legislation, initially because the legislative reforms were criticized for too little liberalization rather than too much. With the impending privatization of TF1—a step which would completely overturn the existing public/private balance, TF1 then capturing 40 per cent of the French television audience—it seemed possible that paragraph nine might come into its own.

Although paragraph nine was raised by the deputies in their reference to the Conseil over the proposed 1986 legislation, it was acknowledged that the Conseil had previously held that it was a matter for legislative appreciation whether goods or enterprises could be transferred from the public to the private sector. In making such a transfer the legislator was merely required to respect the rules and principles of constitutional value. The deputies thus deployed paragraph nine to argue, not that TF1 should remain publicly *owned*, an argument they were unlikely to win, but that it be subject to the *public-service regime* of state concession rather than the proposed administrative authorization. The latter would impose upon the contracting party the obligation to conform to established rules governing the public service, namely, equality of access, continuity of service, and neutrality. But again the complaint was rejected on the ground that the choice of licensing system fell within the competence of the legislature. Paragraph nine has therefore had little impact on the French broadcasting sector and its *requirement* that national public services be publicly owned, in contradistinction to Article 43 of the Italian Constitution which is framed in facultative terms, may go some way to explaining why the Conseil was prepared to hold in its 1986 judgment that hertzian television could not be characterized as a public service.[59]

In holding that hertzian television was not a public-service activity having its foundations in the constitution the Conseil constitutionnel struck at the very basis on which French broadcasting had been organized since the Second World War. The acknowledgment that it was within the legislator's field of competence to introduce a television sector which was outside the public-service regime and subject to authorization rather than concession must have been music to the ears of those who had drafted the

---

[59] Dec. 86–217 of 18 Sept. 1986 [1986] JO 11294 at 11295.

1986 legislation specifically to open the way to private enterprise. The import of the Court's reasoning was lessened, however, by the affirmation that all aspects of broadcasting, be they in the public or private domain, were subject to certain basic constitutional prerequisites. If the outer manifestations of public and private sectors had become misleading in the audiovisual sector, the Court was prepared to cut across the distinction and impose its own wide-ranging requirements: where the Socialist deputies had called for the notion of the 'public domain' to be replaced by that of 'public service' the Conseil constitutionnel took the argument one stage further, replacing 'public service' with 'objectives of constitutional value', among them the value of pluralism.

To summarize, the Conseil constitutionnel, unlike the Italian Constitutional Court, has not been required to determine the constitutional legitimacy of the state broadcasting monopoly, whether in transmission or programming. Though the issue arose in the 1978 reference it was not considered to fall within the Conseil's jurisdiction. Instead, the Conseil has been faced with legislative proposals designed both to create a new private sector and to introduce a shift from public to private ownership. Though inevitably containing the growth of the public sector, and in the case of TF1 reducing its existing scope, the Conseil has not held such initiatives to be unconstitutional. Instead, it has made it increasingly clear that it does not consider the presence of either public or private actors to be constitutionally necessitated, rather the decision to allocate ownership between a number of state or private actors is a matter lying within the overall competence of the legislature, in accordance with Article 34 of the 1958 Constitution. The introduction of private actors has thus been held entirely permissible while the total dismantlement of remaining pockets of state ownership appears neither necessitated nor prohibited, so long as the recognized constitutional imperatives are respected.

If the nature of constitutional review in France and Italy has led the two courts to take divergent paths, they appeared by the late 1980s to have reached a similar end-point: recognition of the legitimacy of a system embracing both public and private operators. Nevertheless, the similarity should not be overstressed. In Italy the public and private sectors are seen to further the goal of pluralism in distinct, yet mutually complementary, ways, each has a separate claim to constitutional protection. In France neither has a claim of right to protection: each sector is viable only as long as it gives effect to the Conseil's functional view of a constitutionally legitimate broadcasting sector. The French Conseil's stress on substance rather than form has left the public sector exposed: further moves to privatize the remaining public domain can be countered at the constitutional level only through evidence that this would jeopardize the realization of a constitutional (plural and honest) broadcasting system. Although the legislature's discretion in determining the matrix of audiovisual ownership is not unbounded—it can only be exercised to *further* and *not restrict* the public's enjoyment of its constitutional freedoms, or to reconcile these freedoms with other constitutional rules and values—the need to establish that government policies will inevitably imperil constitutional interests imposes a difficult evidentiary burden to overcome.[60]

(iii) Britain

British courts, because of the consitutional limitations discussed in Chapter 4, have had no influence on the basic structure of British broadcasting and were not used to challenge the early monopoly of the BBC or the subsequent BBC/ITV duopoly. This has been seen as an essentially political determination, outside the judicial realm.

3. OPENING STATE BORDERS TO FOREIGN COMPETITION: NATIONAL MONOPOLIES AND EUROPEAN REGULATION

If we turn to examine developments at the level of the Council of Europe and European Community it will be seen that state monopolies have, until relatively recently, undergone very little by way of direct challenge. Instead it is the viability, rather than the legitimacy, of these institutions which has been brought into question by the dismantling of the national boundaries within which their power was centred. Both the European Community and Council of Europe have sought to lift restrictions on cross-border transmissions, and in so doing they have exposed national broadcasters to new competition from foreign off-air and satellite services. State monopoly broadcasters may continue to retain control over nationally allocated *frequencies* but they can no longer dictate the *range of services* accessible to the national audience: protected from within, such monopolies have been undermined from without.

(i) The Council of Europe

In looking first at the approach taken by the European Commission and Court of Human Rights it will be seen that the legal debate has centred on the meaning to be ascribed to Article 10 of the 1950 European Convention

---

[60] See the *saisines* and Dec. 86–210 of 29 July 1986 [1986] JO 9383 ff. on the proposed 1986 legislation introducing new provisions relating to press concentrations. The case is interesting in that, although the Conseil identified certain noticeable gaps in the legislation which would have opened the way for evasion, it was reluctant to challenge the government's assessment of the required transparency measures. The Conseil held that the fact that the provisions were *less rigorous* than those contained in prior legislation was not of itself sufficient to found a case of unconstitutionality.

on Human Rights, a provision which specifically recognizes the right to impart information and ideas 'regardless of frontiers'.[61] It has been suggested that Article 10, correctly interpreted, precludes the creation of state broadcasting monopolies. The third sentence of Article 10(1) provides '[t]his article shall not prevent States from requiring the licensing of broadcasting, television or cinema enterprises' and some have seen the use of the term 'licensing' to 'point in favour of radio and television corporations being operated by private enterprises rather than by state monopoly.'[62] This, and the argument that the use of the plural term 'enterprises' indicates that the grant of licences to more than one broadcasting body was envisaged, are not, however, entirely convincing.[63] In the first place there is no reason why licences cannot be awarded to public bodies, the BBC for example, operates under a charter and licence, and the use of the plural term 'enterprises' can hardly be read in these circumstances as outlawing the grant of a unique licence: use of the singular term 'enterprise' would have been grammatically incorrect, given that it refers to three distinct sectors—broadcasting, television, and cinema.

We have already seen how, in the aftermath of the Second World War, a number of European countries established state broadcasting monopolies under close government supervision. It is unlikely that these countries would have signed a Convention outlawing such practices, and it is probable that the licensing clause was designed to reassure them that they would not be bound to apply principles considered relevant in the domain of the press—notably the prohibition of prior authorization—to the audiovisual sector. A licensing system can be used to fulfil a number of distinct objectives: it may be used to allocate the use of resources, it may also help to prevent legal wrangles over entitlements and interference and, finally, the award of licences may be used to impose operating terms on the chosen licensees. The licensing clause of Article 10 can be read simply as indicating the legitimacy of a licensing regime, that is the award of permits, and as providing no guidance on which criteria may be deployed in allocating licences, or which operating terms, if any, will be compatible with the Convention.[64] It is probable, however, that many of the states which signed and ratified the Convention regarded the third sentence of Article 10(1) as authorizing not merely the grant of licences but also the imposition of extensive technical and programming requirements: an

---

[61] The full text is set out in the App.   [62] G. Malinverni (1983), 458.

[63] The argument that the term 'enterprises' indicates that licences must be given to more than one organization was put forward by the applicants but was not accepted by the European Commission on Human Rights in App. No 3071/67, *X* v. *Sweden*, 26 Coll. 71.

[64] This was the approach adopted by the European Court of Human Rights in the *Groppera* case, (1990) 12 EHRR 321, on which see below.

endorsement, that is, of the existing status quo. It was the fear that such a clause would indeed be construed to afford states a completely free hand in determining licensing terms that led the drafters of the 1966 International Covenant on Civil and Political Rights to reject incorporation of a similar clause in Article 19 which, in other respects, follows Article 10 quite closely.[65]

How then has Article 10 been interpreted in practice? In line with the early approach of the Italian Constitutional Court, the Human Rights Commission at first indicated that it was unwilling to challenge the widespread European presence of public broadcasting monopolies. In 1967 the Commission was called upon to consider whether the Swedish broadcasting monopoly was contrary to Article 10(1) of the Convention.[66] It concluded that the licensing clause afforded states considerable discretion in determining the public or private make-up of their broadcasting systems. They were consequently free to decide whether or not to grant 'a monopoly in the field of this particular activity or whether there must be competing enterprises at the same time'. This approach was confirmed four years later when the British broadcasting sector came under scrutiny in *X* v. *United Kingdom*, the Human Rights Commission again holding that the term 'licensing' 'could not be understood as excluding in any way a public television monopoly as such'.[67] By 1976, however, a change in attitude could be discerned, and the Commission indicated that it was no longer prepared to maintain this point of view 'without further consideration'.[68] This refusal simply to endorse existing state broadcasting structures was undoubtedly triggered by a growing awareness both of the level of public dissatisfaction with these institutions' lack of political accountability and of the new opportunities for alternative broadcasting outlets, outlets such as cable which had already found a legal champion in the Italian Constitutional Court.[69] It must, therefore, have been apparent that in swimming with those member governments of the Council of Europe which wished to retain their broadcasting monopolies the Commission and Court risked finding themselves increasingly at variance with national constitutional courts.

These issues were further examined by the European Court of Human Rights in two recent cases: *Groppera Radio AG* v. *Switzerland* and

---

[65] G. Malinverni (1983), 457, n. 79.
[66] App. No 3071/67, *X* v. *Sweden*, 26 Coll. 71.
[67] App. No 4750/71, *X* v. *UK*, 40 Coll. 29.
[68] App. No 6542/74, *Sacchi* v. *Italy*, 5 D & R 43.
[69] In Res. 428 (1970) of the Consultative Assembly of the Council of Europe (DH–MM(89)6), for example, it was held that '3.[n]either individual enterprises, nor financial groups should have the right to institute a monopoly in the field of press, radio or television, nor should government-controlled monopoly be permitted.'

Informationsverein Lentia and others v. *Austria.*[70] In the *Groppera* case the Court acknowledged that a number of technical and economic considerations, as well as the desire of several states that broadcasting remain 'the preserve of the State', had underscored the insertion of the licensing clause in Article 10 of the Convention. Although the Court recognized the considerable technical and structural changes which had taken place in the broadcasting environment since the drafting of the Convention, in particular the demise of state monopolies in many European countries, it continued to see the third sentence of Article 10(1) as confirming 'that States are permitted to control by a licensing system the way in which broadcasting is organized in their territories, particularly in its technical aspects'. The Court, however, went on considerably to reduce the potential import of the licensing clause by holding that 'licensing measures' must conform to the requirements of Article 10(2). The justifications contained in Article 10(2) for imposing restrictions on freedom of expression are quite limited, although in *Groppera* there are indications that the Court considered the phrase 'the protection of . . . the rights of others' broad enough to cover regulations designed to ensure pluralism, particularly in the information field. Although this would seem to open the door for a Convention state to argue that its broadcasting monopoly served to ensure the provision of plural programming, Article 10(2) also requires that any restriction on freedom of expression be shown to be 'necessary in a democratic society'. In the *Groppera* case Switzerland had acted to restrict cable relay in Switzerland of an Italian radio channel intended for a Swiss audience. The owners of the station had deliberately evaded Swiss licensing requirements by establishing a powerful transmitter on the Italian border, and in these circumstances the restriction was held to be proportionate. The Court was not called upon to consider the more wide-ranging question whether a state broadcasting monopoly could ever be held to conform to the Convention.

This was, however, the issue in the *Lentia* case, where the Court adopted a rather different approach to the relationship between the licensing clause and the second paragraph of Article 10. Here, the radio and television monopoly of the Austrian Broadcasting Corporation, ORF, was directly challenged by five applicants who wished to set up their own cable or radio stations. Both the Commission and the Court started from the premise that the applicants' rights to expression under Article 10 had been infringed. The position of the licensing clause in the first paragraph of Article 10, which defines the scope of freedom of expression, rather than in the second paragraph, which establishes permissible derogations to it, might have led

---

[70] *Groppera Radio AG* v. *Switzerland* (1990) 12 EHRR 321 and *Informationsverein Lentia and others* v. *Austria* (1994) 17 EHRR 93.

to the conclusion that it was intended to limit the scope of the right itself. In the case of *X* v. *Sweden* the Commission had indeed indicated that the right to freedom of expression would be more restricted in a state which required the licensing of radio and television enterprises than in one which did not.[71] In *Lentia*, however, the Court, without further exposition, concluded that the applicants' freedom to impart information and ideas had been infringed.[72] It was irrelevant when considering the existence of an infringement that the Austrian regulations sought to promote the transmission of 'well-balanced, objective and pluralistic programmes'; this was important only when considering whether those regulations, as restrictions on freedom of expression, could be justified.

Although finding that the applicants' freedom of expression had been infringed, the Court, somewhat paradoxically, did not conclude that they were therefore entitled to broadcasting licences. The right at issue was not the applicants' individual right to broadcast but their right that an unspecified number of private licences be set aside for private operators. It was precisely because the Court considered the applicants' claim that they would have been granted licences if permitted to apply for them to be speculative that it refused to award financial compensation. This was in line with previous Commission statements to the effect that individuals do not enjoy a 'right' to a broadcasting licence: in *X and Association Z* v. *United Kingdom*, for example, it held that freedom of expression does not embrace 'a general and unfettered right for any private citizen or organisation to have access to broadcasting time on radio and television in order to forward its opinion'.[73]

If there is a right under Article 10 to apply for a private broadcasting licence, though not an individual right to obtain one, how extensive must the private sector be? The answer would appear to be as extensive as possible, with only such restrictions to its scope as can be convincingly justified by the state in question. In considering the nature of these restrictions the Court and Commission adopted different lines of argument. The Commission followed *Groppera* in holding that only those restrictions which fell within the list set out in Article 10(2) would be

[71] App. No 9297/81, *X* v. *Sweden*, 28 D & R 204 at 205.

[72] The Commission explicitly held that the licensing clause did not limit the rights guaranteed in the first two sentences of Art. 10(1), although there are some indications that it would not regard the refusal of a licence on purely technical grounds to be an interference with the applicant's rights, see paras. 61, 64, and 65. For further comment see R. Craufurd Smith (1995).

[73] App. No 4515/70, *X and Association Z* v. *UK*, 38 Coll. 86 at 88. See also App. No 10746/84, *Verein Alternatives Lokalradio Bern* v. *Switzerland*, 49 D & R 126. In both cases the Commission recognized that recourse to the Court might be possible using Art. 10 in combination with Art. 14 where licences have been awarded on a discriminatory basis.

acceptable, while the Court indicated that justification could be found in the more general licensing clause in Article 10(1). According to the Court the licensing clause enabled states to take into account a wide range of considerations when awarding licences, some of which would not fall within the more limited scope of Article 10(2). Nevertheless, elements of Article 10(2) were selectively cut loose to exert a restraining brake on state discretion: once a restriction is found to correspond to a 'legitimate aim' it must still be shown to have been 'prescribed by law' and to be 'necessary in a democratic society'.

Although the Commission and Court approached Article 10 differently they came to a similar conclusion regarding the Austrian broadcasting monopoly. Neither ruled out in principle the legitimacy under the Convention of public broadcasting monopolies but it is apparent from their reasoning that, given the expansion in broadcasting outlets and the concrete realities of cross-border broadcasting, states will now find it difficult, if not impossible, to justify the total exclusion of private broadcasters from the audiovisual sector. The Commission was of the opinion that a state monopoly would now be acceptable only if it made sufficient provision for independently produced programmes and specific-ally referred to openings for private expression at the local or regional level: absent such provision the licensing of private broadcasters would be required. The Court held that the extreme restriction on freedom of expression which a state monopoly necessarily entailed could not, in the Austrian context, be held proportionate to the aim of the Austrian government in ensuring the 'objectivity and impartiality of reporting, the diversity of opinions, balanced programming and the independence of persons and bodies responsible for programmes'. Such concerns could less intrusively be addressed by issuing private licences subject to specified content requirements and the introduction of adequate anti-trust regula-tions.[74]

Finally, it may be noted that the European Court of Human Rights in the case of *Autronic AG* v. *Switzerland* indicated that it will be exceedingly difficult for states to justify restrictions on the *reception* of unencoded foreign broadcast signals within their territory, whether the signals are from fixed or direct broadcasting satellites.[75] Application of the Article 10 right to receive and impart information and ideas 'regardless of frontiers' consequently serves to undermine the ability of nation states to monopolize

---

[74] *Informationsverein Lentia and others* v. *Austria* (1994) 17 EHRR 93, Commission at para. 84, Court at para. 39.
[75] *Autronic AG* v. *Switzerland* (1990) 12 EHRR 485. The 1989 European Convention on Transfrontier Television was intended to reduce the incidence of conflicts over cross-border broadcasts by getting contracting states to agree basic ground rules in areas, such as advertising, where disagreement seemed likely.

their citizens' access to broadcast material whether that comes from within or from outside the national territory.

To conclude, we may say that although public broadcasting monopolies have not been held in principle to infringe the fundamental rights set out in the European Convention it is unlikely that, in a given concrete situation, such a monopoly would be found necessary to meet legitimate licensing objectives. The Austrian broadcasting case represents a clear warning to those pockets of public monopoly which may still exist. Although an element of public ownership may continue to be justifiable under the Court's somewhat open-ended interpretation of the licensing clause, it is apparent that primacy has been afforded private expression. Public channels are granted merely provisional legitimacy: acceptable only while states can establish convincing justification for their scale and remit. From this perspective parallels can be drawn with the early decisions of the Italian Constitutional Court, where the public sector was held admissible only while technical or financial limitations prevented the realization of a competitive broadcasting sector; a position departed from in the Court's 1988 decision which emphasized the essential nature of both public and private sectors in guaranteeing the provision to the public of diverse information.[76]

(ii) The European Community

Although Article 222 of the EC Treaty stipulates that the 'Treaty shall in no way prejudice the rules in Member States governing the system of property ownership' it has become increasingly apparent that Community law can have a significant impact on the way in which property is enjoyed and exploited.[77] Article 90(1) of the Treaty undoubtedly envisages the continuing existence of public undertakings, but requires Member States in relation to such undertakings, or undertakings to which they grant special rights, to refrain from introducing measures contrary to the rules set out in the Treaty, in particular the competition and free-market provisions. Article 90(2) goes on to provide that the activities of '[u]ndertakings entrusted with the operation of services of general economic interest or having the character of a revenue-producing monopoly' are also to be subject to the rules contained in the Treaty, in particular to the rules on competition, but provides for derogations from these rules where compliance would obstruct their performance of the particular tasks assigned to them.

In *Italy* v. *Sacchi* the European Court of Justice applied Article 90(1) to

---

[76] Dec. 826/1988 [1988] Foro it. 2477, 2499.
[77] See, e.g., Joined Cases C–241–242/91P, *Radio Telefis Eireann and Independent Television Publications Limited* v. *Commission* [1995] 4 CMLR 718.

the audiovisual media and held that there was 'nothing in the Treaty to prevent Member States, for considerations of public interest, of a non-economic nature, from withdrawing radio and television broadcasts, including broadcasts by cable, from the field of competition, by conferring on one or more institutions the exclusive right to operate in this field'.[78] In the subsequent case of *Höfner and Elser* the Court held, however, that where a state grants an undertaking exclusive rights to provide a particular service and that undertaking is not able to meet the demand for that service, then the State may be in breach of Article 90(1) in co-ordination with Article 86 which prohibits the abuse of a dominant position.[79] The broad remit which the Court has recently given to Article 90(1) leads one to question whether, if the legitimacy of a state broadcasting monopoly were now to be raised before the Court, it would consider such an undertaking able to meet the demand for broadcasting services. Moreover, the *Corbeau* case indicates that where an undertaking has been entrusted with responsibility for providing a 'service of general economic interest' within Article 90(2) it will have to show that *all* its activities are necessary for it to provide that service.[80] In the broadcasting context this would mean that a public broadcaster with extensive exclusive rights would have to show that it was necessary for it to have those rights not only in the field of scheduling, but also in the other fields assigned to it such as transmission and production. Article 90(3) of the Treaty authorizes the Commission to pass directives in order to ensure compliance with the provisions of Article 90(1) and (2), a power it has utilized, most noticeably in the telecommunications sector, to prohibit the continuing exercise of certain exclusive rights which impede market competition.[81]

After the *Sacchi* decision the legitimacy of a state broadcasting monopoly was to arise once again in the *ERT* case.[82] Here, the European Court of Justice held that although the Greek public-broadcasting monopoly did not of and in itself contravene Community law, it was still possible that the manner in which the monopoly was *'organized or exercised'* might infringe the rules of the EC Treaty. In particular, the Court noted that the award to ERT of a monopoly not only to broadcast its own programmes but also to relay foreign channels could lead to discrimination against foreign stations contrary to the rules on freedom to provide goods or services, or to an abuse of a dominant position. The

---

[78] Case 155/73, *Italy* v. *Sacchi* [1974] 2 CMLR 177, 203. For comment see A. Decocq (1989), 363.

[79] Case C–41/90, *Höfner and Elser* v. *Macrotron GmbH* [1993] 4 CMLR 306.

[80] Case C–320/91, *Paul Corbeau* [1995] 4 CMLR 621.

[81] See, e.g., Commission Dir. 95/51/EC [1995] OJ L256/49.

[82] Case 260/89, *Ellinka Radiophonia Tileorassi—Anonimi Etairia* v. *Dimotiki Etairia Pliroforissis* [1991] ECR 2925.

Court referred the matter back to the national court to consider whether, on the facts, such contraventions of the Treaty could be established.

The approach adopted by the Court in the *Sacchi* and *ERT* cases is mirrored also in official statements of Community policy. The preamble to the 1989 Television Directive is careful, for example, to affirm that its provisions do 'not affect the responsibility of the Member States and their authorities with regard to the organization—including the systems of licensing, administrative authorization or taxation—financing and the content of programmes'.[83] In 1991 the Commission, in a written question, was asked whether state broadcasting monopolies were compatible with 'Community principles of freedom of movement for services and goods and the rules concerning competition' where other organizations sought permission to broadcast. Replying for the Commission, Mr Bangemann stated that '[u]nder Community law, Member States are free to determine the number and the public or private status of television broadcasting organizations that may be authorized to broadcast programmes within their territory', so long as the authorization procedures and the companies granted broadcasting permits comply with 'the fundamental principles of freedom of establishment and free movement of persons, services and capital and with the rules of competition laid down in the EC Treaty'.[84]

This response clearly reveals the extent to which public-broadcasting activities may in fact be circumscribed by the exercise of Community rights. Thus, despite the freedom seemingly afforded to states in the first sentence, it is apparent that the competition principles referred to at the end of the statement open the door to Commission scrutiny of the activities, if not the existence as such, of public broadcasters. It is, of course, possible for Article 90(2) undertakings to argue that compliance with the competition rules would obstruct the realization of the particular tasks assigned to them. A reading of the *Corbeau* case suggests that an enterprise required to provide key services on a universal basis, at a uniform tariff, and of consistent quality, would be considered an undertaking providing a service of general economic interest.[85] Public-service broadcasters have traditionally sought to fulfil these objectives, and the Commission in its 1993 EBU decision acknowledged that they may indeed be considered general-interest undertakings within Article 90(2). The burden of proof imposed on such undertakings when seeking to justify infringment of the competition rules is, however, a heavy one, for it is impossibility and not merely inconvenience or additional expense in

[83] Dir. 89/552/EEC [1989] OJ L298/23.
[84] Written question 2225/91 by Mr Victor Manuel Arbeloa Muru, printed, with Mr Bangemann's response of the 8 Jan. 1992, in [1992] OJ C78/41.
[85] Case C–320/91, *Paul Corbeau* [1993] ECR I–2533.

carrying out its public mission which must be shown. The Commission in its 1993 EBU ruling was clearly of the opinion that public broadcasters were not then in a position to show that compliance with the competition rules rendered performance of their public mission impossible.[86] Public-service broadcasters are consequently subject to the normal application of the Community competition rules.

Under Community law it is now well established that the transmission of television signals and the relaying of such signals by cable fall to be considered under the Treaty rules relating to the provision of services.[87] National restrictions on the cross-border provision of such services will thus have to be justified, where discriminatory, under one of the limited heads set out in Article 56 of the Treaty (applied to the service provisions by Article 66) or, where applied to national and foreign broadcasts alike, as being in the public interest, objectively necessary, and proportionate to the aims pursued.[88] In many areas, such as advertising, the scope for domestic regulation of television broadcasts transmitted from abroad has now been pre-empted by the 1989 Television Directive.[89] There is thus a strong presumption under Community law against the imposition of restrictions on foreign broadcasts, and it is apparent that the Commission perceives the scope for successful justification to be highly circumscribed, not least because the free movement of broadcasting services across frontiers is considered 'a specific manifestation in Community law of a more general principle, namely the freedom of expression as enshrined in Article 10(1)' of the European Convention.[90]

Opening national broadcasting 'markets' to foreign competition clearly curtails the capacity of the Member States to regulate the flow of advertising revenues to national broadcasters: the 'public-service' nature of the British commercial ITV channel, for example, was built on its monopoly of advertising revenue, its 'licence to print money'. Public-service broadcasters may be badly hit by additional commercial competition, particularly where they are subject to strict limits over advertising times and scheduling: over a five-year period between 1986 and 1991, for example, advertising revenues of the German private commercial station SAT 1 rose from 22.4 million DM to 653.9 million DM, while the revenues of the public broadcaster ARD fell from 1,102.2 million DM to 483 million

---

[86] Dec. 93/403/EEC, *Re the Application of the European Broadcasting Union* (Case IV/32.150) [1995] 4 CMLR 56, 81.

[87] Case 52/79, *Procureur du Roi* v. *Debauve* [1981] 2 CMLR 362.

[88] Case C–384/93, *Alpine Investments BV* v. *Minister van Financiën* [1995] ECR I–1141.

[89] Dir. 89/552/EEC [1989] OJ L298/23.

[90] Preamble to the 1989 Television Dir. For details of the EC Commission's attitude to the extent of 'general-interest' justifications for national restrictions on cross-border broadcasts see EC Commission (1984), 169 ff. and Ch. 7 below.

DM.[91] Similarly, between 1989 and 1993, RTL4 and RTL5, broadcasting out of Luxembourg and relayed over Dutch cable systems, were together able to capture 30 per cent of the Dutch audience and 53 per cent of total advertising revenues, taking full advantage of the lighter Luxembourg regulatory regime.[92] Thus, although the liberalization of cross-border broadcasting may indeed, as the 1989 Directive indicates, have no effect on the 'responsibility' of Member States to organize their national broadcasting systems, it clearly circumscribes their regulatory options. As de Witte noted in 1987 'it is not difficult to predict that a free flow of foreign broadcasts might cause a rapid collapse of several national broadcasting systems; States will be denied the eminently cultural policy choice between public monopoly and commercial broadcasting'.[93] The Commission's initiatives to 'liberate fully' the competitive potential of the audiovisual sector and encourage the development of a secondary rebroadcasting market have undoubtedly offered all broadcasters, public among them, new opportunities to market their programmes and services.[94] Nevertheless, the question remains to what extent an increasingly competitive outlook will undermine the non-commercial objectives on which the public-service broadcasting stations have been based.

4. PUBLIC OWNERSHIP OF THE AUDIOVISUAL MEDIA AND THE COURTS: AN APPRAISAL

The above analysis has served to highlight the by no means surprising fact that courts of law have, from the 1960s onwards, been willing to adapt existing constitutional provisions to the changing technological, political, and social environment which was discussed in Chapter 4. Initially prepared to endorse state claims as to the legitimacy of public broadcasting monopolies, though with the caveat that these should be more politically independent and accountable, they have moved on to accept a mixed broadcasting system. The forces favouring privatization of the audiovisual media have been substantial, and courts of law have in the end proved willing to accommodate, if not actually further, them. At the one end of the spectrum might be placed the German Constitutional Court, which has sought to contain the forces of private capital, at the other the Italian Constitutional Court, which opened local broadcasting to private operators.

---

[91] Dec. 93/403/EEC, *Re the Application of the European Broadcasting Union* (Case IV/32.150) [1995] 4 CMLR 56.   [92] B. Sturgess *et al.* (1995), 25.
[93] B. de Witte (1987), 268.
[94] Communication from the Commission to the Council and Parliament on audiovisual policy: COM(90)78 final, 21 Feb. 1990.

Some may consider that the courts have created an unduly expansive 'margin of state appreciation', their case law simply keeping pace with the political swing in favour of private broadcasting. But it would be fairer to conclude that the courts have tried, albeit in a field of considerable political sensitivity, to establish an agenda of their own which goes beyond mere time-serving.

To some extent the political and legal agendas have overlapped; constitutional guarantees of free speech provide at least one basis for the courts to champion individual, private, expression and the democratic failings of the frequently government-dominated public sector have provided another. This is not to say that political and judicial operators share the same underlying objectives: politicians have clearly been motivated by a desire for 'high-tech' industrial development, for international competitiveness, and in some quarters by the desire to marginalize a public sector which was seen as unduly bureaucratic and increasingly difficult to 'control'. Such considerations find little foothold in a rights-based legal analysis. Nor indeed do political operators themselves share a common image of what form the audiovisual landscape should take, as the bitter political disagreements which accompanied the passage of the 1990 Italian broadcasting legislation so clearly illustrate. Political blueprints for broadcasting are as varied as the political fortunes which spawn them, but there is now wide acceptance of the legitimacy of a private broadcasting sector.

If courts and legislatures have been moving gradually in the same direction towards a mixed broadcasting environment, albeit with different benefits in mind, they have been moving at very different rates. Court action, as we have seen, is bound by operational rules which may, as in the French situation, relegate it to a reactive, though by no means unimportant, role or which, as in the Italian situation, may enable the courts directly to challenge the broadcasting status quo. In Italy the Constitutional Court showed that it was responsive to social and political demands which went beyond the ruling parties' self-interested protection of the public broadcasting sector. Calling first for reform and then actively dismantling the established structure, it worked to an agenda not shared by the powerful Christian Democratic Party. In France, the Conseil constitutionnel, faced with political action rather than inaction, felt able to step back from the increasingly blurred public–private debate and establish an essentially functional view of broadcasting. In consequence, when the Conseil came to examine the privatization of the central public-sector channel, TF1, it considered that no constitutional difficulties arose simply from the station's move to private ownership.

This last point reveals the extent to which legal questions in the broadcasting field have shifted over time. The question now is not so much whether broadcasting outlets should be publicly or privately owned but the extent to which broadcasters should be regulated and whether the regulatory load should vary from one broadcaster to another. Thus, although the Italian Constitutional Court's growing emphasis on the constitutional value of 'pluralism' helped it to validate the public sector in its own right, it does not appear to require that the public sector be publicly owned. In Italy the market is consequently to be divided between a private and public sector, identifiable according to the spread of regulatory burdens and advantages. In France, the position is not quite so plain in that the Conseil constitutionnel did not itself seek to demarcate a specific area subject to public-service regulation; it was essentially for the state to determine how the consitutional objective of pluralism might be realized through public or private ownership, regulation, and commercial competition.

In determining the number of broadcasting outlets and the applicable regulatory regime political and legal agendas may, however, continue to diverge. Vincent Porter and Suzanne Hasselbach have noted how in Germany the courts and *Länder* have worked to different paradigms: the Constitutional Court considers the public sector to be the central plank of the German broadcasting order and has required at least a 'basic' commitment to public-service principles from private operators, while the *Länder* have sought to ensure that private operators are not burdened with uneconomic obligations which, in a competitive environment, could challenge their survival.[95] Indeed as competition, national and international, intensifies governments may be tempted to lighten the private sector's regulatory load and, where they do not do so, we can expect to see private companies increasingly looking to the courts to overturn remaining public-service obligations. It is the theoretical foundations and practical scope for judicial resistance to such moves which together constitute the subject of the next chapter.

[95] V. Porter and S. Hasselbach (1991).

7
Pluralism and Freedom of Expression: Constitutional Imperatives for a New Audiovisual Order

> If the claims of two (or more than two) types of liberty prove incompatible in a particular case, and if this is an instance of the clash of values at once absolute and incommensurable, it is better to face this intellectually uncomfortable fact than to ignore it, or automatically attribute it to some deficiency on our part which could be eliminated by an increase in skill or knowledge; or, what is worse still, suppress one of the competing values altogether by pretending that it is identical with its rival—and so end by distorting both.[1]

In the preceding chapter we charted the gradual accommodation within legal theory of a 'mixed' broadcasting system embracing both public and private operators. Inevitably the development of private broadcasting has sparked off, as in a chain reaction, a series of further questions concerning the legitimate scope of state regulation in the audiovisual sector. With the growth of an audiovisual 'market', new controls have been established to keep in check the activities of private and public operators, leading to the 're-regulation' of European broadcasting. The considerable complexity of much of this regulation is well illustrated by the UK Broadcasting Act 1990 and its impenetrable provisions on cross-media ownership. Although national regulation has increasingly concerned itself with competition aspects of the industry, the determination of European governments to maintain at least skeletal controls over programme content in the face of new commercial, especially international, challenges reveals an unwillingness to forgo all influence over the audiovisual media, if not a continuing commitment to certain of the public-service ideals which have dominated the past.

This Chapter will examine in rather more detail the theoretical foundations for judicial intervention in the audiovisual field, and how legal

[1] I. Berlin (1969), 1.

principles have been developed in order to adapt to changing technological and political circumstances. As we have seen, there has been a judicial tendency not to oppose in principle the possibility of structural change; indeed the Italian Constitutional Court has explicitly required it. Instead, national courts in a number of European countries have set about establishing regulatory guidelines for a 'mixed' market. In both Italy and France they have drawn heavily on constitutional guarantees of freedom of expression and given prominence to the related principle of informational pluralism. The elevation of the concept of pluralism to a position of prominence raises a number of interconnected questions: what are its constitutional foundations and how does it relate to the well-established right to freedom of expression, generally considered to determine the parameters of legitimate press regulation? Although these questions may appear unduly theoretical, their answers have important practical implications for the audiovisual media, implications for the size and competitiveness of the broadcasting sector, for the selection of broadcasters on ethnic, religious, or political lines, and for the legitimacy of content regulations.

The nature of the right to freedom of expression has been, and remains, hotly contested, but, in the context of the printed press, it is often considered, as we noted in Chapter 1, to be based on a 'negative-liberty' or 'no-censorship' theory of speech rights. Such a theory focuses on the need to prevent the censorship of specific ideas and the corresponding right to say what one wishes, however distasteful, free from external restraint or sanction. Traditionally, the theory has been called in aid to protect individual expression from state intervention, rendering the printed press 'off limits' for government regulation. Those seeking to open up and deregulate the broadcasting industry have built on historical anxieties over state power to affirm a narrow formulation of the negative-liberty principle, one that protects individual autonomy from public but not private threats. The problems posed by the promotional power of private capital are simply not addressed by such a theory, nor is the fact that individual speech may be as dangerously distorted in private as it is in public hands. Viewed from this perspective, individual expression has a status akin to that of private property: although the costs involved in running a national newspaper or television station put their ownership beyond the reach of most individuals, state intervention to redress any resulting expressive imbalance in society is regarded an unacceptable intervention in the private domain.[2] The ramifications of such an approach

---

[2] It should be noted that property rights, though afforded a high level of protection, are not generally held to be inviolable, and in certain circumstances property may be regulated or even appropriated by the state in the 'public interest'. Moreover, there are some activities and entities, such as the right to vote, which are deemed so important for the individual or state

for media regulation are clearly considerable, and for those, like David Kelley and Richard Donway, who emphasize the importance of the private market in promoting individual freedom, calls for access rights or other forms of market intervention are seen as nothing more than 'particularly egregious' examples of 'demanding a right to the labor of others'.[3]

Matched against such a theory the reality of broadcasting regulation in Europe, with its system of limited licences and institutional programme controls, could not fail but be found wanting. Central to the more limited 'negative-liberty' view of free speech outlined above is an irrefutable presumption against state intervention: even if state intervention could immediately be brought into play to enhance individual autonomy by maximizing the number of speakers through access or antitrust provisions, the potential long-term dangers of public regulation are considered to outweigh any more immediate benefits. Even the most benign state regulation is seen as starting the slide down a dangerous slippery slope, leading if not to outright censorship then to an even more pervasive and difficult to identify practice of self-censorship.

Though extreme in its implications and *prima facie* at odds with the level of state intervention to be found in the European broadcasting sector, this emphasis on individual expression, with its concern for the interests of the speaker, seems to accord with the way in which the press and other communicative freedoms have been framed in the Italian and French constitutional texts. Both Article 11 of the French 1789 Declaration of the Rights of Man and Article 21 of the 1948 Italian Constitution focus on the act of expression, the French provision stating that every citizen may speak, write, and publish freely; the Italian that everyone has the right to express freely his own thoughts in words, writing, or by any other means of diffusion.[4] More specifically, Article 21 of the Italian Constitution provides that the press is not to be subjected to a system of authorization or censorship. Despite this textual emphasis on individual expression the Italian and French Constitutional Courts have recognized that the audiovisual media perform a variety of important social as well as individual functions and have interpreted the constitutional provisions accordingly. In doing so they have stopped well short of outlawing all state intervention in the broadcasting sector and rejected an extreme 'negative-liberty' approach to freedom of expression.

---

that we do not allow them to be sold. The fact that it is *possible* for money to buy speech is not, therefore, a convincing argument that it should be allowed to do so: we must push the question back a stage and ask whether speech exhibits characteristics which render its commodification contrary to recognized individual or social needs.

[3] D. Kelley and R. Donway (1990), 81.
[4] The full texts are set out in the App., below.

1. PLURALISM AND FREEDOM OF EXPRESSION IN ITALIAN CASE LAW

The Italian audiovisual cases reveal a shifting and uncertain attitude to the relationship between the right to free speech and the interest in programme pluralism. As one might expect, given the then state stranglehold of the audiovisual media, the Italian Constitutional Court in its early ruling in 1960 did not decide that the constitutional protection afforded to freedom of expression precluded all state regulation of radio or television.[5] After holding that the ultimate objective in this field was that as many people as possible should have an opportunity to express themselves, not that one or two people should be able to speak freely without state intervention, the Court concluded that, where only a few frequencies were available for broadcast use, state rather than private ownership offered the best possible guarantee that individual access would be made available to those who sought it. It will be apparent that although the desire to facilitate individual expression reflects the 'negative-liberty' preoccupation with individual autonomy, the Court refused to take the second step of holding that all state intervention inevitably damages that autonomy. Though clearly aware of the dangers of state intervention the Court indicated that the suggested alternative, private actors operating in an unregulated market, using speech as a form of property, could equally distort expression or limit access.

Rather than adopt a 'slippery-slope' approach to state regulation the Court set guidelines for the public broadcaster, requiring that complete impartiality be maintained in the award of air-time to third parties. Article 21 of the Constitution was held to necessitate that access be a product not of content, of what the individual wished to say, but rather of whether the individual actually wanted to say something. State ownership could thus be used positively to expand individual speech opportunities and create a '*multiplicity of speakers*', but public broadcasters were debarred from taking a view, negative or positive, on the value of the speech they consequently broadcast.

If Article 21 was seen as designed to facilitate speech opportunities *in principle* on a non-discriminatory basis the Court, in the same 1960 decision, nevertheless accepted that *in practice* some selection would have to be made due to the limited air time. Rather than adopt a 'first come, first served' approach which would have been consistent with its emphasis on non-discriminatory access, it instead referred to the need to consider 'other interests' entitled to protection, namely the variety and worth of programmes. The existence of two distinct interests, each pulling in

---

[5] Dec. 59/1960 [1960] Giur. cost. 759.

potentially different directions, can thus be traced back to the earliest television cases, an interest both in the impartial facilitation of individual speech and in programme variety or pluralism. In particular, the 1960 decision indicated that, in the public sector at least, the principle of pluralism could legitimately be brought into play even where this prevented, on content grounds, those who wished to express themselves having access to the audiovisual media. If the rationale for public ownership was that a private broadcast market would not impartially allow access to all those who might wish to speak, it appeared, somewhat paradoxically, that the allocation of air-time in the public sector could legitimately involve a degree of selection based on the 'variety' or 'worth' of the proposed communication.

It is thus possible to distinguish three aspects of freedom of expression in the initial Italian broadcasting rulings. The first is the negative 'no-censorship' principle which prohibits censorship of particular ideas or opinions on grounds of content; a principle which, as we have seen, some have limited to state intervention and given a wide scope in attacking all forms of state broadcasting regulation. The second is the positive principle that the state should act to further opportunities for individual expression, giving rise to a 'multiplicity of speakers'. The third is the 'plurality of voices' principle which calls for a regulatory framework to facilitate the transmission of a wide variety of viewpoints and opinions. It was not initially clear whether the Constitutional Court considered this last interest in pluralism to be based on Article 21, though there were undoubted indications to that effect. In its 1972 decision on the printed press, for example, the Court held that Article 21 not only protected the right of the *speaker or writer* to give and divulge information but also 'indirectly protected' the 'general interest' of the *recipient* to information.[6] The situation was clarified by Decision 112 of 1993 in which the Court confirmed that Article 21 embraces both 'the right to inform and the right to be informed'.[7] According to the Court, the 'right to information' guaranteed by Article 21 entails four things: a plurality of sources of news and information, providing different points of view and contrasting cultural orientations; objective and impartially presented information; comprehensive and continuous transmission of accurate information; and respect for human dignity, public order, and morality, coupled with the requirement that there should be no distortion of children's moral and psychological development.[8]

The two 'no-censorship' and 'multiplicity of speakers' principles interrelate with the 'plurality of voices' principle in rather different ways. It is

---

[6] Dec. 105/1972 [1972] Giur. cost. 1196.
[7] Dec. 112/1993 [1993] Foro it. 1339 at 1349.   [8] *Ibid.*

usual to find certain categories of speech, even within the most liberal democracies, which are prohibited because of their capacity to endanger life or undermine other recognized rights to, for example, racial or sexual equality. The scope of these prohibitions varies from one country to another, but outside this restricted area there is a general presumption that people should be allowed to write and say what they think. To allow governments or private individuals systematically to intervene in order to restrict such expression is clearly capable of limiting not only the number of speakers but also the range of opinions circulating in society. From this perspective compliance with the no-censorship principle appears a necessary, though not sufficient, condition for realization of the other two principles.

As we have seen, however, the no-censorship principle is sometimes used to attack not only negative but also positive state intervention in the mass media on the ground that any regulation has the capacity to alter the specific content of what would otherwise be broadcast. Concern over the way in which governmental intervention may 'accentuate the distortions in the system', affording officially sanctioned speech a privileged place on the airwaves, has led Thomas Emerson to suggest guidelines for determining when state involvement is acceptable.[9] He distinguishes 'macro' intervention, where the government seeks to *support* speech in a particular area, for example by calling for a certain proportion of television time to be dedicated to current affairs, from 'micro' intervention, where the government seeks to *dictate* the specific content of speech in that area by, for example, requiring that an international incident is covered from a particular, 'government-friendly', perspective.[10] Macro intervention is less likely to involve the deliberate distortion of information for the government's own ends than intervention at the micro level, and for this reason may prove more acceptable. Regulations designed to ensure a multiplicity of speakers and the transmission of a plurality of voices are arguably forms of macro intervention, in that they are not generally framed to require the transmission of specific information or opinions. It is only if we consider the no-censorship principle to exclude *both* macro and micro regulation that conflict between the three principles becomes inevitable.

Such a conclusion is not without its proponents, and it is interesting to note that in the US Supreme Court case of *Turner Broadcasting* the judges were divided on whether American 'must-carry' rules, requiring cable operators to relay a certain percentage of over-the-air broadcasting television stations, constituted content-based regulations necessitating strict judicial scrutiny.[11] The majority held that they were not 'designed to

[9] T. I. Emerson (1981).   [10] *Ibid*. 803–4.
[11] *Turner Broadcasting System, Inc.* v. *FCC* (1994), 114 S Ct. 2445.

favor or disadvantage speech of any particular content', while the minority considered the Court to be 'mistaken in concluding that the interest in diversity—in "according access to a multiplicity" of "diverse and antagonistic sources" . . . is content neutral'.[12] In promoting the speech of broadcasters, government was simultaneously excluding the specific speech of those who would otherwise have had access to the cable systems. For Justice O'Connor such regulations constituted an impermissible restriction on the editorial freedom of cable operators, the main threat to freedom of expression being governmental and not private power.

The scope for conflict between the multiplicity of speakers and plurality of voices principles is equally all too apparent. Creating a plurality of voices may, owing to economic pressures, involve restricting the number of individuals permitted to speak, selecting among those who wish to speak on the basis of what they have to say, or requiring that those who do speak adopt a certain form and content. The conflict thus turns on whether we prefer to carry the principle of individual equality over to individual expression, with a consequently neutral approach to what is said, or whether in a particular context, such as the mass media, we prefer to put our interest in the expression of ideas over and above that of the individual interest in expression.

The tension between the multiplicity of speakers and plurality of voices principles may be dealt with in a number of ways. One is to hold that in practice the two are generally quite compatible: in facilitating individual expression one invariably also broadens the available range of ideas. This empirically based 'practical compatibility' approach ignores those economic factors which may lead certain forms of programming to be dropped in an increasingly competitive environment and offers no guidance on how the different interests should be weighted where conflicts arise.[13] Alternatively, it is possible to deny all conflict by holding that constitutional guarantees of freedom of expression have as their object in the media sector the creation of a plurality of voices: establishing a multiplicity of speakers is thus merely a *means* by which the end of pluralism might be attained. Viewed from this 'means/ends' perspective the establishment of a multiplicity of speakers through the introduction of a competitive private market would be only one mechanism for realizing a plurality of voices: where market solutions were not available, or proved ineffective, there would be no theoretical bar to the introduction of content regulation or reversion to public ownership, provided this itself proved an effective means of enhancing pluralism.

In the Italian context the potential for direct conflict between the

---

[12] *Turner Broadcasting System, Inc.* v. *FCC* (1994), 114 S Ct. 2464 and 2477.
[13] For a discussion of the impact of heightened competition on programme choice in the US see J. G. Blumler (1991), 208.

impartial facilitation of individual speech and the promotion of plural programming was initially held in check through an alternative strategy: the gradual association of each interest with the public and private broadcasting sectors respectively. In the public sector the goal to be attained was a plurality of voices, the interest in individual expression giving way to the interest in plural programming. In the private sector the multiplicity of speakers objective remained paramount, with the state's role essentially limited to that of 'policeman of the airwaves'. The underlying judicial tolerance of selection on content grounds in the public sector is illustrated by Decision 225 of 1974 in which the state monopoly over the transmission of foreign broadcasts within Italy was challenged.[14] Here the Constitutional Court held that in order to realize 'a requirement stemming from Article 21' access to television had to be offered impartially and as extensively as possible to political, religious, and cultural *groups*— through which the various ideologies present in society were thought to be expressed.[15] In order to reflect the *pluralità delle voci* present in society reference was thus to be made to established social groups, even where this excluded other individual or heterodox voices. In contrast, the co-terminous Decision 226 of 1974, where the state monopoly over cable broadcasting was under scrutiny, reveals the Court's rather different view of what was constitutionally necessitated in the private field.[16] In the local cable sector it called for a multiplicity of private cable television *networks*, thereby facilitating the free expression of thoughts required by Article 21. Although the state was not precluded from all intervention in the private sector it became increasingly apparent that the Court considered this to be more or less limited to ensuring minimal disturbance and a competitive broadcasting market.[17]

The distinction made as regards the requirements variously demanded of the public and private broadcasting sectors remained a continuous feature of the early Italian decisions. In particular, there was little to indicate that the use of Article 21 to require a competitive private sector was anything other than an attempt to advance the individual interest in self-expression. Even when the Constitutional Court appeared to recognize a causal nexus between individual expression and content pluralism, as in Decision 225 of 1974, it is probable that the Court was highlighting the fortuitous fact that it was possible, through the introduction of private actors, to promote both interests and did not regard private ownership to be merely an effective,

---

[14] Dec. 225/1974 [1974] Giur. cost. 1775.
[15] *Ibid.* 1789.
[16] Dec. 226/1974 [1974] Giur. cost. 1791.
[17] Dec. 202/1976 [1976] Giur. cost. 1267.

though potentially defeasible, mechanism for the attainment of pluralism.[18]

Can one conclude from this that the Court was walling off an area of private expression in which the Article 21 'multiplicity of speakers' principle ruled supreme, a conclusion with not insignificant implications for the regulation of the private sector? Stephen Holmes has suggested that courts will sometimes fix upon a distinction which is conceptually easy to draw to avoid the difficult task of choosing, or in some way accommodating, conflicting principles: by establishing distinct fields, for example the print and audiovisual media, in which the various principles may be compartmentalized and allowed sole play, underlying tensions can be hidden.[19] Moreover, although such divisions may seem arbitrary and thus run counter to our expectations of principled rule-making in the legal field, Lee Bollinger has suggested that they can represent a rational response to conflict between key constitutional values.[20] Where two values both demand support but the realization of one may preclude attainment of the other a 'partial regulatory' approach, with each interest being protected in a distinct sector, enables the benefit of each to be attained. Lee Bollinger considered that the endorsement of differing levels of government regulation in the print and audiovisual sectors could also create a 'beneficial tension' within the system, each sector acting as a potential check on the dangers inherent to the other.

Support can be derived, even from the most recent cases, for the view that the Italian Constitutional Court has in fact adopted such a partial regulatory approach. Despite confirming the desirablity of varied programming in *both* the public and private sectors, the Court has repeatedly held that in the private sector the citizen's right to information has to be tempered (*comporre*) by the need to respect the freedom assured to business by Articles 21 and 41 of the Constitution.[21] In this context the drive to create an internally plural system, open to the various voices present in society, is necessarily restricted. Similarly, in Decision 112 of 1993, the Court drew a clear distinction between the public-service goals and obligations of paramount consideration when awarding licences for the provision of public-service channels, and the interests in freedom of

---

[18] Dec. 225/1974 [1974] Guir. cost. 1775 at 1788, where the Court held that the state monopoly over broadcasting stations relaying foreign channels resulted in an unacceptable narrowing of the sources of information available to the Italian public.

[19] S. Holmes (1990). See, in particular, 50 where Holmes considers the distinction drawn by the US Supreme Court between the electronic and print media: '[a]lthough highly dubious in itself, the drawable line nevertheless symbolized the undrawable one. An implausible distinction allowed the Court to affirm two important constitutional principles: (1) the government deserves distrust, and (2) so do wielders of private power.'

[20] L. C. Bollinger (1976).

[21] Dec. 826/1988 [1988] Foro it. 2477 at 2499, pt. 19.

expression and economic initiative which are to predominate when determining the operating rules in the private sector.[22]

But there are also indications that the Court continues to support the idea of market primacy, a competitive market in broadcasting services being regarded the best mechanism for the realization of freedom of expression. In Decision 420 of 1994, in which the constitutionality of Italy's 1990 broadcasting legislation was examined, the Court held that there would be no need to maintain a state broadcasting service where an adequate antitrust system was already in place.[23] It should be noted that the Court at this point appeared to consider such antitrust legislation necessary to prevent the development of an oligopolistic market or one in which a particular firm achieves a position of market dominance. This clearly falls far short of guaranteeing a multiplicity of sources and a *maximal* level of external pluralism which the Court has held Article 21 to require.[24] It is consequently difficult to see the relevance of antitrust regulations, designed merely to address the risk of oligopoly, given that these are clearly insufficient to guarantee either a multiplicity of speakers or a plurality of voices. As Roberto Pardolesi has pointed out, the reference to antitrust controls is both unnecessary and confusing; such talk properly falls within the domain of Article 41, concerned with facilitating private enterprise; it is simply misleading when it strays into the Court's discussion of Article 21.[25] At point 14.4, however, the Court once again refers to the need to ensure access for the maximum possible number of voices and that it was not just any minimal antitrust regime which would be held to be acceptable.

It is possible, therefore, to glean from the cases support for two completely conflicting approaches: first, that the Court has adopted a partial regulatory approach, protecting freedom of expression and pluralism in the private and public sectors respectively; secondly, that the Court perceives the ultimate goal to be the enhancement of opportunities for individual expression through a competitive market in broadcasting services. There is, however, a third approach clearly evident in the cases decided from the late 1980s onwards which affords priority to the principle of pluralism, a principle held to be equally applicable in both public and private domains.[26] Although there is no explicit mention of pluralism in Article 21 the Court has, as we have noted, now confirmed that this Article serves to guarantee freedom of information, information which, in the

---

[22] Dec. 112/1993 [1993] Foro it. 1339 at 1351, pt. 9.
[23] Dec. 420/1994 [1994] Giur. it. 129.
[24] See, e.g., Dec. 826/1988 [1988] Foro it. 2477 at 2499, pt. 19.
[25] R. Pardolesi (1995).
[26] See, e.g., Dec. 826/1988 [1988] Foro it. 2477 at 2494–5.

broadcasting field, is to be of a plural and unbiased nature.[27] Such pluralism seems to require not only that different views on a particular subject be transmitted but that there be a diversity of programme types or genres, ranging from politics and news to culture and entertainment.[28] This recognition of pluralism not only carries forward one of the key principles underlying the public-service broadcasting concept, but also accords with how many people regard television and radio, not as media for their own personal expression but as important and diverse informational resources.

At least two important consequences flow from this development. The first is that the Italian Court envisages a distinct role for the public-service sector, able to make its own contribution to the attainment of pluralism. The Court appears to take this contribution as read, so that the public-service sector is not considered to be provisional, acceptable only while a competitive private sector cannot be realized. The second is that the private sector is itself valued as a mechanism for furthering a plurality of voices, not simply as a means by which individual expression can be promoted regardless of its content. Such an approach leaves open the legitimacy of introducing content regulations in the private sector where the competitive environment fails to provide sufficiently varied programming, a form of intervention which would be excluded if the only objective were to protect private broadcasters' freedom of expression. Support for this conclusion can be derived from the Constitutional Court's Decision 112 of 1993 in which it considered whether the content restrictions imposed on private broadcasters by legge 223 of 1990, relating, for example, to transmission times for films prohibited to children, contravened their right to freedom of economic activity under Article 41 of the Constitution. The Court held that, in the specific context of broadcasting, private enterprise could be restricted to ensure that it did not prejudice the transmission of plural and impartial information, or, more generally, the values protected by Article 21 of the Constitution.[29]

Though espousing a unifying objective, that of informational pluralism, recent decisions of the Italian Constitutional Court nevertheless make it plain that different regulatory strategies are to be adopted in the public and private fields.[30] In the public sector diverse programming is to be achieved through 'internal pluralism', or content regulation, while in the private

---

[27] Dec. 112/1993 [1993] Foro it. 1339 at 1353.

[28] In Dec. 826/1988 [1988] Foro it. 2477 the Court, at 2495, emphasized that Art. 21 served to protect information understood in a 'wide and comprehensive sense'. Art. 21 was concerned not merely with informational programmes but also those of a cultural nature or capable of inluencing public opinion.

[29] Dec. 112/1993 [1993] Foro it. 1339 at 1352–4.

[30] Dec. 826/1988 [1988] Foro it. 2477 at 2499; Dec. 112/1993 [1993] Foro it. 1339 at 1351; and Dec. 420/1994 [1994] Giur. it. 129 at 142.

sector this is to be promoted primarily through a system of 'external pluralism', designed to ensure that as many individuals holding different opinions as possible will be able to own their own broadcasting stations. It appears that these different regulatory techniques are for the most part restricted to their own particular sector so that the practical implications of this strategy, as outlined by the Court, are consequently very similar to those of the 'partial regulatory' approach discussed above. In Decision 420 of 1994 the Court held that both internal and external pluralism had their own 'dimensions' and place; one technique could not simply be substituted for the other.[31] Such statements lend support to the view that the closely regulated public sector cannot simply be replaced by a lightly regulated competitive private sector, that both work together to fulfil the public's 'right to information' guaranteed by Article 21 of the Constitution. On the other hand, if internal and external pluralism really are no more than regulatory techniques established to realize a given end, then there would seem to be no reason for rigidly confining them, particularly where they do not produce the desired result. The Court has indeed accepted, as we have noted above, that the criteria adopted in the 1990 legislation for selecting applicants for private licences, which include the quality of the proposed service, as well as compliance with the statute's programming requirements for the private sector, are not contrary to Article 21.[32]

It may be objected that the perception of free speech simply as a means to increase the diversity of available information fails to take into account that in certain circumstances the autonomy of the individual in deciding whether or not to communicate is considered paramount, even where this may impede the circulation of relevant information. For example, there are whole areas of human communication, workplace gossip, or family dinner-table discussion, where state intervention to increase the variety of ideas would not only intrude unduly into the private realm of individual thought, but would also largely misunderstand the nature of the activity in question.[33] We do not think it appropriate to *require* our fellow workers, relations, or friends to provide us with a plurality of voices; they may indeed be valuable and desirable sources of information but this is not an official role. Moreover, in certain contexts—the workplace springs to mind, but there are others—there is often a tacit understanding that discussion of contentious matters (religion or politics) should be avoided for fear that personal disagreements may damage employee unity. Only certain individuals or entities in society are expected to labour under a

---

[31] Dec. 420/1994 [1994] Giur. it. 129 at 142, pt. 14.1.

[32] Dec. 112/1993 [1993] Foro it. 1339 at 1351–2.

[33] See J. Lichtenberg (1990), 116, who notes that in such 'private' contexts the interest in privacy may take precedence over other competing claims.

legal obligation to furnish information: these entities range from government itself, through schools, universities, and at least parts of the media to certain private actors, for example companies, variously required to publish annual accounts and provide information to employees on such matters as impending redundancies. It is apparent that the *nature* of the information and the *range of individuals who may have a claim upon it* vary from case to case.

What grounds, then, have been given by the Italian Constitutional Court for preferring the plurality of voices principle in the audiovisual field? It is clear that Article 21 itself gives no guidance on when freedom of expression should be preferred over freedom of information and vice versa.[34] It is also clear that where two potentially conflicting objectives are linked under a single constitutional head there is the danger that a court may justify its preference for one or other objective simply by reference to the relevant Article, without offering a reasoned explanation of why the particular option has been selected. In the audiovisual context the Court's emphasis on pluralism appears to stem from concerns over the potential influence of the mass media on individuals and society. In Decision 148 of 1981 it noted that television penetrated directly into the home and that the combination of words and pictures made it a particularly persuasive medium, a formative influence on public opinion.[35] The election in spring 1994 of Silvio Berlusconi, the owner of three national television channels, as Italian Prime Minister heightened public concern over the political power of television, and there is some evidence to suggest that television may in the past have affected electoral outcomes in Italy.[36] That television may have such an impact would certainly seem to be accepted by the politicians themselves: it is no coincidence that in the run-up to the 1995 broadcasting referenda the Fininvest channels owned by Silvio Berlusconi transmitted 500 advertisements calling for a 'no' vote and only twenty-one in favour.[37]

If concern over the audiovisual media's capacity both to convey and to distort information has led the Court to emphasize the importance of pluralism as a key constitutional value, how can one make sense of those conflicting lines of argument which continue, even in the most recent cases, to point to a partial regulatory approach and the continuing importance of freedom of expression in the private sector? Some of the confusion appears to be caused by the Court's repetition of statements made in earlier cases: a repetition presumably intended to display a degree of doctrinal coherence

---

[34] Dec. 112/1993 [1993] Foro it. 1339 at 1349, pt. 7.
[35] Dec. 148/1981 [1981] Giur. cost. 1379 at 1408.
[36] See S. Ambrosini (1995), 132, n. 11 and E. Barendt (1995), 256.
[37] A. Calabrò(1995).

over time, yet which in reality serves to emphasize the tensions between these cases and the more recent emphasis on pluralism. Nevertheless, there are good grounds for regarding recent references to the importance of freedom of expression as more than merely misguided attempts to affirm that constitutional principles have been applied consistently. Instead, they clearly recognize that there are a number of important interests at stake, not only pluralism, which require some degree of accommodation in the broadcasting field. This accommodatory approach finds explicit recognition in the Court's statement that 'the regulation of the relationship between information enterprises . . . given the incidence of a number of constitutional values, must be inspired by the criteria of harmonious composition and reciprocal co-ordination among such values'.[38]

Rather than promote one interest or approach to the detriment of another the Court consequently appears to slide effortlessly across the different territories it has staked out. While emphasizing the unifying principle of pluralism and the 'right to information', it continues to indicate that, in the private context, content requirements will have to be tempered by the need to respect the individual right to expression and freedom of economic enterprise. To focus solely on pluralism may indeed lead to other aspects of freedom of speech being devalued, in particular that element of individual autonomy so valued by 'negative-liberty' theorists. There may, for example, be good grounds for allowing an orator to continue with her oration even though this merely repeats what has already been said. The chance to speak may not only be of value to the speaker but her repetition of a given idea may tell us something important about its strength and prevalence in a given community which any attempt at measured argument would fail to catch. Ensuring that there is some provision for individual access to established audiovisual media, accorded regardless of the likely originality or contribution to pluralism of the discourse, is one way of responding to these interests. The growth of the Internet has revealed that there is a considerable demand for opportunities for unmediated individual and group communication. Allowing individual ownership of the channels of communication themselves is another.

There can be little doubt that this attempt by the Court to accommodate competing interests will prove to be a continuing focus for legal debate, not least because its implications are sketched out at only the most general

---

[38] Dec. 826/1988 [1988] Foro it. 2477 at 2499, pt. 1. Text reads '*la regolamentazione dei rapporti tra imprese d'informazione . . . data l'incidenza di più valori costituzionali, deve essere ispirata al criterio dell'armonica composizione e del reciproco coordinamento tra tali valori*'. In curtailing any one of these values to further the end of pluralism the Court indicated that the means used must not only be to the point and focused, but also proportional to the objective sought to be obtained. See also Dec. 112/1993 [1993] Foro it. 1339 at 1349, pt. 7.

level. Given the apparent importance, for regulatory purposes, of the distinction between the public-service and private broadcasting sectors it is suprising that the Court has not established clearer guidelines for demarcating the boundary between the two. Just how much pluralism is to be provided by the public-service sector and how many frequencies, cable, and satellite channels are to be allocated to realize its objectives? In its 1988 decision the Constitutional Court held that the 'public-service' should be afforded sufficient finance and frequencies to enable it to fulfil its particular tasks, but when are its tasks to be taken as fulfilled?[39] Despite these continuing uncertainties there can be little doubt that the Italian Constitutional Court has attempted to develop principles which are relevant and meaningful in the broadcasting context, particularly the principle of pluralism, without entirely discounting those other established constitutional interests which have a continuing claim to protection.

2. PLURALISM AND FREEDOM OF EXPRESSION IN FRENCH CASE LAW

Similar ambiguities concerning the nature of the relationship between pluralism and free speech can be detected in the case law of the French Conseil constitutionnel. The tension between the two interests was explicitly recognized somewhat earlier than in Italy, with pluralism identified as a key concept in the audiovisual sector in 1982. In Decision 82–141 the Conseil constitutionnel acknowledged that it was not only the freedom of communication enshrined in Article 11 of the 1789 Declaration (hereafter referred to as 'Article 11') which was applicable to the broadcasting field, but that there were also a number of distinct objectives of 'constitutional value' which had to be taken into account, among them respect for the freedom of others and the 'preservation of the pluralist nature of socio-cultural expression'.[40] Like its Italian counterpart the French Conseil recognized pluralism to be a principle capable of imposing limits on the realization of freedom of communication, holding that it was necessary to *reconcile* (*concilier*) these various interests. The task of reconciliation was, as we have seen in the last chapter, left principally to the legislator and the Conseil has provided little by way of guidance on the limits of this clearly extensive legislative discretion. In its earlier 1982 audiovisual decision, for example, the Conseil constitutionnel did not consider it possible to challenge the legislator's decision to award public-service concessions, subject to *cahiers des charges*, for the new television

---

[39] Dec. 826/1988 [1988] Foro it. 2477, pt. 19.
[40] Dec. 82–141 of 27 July 1982 [1982] JO 2422 at 2423.

channels, despite the potential of such a regime for constraining the station-owner's freedom of expression.

The status of pluralism as an 'objective of constitutional value' was confirmed in the Conseil's 1986 audiovisual ruling, where respect for pluralism was held to be one of the conditions for democracy.[41] The Conseil went on, however, to provide a further justification for constitutional protection stating that programme pluralism, in both the public and private sectors, was a necessary prerequisite to the realization of the freedom to communicate thoughts and opinions guaranteed by Article 11. This is somewhat perplexing, for if pluralism is essential for freedom of communication it is not immediately apparent why the legislator should also have to 'reconcile' the two interests. Nor does access to a diversity of opinions appear strictly necessary for the free communication of thoughts and opinions. It is not unduly difficult to imagine a society in which the ideas in circulation are very limited—individual members of a given society may, for example, be simply too apathetic and lacking in curiosity to expand the range of discourse—but where there are no significant restrictions on people saying what they like or listening quite freely to others. There is a distinction between people being limited in what they say because of social development or indifference and an individual not being allowed to communicate on a given subject because of social or legal restrictions. Access to a diversity of opinions is essential not for communication to take place at all, but for communication to be varied and informed.

Nevertheless, the Conseil came very close to equating freedom of communication with pluralism. Communication is evidently a two-way process, involving a communicator and a recipient: for it to be 'free' in any meaningful sense the communicator must not be prevented from expressing what he or she wishes, and the recipient must be able to receive that message free from extraneous intervention. In its 1986 ruling the Conseil constitutionnel held, in a statement mirroring that of the American Supreme Court in its 1969 *Red Lion* decision,[42] that the main addressees of the Article 11 freedom were the listeners and viewers. What was important, indicated the Court, was that their 'free choice' should not be subverted by either private interest or public power: the freedom of public and private broadcasters to communicate as they wished was clearly

[41] Dec. 86–217 of 18 Sept. 1986 [1986] JO 11294. For commentary see, *inter alia*, P. Wachsmann (1987) and B. Genevois (1988), 205.

[42] 'It is the right of the public to receive suitable access to social, political, esthetic, moral, and other ideas and experiences which is crucial here. That right may not constitutionally be abridged either by Congress or by the FCC': *Red Lion Broadcasting Co., Inc.* v. *Federal Communications Commission*, 23 L Ed 2d 371 at 389.

subordinate to the claims of listeners and viewers to 'choose freely', presumably among diverse information sources.

There are thus two lines of thought apparent in the 1986 broadcasting decision. The first recognizes a distinct constitutional objective, namely the 'preservation of the plural character of the socio-cultural currents of expression', with which Article 11 has to be reconciled. The second considers pluralism to be an essential prerequisite not only for democracy but also for freedom of communication, such that Article 11 embraces both a right to individual expression and a right on the part of citizens to diverse information. If Article 11 does indeed embrace both an individual right to expression and a right to receive diverse information, a further principle *outside* Article 11 is needed to explain why in some cases the interest of the speaker appears to be paramount, while in others, notably in the broadcasting sector, it is that of the 'listener or viewer' which is given primacy. One explanation is the importance of the audiovisual media's provision to the public of 'information, education and entertainment'. It is this informational role which justifies curtailing the speech of some to further the reception of plural programming by others. In order to prevent the importance of this 'external consideration' being lost the 1986 judgment should as a matter of preference be interpreted, despite the indications to the contrary, as recognizing two distinct principles: an Article 11 interest in freedom of expression and a separate, limiting principle of audiovisual pluralism.

The 1986 audiovisual decision is quite specific in holding that the principle of pluralism applies to both the private and public broadcasting sectors. Furthermore, the Conseil constitutionnel was prepared to flesh out certain concrete implications of its theory, going on to consider whether the legislative provisions proposed for each sector, particularly the media-ownership restrictions, were adequate to enable the objective of pluralism to be realized. In addition, it specifically required the regulatory body set up by the 1986 media legislation, the Commission nationale de la communication et des libertés (CNCL), to preserve 'as a priority' when exercising its powers the pluralist expression of opinions.[43] Given the absence in French law of direct individual recourse to the Conseil constitutionnel, this was an important recognition of the role which the French administrative courts can play in ensuring that decisions of the audiovisual regulatory bodies pay due consideration to the interest in pluralism.

Indeed, prior to the 1986 decision, the Conseil d'Etat had already proved itself willing to review the award of air-time to religious or political parties. In the *Union des Athées* case its decision did not, however, go in

---

[43] Dec. 86–217 of 18 Sept. 1986 [1986] JO 11294 at 11295, col. 2.

favour of the applicants. Here the Conseil d'Etat held that although the 1974 broadcasting legislation assured equal access for the expression of the principal lines of thought in society, all that was required was that equality be assured across the public-service channels as a whole.[44] The Union of Atheists could not, therefore, use the particular coverage afforded the main religious cults as the foundation for claiming a similar award of air-time. In the later case of *Labbé and Gaudin* the Conseil d'Etat was called to examine the award of television time to political parties.[45] In exercising its power of review it noted that, although the then Broadcasting Authority, the Haute Autorité de la communication audiovisuelle, had a wide margin of administrative discretion, the Conseil was empowered to ensure respect for the key principles of equality, pluralism, and programme balance. Here, too, however, the case went against the applicants, the Conseil d'Etat holding that, where time equal to that afforded to the Prime Minister's monthly comment on current affairs had been awarded to the opposition and majority parties, there could not be said to have been any manifest administrative error.

In its 1986 constitutional ruling the Conseil constitutionnel provided some further indications of how the CNCL should exercise its powers in order to promote pluralism. Where only one frequency was available in a given zone for private broadcasting the Commission would have to impose obligations ensuring a free and plural expression of ideas, but even where there were several frequencies available, and those frequencies had been allocated to different operators, similar provisions would have to be applied if plural programming was still not being produced.[46] The constitutional legitimacy of the imposition of content restrictions on private broadcasters acting in competition with a number of other operators was thus specifically acknowledged.

3. JUDICIAL INTERVENTION IN THE REGULATION OF THE AUDIOVISUAL MEDIA IN ITALY AND FRANCE: SOME CONCLUSIONS

What conclusions can we tease out from the judicial decisions discussed above? It is certainly possible to see clear parallels between the Italian and French cases. In both countries the courts have grappled, often rather confusingly, with the tension between the desire to meet the interests of the listeners in the provision of a varied and reliable broadcasting service and the interests of the broadcasters in seeking to be free from restrictions

---

[44] Dec. 17651 [1980] Rec. déc. Cons. d'Etat 347.
[45] For details see R. Errera (1986), 155.
[46] Dec. 86–217 of 18 Sept. 1986 [1986] JO 11294 at 11296.

on the timing and nature of the programmes they transmit. In both countries the importance of pluralism has been emphasized, even to the degree of accepting that it may entail restrictions on individual expression. As the European Commission Green Paper on Pluralism and Media Concentration in the Internal Market notes

Both in statutes and case-law the link [between freedom of expression and pluralism] is one of derogation from the principle of freedom of expression. Like certain obligations relating to editorial content (morality, impartiality, taste and decency, etc.), the function of the concept is to limit in certain cases the application of the right to freedom of expression to a potential beneficiary.[47]

Although both Courts seem to have relied on the constitutional guarantee of freedom of expression as the basis for establishing this principle of pluralism, such a step was neither necessary nor, perhaps, desirable, given that we are here dealing with two separate interests. A distinct constitutional basis can be constructed, even though this may share objectives traditionally thought to underpin the guarantee of freedom of expression.

As we have seen, Article 3 of the Italian Constitution imposes upon the Republic the task of 'removing the obstacles of an economic and social nature, which restricting the freedom and equality of citizens, hinder the full development of the human person and the effective participation of all workers in the political, economic and social organisation of the country'.[48] Similarly, paragraph 10 of the Preamble to the 1946 French Constitution establishes that the state is to assure to individuals 'the conditions necessary for their development', and paragraph 13 provides that it will guarantee 'to children and adults equal access to education, professional training and culture'. Individuals are often thought to be the best judges of how to lead their own lives and to seek out what is good for them: the constitutional provisions cited above indicate that for this to be possible they must be educated in the linguistic and conceptual tools which will enable them to understand the society around them. Access to information about the world and the ability to express their own perceptions and needs afford individuals some capacity to direct their own lives.

It is, of course, possible to regard this view as naïvely utopian. P. H. Schuck warns that the scope of individual autonomy is heavily curtailed; for him society 'is pathological and the individual its victim. His desires, capacities, self understanding, and behaviour reflect the play of large social forces beyond his control'.[49] Nevertheless, the exposure to a range of ideas and information may help foster a critical facility capable at times of going beyond and challenging the accepted confines of daily life, even the agenda

---

[47] EC Commission (1992), 15.   [48] See App. for full text.
[49] P. H. Schuck (1983), 1605.

set by the mass media themselves, a facility essential for social change which lies at the very root of liberal democratic theory.[50] The wide-ranging transfer of information is thus vital in enabling individuals to build on the past to develop, combine, and experiment with established cultural and social forms.

The introduction of public education, public libraries, and public broadcasting was seen, at least in part, as a means of opening access to such information even to the most socially disadvantaged. Thus, in its 1960 audiovisual ruling, the Italian Constitutional Court noted the very great importance of television in satisfying both individual and social needs for information, culture, and entertainment.[51] This view was confirmed in 1981 when the Court, drawing on previous judgments, held, first, that the audiovisual sector performs a fundamental informational role; secondly, that it contributes to the cultural development of the country; and, thirdly, that the programmes thereby transmitted are capable of influencing public opinion.[52] Similarly, the Conseil constitutionnel in its 1986 decision recognized the constitutional importance of social and cultural pluralism and the role played by the broadcasting media in conveying that pluralism to viewers and listeners through providing access to varied programming.[53]

But there are other constitutional foundations for the principle of pluralism beyond individual and cultural development. The Conseil constitutionnel in its 1986 decision also considered respect for pluralism to be one of the conditions of a democracy and the Italian Constitutional Court, in seeking to prevent the broadcasting sector falling into the hands of one or two private entities, stressed that this was an 'activity which, far beyond its economic relevance, touches very closely fundamental aspects of the democratic life'.[54] This was confirmed in 1993 when the Court held that the founding principles of the Italian state set out in the Constitution required that democracy be based on free public opinion, capable of development through the ability of all to compete in the formation of the general will.[55]

The mass media are now seen as integral elements, a fourth arm, of modern democracies, providing the electorate with the information

---

[50] See S. Macedo (1991), 204: 'Liberal politics, the rule of law and individual rights, protects the liberty to explore various ways of realizing the good life, and to exercise self-critical, self-transforming reflective capacities. For liberalism, autonomy is something more than one personal ideal among others'.

[51] Dec. 59/1960 [1960] Giur. cost. 759 at 781.

[52] Dec. 148/1981 [1981] Giur. cost. 1379 at 1404.

[53] Dec. 86–217 of 18 Sept. 1986 [1986] JO 11294 at 11295.

[54] Dec. 225/1974 [1974] Guir. cost. 1775 at 1787 ('*si tratti di attività che, ben al di là della sua rilevanza economica, tocca molto da vicino fondamentali aspetti della vita democratica*').

[55] Dec. 112/1993 [1993] Foro it. 1339 at 1350.

necessary to evaluate the performance of political representatives and make reasoned decisions on how society should be governed. For many people the audiovisual media provide the only regular source of information about the day's major political events; reliance on them as sources of 'news' exacts a heightened responsibility to give issues wide and fair coverage.[56] Moreover, the act of seeking out and relaying such information to the public can open government to healthy scrutiny and criticism, criticism which other vested interests may be unwilling to voice. The benefits of this watchdog function can be felt beyond the central confines of government when the media turn to examine the activities of other influential bodies in society: the financial institutions, multinational companies, even the media themselves. Given these considerations it is difficult to agree with the observation made by the European Commission in its Green Paper on Media Concentration that pluralism is not itself a human or basic right: media pluralism meets not only social but also individual needs and plays an established role in the democratic process.[57] It is precisely these concerns which have led to the judicial endorsement of pluralism as a constitutionally recognized principle.

4. FREEDOM OF EXPRESSION: AN UNCERTAIN VARIABLE IN BRITISH CASE LAW

The development of pluralism as a distinct legal principle by the French and Italian constitutional courts has no parallel in the British context. Although British courts have at times shown themselves to be sensitive to the informational needs of the public and, through the public, to the interests of the press, such steps have tended to be taken under a poorly theorized concept of freedom of expression, rather than a specific interest in informational pluralism. Freedom of expression is recognized as a distinct public interest, to be balanced against other competing interests, but the weight afforded freedom of expression by British courts has been very variable. Despite the well-documented cases in which the European Court of Human Rights and House of Lords have disagreed over the practical level of protection to be afforded to freedom of expression in a democratic society,[58] English judges have expressed their conviction that there is no difference between English law and Article 10 of the European

---

[56] J. Lichtenberg (1990), 123.

[57] EC Commission (1992), 15. It may be noted that the Italian Constitutional Court in its 1988 audiovisual ruling referred to pluralism as a 'fundamental' value or principle.

[58] See, e.g., *The Sunday Times* v. *UK (No 2)* (1992) 14 EHRR 229, and *The Observer and The Guardian* v. *UK* (1992) 14 EHRR 153. For detailed consideration of the impact of the European Convention in UK courts see A. Clapham (1993), ch. 1.

Convention on Human Rights. Thus, Lord Goff in *Attorney-General* v. *Guardian Newspapers (No 2)* held that:

The only difference is that, whereas Art. 10 of the Convention, in accordance with its avowed purpose, proceeds to state a fundamental right and then qualify it, we in this country (where everybody is free to do anything, subject only to the provisions of the law) proceed rather on the assumption of freedom of speech, and turn our law to discover the established exceptions to it.[59]

Although a plaintiff cannot use the Convention as a direct source of rights before an English court, judicial statements such as those of Lord Goff might lead one to conclude that, if a person could point to the likelihood of his or her interest in expression being protected under the Convention, a similar level of protection would be provided by the English courts. In the context of judicial review, however, the courts have continued to assess administrative action in terms of reasonableness, and have stood back from applying what they consider to be the potentially more intrusive proportionality test employed by the European Court of Human Rights when evaluating the legitimacy of restrictions on freedom of expression.[60] This does not, however, mean that English courts simply ignore the existence of human rights when reviewing administrative decisions. The recent Court of Appeal ruling in *ex parte Smith*[61] confirmed that, when considering the reasonableness of administrative action, English courts are cognizant of the importance of protecting human rights and the more substantial the infringement of human rights the more the court will require by way of justification before it will be satisfied that the decision taken was reasonable. Nevertheless, English judges in such circumstances do not see themselves as 'primary decision-makers', and differences in the application of the reasonableness test and the European Convention test of proportionality leave scope for continuing divergence in the appreciation of those restrictions on freedom of expression which are thought legitimate.

Although, as we noted in Chapter 4, British courts have, in extreme circumstances, been willing to ensure that broadcasting companies operate to provide fair coverage of a range of political views in accordance with statutory or contractual requirements, they are in general unwilling to reappraise the programming decisions taken by broadcasting organizations. This unwillingness in the context of review indicates a more general problem for judicial enforcement of programme pluralism. There are so

[59] [1988] 3 WLR 776 at 808.
[60] *R* v. *Sec. of State for the Home Department, ex p. Brind* [1991] 1 All ER 720. For comment see E. Barendt (1990) and T. Allan (1991).
[61] *R* v. *Ministry of Defence, ex p. Smith* [1996] 1 All ER 257.

many different ways of achieving pluralism, and so many different gradations of achievement, that the strong subjective element in programme policy is likely, and not without good reason, to deter judicial evaluation in all but the clearest cases of failure. The judicial unwillingness to overturn the decisions of specialist bodies, coupled with the costs and delays of legal adjudication, has tended to protect British broadcast companies from legal challenge, complaints from the public being handled either internally or, where applicable, by the Broadcasting Complaints Commission or Broadcasting Standards Council (now replaced by the Broadcasting Standards Commission).

The reluctance to overturn decisions taken by administrative or professional bodies, even where their results appear random or ineffective, is again illustrated by the *Brind* case.[62] Here, the House of Lords refused to find unreasonable the Home Secretary's order prohibiting the direct broadcasting of statements made by representatives of certain Northern Irish organizations, even where it remained possible for broadcasters to show film footage with the voices of the representatives of these proscribed organizations dubbed by actors. Paradoxically, it was precisely because the ban merely required the voices to be substituted that led the European Human Rights Commission to conclude that the restriction was not disproportionate.[63]

The second area where the right to freedom of expression may be taken into account is in the interpretation of statutes. Here, British courts have proved willing to enhance free-speech interests, recognizing a 'presumption, albeit rebuttable, that our municipal law will be consistent with our international obligations'.[64] Thus in both *Attorney-General* v. *BBC*[65] and *Marshall* v. *BBC*[66] courts used their powers of interpretation to facilitate media coverage of certain tribunal and election activities. Access to information is clearly essential for meaningful reporting, and these decisions indicate the important role which courts can play in creating conditions conducive to the relaying of relevant information to the public.

Similarly, in the recent case of *R.* v. *Broadcasting Complaints Commission, ex parte BBC*, Brooke J was undoubtedly influenced by the BBC's stated concern that journalists might be deterred from tackling controversial issues if access to the Broadcasting Complaints Commission was made widely available.[67] Under the 1990 Broadcasting Act the Broadcasting Complaints Commission was empowered to consider complaints of unfair treatment from individuals or organizations with a 'direct interest' in

---

[62] *R* v. *Sec. of State for the Home Department, ex p. Brind* [1991] 1 All ER 720.
[63] App. No. 18714/91, *Brind et al.* v. *UK*, 77–B D & R 42.
[64] Lord Scarman in *Attorney-General* v. *BBC* [1981] AC 303 at 354.
[65] *Ibid.*   [66] [1979] 1 WLR 1071.   [67] *The Times*, 24 February 1995.

the programme referred to it. The Commission's decision to accept a complaint from the National Council for One Parent Families was successfully challenged in the High Court where it was held that a pressure group interested in only a general way in the issues raised, and not itself featured in the programme, could not be held to have a 'direct interest'. The judgment greatly curtails the ability of interest groups and individuals to initiate an external investigation into broadcast decisions, and Helen Power, in considering the role of review in this area, has noted a judicial reluctance to interfere with the Commission's substantive work 'coupled with a determination . . . to ensure that it does not expand its remit in terms of the complainants with whom it deals'.[68] Judicial rulings in this area have not, however, been entirely consistent, and in January 1995 Schiemann J found that the Broadcasting Complaints Commission had acted within its powers in accepting a complaint by a Parish Council troubled by a programme which examined the existence of racism in its area.[69] The judge held in this case that the phrase 'direct interest' should be given a broad meaning, and that the Commission had been justified in considering the complaint.

English courts have, however, proved less willing to assist journalists in their investigative enquiries where information obtained by them could have a bearing on legal proceedings.[70] Although the majority of US states and a number of European countries allow journalists a measure of protection from revealing their sources, English courts, under the terms of section 10 of the Contempt of Court Act 1981, can require disclosure of confidential information where this is considered necessary in the interests of justice or national security or for the prevention of disorder and crime. As the *William Goodwin* case illustrates, judges have been unwilling to afford the press any special privileges in the light of the mass media's investigative and informational roles.[71] William Goodwin, a trainee journalist, refused to hand over to the court notes which would have revealed the identity of the person who had passed on to him confidential company information. The company wished to take legal action against the source and Goodwin was found guilty of contempt. The case was referred on to Strasbourg where the European Court of Human Rights ruled that the order for disclosure contravened the journalist's right freely to receive and impart information under Article 10 of the European Convention on Human Rights. Although the company had a legitimate interest in

---

[68] H. Power (1994), 130.

[69] *R.* v. *Broadcasting Complaints Commission, ex p. Channel Four Television Corporation*, *The Times*, 4 January 1995.

[70] *BSC* v. *Granada Television* [1980] 3 WLR 774.

[71] *X Ltd and Another* v. *Morgan-Grampian (Publishers) Ltd and Others* [1990] 2 WLR 421; and see also *Sec. of State for Defence* v. *Guardian Newspapers Ltd.* [1985] AC 359.

172 *Broadcasting Law and Fundamental Rights*

disclosure of the source to prevent further dissemination of the information and to facilitate termination of the source's employment, these were outweighed by the interest of a democratic society in a free press.[72]

It is undoubtedly the case that English courts have, in their development of the common law, sometimes given greater weight to self-expression and the receipt of information than other established private interests. Thus in *Guardian Newspapers Ltd (No 2)* Scott J in the High Court and the judges in the House of Lords recognized the existence of an admittedly limited defence to an action for breach of confidence, namely that the information was disclosed to reveal 'iniquity'.[73] There was, however, disagreement whether the defence could be made out on the facts of the case, revealing different judicial appreciations of the protection to be afforded the mass media. Scott J emphasized the media's 'watchdog role', holding the ability of the press to report allegations of scandal in government to be 'one of the bulwarks' of a democratic society. Although the Law Lords recognized both the public interest in freedom of speech and 'the right of the people in a democracy to be informed by a free press', they did not consider that the iniquity defence could be used to protect unconfirmed allegations of the sort made by Peter Wright in his book.[74]

In the field of defamation the House of Lords has afforded the press considerably more scope to impugn the actions of local or central government, and has not imposed a standard of responsible reporting along the lines indicated by their Lordships in the *Spycatcher* decision. In *Derbyshire County Council* v. *Times Newspapers* the House of Lords held that a local authority could not sue in libel and stressed that it was of the 'highest public importance' that any government body be 'open to uninhibited public criticism'.[75] Concern was expressed that libel actions, or indeed the threat of such actions, could 'chill' legitimate reporting. A complete defence was consequently made available to the press, whether or not the allegations made were the result of careful investigations. This approach differs from that of the High Court of Australia in the *Theophanus* and *Stephens* cases.[76] Both involved actions for defamation brought by Members of Parliament regarding reports which appeared in the defendants' newspapers. The High Court ruled in *Theophanus*, and followed this reasoning in *Stephens*, that an effective representative

[72] *Goodwin* v. *UK* (1996), 22 EHRR 123. For a rather different attitude to disclosure by the European Human Rights Commission in a case where confidentiality was not in issue see App. No. 25798/94, *BBC* v. *UK*, 84–A D & R 129.
[73] *Attorney-General* v. *Guardian (No 2)* [1988] 3 WLR 776.
[74] A helpful summary of the various *Spycatcher* cases is provided in C. Turpin (1995), 121–4. [75] [1993] AC 534.
[76] *Theophanus* v. *Herald and Weekly Times Ltd and Another* (1994) 124 ALR 1 and *Stephens* v. *West Australian Newspapers Ltd* (1994) 124 ALR 80.

democracy did not require that the press be afforded absolute freedom to discuss public affairs with impunity. Liability could still arise where a journalist published a defamatory statement which he or she knew to be false, or with reckless disregard for the truth or untruth of the material published.[77] When compared to the Australian cases and the approach of the House of Lords in *Guardian Newspapers Ltd (No 2)* the considerable weight given to the citizens' interest in access to information on public affairs in the *Derbyshire County Council* case becomes apparent, though in *Guardian Newspapers (No 2)* the Law Lords did ultimately refuse to grant a permanent injunction on the basis that the information under dispute was already in the public domain.[78]

Such cases indicate a healthy respect for public access to information, but they constitute only one end of a spectrum which also comprises decisions in which freedom of expression has certainly not been afforded the same deference. In fields such as the award of interlocutory injunctions the weight and status to be granted to freedom of expression have varied from one action to another.[79] The litigation concerning the award of an interim injunction in the *Spycatcher* case[80] reveals not only the very different weight which judges may afford to the public interest in freedom of expression, but also that even where they remodel their approach along the lines of Article 10 of the Human Rights Convention, as did Lord Templeman, and consequently afford freedom of expression primacy, they may still be more generous in their estimate of those restrictions which are 'necessary in a democratic society' than the European Court of Human Rights.[81] Moreover, far from being considered a unique conduit of information to the public, there are clear dicta to the effect that the mass media will not be afforded any special protection above and beyond that offered to individual citizens, as Sir John Donaldson stated during the *Spycatcher* litigation, the media's 'right to know and their right to publish is neither more nor less than that of the general public'.

There is thus no consistent body of doctrine in the area of free speech: in some cases the protection afforded to freedom of expression has appeared, if anything, overbroad, in others particularly restrictive. Differing levels of protection have been afforded to speech, depending on the nature of the action brought and even the parties to the litigation, making principled analysis difficult. Ultimately, however, it must be noted that the structural

---

[77] (1994) 124 ALR 1 at 21 (Mason CJ, Toohey, and Gaudron JJ).

[78] For another robust judicial statement of the importance of freedom of expression see Hoffmann LJ in *R.* v. *Central Independent Television plc* [1994] 3 All ER 641.

[79] A. E. Boyle (1982), 581–5.

[80] *Attorney-General* v. *Guardian Newspapers Ltd and Others* [1987] 1 WLR 1248.

[81] *The Sunday Times* v. *United Kingdom (No 2)* (1992) 14 EHRR 229 and *The Observer and The Guardian* v. *United Kingdom* (1992) 14 EHRR 153.

evolution of the audiovisual media in Britain has been determined almost exclusively in the political arena. Principally because of the constitutional position of the judiciary there has been no consistent analysis of the distinct role of the print and audiovisual media comparable to that developed by the French and Italian Constitutional Courts, nor the establishment of constitutional parameters for government regulation in the audiovisual field.

5. PLURALISM AT THE EUROPEAN LEVEL: PRELIMINARY BUT DECISIVE RECOGNITION

(i) The Case Law of the European Commission and Court of Human Rights

It is not only at the national level that the principle of pluralism has been recognized; concern for pluralism underscores many of the recommendations and resolutions adopted by the Committee of Ministers, the Parliamentary Assembly, and the Consultative Assembly of the Council of Europe in the media field.[82] The importance of pluralism has also been recognized by the European Court of Human Rights in the *Lentia* and *Groppera* decisions, considered in Chapter 6.[83] Prior to the *Groppera* judgment the Commission of the European Communities had expressed the view that domestic regulations designed to promote programme pluralism would, if applied to foreign channels, restrict the foreign broadcasters' freedom of expression under Article 10(1) and would not be justifiable under any of the limited exceptions set out in Article 10(2) of the European Convention on Human Rights. It consequently suggested that the imposition of 'minimum requirements as regards the expression of different opinions or the balance of programmes', or restrictions relating to the nature, quality, orientation, and reliability of information, would be contrary to Article 10.[84] Given the legislative competence of the European Community, the Commission of the European Communities was primarily interested in restrictions on the free flow of broadcasts from one Community country to another, but its observations clearly point to a further question: can states justify such programming regulations under the European Convention on Human Rights when they are imposed, not on

---

[82] See, e.g., Res. (1974) 43 on Press Concentrations (DH–MM (91)1), Rec. 747 (1975) on Press Concentrations (DH–MM (89)6) and the Committee of Ministers' Declaration on the Freedom of Expression and Information, adopted 29 Apr. 1982 (DH–MM (91)1).

[83] *Informationsverein Lentia and others* v. *Austria* (1994) 17 EHRR 93; *Groppera Radio AG* v. *Switzerland* (1990) 12 EHRR 321.

[84] EC Commission (1994), 174.

domestic and foreign broadcasters alike, but solely on their own domestic broadcasters?

It is undoubtedly the case that in both *Lentia* and *Groppera* the European Court of Human Rights considered that the various restrictions on the award of broadcasting licences and cable programming interfered with the applicants' freedom to 'impart information and ideas' within Article 10(1). Nevertheless, the Court in *Groppera* accepted the Swiss government's submission that its restriction on the relaying by Swiss cable organizations of radio signals broadcast by Groppera Radio from Italy was for the 'protection of the . . . rights of others', within the second paragraph of Article 10. The government argued that the regulations protected such rights because they were '*designed to ensure pluralism, in particular of information*, by allowing a fair allocation of frequencies internationally and nationally'.[85] The Court held that the cable regulations did indeed protect the 'rights of others' but did not provide any further explanation of the nature of these rights. It is possible that the Court in this case accepted the government's justification for its intervention, namely the protection of pluralism, but the elliptical judgment is far from conclusive on this point.

The *Groppera* decision does not, therefore, firmly establish the nature of the 'rights of others' mentioned in Article 10(2), and the question is inevitably raised whether these are rights to diverse information relayed over the media, or other rights which merely happen to promote media pluralism. It is possible to argue that, despite the Swiss government's explicit reference to pluralism, this principle plays little, if any, substantive role in the decision. The relay restriction was merely a necessary adjunct to the government's attempt to prevent the use of what, when employed over Swiss territory, were technically Swiss frequencies, frequencies which at some point in the future it might wish to allocate to an organization other than Groppera Radio. On this view, the regulation undoubtedly protected the rights of others, but they were the rights of *governments* under international telecommunications law to regulate their own national frequencies free from unwarranted interference, not the rights of *viewers and listeners* to plural programming. The Swiss government's attempt to justify its cable regulations on the basis that they protected the rights of others can thus be seen as adding little to its other specified objective, namely the 'prevention of disorder in telecommunications'.

Though plausible, such an interpretation seems unduly restrictive. It should be noted that the European Court of Human Rights specifically recognized the importance of *both* aims put forward by the Swiss government, indicating that it perceived the second aim, protection of the rights of others, to add to, and not merely reformulate, the prior objective

[85] *Groppera Radio AG* v. *Switzerland* (1990) 12 EHRR 321 at 342, emphasis added.

of 'preventing disorder in telecommunications'. The Commission of the European Communities, softening its earlier views on the status of diversity-related programme restrictions, has adopted the wider interpretation of the *Groppera* case, acknowledging in its Green Paper on Pluralism and Media Concentration that the European Court of Human Rights 'takes the view that pluralism is an exception to the principle of freedom of expression, designed to protect the rights of others' within the meaning of Article 10(2).[86]

It is at least possible that the majority of the Court considered the cable restrictions to be a genuine attempt to protect, admittedly in the long term, the plurality of Swiss broadcasting services. The range of programmes made available to the public by Swiss broadcasters could be curtailed if national broadcasts, under licences carefully planned and allocated by the Swiss government, were to be freely interrupted or pre-empted by transmissions from abroad. Relaying of the Italian signal by the cable co-operative would have supported this unjustified and potentially disruptive service. The facts of the *Groppera* case may be seen, therefore, as going no further than confirming that audiovisual regulations designed to protect the planned allocation of national frequencies from foreign interruption will be acceptable as genuine and proportionate attempts to further pluralism. On the more general questions of how far this interest in media pluralism might be extended to justify other forms of national regulation, or who is entitled to act to protect it, the judgment remains silent.

If the 'rights of others' in Article 10(2) do indeed include a right to 'pluralism, in particular of information', how does this right relate to the right to freedom of expression protected by paragraph one? The categories established in Article 10(2) set out permitted *derogations* from the rights enshrined in Article 10(1) and, as exceptions to the general rule, are to be interpreted restrictively.[87] Moreover, despite the reference to 'duties and responsibilities' at the beginning of paragraph two and the requirement that such derogations be 'necessary in a democratic society', their introduction would appear to be essentially facultative rather than mandatory. Paragraph two provides that such freedoms '*may* be subject to such formalities', thereby enabling contracting states to justify particular restrictions, it does not impose upon them a distinct set of obligations in their own right. If this is so, then the principle of pluralism recognized in the *Groppera* case receives only the weakest protection under the terms of the European Convention on Human Rights. It serves to protect national regulations promoting pluralism from allegations of illegal interference with individual expression, but offers no substantive help to those seeking to ensure such regulations are maintained or put in place.

[86] EC Commission (1992), 16, emphasis added.   [87] D. Korff (1988), 144.

The recent *Lentia* case allows states rather more regulatory autonomy under the European Convention on Human Rights than *Groppera* had indicated was possible. In *Lentia* the Court held that the third sentence of Article 10(1), which accepts the principle of state licensing, could be used to justify restrictions on expression even where the objectives underlying such restrictions do not correspond to any of the aims set out in Article 10(2). In *Groppera*, on the other hand, the Court had indicated that measures imposed by virtue of the state's licensing regime would still have to be justified as falling within one or other of the limited number of heads established in Article 10(2). Any remaining uncertainty about the protection afforded to regulations designed to promote programming pluralism by Article 10(2) is consequently rendered less important, given that such regulations will probably now be held to fall within the scope of the licensing clause in Article 10(1). State discretion is not, however, absolute, and only those licensing requirements considered to pursue a legitimate aim will be protected by Article 10(1). In addition, the Court requires licensing regulations to meet two of the specifications contained in Article 10(2): they must be 'prescribed by law' and be 'necessary in a democratic society'.

What guidance has the Court given on the type of regulations which will be held to pursue a legitimate aim? Apart from technical requirements, the *Lentia* decision indicates that states will be able to take into account a wide range of considerations when awarding licences. These include 'the nature and objectives of a proposed station, its potential audience at national, regional or local level, the rights and needs of a specific audience and the obligations deriving from international instruments'.[88] Restrictions capable of contributing to the 'quality and balance of programmes' were also indicated to be legitimate. Since regulations intended to promote pluralism are usually designed to take into account the needs and interests of the constituent members of the audience and to ensure the transmission of a balanced variety of programmes, there would seem to be little difficulty bringing such regulations within the protection offered Article 10(1).

Where a regulation designed to promote pluralism has passed the first hurdle and been held to fall within Article 10(1), in what circumstances will the Court go on to consider it 'necessary in a democratic society', a provision taken to require the existence of a 'pressing social need'?[89] In *Lentia* the Court repeated earlier statements to the effect that, though states are afforded a certain margin of appreciation in deciding which measures are necessary to further cultural and social pluralism, this margin of appreciation is not unlimited: European supervision is strict where

[88] *Informationsverein Lentia and others* v. *Austria* (1994) 17 EHRR 93 at 112.
[89] *Sunday Times* v. *UK* (1979), 2 EHRR 245.

Article 10 rights are concerned.[90] The *Autronic*[91] case suggests that a total ban on reception, as opposed to relaying, of foreign signals which comply with their domestic regulations will not be held to be necessary to protect pluralism, while in *Groppera* the Court noted with approval that the Swiss government had not sought to jam the Groppera signal. The Court also emphasized that the cable regulations did not constitute 'a form of censorship directed against the content or tendencies of the programmes concerned'—indicating that it might be easier for states to justify as necessary technical, as opposed to content-related, regulations.[92]

There are echoes here of the dispute in the American *Turner Broadcasting* case, considered earlier in this Chapter, where the issue was whether requirements mandating that cable companies carry certain signals amounted to a restriction on content requiring strict judicial scrutiny. In *Groppera* it was certainly arguable that the Swiss government was not seeking to censor anything specific which the Italian station was relaying; it simply did not wish to have unauthorized stations using Swiss frequencies. The restriction was, to use Thomas Emerson's terminology, a legitimate form of 'macro intervention'.[93] Looked at from the perspective of the *Groppera* station, however, it is apparent that it was prevented from relaying the specific programmes which it would have scheduled if it had had an audience. It is consequently difficult to see, as a matter of practical reality, how the Swiss government's action could have been anything other than an attempt to censor the Groppera Radio signal, and Judge Pettiti, in his dissenting opinion, asked rhetorically whether preventing a broadcast did not in fact amount to censorship. Indeed, the Court noted in its subsequent *Autronic* decision that 'Article 10 applies not only to the content of information but also to the means of transmission or reception since any restriction imposed on the means necessarily interferes with the right to receive and impart information'.[94] It is consequently worth remembering that whether one sees a particular restriction as an impermissible attempt to curtail specific speech or not may well depend on whose shoes one places oneself in.

How, then, is it possible to reconcile the Court's apparent antagonism to content regulations in *Groppera* with the, at least provisional, acceptance of such restrictions in *Lentia*? One approach would be to take the rather narrow view of the *Groppera* case considered above. From this perspective the Swiss government's action was founded on the premise that the Italian signal should not, under international telecommunication regulations,

---

[90] *Informationsverein Lentia and others* v. *Austria* (1994) 17 EHRR 93 at 112.
[91] *Autronic AG* v. *Switzerland* (1990) 12 EHRR 485.
[92] *Groppera Radio AG* v. *Switzerland* (1990) 12 EHRR 321 at 343.
[93] Discussed in sect. 1 of this Ch.   [94] (1990) 12 EHRR 485 at 499.

have been broadcast at all, regardless of its content. Parallels can here be drawn with the circumstances of the '*Radio Caroline*' dispute which concerned the advertisement, using stickers affixed to cars, of a pirate radio station. Given that the service had no official broadcasting licence, prohibition of the advertisements was considered not to contravene Article 10.[95] Support for this interpretation can be found in the Court of Human Rights' express acknowledgment in the *Groppera* decision that the cable regulations could well have been 'necessary in order to prevent evasion of the law'.[96]

Alternatively, it is possible to read the Court in *Groppera* as indicating that attempts to censor *particular* views or opinions, thereby limiting the range of ideas in circulation, would be likely to fall foul of Article 10, or Article 10 operating in tandem with Article 14 of the Convention to prevent discrimination. In contrast, the type of content restrictions considered by the Court in *Lentia* were designed positively to widen, not diminish, the range of opinions given access to the media; a form of 'macro' as opposed to 'micro' intervention. *Lentia* can thus be seen as leaving open the possibility of justifying content regulations designed to enhance media pluralism whether these are imposed on national or foreign broadcasters.

A final reading of these cases is that in *Groppera* the Court was indicating that the imposition of content requirements on foreign broadcasters, even those designed to promote content diversity, would not be considered necessary in a democratic society, while *Lentia*'s endorsement of content regulations was solely in relation to their imposition by states on their own domestic broadcasters. The facts of *Groppera* involved an attempt to impede the relaying in Switzerland of Italian radio signals, while in *Lentia* the dispute concerned the allocation within Austria of Austrian broadcasting licences. Thus, even, if we take the Court's expression of concern over content regulations in *Groppera* at face value, it is possible to restrict its implications to the context of foreign transmissions. It need not be seen as undermining the apparent acceptance of the Court in *Lentia* that states may continue to adopt regulations which contribute to the 'quality and balance' of domestic broadcasting services.

But whichever view one takes, it is apparent that *Lentia*, like *Groppera* before it, affords only limited protection to the principle of pluralism. Although states remain free to regulate, at the very least, their domestic audiovisual media in the pursuit of pluralism, such regulations continue to be categorized as legitimate *restrictions* on freedom of expression, rather

---

[95] App. No. 8266/78, *X* v. *UK*, 16 D & R 190. It should, however, be noted that there was considerable uncertainty during the *Groppera* case whether the Italian broadcasts were illegal under Italian law.　　　　　　　　　　　　　　[96] (1990) 12 EHRR 321 at 343.

than essential requirements for its realization. It follows that states are
under no duty to establish, or indeed maintain, such regulations once in
force. Given the limited protection afforded to the principle of pluralism
by the state-licensing clause in Article 10(1) and by Article 10(2), it is
worth examining whether pluralism might be given a more entrenched
status, imposing on Convention states specific obligations, rather than a
mere licence to regulate.

Unlike the French and Italian Constitutions there is little in the text of
the European Convention on Human Rights on which to found a distinct
right to media pluralism. The most convincing provision is in fact the first
paragraph of Article 10, with its reference to the right to '*receive* and
impart *information and ideas* without interference by public authority and
regardless of frontiers'. Doubts have, however, been expressed whether
Article 10(1) can be read as establishing a positive right to receive
particular information, as opposed to the right to receive such information
as is readily available free from interference by public authority.[97]
Commentators such as Christoph Engel, who consider Article 10 to be
essentially concerned with the protection of individual rights to expression
or reception, have been led to conclude that such rights would adequately
be catered for by the sale of all transmitting facilities to 'stations that
broadcast mostly soap operas. As freedom of reception under the Human
Rights Convention is a right of individuals and as no one individual can
have a right to reception greater than any other, there can consequently be
no violation of the freedom of reception'.[98]

Such a view is undoubtedly supported by the *Lentia* decision in which the
Court accepted that the Austrian licensing regulations interfered with the
applicants' right to *impart* information without considering whether the
scope of this right might itself be restricted by a competing public interest
in the *receipt* of diverse information. This essentially untheorized presumption of private broadcasting rights places, as we have noted, the burden on
the state to justify all forms of public intervention, in particular the
imposition of regulations designed to promote informational pluralism.
Such an approach differs markedly from the Italian Constitutional Court's
willingness to accept that the constitutional guarantee of freedom of
expression embraces not only a right to inform but also a right to be
informed, the latter requiring public access to different points of view and
cultural trends.[99]

The European Court of Human Right's conclusion in the *Groppera* case
that the Swiss Government's regulations were designed to protect the
'*rights* of others' has still, however, to be explained. If these rights do

---

[97] This point is considered by G. Malinverni (1983) and M. Bullinger (1987).
[98] C. Engel (1987), 64.   [99] Dec. 112/1993 [1993] Foro it. 1339 at 1350.

indeed include, as has been suggested above, a right to media pluralism, then a positive state obligation to facilitate its creation may not be far behind. The Council of Europe insitutions, acting in their political capacity, have certainly indicated that they regard Article 10 to embrace a principle of pluralism. It has been suggested, for example, that the 1982 Committee of Ministers Declaration on the Freedom of Expression and Information 'transposes' the principles enshrined in Article 10 'into major policy principles'.[100] The Declaration provides at point 6 that 'states have the duty to guard against infringements of the freedom of expression and information and *should adopt policies designed to foster as much as possible a variety of media and a plurality of information sources*, thereby allowing a plurality of ideas and opinions'.[101] In addition, the Consultative Assembly of the Council of Europe held in Resolution 428 of 1970 that the duty of the mass media to give complete and general information on public affairs 'corresponded' to the right to freedom of expression. Similarly, the Committee of Ministers in its 1974 Resolution on press concentrations held that the 'existence of a large diversity of sources of news and views available to the general public' was of capital importance for the free receipt and communication of information guaranteed by Article 10.[102] Such declarations do not, of course, constitute legally binding interpretations of Article 10, nor do they refer explicitly to the first paragraph of that Article, but they do indicate a readiness to consider pluralism as an essential element of freedom of expression, rather than simply a tolerated restriction on that right, brought into play under Article 10(2).

More concrete support for the proposition that states have a positive, enforceable obligation to further pluralism under the terms of Article 10 may be gleaned from a number of Court and Commission decisions. In *De Geillustreerde Pers NV* v. *Netherlands* the Commission suggested that states have 'a duty' under Article 10 to protect against excessive press concentrations,[103] while in *Verein Alternatives Lokalradio Bern* v. *Switzerland* it held that 'a licensing system not respecting the *requirements of pluralism*, tolerance and broad-mindedness without which there is no democratic society' would thereby infringe Article 10, *paragraph one*, of

---

[100] Jane Dinsdale, Head of the Media Section of the Council of Europe, in A. Cassese and P. Clapham (1990), 216.

[101] Committee of Ministers Declaration on the Freedom of Expression and Information, adopted 29 Apr. 1982 (DH–MM (91)1), emphasis added.

[102] Res. 428 (1970) containing a Declaration on Mass Communication Media and Human Rights (DH–MM(89)6) at pt. A.3, and Res. 43 (1974) on Press Concentrations (DH–MM(91)1) at paras. 1 and 2 of the preamble. It may be noted that the 'right of the public to information' and access to events of 'high public interest' were also recognized in Art. 9 of the 1989 European Convention on Transfrontier Television, Council of Europe, European Treaty Series No. 132.

[103] App. No 5178/71, *De Geillustreerde Pers NV* v. *Netherlands*, 8 D & R 5.

the Convention.[104] It is possible to envisage a claimant turning the Swiss government's submissions in *Verein Alternatives Lokalradio Bern* to their own advantage by arguing that a state, in refusing them a licence, had failed adequately to take into account such criteria as 'cultural and linguistic pluralism', or the fact that a considerable proportion of the inhabitants in a given reception zone would, absent their station, be 'deprived of broadcasts in their mother tongue'.

Further assistance may be obtained from a series of cases in which the Court has held that not only has the press the task of imparting information and ideas, but that 'the public also has a right to receive them'.[105] The suggestion that the press has the 'task' of conveying information may seem surprising, given that the Convention imposes obligations on contracting states and is not binding directly on private individuals. Nevertheless, the Convention may in certain circumstances impose on states an obligation to take measures to ensure that their citizens conform to given standards of behaviour.[106] It is consequently possible to understand these references to the role of the media as indicating to states that they have a positive duty to intervene if the press fails to fulfil its allotted task. In *Lentia* itself the Court noted that:

it had frequently stressed the fundamental role of freedom of expression in a democratic society, in particular where, through the press, it serves to impart information and ideas of general interest, *which the public is moreover entitled to receive*. Such an undertaking cannot be successfully accomplished *unless it is grounded in the principle of pluralism, of which the State is the ultimate guarantor.*[107]

The actual level of support to be obtained from these cases is, however, limited. It is worth noting, for example, that the Court in *Lentia* did not hold that the state, as 'guarantor' of the communication of information and ideas to the public, was also under a legal obligation to ensure its provision. Similarly, the word 'task' may have been chosen to indicate that we are here in the world of moral aspirations rather than legal obligations. Martin Bullinger has suggested that one cannot conclude from judicial references to the right to receive information that the 'Court had in mind the recognition of an individual right, under Art. 10, of each member of the public to be informed by the mass media'.[108] Moreover, the European Human Rights Commission has not in the past considered individual

[104] App. No 10746/84, *Verein Alternatives Lokalradio Bern* v. *Switzerland*, 49 D & R 126.
[105] *The Observer and The Guardian* v. *United Kingdom* (1992) 14 EHRR 153 at 191; *The Sunday Times* v. *United Kingdom (No 2)* (1992) 14 EHRR 229 at 241; and *Jersild* v. *Denmark* (1995) 19 EHRR 1 at 25–6.
[106] For detailed discussion on the extent to which the Convention is capable of binding individuals see A. Clapham (1993), ch. 4.
[107] *Informationsverein Lentia and others* v. *Austria* (1994) 17 EHRR 93 at 113, emphasis added.   [108] M. Bullinger (1987), 106; and see also G. Malinverni (1983), 450.

viewers and listeners to have sufficient standing to call for correction of misleading information which does not affect them directly.[109]

In conclusion, it appears that the principle of informational pluralism enjoys only a weak status under the European Convention on Human Rights. The European Court of Human Rights does not regard the principle to be an integral component of the guarantee of freedom of expression in Article 10(1), and it is considered merely as a potentially legitimate ground for restricting that freedom. *Lentia* undoubtedly looks favourably upon state regulations designed to ensure that the public has access to a wide range of information, and it is probable that the Court would consider such regulations to be 'necessary in a democratic society'. Nevertheless, there appears to be no obligation on states under the Convention to introduce such measures where their mass media fail to provide an adequate level of diversity, or possible sanction where such requirements are removed in an attempt to lighten the regulatory burden on domestic broadcasters. The *Groppera* decision does indeed hint at a positive right to information, and there are various judicial dicta which can be called in aid to bolster the case for such a right, but support to date remains slight and a firm basis in the Convention has yet to be established.

(ii) Pluralism and the European Community

At the European Community level the issue of media pluralism has been the focus of considerable judicial and political attention. The approach of the Community institutions to the principle of pluralism seems at times confusing, even schizophrenic. This is in part because the various insitutions, and indeed different divisions within these institutions, have approached audiovisual issues from diverse perspectives. The absence of any clear cultural remit in the original EEC Treaty led to early initiatives in the broadcasting field being based essentially on economic, internal market rationales. This alarmed countries such as Denmark and the United Kingdom which focussed on the cultural aspects of broadcasting and disputed the legitimacy of Community intervention. Other countries such as France have taken a more pragmatic approach and attempted to harness the legislative power of the Community to support the audiovisual sector, not simply because of its economic but also because of its social and cultural importance. Although, as we noted in Chapter 4, Article 128(4) of the EC Treaty now requires the Community to take 'cultural aspects into account in its action under other provisions of the Treaty', the Community

---

[109] App. No 3071/67, *X* v. *Sweden*, 26 Coll. 71. The complainant alleged that Swedish television had given a misleading impression of a company in Liberia. The Commission held that he was not a victim under Art. 25 on this count because he was not affected *personally* by the report.

continues to have limited direct legislative competence in the cultural field and it is the Treaty Articles relating to the free movement of goods, services, persons, and capital which continue to serve as the primary motor for regulatory change.

Pressure for specific Community action to tackle the concentration of ownership within the European media came initially from the European Parliament in a series of resolutions dating back to 1990.[110] These resolutions prompted the Commission to adopt, in 1992, a Green Paper on Pluralism and Media Concentration, which explored the scope for a Community initiative in this area.[111] The Commission's approach to the problem was, however, noticeably different from that of the European Parliament. While the Parliament was primarily concerned about the power which wide-scale media holdings afforded individuals such as Silvio Berlusconi and Rupert Murdoch, the Commission focused on the potential distortion of the Internal Market caused by the different national media concentration rules. This shifted the terms of the debate onto economic matters, the Commission suggesting that 'implementation of industrial policy might justify a dynamic approach to secure the speedy elimination of obstacles to [structural] adjustment by harmonizing media-specific anti-concentration laws'.[112] The Commission noted that pluralism was not itself an objective specified in the EC Treaty, so that the Community had no power to act directly to protect pluralism in its own right: the Community was merely required to take the need for pluralism into account when exercising those powers it did enjoy under the Treaty.

The Commission's 1992 Green Paper on Pluralism did not draw any firm conclusions on the need for harmonization of national media concentration provisions. Political sensitivities, the concern to ensure a sound legal base for intervention, and the need to obtain reliable data have led to a cautious, step-by-step approach in the formulation of concrete proposals. As a follow-up to the Green Paper the Commission sent additional questionnaires to governments, the broadcasting industry, and other interested parties concerning a possible Community initiative; it also commissioned research on the availability within Member States of comparable data recording audience levels for the various media. Although the Community investigations revealed significant support for a Community initiative, certain governments and industry operators have continued to express concern. The UK government has argued, for example, that Member States, not the Community, are best equipped to

---

[110] Res. on media takeovers and mergers [1990] OJ C68/137; Res. on media concentration and diversity of opinions [1992] OJ C284/44; and Res. on the Commission Green Paper 'Pluralism and media concentration in the internal market' [1994] OJ C44/177.
[111] EC Commission (1992).   [112] *Ibid.* 101.

intervene to protect pluralism, and that the legal basis for legislation at the Community level has not been made out.[113] A draft directive has, however, been prepared by DG XV, although at the time of writing, in summer 1996, it has still to be agreed by the Commission. The Commission has indicated that it wishes to combine in its proposals a high level of protection for pluralism with support for the communications sector through the establishment of a 'level playing field' created by uniform ownership thresholds. It is expected to propose that no individual will be allowed to own radio or television stations which command more than 30 per cent of the audience share for that particular medium, or, where an individual owns a mixture of radio, television, and newspaper outlets, the average audience share across these media is not to exceed 10 per cent. The provisions would apply prospectively only and would not invalidate media holdings already acquired.

The Green Paper at times seemed to depict media pluralism as an inevitable and beneficial consequence of the realization of Community freedoms and, at others, as a legitimate, if rather regrettable, restriction upon them.[114] It is a short, but erroneous, step from holding that pluralism may result from realization of the EC Treaty provisions relating to, say, free movement of goods and services, to the suggestion that pluralism is in some way personified by, or the same thing as, those freedoms. On this latter view any attempt by Member States to restrict the exercise of the various Community freedoms in the name of pluralism could paradoxically be regarded as an impediment to its realization. In its recent communication on the consultation process which followed the Green Paper, the Commission took pains to stress, however, that it was wrong to contrast the objective of completing the Internal Market with that of safeguarding pluralism.[115] Though national rules designed to promote pluralism may impede the exercise of certain Community freedoms, such as freedom of establishment, harmonization of those rules has, according to the Commission, to take into account the interest in media diversity. The Commission has stressed that the Internal Market is not a 'free market', and that the interest in pluralism has to be respected in the harmonization process. In its opinion, the pursuit of pluralism and completion of the Internal Market are not in practice antagonistic and will be seen as such only if the application of Community rules is regarded as pushing inevitably in the direction of deregulation.[116]

---

[113] UK Response to the European Commission questionnaire on media concentration and pluralism in the internal market, Department of National Heritage, July 1995.

[114] EC Commission (1992), 62.   [115] EC Commission (1994c), 27.

[116] It may, however, be noted that at other times the Commission has talked of striking a balance between the 'need to guarantee the diversity of media controllers and the need to

Parallels have undoubtedly been drawn between the free movement of services and freedom of expression, considered to be mutually enhancing. The then director of the Internal Market Directorate of the European Commission, Ivo Schwartz, speaking at a colloquium in 1989, suggested that the freedom to provide services under Community law would facilitate freedom of expression,[117] while the preamble to the 1989 'Television Without Frontiers' Directive specifically links freedom to provide broadcasting services with Article 10.[118] It is, however, apparent that the protection of freedom of expression under Article 10 and the provision of services under Community law have distinct underlying goals and spheres of operation, as the *Grogan*[119] and *Open Door Counselling*[120] cases indicate. In *Grogan* the European Court of Justice held that the provision of information to nationals of Member States concerning the location of abortion clinics abroad would not constitute a service within the meaning of Article 60 of the EC Treaty where the information was not distributed on behalf of an economic operator established in another Member State. This factor did not prevent the European Court of Human Rights in the *Open Door Counselling* case from deciding that restrictions on the provision of such information by advisory clinics in Ireland contravened Article 10 of the Human Rights Convention. In particular, the Community focus on commercial activities contrasts markedly with the reduced level of protection offered to commercial speech by the Human Rights Commission. In *De Geillustreerde Pers NV* v. *Netherlands*, for example, the Commission specifically noted that it did not consider protection of the commercial interests of particular newspapers to be contemplated by Article 10 of the Human Rights Convention.[121] The simple equation of the freedoms protected under the EC Treaty with those set out in the European Convention on Human Rights may thus serve to obscure their differing scope and emphasis.

During the course of the 1980s a number of references were made to the European Court of Justice in which it was alleged that certain state broadcasting regulations infringed Community law. These cases served to emphasize that Member-State jurisdiction in the audiovisual sector was directly circumscribed by the EC Treaty. Domestic restrictions which overtly discriminate against broadcasting services provided from another

---

facilitate access to media activities so as to promote the development of the media industry', which implies a degree of co-ordination between competing objectives: European Commission (1994c), 28 and 41.

[117] I. E. Schwartz in A. Cassese and A. Clapham (1990), 166.

[118] Dir. 89/552/EEC [1989] OJ L298/23.

[119] Case C–159/90, *Society for the Protection of the Unborn Child* v. *Grogan* [1991] 3 CMLR 849.

[120] *Open Door Counselling and Dublin Wellwoman* v. *Ireland* (1993) 15 EHRR 244.

[121] App. No 5178/71, 8 D & R 5.

Member State will be legitimate only if they have been imposed for 'public policy, public health or public security' reasons within the terms of Article 56 of the EC Treaty, applied to the service provisions by Article 66. The European Court of Justice clearly stated in *Commission* v. *Belgium* that the pursuit of cultural objectives, including media pluralism, could not be held to fall within any of these categories, which are strictly construed.[122] This was also the view taken by the Commission of the European Communities in its Green Paper on Pluralism, in which it stated that '[p]luralism . . . cannot be associated with any of these three reasons'.[123] In its decision in *Bond van Adverteerders*, a case involving Dutch restrictions on the cable relay of foreign programmes containing advertisements intended for the Dutch audience, the European Court of Justice also held that economic aims, such as 'securing for a national public foundation all the revenue from advertising' intended for the public of that country 'cannot constitute grounds of public policy within the meaning of Article 56 of the Treaty'.[124]

Non-discriminatory national provisions which impede the Community freedom to provide services can, however, be justified if found to be in the 'general interest'. The European Court of Justice in its *Veronica* judgment held that the establishment of 'a pluralist and non-commercial broadcast system' is a cultural policy aim within the category of general-interest objectives recognized by Community law.[125] Thus, non-discriminatory provisions designed to safeguard 'the freedom of expression of the various components, in particular, the social, cultural, religious or philosophical components' of a particular society will be considered legitimate, even where they impede the flow of goods, services, and capital or restrict freedom of establishment—on condition that they can be shown to be 'proportionate'. Such restrictions on Community freedoms will be considered proportionate only where they are both appropriate and necessary for attaining the objective sought, and in such circumstances the Court of Justice will also seek to be assured that there was no less restrictive way of achieving the intended objective.[126] The stringency of this test means that in practice many of the regulations considered by the Court will not, in the

---

[122] Case C–211/91 [1992] ECR I–6757.
[123] European Commission (1992), 66.
[124] Case 352/85, *Bond van Adverteerders and Others* v. *The Netherlands* [1989] 3 CMLR 113, para. 34.
[125] Case C–148/91, *Vereniging Veronica Omroep Organisatie* v. *Commissariat voor de Media* [1993] ECR I–487. The Court also acknowledged that the promotion of media pluralism could be held to be in the general interest in the earlier Case C–353/89, *Commission* v. *Netherlands* [1991] ECR I–4069. For a helpful case note on *Veronica* see W. Hins (1994).
[126] For a discussion of how the 'proportionality test' is applied with varying intensity by the ECJ depending on the subject matter in dispute see P. Craig (1994), 418–21.

final analysis, be found sufficiently proportionate for the attainment of media pluralism.

The Commission of the European Communities has made it clear that it will consider any move to extend national programme diversity or ownership rules to foreign stations or their owners an unjustified attempt to give extra-territorial effect to the state's conception of pluralism. In its Green Paper on Pluralism it noted that '[c]ertain obligations could not reasonably be imposed (threatening a ban on retransmission) on a cross-border channel, such as those requiring the various shades of opinion in society to be reflected'.[127] The Commission's view that foreign broadcasts are intrinsically valuable additions to domestic services, even when these are commercial channels which would not be allowed nationally, found expression in the 1984 Television Without Frontiers Green Paper, the precursor to the 1989 Television Directive.[128] In the context of discussing what were in fact discriminatory restrictions on foreign stations the Commission stated:

The dialogue between different cultures and their interpenetration and cross-fertilization, nurtured as they are by radio and television, do not pose a threat to a country's public policy but preserve it from isolation, one-sidedness and nationalism by imparting a European dimension. It is not evident to what extent this additional source of information, opinions, ideas, culture, entertainment, *etc.*, from other Member States could constitute a threat to national public policy in the manner described.[129]

If foreign broadcasts are seen as inevitably enhancing pluralism, then, as we have noted above, Member States are unlikely to win the argument that 'levelling the playing field' by extending national content regulations to foreign stations will protect existing programme diversity. It is probable that it was because the Commission considered that regulations requiring programme diversity would not be considered lawful were their application to impede the free flow of broadcasts across borders that no specific Community requirements in this field were included in the 1989 Television Directive.

The European Court of Justice appears to have been similarly rigorous when evaluating whether state regulations, directed variously at domestic or foreign broadcasters or both, are necessary to protect pluralism. In Cases C–288/89 and C–353/89 the Court was asked to examine a number of different restrictions contained in the Dutch media law.[130] One of these

---

[127] See EC Commission (1992), 69–76.   [128] EC Commission (1984).
[129] *Ibid.* 136–7.
[130] Cases C–288/89, *Stichting Collectiëve Antennevoorziening Gouda and Others* v. *Commissariaat voor de Media (CM)* [1991] ECR I–4007 and C–353/89, *Commission* v. *Netherlands* [1991] ECR I–4069.

restrictions required domestic broadcasters to commission the production of all or part of their programming material from a particular Dutch undertaking, NOPB, thus preventing them looking not only to other domestic but also to other EC companies for their programming commands. The Dutch government argued, drawing parallels with the Italian government's success in defending its public broadcasting monopoly in the *Sacchi* case,[131] that the removal of programme production from the sphere of free competition should be considered a legitimate strategy to ensure that domestic broadcasters had access to quality products at the lowest cost. The European Court of Justice rejected this proposition, holding that the prohibition exceeded its aim of protecting freedom of speech: '[p]luralism in the audiovisual sector of a Member State could not in any way be affected by enabling the various national broadcasting organisations to call upon the services provided by persons established in other Member States'.[132]

The second provision of the Netherlands' media law considered by the Court permitted cable retransmission of foreign channels containing advertisements intended for the Dutch audience only where the advertisements did not exceed 5 per cent of the total air time, were not broadcast on Sundays, and were clearly separated from programmes. In addition, the transmitting company was required to be non-profit-making, was not to assist third parties to make a profit, and had to employ an independent entity to manage its advertising. Here, too, the Court found against the Dutch government, concluding that these specific regulations were not appropriate for attaining the desired goal. Mirroring the European Commission's approach to restrictions on foreign broadcasts, the Court found there to be no 'necessary connection' between the restrictions concerning the structure of foreign broadcasters and the cultural policy in question, namely, safeguarding the freedom of expression of the various components (in particular social, cultural, religious, and philosophical) of Dutch society. The Court went on to state that:

In order to ensure pluralism in the audiovisual sector, it is not indispensable for national legislation to require broadcasting bodies established in other Member States to align themselves on the Dutch model should they intend to broadcast programmes containing advertisements intended for the Dutch public. In order to secure the pluralism which it wishes to maintain the Netherlands' Government may very well confine itself to formulating the statutes of its own bodies in an appropriate manner.[133]

---

[131] Case 155/73, *Italy* v. *Sacchi* [1974] 2 CMLR 177.
[132] Case C–353/89, *Commission* v. *Netherlands* [1991] ECR I–4069, para. 30.
[133] *Ibid.*, para. 42.

The Dutch advertising restrictions were considered by the Court to be protectionist measures, designed to shield the centralized Dutch advertising foundation, STER, from external competition: 'by controlling the transmission of the advertisements, the legislation curtailed the competition from foreign broadcasting organizations to which that foundation could be exposed . . . [t]hat objective could not, however, justify restrictions on the freedom to provide services'. Thus, although it was permissible for the Dutch media law to establish a central advertising body independent of, and consequently designed to maintain, the non-commercial nature of the Dutch broadcasting organizations, the government could not seek to prevent the relaying of foreign commercial channels in competition with those domestic stations.

Although the above cases indicate that Member States have little scope to rely on cultural policy objectives in justifying broadcasting regulations which restrict one or other of the Community freedoms, the subsequent *Veronica* decision may represent a rather more circumspect approach to national, culturally-oriented regulations.[134] Here the European Court of Justice accepted that certain provisions of the Dutch media law were justifiable in order to protect the pluralist and non-commercial nature of the national broadcasting system. The restrictions in question prevented the domestic broadcaster, Veronica, from helping to establish a Luxembourg-based commercial television service intended for reception in the Netherlands. The Dutch station had provided the Luxembourg station with both legal advice and financial assistance. It should be noted that the restrictions, like those on production considered in Case C–353/89, were imposed on *national* broadcasters, but in this case, as well as restricting the free flow of services, it was argued that they also impeded the free flow of capital. It appears that the Court considered the Dutch provisions to be legitimate both on cultural policy grounds and on the basis that Veronica was acting to assist a foreign company to circumvent Dutch restrictions,[135] under the legal doctrine which has come to be associated with its judgment in the *van Binsbergen* case.[136] The Court accepted that the regulations could be justified on grounds of cultural policy, in that they were designed to ensure *domestic* broadcasters concentrated on the legitimate public tasks assigned them and did not dissipate income to commercial ventures. It did not, however, specifically examine the question of proportionality, and instead passed quickly on to the second limb of its decision, holding that it was open for a Member State to take measures to prevent Community

---

[134] Case C–148/91, *Vereniging Veronica Omroep Organisatie* v. *Commissariat voor de Media* [1993] ECR I–487.   [135] *Ibid.*, paras. 11 and 12.
[136] Case 33/74, *Johannes Henricus Maria van Binsbergen* v. *Bestuur van de Bedrijfsvereniging voor de Metaalnijverheid* [1974] ECR 1299.

rights being used deliberately to circumvent national rules of a particular Member State, rules which would have been applicable to the organization in question if established in that state. Veronica, in assisting a foreign commercial station to broadcast into the Netherlands, was thereby acting to circumvent domestic laws intended to protect the non-commercial nature of Dutch broadcasting.

Similar issues were raised in the *TV10* case which was referred to the European Court of Justice for a preliminary ruling by a Dutch court.[137] The European Court of Justice confirmed its ruling in *Veronica*, holding that states could take action to prevent the circumvention of domestic rules by organizations directing their services 'entirely or principally' at their territory from abroad. In the *TV10* case there was evidence that such targeting had taken place, in that TV10, which broadcast from Luxembourg, had concluded cable relay contracts solely with operators in Luxembourg and the Netherlands, the target audience for the service was the Dutch public, the advertisements were made in the Netherlands, and most of those working for TV10 were Dutch. In many instances, however, it will be difficult for Member States to make out such an argument: establishing the requisite intention to circumvent a given country's broadcasting regulations may not be easy, particularly where the broadcast signal covers a number of different countries. Moreover, the circumvention argument will not be open to a state where the Community has already intervened to regulate the area under dispute. Thus, in a recent case in which Norway sought to enforce against a station broadcasting from the United Kingdom into Scandinavia domestic prohibitions on advertising targeted at children, the EFTA Court held that television advertising was covered by the 1989 Television Directive (applicable within the EFTA area), so that the circumvention argument was inapplicable. The Court noted that, although looked at from a national perspective, 'this result might well be viewed as a circumvention of national law', looked at from 'an EEA context it is, however, a logical and necessary consequence of the main principles of the directive'.[138]

Finally, Member States may find it difficult to justify measures designed to ensure the preservation of a range of various media outlets—newspapers, television, radio—by restricting the ability of certain media to obtain revenues in the hope that this will filter over to the other sectors. This was the argument of the French government in the *Leclerc-Siplec* case, where it maintained that French regulations prohibiting distributors from advertising on television would protect the regional press and guarantee pluralism in

---

[137] Case C–23/93 *TV10* v. *Commissariaat voor de Media* [1994] ECR I–4795.
[138] Joined Cases E8–9/94 *Forbrukerombudet* v. *Mattel Scandinavia A/S and Lego Norge A/S* [1996] 1 CMLR 313 at 328.

the media.[139] The intention was that distributors would look elsewhere for an advertising outlet, ultimately choosing the regional daily press. Advocate General Jacobs, though recognizing in principle that such an argument might be acceptable, held that the measures in question were clearly disproportionate with regard to the projected aim. There was no guarantee that distributors would turn to the press; they might, for example, use radio stations or billboards. Moreover, there were other measures which the Advocate General considered equally effective but less detrimental to trade between Member States, for example, a restriction on the total amount of advertising time on domestic television and radio stations, tax benefits, or direct subsidies, as long as the Treaty provisions on state aid were respected. There also appeared to be no reason why distributors should be singled out to bear the burden of supporting the newspaper industry, and for this reason as well the provisions were considered arbitrary.[140] The Advocate General did not in fact consider the restrictions to be caught by Article 30 and the Court, employing different reasoning, concluded that the regulations fell outside the scope of Article 30 and so did not examine the question of justification.

If we review these broadcasting cases, the distinctions established by the European Court of Justice appear at times exceedingly fine. For example, Member States may choose to monopolize their broadcasting industry in public hands, but may not insist that national companies use a particular domestic production company; they may prohibit national, non-commercial companies from assisting foreign commercial companies located outside their borders in order to protect the non-commercial, pluralist nature of the domestic broadcasting service, but cannot require that stations broadcasting to their territory from abroad, save possibly in cases of deliberate circumvention, adopt similar non-commercial structures or strategies, nor can they restrict the relaying of such stations by national cable companies. Such decisions clearly attempt to strike something of a balance. On the one hand they espouse a policy of open borders; on the other, they offer a degree of protection for domestic broadcasting systems through the doctrine of deliberate circumvention and the application of general-interest justifications, the latter embracing cultural-policy object-ives and media pluralism. Throughout they display a genuine concern to ensure that Member States do not unjustifiably attempt to protect their domestic industries from foreign competition under the guise of cultural concerns. Given the ease, however, with which broadcasting operations may relocate from one country to another and the difficulties inherent in establishing deliberate circumvention, the goal of facilitating cross-border

---

[139] Case C–412/93, *Société d'Importation Edouard Leclerc-Siplec* v. *TF1 Publicité SA and another* [1995] ECR I–179.   [140] *Ibid.*, paras. 61 and 62.

services may ultimately undermine national broadcasting policies. Member States which wish to continue to impose content regulations on domestic broadcasters in order to further programme diversity will find this increasingly difficult to enforce as commercial competition heightens. For how long will companies which rely on advertising, or indeed subscription revenues, continue to be willing to incur the costs of scheduling programmes which do not attract maximal audiences? Those which do are likely to be only those organizations which receive some form of compensating subsidy from public funds.

More generally, the cases discussed above highlight the potentially wide scope for Community action in the cultural field, with scrutiny extending not only to restrictions addressed to both national and foreign stations but also to those binding only on national broadcasters where these impede the realization of the Internal Market. Indeed, recent decisions such as *Gebhard* v. *Consiglio dell'Ordine degli Avvocati e Procuratori di Milano* indicate that the European Court of Justice is prepared to evaluate any Member State's measure which curtails the exercise of Community freedoms, whether or not it discriminates directly or indirectly against other Community goods, services, or service providers.[141] *Gebhard* itself suggests that Member States may be required, at the suit of a foreign EC national established in their country, to demonstrate that domestic regulations—whether relating to programmes or ownership of the media— both pursue legitimate objectives and are proportionate. In such circumstances it is, however, probable that the Court would show a degree of deference to the host state's assessment of those regulations deemed necessary to realize domestic social and cultural policy objectives within its own territory. A truly 'indigenous' national broadcaster would not, of course, be able to rely on the establishment provisions to challenge domestic regulations. In this case the individual or company might consider falling back on the service provisions of the EC Treaty, arguing that its ability to provide competitive services abroad was unduly restricted. The Community refuses, however, to intervene in cases of 'reverse discrimination', namely where an EC national complains that the national restrictions to which he or she is subject are more onerous than those imposed on competitors established abroad by the competitors' own state. In such circumstances, therefore, no Community remedy would be available.

If we turn to consider the domestic anti-concentration regulations of the type currently under examination by the Commission—limits on the number of licences any one entity can hold, restrictions on shareholdings to a certain percentage, etc.—the *Veronica* decision indicates that, if challenged

---

[141] Case C–55/94 *Gebhard* v. *Consiglio dell'Ordine degli Avvocati e Procuratori di Milano* [1995] AU ER (EC) 189.

before the European Court of Justice, these regulations may very well be held to be legitimate, designed as they are to protect pluralism in the media. It is precisely because the Commission considers that they would be held to be legitimate that it is considering a directive to harmonize them. To date the Commission has limited itself to exploring the need for Community measures in the field of structural regulations, and has avoided intervention in the field of regulations which specifically require diverse programming, an alternative mechanism for achieving the same end. In its 1992 Green Paper the Commission confirmed that '[h]armonization would focus on national, media-specific anti-concentration rules and not on the pluralism rules relating to programme content.'[142] As we have noted above, the Commission considers it unlikely that the imposition of diversity requirements on foreign broadcasters would be held a proportionate strategy for furthering media pluralism—but what of diversity requirements imposed by Member States on their own domestic broadcasters? The Commission has sought to justify its plans to harmonize national ownership regulations on the basis that these impede the exercise of the freedom of establishment[143] and the freedom to provide services: the diversity of national rules is thought to create uncertainty and lead to circumvention. The programming rules which Member States impose on their domestic broadcasters are similarly diverse and may discourage foreign firms from entering that market, or lead domestic firms to consider broadcasting from a foreign base, though such restrictions merely make the provision of the domestic service comparatively expensive. Moreover, the move, facilitated by the 1989 Television Directive, to open domestic borders to foreign broadcasting services can impose deregulatory pressures which Member States may find it difficult to withstand, in such circumstances there seems to be a strong argument in favour of considering the adoption of a supra-national level of remedial strategies, whether under the auspices of the European Community or Council of Europe, to ensure that widely recognized objectives are not lost in the heightened competition.

Nevertheless, the political difficulty of agreeing even the most basic programming commitments at Community level is likely to deter any such

---

[142] EC Commission (1992), 105.

[143] There has been doubt whether non-discriminatory national regs. can be held to infringe Art. 52 of the EC Treaty and the Commission in its Green Paper on Pluralism initially indicated that ownership regs. could not be held contrary to the rules on freedom of establishment: EC Commission (1992), 90–1. The recent case of C–55/94, *Gebhard* v. *Consiglio dell'Ordine degli Avvocati e Procuratori di Milano* [1996] 1 CMLR 603 indicates, however, that similar rules apply to all the Community freedoms so that non-discriminatory provisions may restrict the freedom of establishment and require objective justification. In recent statements the Commission has suggested that action to harmonize national ownership rules may be based on the need to prevent impediments to freedom of establishment: EC Commission (1994c), 33, 41.

attempt. The exhortation in Article 4 of the 1989 Television Directive to Member States to ensure that domestic broadcasters schedule a majority of European productions was designed to encourage the European programme industry faced with competition from comparatively cheap American programmes which had already recovered their costs on the American market. Yet it was introduced only in the face of fierce criticism, and in its final form merely imposed on Member States the weak obligation to act 'where practicable and by appropriate means'. With the 1989 Directive now under review, the European quota provision continues to excite heated controversy.[144] Such experience is unlikely to encourage further attempts to impose positive programme requirements.

Moreover, which services should be subject to regulations requiring content diversity even if they could be agreed? The providers of newer audiovisual services such as video-on-demand argue that they are distinct from traditional broadcast services since they are provided on a one-to-one basis, and reject the suggestion that they should be subject to established broadcasting regulations.[145] Many of the newer stations are thematic and could not plausibly be expected to carry a range of different programmes. An alternative strategy would be to impose a financial levy which could be used to subsidize production of a variety of programmes which would not otherwise be aired.

Adoption by the Community of a common framework of rules regulating media ownership may undoubtedly have beneficial consequences, particularly in those countries where national governments have proved reluctant, often for self-interested reasons, to prevent media concentrations. It is interesting to note, however, that the Commission proposals appear likely to require the existence of only four operators in any media sector and will only cover the printed press where holdings are combined with interests in other sectors. Despite early indications that the Community would seek to ensure that 'there is the greatest possible number of media and that these are independent of one another'[146] the final result may thus be a toleration of media markets dominated by three or four large operators in any sector with sufficient size to compete internationally. Such concentration may ultimately facilitate the continuing imposition of programming requirements. Another scenario is, of course, that growing competition for revenues, programmes, and audiences will continue to impose on those who shape the programming schedules inescapable pressure to conform to the logic of the market and offer only those programmes which maximize

---

[144] [1996] *Agence Europe*, no. 7404, 8.

[145] For brief commentary on the debates surrounding the European Parliament's consideration of whether the 1989 Television Dir. should be extended to cover the new video-on-demand services see [1996] *Agence Europe*, no. 6670, 15, and no. 7404, 8.

[146] EC Commission (1992), 105.

ratings. Community law has gradually restricted Member States to regulating their own domestic media, and even here there have been Community inroads into Member State jurisdiction. In an open, pan-European market Member States acting individually may no longer have sufficient control to ensure that the various social and cultural functions traditionally performed by their radio and television services continue to be provided.

6. PLURALISM: A LEGAL LODESTAR FOR THE AUDIOVISUAL MEDIA?

The above discussion reveals that, over the course of the last fifteen years, there has been widespread judicial acknowledgement of the existence of a distinct legal principle of pluralism, applicable in the broadcasting context. The weight afforded to pluralism in the face of other competing interests has, however, varied markedly from one jurisdiction to another, as have the various regulatory techniques which judges have employed for its realization. Much of the uncertainty stems from the somewhat ambiguous relationship between pluralism and the principle of freedom of expression. Although freedom of expression and access to diverse information both depend for their effective realization on the general absence of content-specific censorship, they differ in their focus and objectives. The primary aim of freedom of expression is to protect the right of individuals to express themselves without sanction; a right which may, but need not, lead to the transmission of a variety of ideas and information. The objective underlying media pluralism is, on the other hand, the communication to the public of diverse ideas and information; an objective which is itself likely to benefit from an expansive, individual right to expression, but which may also lead to certain individuals being refused access to the media. The act of selection and mediation of ideas by journalists, editors, and producers in television and radio is clearly far removed from the impartiality among those wishing to speak which freedom of expression would seem to entail. Whatever the exact points of contact between these two principles, many of the decisions considered above clearly recognize an individual need not only for self-expression but also for information.

It will also be apparent from the above discussion that both French and Italian courts consider pluralism to be a distinct constitutional principle requiring positive promotion. For these courts pluralism appears to be linked to, if not an aspect of, freedom of expression, and is far from being regarded as merely another ground which states may use when justifying restrictions upon this latter right. The European Court of Human Rights, on the other hand, does appear to see pluralism as a *restraint* on the primary interest of freedom of expression, an approach which reduces the protection afforded to pluralism under the European Convention on Human Rights. Similarly, the European Court of Justice, though acknowledging media pluralism to be a legitimate national objective, has sought to keep its application within carefully monitored limits because of its capacity to restrict established Community freedoms. Both at the Council of Europe and European Community levels a major concern has been to facilitate the flow of broadcasting services across borders, greater tolerance being afforded those national restrictions aimed primarily at domestic media and which have little impact on foreign stations, though the possibility of challenges to such regulations as ineffective and unnecessary should not, however, be ruled out.

Whether or not pluralism should be seen as an aspect of, restriction upon, or principle distinct from freedom of expression, the question remains why certain courts should have singled out the audiovisual media for this particular informational burden. Why, that is, should broadcasters be required to pay the regulatory costs of keeping us informed? It is probable that the historical development of television and radio as public services, however flawed the match of theory and reality may have been, has left an enduring perception that this form of communication should indeed be used to 'inform, educate and entertain'. Television, even more than radio or the press, has considerable audience reach throughout Western Europe, with, for example, British viewers constituting about 98 per cent of the population and watching, on average, something in the order of twenty-five hours' television a week.[147] Part 1 of this book has highlighted the extent to which this particular perception of the audiovisual media came to permeate both the attitudes of professional broadcasters and public expectations. It is, moreover, an ideal which continues to exert a powerful influence on those who frame the regulations for the broadcasting media. The French loi 89–25 of 1989, for example, acknowledges in its first Article that freedom of expression may legitimately be restricted in order to further pluralism and calls on the Conseil supérieur de l'audiovisuel to watch over the quality and diversity of the programmes transmitted; the Italian legge 23 of 1990 provided in its first Article that pluralism, objectivity, and complete and impartial information are among the fundamental principles of the broadcasting order; while in Britain the government accepts that there remains a place for the BBC, broadcasting 'a wide range of radio and television programmes for people with different tastes and interests and of all ages'.[148] In establishing a distinct role for the

---

[147] Booz Allen and Hamilton (1992), 3, chart 2.3; the British data were recorded in *Guardian*, 25 May 1993.
[148] French loi 89–25 of 17 Jan. 1989; Italian legge 223 of 1990; and British Government (1994), 1.

principle of pluralism in the broadcasting sector courts of law have been swimming against strong ideological and commercial currents, but the tide has yet to turn completely, and there continues to be influential support for their position.[149]

Given that it is not only the audiovisual media which perform a key informational role, it is worth considering whether the legal requirement of pluralism might not, in fact, extend to other sectors. Is it, for example, applicable in the field of the printed press? The rhetoric of freedom of the press, particularly that espoused by the press itself when seeking to protect its interests, could lead one to conclude that, unlike the broadcasting media, this institution does and should enjoy almost unrivalled freedom from regulatory control. It is undoubtedly possible to point to considerable differences in the regulatory regimes established for the two media. Thus the French Conseil constitutionnel has concluded that a licensing system can legitimately be employed in the audiovisual sector but that its use in the context of the printed press would clearly be unconstitutional.[150] Similarly, Article 21 of the Italian Constitution specifically provides that the press is not to be subjected to a system of authorization and, for reasons considered in Chapter 2, no comparable provision was included for the audiovisual media. The Italian Constitutional Court has accepted this dichotomy and has refused to extend the 'specific discipline' applicable to the press into the audiovisual domain.[151] One reason for this acceptance was given in the 1981 broadcasting case in which the Court emphasized what it considered to be the particularly suggestive nature of the audiovisual media stemming from their direct entry into the home and persuasive combination of words and pictures.[152] It was thus the *impact* of the audiovisual media which justified a distinct regulatory regime.

A similar attempt to distinguish between the print and audiovisual media, this time focusing on the way in which they are accessed by the public, was made in the recent English case of *R.* v. *Radio Authority, ex parte Bull and another*.[153] Here, the applicants applied for judicial review of the Radio Authority's decision to prohibit radio advertising by the humanitarian pressure group, Amnesty International. The Radio Authority had concluded that Amnesty's advertisements would be in breach of section 92(2)(a)(ii) of the 1990 Broadcasting Act which prohibits the insertion of advertisements by bodies of a 'wholly or mainly political nature', or advertisements 'directed towards a political end'. There is no equivalent restriction preventing political advertising in the printed press. Counsel for the Radio Authority argued that '[w]hen an advertisement was

---

[149] See Ch. 3, sect. 4.   [150] Dec. 82–141 of 27 July 1982 [1982] JO 2422.
[151] See, e.g., Dec. 226/1974 [1974] Giur. cost. 1791 at 1798.
[152] Dec. 148/1981 [1981] Giur. cost. 1379 at 1408.   [153] [1995] 4 All ER 427.

on a hoarding or in a newspaper the reader could decide at a glance how much of it he wished to read' while if 'it was inserted into a radio programme which he wanted to hear he had no similar way of curtailing it'.[154] Kennedy LJ, dismissing the application for review, appeared to accept that such a distinction could reasonably be made, concluding that 'in addition to freedom of communication there were other rights to be protected, such as freedom from being virtually forced to listen to unsolicited information of a contentious kind'.[155] Although this distinction may have some cogency in the advertising context it seems less relevant in the field of programming requirements: individuals are not 'forced' to listen or watch a particular programme, and can always switch off their television or radio sets. Moreover, the widespread use of remote controls and video recorders undermines attempts to draw a similar distinction between television and the press.

These differences in the regulation of the audiovisual and press sectors have inevitably led to allegations of 'double standards' and to calls for the extension of the less interventionist press regime to radio and television.[156] Certainly, the justifications given by the courts for maintaining this disparity do not, without further evidence, appear entirely convincing. The emotive power thought to be derived from the combination of words and pictures clearly cannot be a relevant consideration in the radio sector, which is nevertheless subject to many of the regulatory burdens imposed on television. Newspapers may contain an equally powerful, if not more enduring, juxtaposition of words and pictures, and if radio and television are capable of directly penetrating the home, then newspapers can at least find their way onto the doorstep. Moreover, the distinction between the printed press and the audiovisual sector is becoming increasingly blurred with the development of on-line news services.

Though the Italian Constitutional Court initially appeared to adopt a 'technology determinist' approach to media regulation, justifying intervention in the broadcasting sector on the basis of spectrum scarcity,[157] it quickly shifted its position by noting that access to the media could be impeded by economic as well as technological factors.[158] Economic barriers to entry are not restricted to the broadcasting media, nor do they necessarily characterize all broadcasting services, and the Court's more general concern with access and pluralism may be seen as preventing an artificial wall being built around the broadcasting media, as the sole sector

---

[154] *Ibid.* 437.   [155] *Ibid.* 440.
[156] D. Kelley and R. Donway (1990), 66.
[157] Dec. 59/1960 [1960] Giur. cost. 759 at 781, pt. 5.
[158] See, e.g., Dec. 148/81 [1981] Giur. cost. 1379 at 1407, confirmed in Dec. 112/1993 [1993] Foro it. 1339 at 1350.

in which extensive content and structural regulations would be held acceptable. In the United States, however, technological determinism does appear to have taken firm root. In *Turner Broadcasting* the Supreme Court held that 'it was the special physical characteristics of broadcast transmission, not the economic characteristics of the broadcast market' which justified the more intrusive regulation of broadcasting as opposed to cable services. Newspapers and cable television were also thought to display important technological differences. Cable operators in America generally control access to all television programming entering an individual's home, whereas a newspaper proprietor is usually responsible for arranging the distribution of its own product and not that of competing papers. Spectrum scarcity does not characterize the cable sector but cable-operator bottlenecks do.

The medium-specific approach of the American courts evident in both *Turner* and the recent *American Civil Liberties Union et al.* v. *Janet Reno*[159] case may serve to obscure valid concerns which cut across all the mass media: distribution bottlenecks would, for example, be just as worrying in the print as they are in the cable sector. The ease with which services from one sector, for example analogue broadcasting, may now move to deploy alternative forms of transmission, for example cable relay, cautions against developing an inflexible approach to regulation tied to transmission technologies. For the viewer, television and radio services are the same whether they are broadcast or transmitted over a wire. Moreover, how should new transmission technologies be classified: with print, off-air broadcasting, cable television, or the telephone? In the *American Civil Liberties Union* case Judge Sloviter considered the Internet to be more akin to telephone communications than to broadcasting, because, as with the telephone, an Internet user has to act affirmatively and deliberately to receive specific information. But it is not impossible that the bulk of our communication services, including news and entertainment television programmes, will soon be available online, so that our access to video programming becomes as 'affirmative and deliberate' as our access to the Internet.[160]

Returning to the European context, a rather more detailed examination of the rules applicable in France and Italy to the printed press provides support for the view that, despite initial appearances, the regulatory dividing lines between the various media are considerably more complex than is suggested by a simple press–audiovisual dichotomy. It quickly

[159] *American Civil Liberties Union et al.* v. *Janet Reno* [1996] US Dist., LEXIS 7919.
[160] British Sky Broadcasting, for example, plans to offer access to the Internet through convential TV sets in a package which is intended to include video and other interactive services such as home banking: *Financial Times*, 23 August 1996, 1.

becomes apparent that in neither country has there been a complete rejection of state regulation in the press field: both have established specific antitrust measures and introduced a number of fiscal and other financial, for example postal, advantages. Moreover, Article 21 of the Italian Constitution expressly provides that the means by which the periodical press is financed may be regulated by law. Nor do the respective constitutional courts consider that the only basis for press regulation is the protection of individual autonomy, indeed, the underlying theoretical basis for regulation in *both* the audiovisual and press sectors appears to be a common concern with informational pluralism.

Thus, the French Conseil constitutionnel has explicitly recognized that the public has an interest in a diverse and varied press.[161] Decision 84–181 records that '*en définitive l'objectif à réaliser est que les lecteurs qui sont au nombre des destinataires essentiels de la liberté proclamée par l'Article 11 de la Déclaration de 1789 soient à même d'exercer leur libre choix sans que ni les intérêts privés ni les pouvoirs publics puissent y substituer leurs propres décisions ni qu'on puisse en faire l'objet d'un marché*', a statement which was to be endorsed by the Conseil in its later 1986 broadcasting decision.[162] The Italian Constitutional Court in Decision 105 of 15 June 1972 also held the press to be an irreplaceable source of public information, serving to create an aware and knowledgeable citizenry.[163] Article 21, said the Court, protected not only the *freedom to divulge* news but also a general interest in the *receipt of information*, which required public access to a plurality of information sources. Moreover, the degree of press regulation in Italy, which affords individuals a right to rectification and reply where their dignity has been damaged, or where they have been subject to false allegations, goes well beyond the level of intervention tolerated in countries such as America, where the publication rights of the speaker are ranked above that of the newspaper-reading public.[164] In *Miami Herald Publishing Co.* v. *Tornillo*, for example, the US Supreme Court invalidated a Florida statute which established a right of reply for political candidates 'assailed' by newspaper coverage.[165] The Court noted that it had yet to be

---

[161] Dec. 84–181 of 10 and 11 Oct. 1984 [1984] JO 3200 and Dec. 86–210 of 29 July 1986 [1986] JO 9393.

[162] Dec. 84–181 of 10 and 11 Oct. 1984 [1984] JO 3200 at 3202: 'Finally the objective to be realized is that the readers, who are the essential addressees of the freedom proclaimed by Article 11 of the 1789 Declaration, should be able to exercise their free choice without private interests or public powers being able to substitute their own decisions or render such choice the object of a market'.

[163] Dec. 105/1972 [1972] Giur. cost. 1196.

[164] The registration requirement is contained in Art. 5 of legge 47 of 1948, while the right of reply is to be found in Art. 42 of legge 416 of 1981. Legal regulation of the Italian press is considered in some detail by R. Lanzillo (1990), 179 ff.

[165] *Miami Herald Publishing Co* v. *Tornillo*, (1974) 418 US 241.

demonstrated how governmental regulation of the editorial process 'can be exercised consistent with First Amendment guarantees of a free press as they have evolved to this time'.[166]

Although the different levels of state intervention in the press and audiovisual sectors could lead one to conclude that principles have been inconsistently applied or that the two media are essentially different in kind, the French and Italian cases discussed above indicate a willingness to see newspapers and the audiovisual media as part of a wider communications sector governed by common principles.[167] The diverse strategies for realizing common objectives employed in the press and audiovisual media stem from their different historical development and public perceptions of the way in which they convey information. As we have seen, for much of its history the printed press in Western Europe was politically partisan and there remains a general expectation that, at least at the national level, newspapers will display a variety of 'political leanings'. Such leanings are not thought to impede a lively exchange of diverse opinions, indeed they are widely considered to foster informational pluralism, so long, that is, as a sufficient range of newspapers continues in existence to express these views. Where newspaper ownership becomes unduly concentrated, or significant currents of thought become excluded, the principle of pluralism indicates that state intervention may be justified.[168] The problem in such circumstances is not, therefore, one of the *legitimacy* of regulation, but an equally fundamental one of *efficacy*: how is it possible to promote greater diversity in the printed press?[169] The requirement that the audiovisual media meet certain standards of balance and diversity is simply a different regulatory strategy for attaining the same end.

Recognition that the press and audiovisual media share certain common objectives should encourage a greater willingness to experiment with new regulatory forms. Clearly delimited parts of the broadcasting sector, for example, could become more like the press, offering 'conviction programming' without the requirement methodically to balance views or opinions. Alternatively, where diversity in the press is shown to be failing, financial or other forms of intervention should at least be considered, and not ruled out of court as an unacceptable form of interference with press freedom;

---

[166] *Miami Herald Publishing Co.* v. *Tornillo* (1974) 418 US 258.

[167] Didier Truchet has argued that it is possible to distinguish the development in France of a common law of communication, with distinct rules on concentrations, transparency, and pluralism. Although these rules are not yet universally applicable in all media sectors they nevertheless reveal a degree of convergence: D. Truchet (1987).

[168] As R. H. Coase (1977), 8, has argued 'we cannot rule out regulation in any market as being undesirable on an *a priori* basis'.

[169] For consideration of the problems inherent in any attempt to alter press output see R. Negrine (1989).

action to prevent anti-competitive practices should be speedy and robust. The disappearance of competing newspapers from most of the large cities in the United States indicates that leaving this sector to be regulated simply by market forces may destroy that very diversity and choice promised by proponents of market regulation. We are not faced, when considering how to regulate new media services such as video-on-demand, with a simple choice between an idealized press or audiovisual model. There may well be obligations which the new information services could reasonably be expected to bear, support, for example, for indigenous production or subsidized access for schools and libraries, to mark their participation in a wider communications sector. The ability to build on both the successes and failures of the print and electronic media, rather than to view each as walled off in its own distinct ideological domain, not only accords with a growing convergence within the mass media but also facilitates a more sensitive response to the rapid technical and financial changes which have characterized the last decade.

8
Theory into Practice:
Judicial Guidelines for the
Audiovisual Sector

> Legal rules are, however, often inadequate to shape a society having
> the characteristic of freedom of speech because many different forms
> of a society are consistent with that principle. The concept of 'freedom
> of speech' is too complicated and indeterminate to be a useful guide in
> resolving many specific disputes.[1]

The last two chapters have considered how particular courts of law have
responded to the technological and ideological changes which have caused
such turmoil in the communications sector over the last two decades. In
doing so they have isolated a number of principles, pluralism among them,
which are of particular relevance to the audiovisual media. What,
however, are the *practical* implications of this developing case law: to what
extent has it been, or is it, possible to convert this theory into meaningful
imperatives for the mass media? This question is important for those in
Britain who are concerned at the precarious nature of fundamental rights
in the domestic legal order and who look for a solution in the adoption of a
Bill of Rights or incorporation into domestic law of the European Human
Rights Convention.

We have seen that among the legal principles applied to the audiovisual
sector freedom of expression, the right to information, and pluralism have
assumed a central role. It is the Italian Constitutional Court which,
perhaps more explicitly than any other, has set out what it considers to be
the basic requirements for a legitimate broadcasting order. In Decision 112
of 1993 the Court stated that such a service should provide, first, a plurality
of sources of news and information, comprising different points of view
and contrasting cultural orientations; secondly, objective and impartially
presented information; thirdly, a continuous and comprehensive transmission of accurate information; and, fourthly, programmes which respect
human dignity, public order, and morality, and which are incapable of
distorting children's moral and psychological development.[2] The Court
also indicated that it was desirable to have services universally available

---

[1] R. F. Nagel (1984), 321.   [2] Dec. 112/1993 [1993] Foro it. 1339 at 1350.

across the whole of the national territory in its 1960 judgement.[3] It will be readily apparent that these *constitutionally* mandated standards incorporate familiar elements of the public-service broadcasting ethos. The French Conseil constitutionnel has similarly adopted a functional view of broadcasting and has stressed the importance of public access to 'honest' information and diverse programmes.[4] The European Court of Human Rights and European Court of Justice have instead tended to emphasize the broadcasters' freedom to communicate and provide services, particularly across frontiers, with pluralism considered a potential justification for the imposition of regulations which constrain these freedoms.

Before we turn to evaluate how effective judicial intervention in the audiovisual sector has been in practice, it may be helpful to draw together from the preceding chapters some of the central aspects of radio and television regulation which have been the subject of judicial scrutiny. What impact have the objectives identified above had on the day to day running of the audiovisual sector? As we have seen, views differ as to the most effective way of creating diverse programming and promoting public choice. For this reason the courts have afforded states a margin of appreciation in deciding how best to pursue the various constitutional objectives. There are, however, outer limits to this discretion, and the courts have not been slow in developing concrete requirements for the audiovisual media, for example, that ownership of the media be 'transparent',[5] or that regulatory agencies be free from government influence,[6] which they regard as necessary to promote pluralism and freedom of expression. Consideration is given in this Chapter to the impact of judicial decisions on the licensing system itself, on ownership and content requirements and on the nature and level of competition advocated by the courts in the various media sectors. Although intervention has differed markedly from jurisdiction to jurisdiction the brief overview which follows should indicate the breadth of the issues which have been, and remain, potentially open to judicial scrutiny.

1. THE LICENSING SYSTEM

One of the key defining elements of audiovisual regulation has been the reliance on national licensing systems to apportion entitlements. Through

---

[3] Dec. 59/1960 [1960] Giur. cost. 759 at 781.

[4] Dec. 86–217 of 18 Sept. 1986 [1996] JO 11294 at 11295.

[5] Dec. 826/1988 [1988] Foro it. 2477 at 2502, where the Court considered that, given its importance for the principle of pluralism, transparency also enjoyed constitutional status. The French Conseil constitutionnel in its press Dec. 86–210 of 29 July 1986 [1986] JO 9393 also held, at 9394, that transparency facilitates the realization of freedom of expression.

[6] Dec. 225/1974 [1974] Giur. cost. 1775 at 1789.

the award of licences and the power to rescind them, governments have kept ultimate control over the shape and content of domestic radio and television services. Perhaps, therefore, the most striking aspect of judicial appraisal in this field has been the general unwillingness to challenge the licensing system itself. At the centre of broadcasting regulation, and supported by an intricate web of international telecommunication agreements,[7] the principle of 'licensed' communication, though constitutionally unacceptable in the print sector, may have seemed too significant and well-established an element to overturn—even in the cable field where problems relating to the finite number of available frequencies and programme interference do not arise. Thus the European Court of Human Rights in its *Groppera* decision justified the continuation of licensing regimes on the need to ensure compliance with international obligations and maintain order in the telecommunications sector: the purpose, it held, of the third sentence of Article 10(1) of the Convention was to 'make it clear that States are permitted to control by a licensing system the way in which broadcasting is organised in their territories, particularly in its technical aspects'.[8] A further justification for state licensing used by the Italian Constitutional Court stems from the technical characteristics of the broadcast medium. On a number of occasions the Court has held that broadcasting stations use a common element, the ether, which, being a limited commodity, requires specific assignation.[9] The explanation is, however, unsatisfactory, and not merely for its outdated reference to the 'ether', formerly considered the medium through which electromagnetic waves were transmitted, for it again fails to explain the grant of licences in the cable sector which is not dependent on hertzian relay. Perhaps for this reason the French Conseil constitutionnel has preferred not to draw any particular regulatory conclusions from the use of hertzian relay and refrained from determining the exact legal status of the airwaves.[10]

In accepting state licensing, courts have rejected the alternative 'private-property-rights' solution to allocating resources, equally capable of dealing

[7] Reg. 2020 of the Radio Regs., supplementing the International Telecommunications Convention, provides that '[n]o transmitting station may be established or operated by a private person or by any enterprise without a licence issued in an appropriate form and in conformity with the provisions of these Regulations by the Government of the country to which the station in question is subject'.

[8] *Groppera Radio AG* v. *Switzerland* (1990) 12 EHRR 321 at 338 and 339.

[9] Dec. 102/1990 [1990] Giur. cost. 610 and Dec. 112/1993 [1993] Foro it. 1339 at 1352.

[10] Dec. 86–217 of 18 Sept. 1986 [1986] JO 11294. For a helpful summary of the arguments concerning ownership of the airwaves see B. Delcros and D. Truchet (1989). Art. 10 of the loi 89–25 of 17 Jan. 1989 provides that use of the radio frequencies available over the French Republic by the holders of authorizations constitutes a privative occupation of the public domain belonging to the state, though there remains some uncertainty what exactly constitutes the public domain: is it the airspace or the frequencies?

with the problem of signal interference. That such an option was not merely of theoretical interest is revealed by the response of Italian courts, called to decide disputes between competing users of the same frequency, after the Constitutional Court's 1976 ruling that the state broadcasting monopoly was unconstitutional at the local level.[11] Gradually, legal rules were developed which granted status and protection to the prior user of a frequency, protection similar to that afforded the owner of private property.[12] Despite this possible approach, courts of law have ultimately stood back from challenging the principle of state licensing which, at the end of the day, offers scope not only for rational spectrum-allocation but also continuing political supervision: the grant of a revocable licence imposes extra pressure on licensees to comply with state regulations.

One consequence of this approach has been that judges have tended to deny the existence of an intrinsic, individual right to broadcast. In Italy, uncertainty over this issue was finally resolved by the Constitutional Court in 1990. The Court categorically denied the existence of an individual right to establish or operate a radio or television station, holding instead that there was only a 'legitimate interest' in the correct exercise of the administrative power to assign and oversee the use of frequencies.[13] This was confirmed in Decision 112 of 1993 in which the Court held that the grant of a concession was a necessary prerequisite to the exercise of an individual's freedom to express him- or herself by means of the broadcasting media. The grant of the concession did not, therefore, so much limit the exercise of a right as condition its existence.[14] Similarly, in 1982, the French Conseil constitutionnel refused to hold that the grant of public-service concessions for private television services served to restrict the constitutionally protected right to freedom of expression.[15] The European Human Rights Commission in its opinion in the case of *Verein Alternatives Lokalradio Bern* also concluded that broadcasting enterprises have no right to a licence under Article 10 of the Human Rights Convention.[16] In the subsequent *Lentia* case the European Court of Human Rights, though holding that the applicants' freedom to impart information and ideas had been violated, did not consider them to be entitled to the grant of a broadcasting licence, and consequently refused their request for financial compensation. The applicants were merely

---

[11] Dec. 202/1976 [1976] Giur. cost. 1267.
[12] These cases are discussed by G. Rao (1988), 26–8 and see also Dec. 4355/1989 [1989] Giur. it. 401. For consideration of the reasons underlying the American rejection of the property rights option see T. W. Hazlett (1990).
[13] Dec. 102/1990 [1990] Guir. cost. 610.
[14] Dec. 112/1993 [1993] Foro it. 1339 at 1352.
[15] Dec. 82–141 of 27 July 1982 [1982] JO at 2422.
[16] App. No 10746/84, *Verein Alternatives Lokalradio Bern* v. *Switzerland*, 49 D & R 126.

entitled to the establishment of a particular system of regulation, namely one which afforded private operators an opportunity to compete for a broadcasting licence.[17]

In conclusion we can see that courts have stood back from mandating the creation of a private market in broadcasting services and have left intact the key mechanism by which the audiovisual sector has traditionally been regulated. This willingness to accept the legitimacy of state licensing, even in the cable and satellite sectors, undoubtedly impedes the ability of any given individual to communicate using the audiovisual media, though the extent of this impediment will depend on such factors as the number of licences made available for private broadcasting and the nature of the criteria adopted by the state for selecting licensees.

2. OWNERSHIP REQUIREMENTS

Though conceding the principle of state licensing in the audiovisual sector, the French and Italian Constitutional Courts, together with the European Court of Human Rights, have confirmed that in practice state discretion in awarding licences is not unlimited. Indeed, it is through the imposition of legal boundaries to this licensing procedure that judges can influence the structure and content of audiovisual services. A number of techniques for attaining a plurality of voices have been discussed in the judicial forum, among them the selection of those to be granted licences or air-time and the imposition of content requirements.

If we concentrate first on the issue of ownership, it will be apparent from Chapter 6 that the *legitimacy of state ownership* was one of the earliest questions relating to broadcasting regulation to be referred to courts of law. The judicial response has been far from uniform. At the risk of some simplification it is possible to conclude that the French Conseil constitutionnel has been the most agnostic over the extent to which the audiovisual media should be in either public or private hands. Though keen to ensure that the system as a whole offers a diversity of programmes, it has left the legislature considerable discretion to determine what balance of public and private ownership will best promote such diversity.[18] The Italian Constitutional Court has taken a more interventionist stance, moving from its early endorsement of the primacy of the market to a position which now regards both public and private sectors to be constitutionally mandated. It is, however, apparent from the Constitutional Court's examination of the questions raised in the 1995 broadcasting referenda that it is not necessary

---

[17] *Informationsverein Lentia and others* v. *Austria* (1994) 17 EHRR 93.
[18] Dec. 86–217 of 18 Sept. 1986 [1986] JO 11294.

for the public-service sector to be publicly owned. What the Court seems to require is the existence of a specific broadcasting sector set up to operate in the national interest, providing a complete range of 'objective, impartial and balanced'[19] programmes in exchange for financial and operational advantages.[20]

The European Human Rights Commission, sensitive to the changing technical environment and the growing involvement of private operators in the audiovisual sector, stated in 1976 that it was no longer prepared to maintain 'without further consideration' its prior acceptance of the legitimacy of public television monopolies.[21] The opinions of both the Court and the Commission in the *Lentia* case have now confirmed that a state monopoly is unlikely to be found a proportionate mechanism for attaining pluralism or, for that matter, any other objective in the audiovisual field.[22] Although the Commission indicated that particular state monopolies might be acceptable if suitably open to private initiative and third-party access, the subsequent decision of the Court raises real doubts whether even this would now be acceptable. With the move in most European countries to a 'mixed' broadcasting system, the discussion of state monopolies appears somewhat academic; nevertheless the approach taken by the Court in *Lentia* does have more general implications for public ownership. Under this ruling public channels are afforded merely provisional legitimacy: acceptable only while states can establish that they are strictly necessary in a democratic society. On this basis it would be open to a private operator to argue that a similar quality of service could be provided by private broadcasters so that the frequencies used by publicly-owned stations should be made available to the private sector.

The European Court of Justice acknowledged the legitimacy of the Italian state broadcasting monopoly in the *Sacchi* case[23] and the Commission of the European Communities has indicated that it does not consider state monopolies *per se* to be precluded by Community law. Nevertheless, it appears that Member States may be required to show that an authorized monopoly is no more extensive than absolutely necessary to achieve the general-interest objective being pursued,[24] while the *ERT* case serves to emphasize that the manner in which a monopoly is '*organized or exercised*' may also infringe the rules on free movement and competition

---

[19] Dec. 826/1988 [1988] Foro it. 2477 at 2499.

[20] Dec. 7/1995 [1995] I Gius. civ. 331.

[21] App. No 4750/71, *X* v. *UK*, 40 Coll. 29. This contrasts with the earlier acceptance of such a monopoly in App. No. 6542/74, *Sacchi* v. *Italy*, 5 D & R 43. For more detail see Ch. 6, sect. 3(i) above.

[22] *Informationsverein Lentia and others* v. *Austria* (1994) 17 EHRR 93.

[23] Case 155/73, *Italy* v. *Sacchi* [1974] 2 CMLR 177, 203.

[24] Case C–320/91, *Corbeau (Paul)* v. *Belgian Post Office* [1995] 4 CMLR 621.

set out in the EC Treaty.[25] Undertakings having the character of a revenue-producing monopoly are required, under Article 90(2) of the EC Treaty, to comply with Community competition rules, though a derogation is provided where compliance would impede attainment of the tasks assigned to them.[26]

The choice between public and private ownership is clearly only one of the many licensing decisions which states have to make in regulating their audiovisual media, and in most countries governments award licences on the basis of a wide range of other criteria.[27] The British Broadcasting Act 1990, for example, prohibits certain political and religious bodies from owning broadcasting licences,[28] while Article 16(13) of the Italian legge 223 of 1990 forbids the grant of licences to those previously found guilty of certain offences.[29] One group of operators which have generally been excluded from obtaining broadasting licences are telecommunications companies. In the United States of America telecommunications companies have successfully turned to the courts for assistance, arguing that by excluding them from the video programming sector the government has infringed their freedom of expression.[30] In Europe this issue has yet to receive judicial scrutiny but, with Member States of the European Union required to liberalize their telecommunications sectors by January 1998, and the previously protected state telecommunications monopolies subject to growing competition, recourse to the courts can be envisaged if legislative solutions prove slow to materialize. To date Community initiatives have gone only as far as requiring that cable television networks be permitted to offer telecommunications services,[31] but the Commission has committed itself to reviewing the position of telecommunications operators which wish to provide video programming by January 1998.[32]

If we turn to consider the approach of the Italian Constitutional Court when addressing the legitimacy of ownership restrictions in the private sector, it is apparent that the Court initially considered the discretion of the administrative authorities in awarding private local licences to be limited, designed merely to ensure the rational use of the airwaves and to minimize station interference, particularly to the public channels.[33] Local licences

---

[25] Case 260/89, *Ellinka Radiophonia Tileorassi—Anonimi Etairia* v. *Dimotiki Etairia Pliroforissis* [1991] ECR 2925.

[26] For further discussion see Ch. 6, sect. 3(ii) above.

[27] See, for details, EC Commission (1992), 39 ff. and E. M. Barendt (1993), 85 ff.

[28] Broadcasting Act 1990, Sched. 2, Pt. II, paras. 1–6.

[29] Legge 223 of 1990, Art. 16, paras. 13 and 17.

[30] *Chesapeake and Potomac Telephone Company of Virginia, et al.* v. *US* 830 F Supp. 909 (ED Va 1993). The cross-ownership rules have, however, recently been relaxed under the 1996 Telecommunications Act.   [31] Dir. 95/51/EC [1995] OJ L256/49.

[32] M. Haag (1996), 119.   [33] Dec. 226/1974 [1974] Giur. cost. 1791 at 1800.

took the form of administrative authorizations rather than concessions, and this was widely thought to indicate the prior existence of an individual right. Such a right was, however, firmly rejected by the Constitutional Court in its 1990 ruling,[34] and Article16(1) of legge 223 of 1990 broke with the past in establishing that concessions, rather than authorizations, were to be awarded for both national and local broadcasting services. The legitimacy of this approach was confirmed by the Constitutional Court in Decision 112 of 1993, in which it held that one could not conclude whether or not an individual had a pre-existing legal right merely from the type of licence, administrative authorization, or concession granted.[35]

The early perception of local broadcasting as an expansive resource, offering all those wishing to try their hand an opportunity to broadcast, meant that little attention was given by the Italian Constitutional Court to the principles which might be adopted in selecting applicants. In Decision 202 of 1976 the Court did, however, note the need to ascertain that those granted licences would manage their transmissions 'correctly' and 'responsibly',[36] and in Decision 826 of 1988 it held that it was important that those holding differing opinions should be able to express themselves over the air, arguably opening the door to some administrative selection on the basis of the type of programmes—jazz, political affairs, entertainment, etc.—proposed by prospective candidates.[37] Finally, in Decision 112 of 1993 the Court held that for there to be compliance with Article 21 of the Constitution licences would have to be awarded under conditions which assured maximum objectivity and impartiality, and according to criteria with clearly defined parameters which did not leave too much discretion to the administrative body.[38] It concluded that the selection criteria established in Article 16(17) of Italian legge 223 of 1990, by virtue of which the technical plans, economic potential, and the quality of the proposed service, or past services where the applicant had already been operating, would all be taken into account, did not go beyond these confines and were suitably clear and objective.[39]

Although selection criteria clearly do discriminate among putative broadcasters, it seems that as long as governments can put forward some reasonably plausible justification the courts will be reluctant to overturn

---

[34] Dec. 102/1990 [1990] Giur. cost. 610.

[35] Dec. 112/1993 [1993] Foro it. 1339 at 1352, pt. 10. It may, however, be noted that Art. 3 of the 1990 statute retained a system of authorizations for broadcasters relaying foreign stations, a distinction which was unsuccessfully challenged in this case as contrary to the principle of equality enshrined in Art. 3 of the Constitution.

[36] Dec. 202/1976 [1976] Giur. cost. 1267.

[37] Dec. 826/1988 [1988] Foro it. 2477 at 2495.

[38] Dec. 112/1993 [1993] Foro it. 1339 at 1352.

[39] A finding confirmed in Dec. 420/1994 [1994] Giur. ital. 129 at 141, pt. 12.

them. In Decision 81–129 of 1981 the French Conseil Constitutionnel refused to accept that the provisions of the 1981 broadcasting legislation which restricted the award of radio licences to associations, thereby excluding individual operators, contravened the principle of equality.[40] The European Human Rights Commission in its opinion in *Verein Alternatives Lokalradio Bern* specifically noted that there was often a political element underlying the selection of licensees, and held that the application of 'sensitive political criteria' such as the desire to ensure cultural and liguistic pluralism and to strike a balance between various regions would not render arbitrary the allocation of licences.[41] The wide margin of appreciation enjoyed by states under the European Convention on Human Rights in selecting licensees and imposing operating require-ments was confirmed in the *Lentia* case, where the Commission again noted that state discretion was 'of particular relevance in an area as complex and fluctuating as that of radio and television broadcasting'.[42] The Court itself acknowledged that states could grant *or refuse* licences not merely on technical grounds but could take into account such issues as the quality and balance of programmes and the rights and needs of specific audiences. Any mechanism for selection had, however, to be no more restrictive than necessary to meet the accepted objectives, and states could find themselves open to a charge of discrimination under Article 14 where their selection displayed signs of bias.

Domestic licensing systems, though at first glance a wholly internal matter, may, on further examination, be seen to raise issues of European Community law. One form of selection which Community Member States are prohibited from pursuing is, of course, selection on the basis of Member-State nationality. A Member State which allowed only its own nationals to apply for broadcasting licences would be acting contrary to the principle of non-discrimination in Article 6 of the EC Treaty and the rules on freedom of establishment set out in Articles 52 to 58. The European Commission has argued that national regulations designed to limit the number of television or radio stations any one individual can own are capable, at least where these differ from one country to another, of restricting the freedom of establishment and the freedom to provide services,[43] and there is no apparent reason why provisions which prevent certain categories such as religious or political organizations from holding a licence should in principle be analysed any differently. In both cases such regulations make it impossible for a particular undertaking to obtain an

---

[40] Dec. 81–129 of 30 and 31 Oct. [1981] Rec. Cons. constit. 35.
[41] App. No. 10746/84, *Verein Alternatives Lokalradio Bern* v. *Switzerland*, 49 D & R 126.
[42] *Informationsverein Lentia and others* v. *Austria* (1994) 17 EHRR 93.
[43] EC Commission (1994c), 33; for further discussion see Ch. 7, sect. 5(ii) above.

initial or additional broadcasting licence. As measures which do not discriminate on the basis of nationality but which nevertheless impede the enjoyment of a Community freedom, it would be for the relevant Member State, if such measures were to be referred to the European Court of Justice, to establish that they pursued an objective recognized as legitimate by the Community and were proportionate. Restrictions on the ownership of broadcasting stations by political or religious organizations are imposed to ensure that the information relayed by radio or television stations is both accurate and impartial, and for this reason they constitute a form of consumer protection. The European Court of Justice regards consumer protection to be a legitimate objective which Member States may pursue, even where this leads to the imposition of restrictions on the free movement of goods and services.[44] It is thus probable that the main argument in any case challenging such an ownership ban would turn on the question whether the prohibition was proportionate and whether a less restrictive method of control might have been employed.

3. THIRD-PARTY ACCESS TO TELEVISION AND RADIO STATIONS

Not everyone has the time or resources to run a broadcasting station, and not all those who apply for a licence will obtain one, yet those denied access may still have something interesting or original to say. Alternatively, an individual may wish to reply to a television or radio programme which touches him or her personally. Moreover, as transmission techniques diversify, programme-providers who have traditionally used one method of communication may seek access to alternative facilities in order to maintain their audience reach. This may involve access by 'off-air' broadcasters to cable or satellite systems and the ability to use proprietary encryption technology where this has become the industry standard. Regulations which afford third parties air time clearly restrict the editorial freedom of the station proprietor, one person's access rights becoming, from the perspective of the station owner, onerous content requirements. Whether such provisions are considered acceptable or not by a court of law will ultimately depend on whose interests, those of the station owner or of the individual or group seeking access, the judge considers him- or herself legally bound to prefer.

The Italian Constitutional Court in Decision 225 of 1974 held that the public sector was constitutionally required to make available air time to political, religious, and cultural goups, representative of the various

---

[44] See, e.g., Case C–275/92 *HM Customs and Excise* v. *Schindler* [1994] ECR 1039.

strands of opinion in society.[45] Parliament responded to this by legislation in 1975 which provided for access for representative social groups, an entitlement which was not extended to individuals.[46] Access to the public channels is controlled by the Parliamentary Commission for the supervision of broadcasting services, and it is thought that decisions taken by this body, as a political entity, are not subject to judicial scrutiny or review. The Constitutional Court has, on a number of occasions, avoided determining this jurisdictional point, and the potential absence of review brings into question whether it is at all meaningful to refer, as the Court does for instance in its 1987 Decision, to a 'right of access' under Article 21.[47] In France, too, legislation has awarded access rights to representative groups, the churches, and professional bodies, rather than to individuals. The French Conseil constitutionnel examined the provisions made for third-party access to the public sector in Articles 54 to 56 of the then proposed 1986 broadcasting legislation and considered them adequate to ensure pluralism.[48] Despite the ability in French law to seek review of the broadcasting authorities' award of air-time it cannot, therefore, be said that there exists an *individual* right of access.

The European Human Rights Commission, though denying that Article 10 of the European Convention on Human Rights embraces an individual or, indeed, group right of access, has indicated that there may be a legitimate question concerning compliance with Article 10, in conjunction with Article 14, where there has been a clear act of discrimination against a particular opinion or group.[49] Such an issue would arise, for instance, were one political party to be 'excluded from broadcasting facilities at election time while other parties obtained air time'.[50] Thus, where access has been granted to particular individuals or groups, others may be able to use this as a stepping-stone to air time, even absent an autonomous and direct right of access. The Commission in its opinion in the *Lentia* case also indicated that adequate access facilities should be provided in the public sector where there was no alternative private outlet to which aspiring broadcasters could turn.[51]

In the various countries under examination the question of mandated access to particular delivery systems or proprietary technology is only now

---

[45] Dec. 225/1974 [1974] Giur. cost. 1775.

[46] Legge 103 of 1975. For commentary see R. Lanzillo (1990), 65 ff. and G. Rao (1988), 13.

[47] e.g., in Dec. 194/1987 [1987] Giur. it. 329. For more detailed discussion of access entitlements in Italy see R. Lanzillo (1990), 74 ff. and E. Barendt (1993), 48–9, 150, 155–7, who notes that in Italy viewers' interests are 'institutionally, rather than legally, protected'.

[48] Dec. 86–217 of 18 Sept. 1986 [1986] JO 11294 at 11295.

[49] App. No. 4515/70, *X and Assoc. Z* v. *UK*, 38 Coll. 86.   [50] *Ibid.* 546.

[51] *Informationsverein Lentia and others* v. *Austria* (1994) 17 EHRR 93 at 106.

becoming a major regulatory issue. In the United States of America, however, such issues have for some time received considerable legislative and judicial attention. Most recently cable operators have turned to the courts to challenge the provisions of the Cable Television Consumer Protection and Competition Act 1992, which requires that they devote a portion of their channels to the transmission of local-broadcast television services. In *Turner Broadcasting* a majority of the Supreme Court held that these provisions did not mandate the transmission of particular speech and were thus subject to an intermediate level of judicial review.[52] The District Court, to which the issue was referred back for a final decision, held that Congress, in framing the 'must-carry' rules in order to protect the local broadcasting sector, had drawn reasonable inferences based on substantial evidence.[53] Cable operators tended to be monopoly providers, and because it was now common for them to insert their own advertising into the channels they conveyed or to have interests in cable programmers, there was a clear incentive to drop from their networks broadcasters which competed for advertising revenue. This could have serious repercussions, particularly for public broadcasters working to tight budgets, and there was evidence that significant numbers of local broadcasters had in fact been dropped from the cable networks.

4. CONTENT REQUIREMENTS

If licensee selection is one way of ensuring programme pluralism, content requirements are another. The nature and legitimacy of content regulation has, however, received only patchy and inconclusive judicial analysis, no doubt in large part owing to the widespread and long-established state practice of content regulation. The question can be seen to take two forms: are content requirements *necessary* and are content requirements *legitimate*?

The Italian Constitutional Court held in its 1960 broadcasting decision that it was necessary to regulate the public sector to ensure that its programmes were suitably varied.[54] The Court has continued to endorse this approach, and in its 1988 ruling it confirmed that the public sector should conform to the ideal of 'internal pluralism', operating in such a way that its programmes give voice to the widest possible range of opinions and ideas.[55] Though content requirements have thus been regarded as

---

[52] *Turner Broadcasting Systems, Inc.* v. *FCC* (1994) 114 S Ct. 2445.
[53] *Turner Broadcasting Systems, Inc.* v. *FCC* (1995) 910 F Supp. 734.
[54] Dec. 59/1960 [1960] Giur. cost. 759.
[55] Dec. 826/1988 [1988] Foro it. 2477 at 2499.

imperative in the public sector it appeared, at least initially, that comparable regulation in the private sector would be considered illegitimate. When, therefore, in its 1976 ruling the Court set out those aspects of private broadcasting which required state regulation it focused primarily on technical and not programming matters.[56] The sole recommendation which might be thought to relate to content concerned advertising limits, and this was prompted by a desire to maintain the financial base of both the public broadcasting sector and the printed press. The position, as we saw in Chapter 7, was not entirely clarified by the Court's 1988 ruling, but its emphasis on 'pluralism' as the guiding regulatory principle indicates that the imposition of content requirements in the private sector may in certain circumstances be legitimate. Given the Court's concern to balance, in this context, the interest in pluralism with that of individual expression and the protection of economic enterprise, it seems probable that the level of regulatory intervention regarded as necessary in the public sector would be considered over-intrusive in the private field.[57] In its later 1993 ruling on legge 223 of 1990 the Court upheld the constitutionality of Article 16, which provides for the quality of the proposed programmes to be taken into account when awarding private licences, and requires local broadcasters to dedicate 20 per cent of their weekly programming to local news and programmes of local interest.[58] The Court confirmed that, although private broadcasters enjoyed the protection of Article 41 of the Constitution guaranteeing freedom of economic enterprise, this protection could be limited to prevent Article 21 and its objectives, in particular the provision of diverse and impartial information, being prejudiced.[59] Moreover, Article 41 does not itself provide an absolute guarantee of economic activity, but envisages 'such planning and controls as may be advisable for directing and coordinating public and private economic activities towards social objectives'.

The French Conseil constitutionnel has accepted the legitimacy of content requirements in both the public and private sectors, and has indicated that where there are insufficient broadcasters to provide plural programming or where, for other reasons, this is not forthcoming, then it will be necessary for content requirements to be introduced into the private sector.[60] The Conseil has, however, noted that restrictions on freedom of expression will be legitimate only to the extent they render that freedom

---

[56] Dec. 202/1976 [1976] Giur. cost. 1267. See also Dec. 153/1987 [1987] Giur. cost. 1141 at 1159 for similar indications that only technical restrictions were envisaged.

[57] Dec. 826/1988 [1988] Foro it. 2477 at 2494, pt. 9 and 2499, pt. 19. See also Dec. 420/1994 [1994] Giur. it. 129 at 142, pt. 14.3.

[58] Dec. 112/1993 [1993] Foro it. 1340 at 1352, pt. 11.   [59] *Ibid.* 1353.

[60] Dec. 86–217 of 18 Sept. 1986 [1986] JO 11294 at 11296. For details of the programme requirements imposed on the public and private channels see E. M. Barendt (1995), 108.

more effective or serve to reconcile it with other principles of constitutional value. Content restrictions designed to further pluralism will consequently have to be carefully tailored to that objective and will be open to challenge where, for example, they do not appear to add to the diversity of programmes already available.[61]

Under the European Convention on Human Rights content restrictions imposed on domestic broadcasters to enhance programming pluralism can be justified as designed to protect the rights of others under Article 10(2),[62] and it is now apparent after *Lentia* that a wide range of content requirements, not merely those designed to enhance programme diversity, may be legitimate under the licensing clause of Article 10(1) provided, of course, that they can be shown to be 'necessary in a democratic society'.[63] Thus it is open to states to impose on domestic broadcasters conditions relating to the 'nature and objectives of the proposed station, its potential audience at national, regional or local level [and] the rights and needs of a specific audience'.[64] Despite statements by the European Commission and Court of Human Rights to the effect that the public has a 'right to information', the categorization of pluralism as a restriction on freedom of expression suggests that such measures are merely permissible and not legally required.[65]

With regard to channels broadcast from abroad the *Groppera* decision indicates that the European Court of Human Rights will scrutinize very closely any restrictions imposed on the 'content or tendencies of the programmes concerned'. Though technical specifications may be possible, as well as the exclusion of signals sent from abroad deliberately to circumvent national regulations, the majority of programming requirements appear unlikely to be considered 'necessary in a democratic society'. It is interesting that the 1989 European Convention on Transfrontier Television permits Parties only provisionally to suspend a service from another contracting state where there has been a failure to respect one of a limited number of negative Treaty restrictions on indecent, pornographic, unduly violent, or racist programming, or where scheduling requirements designed to prevent damage to the 'physical, mental or moral development of children and adolescents' have been contravened.[66]

Similarly, under European Community law, the European Court of Justice will consider very carefully any attempt by a Member State to 'export its domestic regulations' by imposing content requirements on

---

[61] Dec. 84–181 of 10 and 11 Oct. 1984 [1984] JO 3200 at 3202.
[62] *Groppera Radio AG* v. *Switzerland* (1990) 12 EHRR 321.
[63] *Informationsverein Lentia and others* v. *Austria* (1994) 17 EHRR 93.
[64] *Ibid.*, para. 32.　　　　　　　　　　[65] See Ch. 7, sect. 5(i) above.
[66] European Treaty Series, No. 132, Art. 7(1) and (2).

foreign broadcasters. Although Member States are currently allowed to introduce non-discriminatory measures which impede the free movement of radio or television services in order to protect the plural nature of their internal audiovisual systems, it is probable that the Court would not consider the imposition of diversity-related programming requirements to be a proportionate method of protection. This is because the foreign stations would themselves be seen as contributing to media diversity by offering views and perspectives additional to those already made available by domestic broadcasters.[67] A parallel may here be drawn with the 1974 Decision of the Italian Constitutional Court which held that a prohibition on the relaying by private operators of foreign channels over Italian territory would result in an undesirable 'national autarchy' of information sources.[68] This view of foreign stations as important additions to domestic services, services which, when faced with issues of national interest may find it difficult to remain critically impartial, appears close to that voiced by the Commission of the European Communities in its 1992 Green Paper on Pluralism and Media Concentration in the Internal Market.[69] Although the imposition on foreign broadcasters of programming requirements designed to enhance diversity would be acceptable under Community law where the foreign broadcaster has deliberately located abroad in an attempt to circumvent the domestic regulations, once the Community has harmonized a particular field Member States can no longer exclude services which conform to the harmonized rules.[70] Member States do, of course, continue to enjoy extensive freedom in regulating their own domestic audiovisual services, though where their regulations are capable of affecting cross-border trade, as in *Commission* v. *Netherlands*, or the freedom of esablishment of operators wishing to relocate from another Member State, they will fall within the ambit of Community law.[71]

What of domestic stations broadcasting abroad? Many states have sought to use international broadcasting to promote their countries' interests abroad, and it is not without significance that BBC World Service Radio is funded by grant from the Foreign Office, not through the licence fee which finances the remaining BBC radio and television services. This desire to ensure good international relations was recognized by the Italian

---

[67] For further discussion of this point see Ch. 7, sect. 5(ii) above.

[68] Dec. 225/1974 [1974] Giur. cost. 1775 at 1788. The Constitutional Court's willingness to accept some restrictions on foreign *advertising*, though not a total ban, on the basis that this was a business enterprise, not speech activity, could be seen as hinting that restrictions on foreign *programme* content would not have been considered constitutionally acceptable: Dec. 231/1985 [1985] Giur. cost. 1879.

[69] EC Commission (1992), 75.

[70] *Forbrukerombudet* v. *Mattel Scandinavia A/S and Lego Norge A/S* [1996] 1 CMLR 313.

[71] Case C–353/89, *EC Commission* v. *Netherlands* [1991] ECR I–4069.

Constitutional Court in its 1987 Decision, in which it indicated that programming policies could be taken into account when awarding or revoking foreign broadcasting authorizations.[72] Somewhat more disconcerting is the observation made by the Court that the Italian state had no responsibility to meet the information needs of citizens living outside its territory.[73] Although the European Community's 1989 Television Directive and the European Convention On Transfrontier Television[74] set out certain minimum requirements to which states must ensure all national broadcasters, in the case of the Directive, or all national broadcasters with a foreign remit in the case of the Convention, conform, there is little economic or political incentive for the imposition of more demanding content requirements on those domestic broadcasters who aim to target a foreign audience: the financial gains made by transborder broadcasting havens may be considerable, as the importance of the satellite industry for the Luxembourg economy illustrates. Although cross-border stations may indeed provide new and varied programming, the possibility that they may also escape all but the most basic level of regulation should not be overlooked when examining the future of Europe's audiovisual media.

But what sort of programme content have the various courts under consideration indicated to be desirable? The guides given have tended to be very general, with, as we have seen, calls for impartiality, objectivity, completeness, balance, honesty, and, of course, pluralism. The European Human Rights Commission in the *Lentia* case indicated that Article 10 of the European Convention on Human Rights did not require each programme to provide a diverse range of opinions: 'one-sided programmes must be possible wherever a sufficient number of frequencies is available'.[75] Both the Italian and French Constitutional Courts have called for the widest possible reflection of the political, social, and cultural thought present in their societies and, in expressing these general principles, they have given legal support to key elements of the established public-service broadcasting ethic. As we saw in Chapter 4, the public sector has sought to justify its position by recourse to a set of particular goals, goals which it has come to claim as particularly its own. On this theory those broadcasters who do not share these aspirations cannot be said to be truly performing a public service, whatever their means of financial support or constitutional structure.[76] These goals have ranged from the production of diverse

---

[72] Dec. 153/1987 [1987] Giur. cost. 1141, at 1158 and 1159.   [73] *Ibid*. 1154.
[74] Dir. 89/552/EEC [1989] OJ L298/23 and European Treaty Series No. 132, edn. Apr. 1990.
[75] *Informationsverein Lentia and others* v. *Austria* (1994) 17 EHRR 93 at 106.
[76] With the public-service broadcasting concept no longer turning on ownership, the relative and potentially subjective nature of certain of the indicative criteria has led to arguments over which stations can legitimately be classified as being of a 'public-service'

programmes—minority as well as mainstream, educational and entertaining as well as informational—to the fostering of national, regional, and community identity, and to high standards of accuracy, responsibility, and independence in reporting. This expansive appreciation of what at least a part of the audiovisual sector should offer is reflected in much of the rhetoric to be found in the decisions of the French and Italian Constitutional Courts, not least in the Italian Court's refusal, in its 1988 Decision, to distinguish news and information from other entertainment services. The Court rejected the suggestion that entertainment programmes fell outside the protection afforded by Article 21 of the Constitution, holding that it understood the term 'information' in a wide and comprehensive sense, embracing all television messages whether of an informational or cultural nature.[77]

Nevertheless, it is apparent that there are certain categories of speech which states are not only not required to provide but are actually allowed to prohibit. Although such speech undoubtedly adds to the diversity of views expressed in the mass media, the fear of social or individual damage has led to its proscription. Not only are there the familiar restrictions on programmes considered obscene, racist, an affront to religious sensitivities, or likely to damage children, but there are also extensive restrictions on television advertising.[78] The various courts under examination have proved willing to tolerate such restrictions, so much so that in 1981 the French Conseil constitutionnel accepted as legitimate the then complete prohibition on private-sector advertising.[79] In 1985 the Italian Constitutional Court, though refusing to accept as legitimate a total ban on all advertising carried on foreign stations relayed over Italy, nevertheless held that advertising did not enjoy the protection afforded to individual expression by Article 21 of the Constitution. Advertising was instead categorized as an 'economic activity' falling within the scope of Article 41, and therefore open to state regulation to further 'social objectives'.[80]

A similar reluctance to place advertising on the same footing as other forms of broadcasting expression is evident at the European level. The Human Rights Commission, though accepting that commercial statements

---

nature. This classification may be important in obtaining certain financial or other benefits, such as entitlement to membership of the EBU and consequent access to the Eurovision system of programme exchange.

[77] Dec. 826/1988 [1988] Foro it. 2477 at 2499.

[78] For detailed consideration of advertising restrictions and constitutional rights in Europe see W. Skouris (ed.) (1994).

[79] Dec. 81–129 of 30 and 31 Oct. 1981 [1981] Rec. Cons. constit. 35. The complainants had argued that the ban interfered with the freedoms not only of expression and association but also of economic enterprise. The Court did not analyse these claims, merely holding that no principle of constitutional value served to impede the ban.

[80] Dec. 231/1985 [1985] Giur. cost. 1879.

could be covered by Article 10 of the Human Rights Convention, has also indicated that commercial speech enjoys a reduced level of protection. In *Markt Intern and Beerman* v. *Germany*, a case which in fact concerned an information bulletin for retailers rather than an advertisement, the Commission suggested that the test of 'necessity' in Article 10(2) could be less strict when applied to commercial advertising.[81] It is undoubtedly the case that European states have traditionally imposed extensive restrictions on both the timing and content of advertisements, and certain of these restrictions were upheld by the European Court of Justice during the course of the 1980s, even though their capacity for disrupting cross-border broadcasts was becoming increasingly apparent. In its 1980 *Debauve* decision the Court held that a Member State retained a residual power 'to regulate, restrict or even totally prohibit television advertising on its territory on grounds of general interest',[82] though the subsequent *Bond van Adverteerders* judgment revealed that such prohibitions would be subject to careful scrutiny by the Court when assessing their proportionality under Community law.[83] It was these cases which spurred the European Commission to propose a threshold approximation of certain national advertising rules, and the resultant 1989 Television Directive was designed to prevent advertising regulations being used to impede the development of a pan-European broadcast market.[84]

5. CHECKING INSTITUTIONAL AND INDIVIDUAL POWER:
PROTECTION FROM STATE INTERVENTION AND UNDUE
CONCENTRATIONS OF MEDIA OWNERSHIP

Judicial calls for the introduction of access entitlements and programming regulations requiring impartial and accurate reporting reflect a more general concern to ensure that neither public nor private operators subvert the media message for their own partisan ends. In the context of public broadcasting the Italian Constitutional Court in its 1974 decision went beyond the question of third-party access to call for important structural reforms designed to make RAI more democratically accountable. Among the 'seven commandments' established by the Court was the requirement that the public sector be free from government intervention and subject to

---

[81] *Markt Intern and Beerman* v. *Germany* (1990) 11 EHRR 212. For argument that Art. 10 should embrace commercial speech see A. Lester and D. Pannick (1985), while R. H. Coase (1977), D. Kellner (1990), and P. P. de Win (1989) discuss the informational and cultural role played by advertising.

[82] Case 52/79, *Procureur du Roi* v. *Debauve* [1980] ECR 833 at 857.

[83] Case 352/85, *Bond van Adverteerders and Others* v. *The Netherlands* [1989] 3 CMLR 113.   [84] Dir. 89/552/EEC [1989] OJ L298/23.

adequate parliamentary supervision. On this occasion the judicial call for political action found a rapid statutory response in legge 103 of 1975.[85] Similar concerns can be detected in the French 1986 decision in which the Conseil emphasized that members of government were constitutionally precluded from being appointed to the audiovisual regulatory body, Article 23 of the 1958 Constitution prohibiting government members from any public employment or professional activity.[86]

It has, however, been in the private sector that courts of law have shown themselves increasingly willing to set ground rules for market competition in an attempt to prevent undue individual influence in the transmission of ideas. The early Italian broadcasting cases were characterized by a marked distrust of private power and the call for adequate antitrust provision has been a continuous theme running through the case law of the Constitutional Court. Moreover, the Court has expressed concern about concentrations in ownership, not only in discrete media sectors, for example, in the cable field, but also in connection with holdings across the whole range of media activities embracing, for example, both print and audiovisual outlets.[87] The Court in its 1981 judgment made specific reference to the need to consider also those operating in the advertising sector, the sale of advertising having become a key tool in the hands of companies seeking to entrench their position in the Italian media field.[88] In particular, the Constitutional Court noted with concern the absorption of local broadcasting outlets by powerful operators to form regional or national networks, and in 1988 called for certain broadcasting frequencies and advertising revenues to be 'ring-fenced' to protect local broadcasting from such attacks.[89]

The expression of these general concerns, however does little more than point to areas for legislative attention, and the Italian Court has provided very little by way of concrete guidance on the exact level of concentration which can be tolerated under the Constitution. The 1988 Decision, for example, merely confirmed the illegality of a polarized industry in which a public sector was 'balanced' by a private sector completely in the hands of, or dominated by, one individual. But it may well be unrealistic to expect courts of law to provide this level of precision, limited as they are in terms of their ability to analyse market trends and predict how different levels of market concentration will actually affect the range of programmes available to the public. It will also be easier for a court to provide specific

---

[85] Legge 103 of 1975. For commentary see R. Lanzillo (1990), 65 ff. and G. Rao (1988), 13.
[86] Dec. 86–217 of 18 Sept. 1986 [1986] JO 11294.
[87] See, e.g., Dec. 826/1988 [1988] Foro it. 2477 at 2498.
[88] Dec. 148 of 21 July 1981 [1981] Giur. cost. 1379 at 1408.
[89] Dec. 826/1988 [1988] Foro it. 2477 at 2499.

guidance when there is legislation already in place which requires evaluation. In its 1994 ruling the Italian Constitutional Court indicated that although it was not possible to isolate one, constitutionally mandated, set of ownership controls, it was not reduced to the role of a mere government cipher and would check to ensure that any regulations in place were designed to further the objective of pluralism. In examining the specific antitrust provisions included in legge 223 of 1990 the Court concluded that to allow one individual to own three out of the nine national channels allocated to private undertakings was to 'underestimate' the required level of diversity. Though affording the recipient of such licences a strong economic position the statute did not take sufficient account of the need to ensure that the 'maximum possible number of voices' gained access to the airwaves. It was consequently impermissible for the government merely to endorse the existing factual position under which one organization enjoyed an exorbitant advantage through its use of frequencies and ability to obtain advertising revenues. The Court left to the legislature the task of formulating a new set of antitrust regulations, with the warning that to allow one company to own a quarter of the available networks would be constitutionally unacceptable.[90] At the time of writing in the summer of 1996 the Italian government has just referred new legislative proposals to the Parliament, the existing rules being again extended until January 1997. The proposals reduce the limit on ownership for national hertzian channels from 25 to 20 per cent, and include new restrictions on the percentage of advertising revenues which operators in the various audiovisual sectors will be allowed to obtain.[91] If implemented they would require the Mediaset company to release one of its hertzian channels and would probably result in one of its three national television channels moving onto satellite.

The French Conseil constitutionnel has provided rather more detailed guidance on the nature of the antitrust provisions which are necessitated by the Constitution.[92] Like its Italian counterpart the Conseil constitutionnel regards the constitutional imperative of pluralism to require the adoption of effective measures to prevent any given entity from dominating either the audiovisual sector taken in isolation or the whole range of communication activities from print to cable. In this the Conseil's emphasis differed from that of the 1986 Chirac government, favourable to a degree of media concentration in order to place the French audiovisual industry in a strong

---

[90] Dec. 420/1994 [1994] Giur. it. 129 at 142–3.

[91] Details of the proposals which would establish a new Authority to regulate the whole of the Italian communications sector and specific antitrust provisions for radio and television can be found in *Il Sole* of 18 July 1996.

[92] Proposals which, after amendment on the basis of the Conseil constitutionnel's decision, were to become loi 86–1067 of 30 Sept. 1986 [1986] JO 11755.

competitive position internationally and to attract foreign investment. The proposals for loi 86–1067 if 1986 had been drafted to allow a 'flexible' response which, in the view of the Conseil constitutionnel, contained a number of loopholes easily exploitable by determined private operators, just as the regulatory uncertainty in Italy during the 1970s and early 1980s had been ruthlessly exploited by the Fininvest company. The areas highlighted by the Conseil included the failure to prevent an individual from holding up to 25 per cent of the capital in any number of national television services; that there were no restrictions on accumulating shareholdings in any number of regional television services; that there were no restrictions on the number of cable authorizations a given entity could acquire; that long wave radio had not been covered; that there was nothing to prevent the cumulation of radio and television authorizations; and that it remained possible for an individual to form a *de facto* national television network through linking local authorizations.[93] New antitrust provisions were formulated to meet these criticisms, the Conseil having successfully pushed the government into adopting a more stringent and sophisticated mechanism for the control of concentrations.[94] The importance of the role played by the Conseil constitutionnel in this development was acknowledged by M. Gouteyron, *rapporteur* for the November proposals in the Senate when he said '*[c]ertes, ce projet de loi est formellement, au sens étymologique du mot, d'origine gouvernmentale, mais son véritable auteur, c'est en quelque sorte le Conseil constitutionnel*'.[95]

It may be noted that the Conseil was rather less demanding when considering the level of *internal* diversity to be required within a given broadcasting organization as opposed to the extent to which a particular entity might diversify its ownership across a number of distinct media outlets. It chose not to overturn the government's flotation strategy for TF1, which permitted 50 per cent of the shares to be sold in a single block, despite the fact that this placed in the hands of one group of shareholders the dominant national television channel, reaching 40 per cent of the television audience. The Conseil noted that the purchasing group had in fact to be composed of at least two distinct individual or corporate entities; that the remaining 50 per cent of the shares were allocated either to company workers or to the public at large; and that there was scope to ensure a plural programming schedule under the terms of the *cahier des charges*. Nor was TF1 considered to be a monopoly within the terms of the

---

[93] Dec. 86–217 of 18 Sept. 1986 [1986] JO 11294 at 11297.
[94] New Arts. 39, 41, and 41–1 were subsequently inserted into loi 86–1067 of 30 Sept. 1986 by loi 86–1210 of 27 Nov. 1986 [1986] JO 14297.
[95] Quoted in B. Delcros and B. Vodan (1987b), 8: 'Certainly, this legal proposal is formally, in the etymological sense of the word, of governmental origin, but its real author is in a way the Conseil constitutionnel.'

ninth paragraph of the preamble to the 1946 Constitution: the Conseil here refused to distinguish the public and private broadcasting sectors, seeing them both as part of a single, unified broadcasting market. The Conseil constitutionnel thus noted that there remained other competing national television stations in the public sector and that there was also scope to license new private television stations in the future.[96]

There is little to indicate that the European Court of Human Rights considers the European Convention on Human Rights to require the adoption by contracting states of measures designed to control media concentrations, though, as we have seen, the Commission of Human Rights has held that Article 10 of the Convention imposes on states 'a duty' to protect against excessive press concentrations.[97] Within the European Community it has been the Commission, rather than the Court of Justice, which has been the focus of attention in the context of media concentrations. Recent indications suggest that the Commission will put forward proposals prohibiting individuals from acquiring radio or television stations where this will give them over 30 per cent of the audience share for that particular medium, and that individuals who own a mixture of radio, television, and newspaper outlets will also be restricted from increasing their interests, where this would lead them to command an average audience share across these media in excess of 10 per cent. At the time of writing no firm text had been adopted by the Commission, and it is not impossible that these limits may be varied in the course of further negotiations. Public-service broadcasters were particularly concerned by the indications in the 1992 Green Paper on Media Pluralism that common concentration thresholds might be applied to both public and private operators.[98] They argued that such an approach fails to take into account the specific obligations which public-service broadcasters are required to fulfil, such as universal coverage and the provision of a varied and impartial service. The imposition of these requirements prevents their success in the audience ratings from constituting a genuine threat to pluralism.[99] There are indications that any future Commission proposal for a directive will contain a provision allowing Member States to exclude certain 'non-profit-making' organizations from its scope, though public-service broadcasters will undoubtedly wish to have further clarification of what exactly is meant by 'non-profit-making', given that they are all involved in a certain level of commercial activity, if only the sale of programme rights.

[96] Dec. 86–217 of 18 Sept. 1986 [1986] JO 11294 at 11297–8.
[97] App. No. 5178/71, *De Geillustreerde Pers NV* v. *Netherlands*, 8 D & R 5.
[98] EC Commission (1992), 106.
[99] A concern taken up by the European Parliament: see, e.g., para. 1(g) of its Res. on the Commission Green Paper 'Pluralism and Media Concentration in the Internal Market': A3–0435/93.

6. COMPETITION AND PUBLIC SERVICE IN AN
EXPANDING MARKETPLACE

Across Europe the established public-service broadcasters are undergoing a difficult period of transition. Like all operators they are having to assess the impact of technological innovation and the gradual erosion of national boundaries, but they have also to determine whether the pursuit of their traditional objectives is either meaningful, or indeed possible, in an increasingly competitive environment. In the past this process of reappraisal has been fuelled by the desire to maintain political support when licenses have been renewed or to stave off popular disatisfaction with an increase in the licence fee. Now, however, the pressure to substantiate and provide quantifiable criteria by which public-service broadcasting can be identified is coming not from politicians, the public, or even broadcasters, but from courts of law applying competition rules. The main focus of attention has centred around the application of European Community competition law, the key provisions of which are directly effective in Member-State courts, and which are also monitored and enforced by the European Commission in accordance with Council Regulation 17.[100]

A central objective of the EC Treaty is the facilitation of trade between the various Member States 'in accordance with the principle of an open market economy with free competition' (Article 3a(1)). The Treaty is thus built around the presumption that all operators in a particular market are to compete on equal terms whatever their nationality, objectives, or mode of ownership. This is particularly apparent from Article 90, which provides, in its first paragraph, that Member States, when regulating public undertakings and undertakings enjoying special or exclusive rights, are to ensure that the rules on free movement and competition are respected. Although the second paragraph of Article 90 states that revenue-producing monopolies and undertakings providing services of general economic interest may be allowed to derogate from these provisions where conformity would impede the realization of their particular tasks, this is framed in terms of a limited derogation from the normal application of Community competition rules, the paragraph confirming for good measure that '[t]he development of trade must not be affected to such an extent as would be contrary to the interests of the Community'. This apparent reluctance to accept the desirability of applying distinct rules when considering the activities of operators charged with performing a public-service is in marked contrast to the approach to public service provision in countries such as France, where state intervention to further the 'general

[100] [1959–62] OJ Spec.Ed. 87.

interest' has been regarded as a central tool in the realization of republican values.[101]

There is certainly scant direct reference within the Treaty to a category of public-service objectives. The provisions on transport mention 'certain obligations inherent in the concept of a public service' (Article 77) and, as we have noted, Article 90(2) uses the term 'services of general economic interest', but this is all. This limited and provisional recognition has led to calls for an amendment of the Treaty to include a specific Article acknowledging that Member States remain free to establish services in the general interest where these are justified by considerations of economic efficiency, consumer protection, social cohesion, or sustainable development.[102] The concerns identified as supporting state intervention, such as consumer protection and social cohesion, in fact find recognition in a number of existing Treaty provisions (Articles 129a and 130a) and serve as a reminder that the Community embraces a range of objectives which extends well beyond the simple facilitation of intra-Community trade.

It has been suggested that the reference to 'services of general *economic* interest' in Article 90(2) was selected in an attempt to distance the Treaty from the ideological baggage carried by the phrase 'public service', to introduce a degree of 'neutrality', and to avoid using a term the meaning of which varies from one Member State to another.[103] Public services have been established to meet the social as well as economic needs of citizens, and the specific reference to 'economic' appears to call into question the legitimacy of these wider aims. From this perspective the substitution of one phrase for another can hardly be considered to further a 'neutral' approach. Nevertheless, it is now apparent that certain characteristics indicative of a 'service of general economic interest' are similar to elements thought to underpin the notion of 'public service'. Recent rulings of the European Court of Justice suggest that the provision of services designed to satisfy an important social need, on a universal basis, at a uniform tariff, and of consistent quality, are factors which point to a 'service of general economic interest' within Article 90(2).[104] The Commission of the European Communities in its 1993 Decision concerning the EBU Eurovision system concluded that 'public mission broadcasters operating under statutory obligations assigned to them by an act of public authority'

---

[101] R. Kovar (1996); M. Voisset (1995).

[102] Centre Européen des Entreprises à Participation Publique (1995), annexe 1.

[103] R. Kovar (1996), 221. CEEP (1995) 43, has suggested that services of general economic interest should be required to respect a certain number of the following obligations: continuity of service, equality of access to users, and equality of treatment, efficiency, quality, adaptability, transparency, and openings for consumer and citizen participation in, e.g., the setting of programming objectives.

[104] Case C–320/91, *Paul Corbeau* [1993] ECR I–2533.

might be regarded as having been entrusted with services of general economic interest.[105] The Commission did not, however, consider that fulfilment of their particular remit, namely 'the provision of varied and balanced programming for all sections of the population, including a certain amount of sport, and the acquisition of the relevant television rights' would be rendered impossible by compliance with the competition rules. The EBU was consequently unable to rely on the special derogation contained in Article 90(2) and the Eurovision system was examined for compliance with the Community competition rules.

In applying Article 85 of the EC Treaty, which prohibits agreements or concerted practices which prevent, restrict, or distort competition within the common market, to the Eurovision system, the Commission concluded that the scheme in fact restricted competition between the EBU members, since they refrained from bidding against one another while Eurovision negotiations were under way. It also distorted competition with regard to non-EBU members, excluded from participating in the rationalization and cost-savings of the Eurovision system. The Commission was, however, prepared to grant the scheme an exemption under Article 85(3) on the basis that it facilitated the joint acquisition and sharing of rights. Transaction costs were reduced, since EBU members did not have to enter into separate negotiations for rights, and there were various cost-savings inherent in the system of programme exchanges under which the EBU member covering the sporting event in question provided its signal free of charge to other members. Consumers across Europe gained access to 'more, and higher quality' sports programmes and the restrictions on competition were held to be indispensable for attainment of these benefits, provision having been made for non-EBU members to purchase the rights to deferred transmission.

On review, the Decision was annulled by the Court of First Instance, which concluded that the Commission had wrongly taken into account factors which, though appropriate in the context of Article 90(2), were not automatically relevant when deciding whether or not to grant an exemption under Article 85(3).[106] These factors were the public-service obligations of EBU members, in particular the 'obligation to provide varied programming including cultural, educational, scientific and minority programes without any commercial appeal and to cover the entire national population irrespective of the costs'.[107] The judgment is not entirely

---

[105] Dec. 93/403/EEC, *Re the Application of the European Broadcasting Union* (Case IV/ 32.150) [1995] 4 CMLR 56, at paras. 78–9 on which see also Ch. 6, sect. 3(ii) above.
[106] Joined Cases T–528/93, T–542/93, T–543/93, and T–546/93, *Métropole Télévision SA, and others* v. *EC Commission*, [1996] 5 CMLR 386.
[107] *Ibid.*, para. 116.

satisfactory on this point, since the imposition of such obligations may not be entirely unconnected with the desire to improve the production or distribution of goods within Article 85(3). Moreover, the Court went on to hold that 'considerations connected with the pursuit of the public interest' could be relevant when deciding whether or not to grant an exemption under Article 85, but did not provide any indication of the sort of public-interest considerations it had in mind. What does, however, come across clearly from the judgment is a general antagonism to the deployment of public-service considerations in the context of Article 85 and a commitment to ensuring that both the positive and negative requirements of Article 85(3) are made out in full by the Commission and supported with concrete economic data.

It is this call for the application of tight criteria and the provision of convincing evidential support for the grant of any exemption from the competition rules which pose a considerable challenge to public-service broadcasters. The Court of First Instance concluded that the Commission had not convincingly established that it was 'indispensable' for EBU members to obtain exclusive sports rights in order to obtain a fair return on their investment. It was not enough to argue that 'the "concept of fair returns cannot be expressed as a precise figure" but corresponds instead to an "overall financial equilibrium on the part of broadcasters" ': a minimum number of actual economic data was required.[108] It is not immediately apparent what the implications of preventing the Eurovision system from obtaining exclusive rights to sporting events would be, but one possible outcome could be the transfer of exclusive rights to the commercial sector. Given the present level of concern over key sporting events being accessible solely on channels with restricted reach or on pay-per-view terms,[109] the ultimate resolution of this dispute may be the establishment of a list of European 'heritage sporting events' over which neither commercial nor public broadcasters enjoy exclusivity. The British government adopted an approach along these lines in Part IV of the 1996 Broadcasting Act which prohibits the grant of exclusive contracts for televising sporting events of national interest.

A second problem for the EBU is that the Court of First Instance also concluded that the Commission had failed to consider, as it was required to do, whether the EBU's membership criteria were established with sufficient clarity. The Court found that the public-service obligations set

---

[108] *Ibid.*, paras. 118–20.

[109] See, e.g., the European Parliament (1996). Art. 9 of the 1989 European Convention on Transfrontier Television, European Treaty Series No. 132, calls on contracting parties to examine legal measures to 'avoid the right of the public to information being undermined due to the exercise by a broadcaster of exclusive rights for the transmission or retransmission . . . of an event of high public interest'.

out in Article 3(3) of the EBU statutes relating to coverage of the population, programming, and programme production were vague and imprecise, leaving too great a scope for subjective application. For public-service broadcasters to gain exemption from the competition rules for co-ordinated activities there must be no possibility that broadcasters which are really commercial operators with no genuine public-service commitment might gain access to their privileged scheme, or that others who in fact perform a public-service might be excluded. Public-service broadcasting objectives are frequently expressed in imprecise and aspirational terms, to provide, for example, a 'range of programmes', and the impact of this decision could well lead to the adoption of tighter and more readily quantifiable criteria.

Finally, the Court held that if the Commission, in granting an exemption under Article 85(3), did take into account, contrary to the Court's own indications that this would be impermissible, the public-service mission of EBU members, it was also required to consider any financial assistance which public broadcasters receive in furtherance of these objectives, such as licence fee revenue, loans, etc. It is not immediately apparent, however, why this consideration should be relevant in the context of an examination under Article 85(3), where the primary concern is to ensure that the challenged agreement improves the production or distribution of goods, or promotes technical or economic progress. The manner in which the relevant undertakings are financed seems to be more relevant to an examination under Article 92, the EC Treaty Article specifically concerned with state aids, and this, indeed, had been the argument put forward by the European Commission. Given the uncertainties which remain after the Court of First Instance's decision and its wide-ranging implications for public-service broadcasters, it is possible that the EBU will seek further clarification through an appeal to the European Court of Justice.

The reference by the European Commission to Article 92 of the EC Treaty in the EBU case serves as a reminder that the activities of public-service broadcasters may come to be scrutinized under a number of different Community competition rules. One of the principal complaints raised by commercial broadcasters is that public-service broadcasters have obtained 'double funding', 'private' finance from advertising and 'public' finance from licence fees and subsidies, which places them at a competitive advantage. These concerns are potentially extremely wide-ranging in that there are very few public-service broadcasters, the BBC being a rare example, which survive without advertising revenues on the basis of licence fees, though it should be noted that even the BBC obtains commercial income from the sale of programme rights, related books, magazines, and merchandise. Article 92(1) prohibits 'any aid granted by a Member State or through State resources in any form whatsoever which distorts or threatens to distort competition by favouring certain undertakings', though certain forms of aid may be considered compatible with the Treaty including 'aid to promote culture and heritage conservation where such aid does not affect trading conditions and competition in the Community to an extent that is contrary to the common interest' (Article 92(3)(d)). The sort of aid capable of falling within Article 92 is extensive and comprises the receipt of licence-fee revenues, other financial subsidies, low interest loans, even authorizations to run budget deficits.

The Commission of the European Communities has received complaints from a number of commercial broadcasters in France, Portugal, and Spain concerning anti-competitive practices, among them the grant of financial assistance to public-service broadcasters. The complaint by the French broadcaster TF1 alleged that state aid had been received by public broadcasters F2 and F3 in the form of licence fees, specific grants of money, and deficit authorizations. This aid could not be justified as compensation to the public channels for their particular public-service remit because, argued TF1, the programming obligations of all three channels were roughly the same. Clearly, where radio or television stations are subject to similar advertising limits and programming requirements, yet one station benefits from additional public finance, that undertaking will enjoy an anti-competitive advantage. The situation is, however, somewhat more complex where the broadcaster in receipt of public finance is required to fulfil particular public-service obligations which are not imposed on the commercial broadcaster, or where its advertising revenue is comparatively restricted. If it is possible for states to justify the grant of financial aid in order to further public-service objectives, and Article 92(3)(d) seems to indicate that it might, how does one evaluate the cost of meeting these public-service objectives in order to ensure that the finance provided is not excessive? Many public-service broadcasters would argue that it is not possible to divide up their transmissions into those parts which are 'public-service' in nature and those which are not: instead, *all* their programmes are produced and scheduled to provide a service which at times informs, at times educates, and at times entertains. Yet the implications of these complaints seem to be that the broadcasters in receipt of aid will be required to establish that the finance they receive matches the cost of the particular public-services they are required to provide.

Faced with these difficulties the European Commission arranged for further research to be carried out into the feasibility of such calculations. Brian Sturgess and a group of researchers at Putnam, Hayes & Bartlett reported in 1995, but concluded that measuring the costs of meeting public-service obligations was extremely difficult: broadcasters were apparently unwilling to divulge sensitive information, and public broadcasters 'lacked the necessary internal systems of management accounting to identify specific costs systematically'. Moreover, it was noted that many public-service obligations are expressed in very general terms, so that it is impossible to determine their real impact on costs. The authors were thus led to conclude that 'the proposition that public-service obligations place additional operating costs upon public broadcasters is not testable in a meaningful way across or within the Member States of the European Union'.

However difficult it may be to calculate the costs of public-service obligations, the Commission is nevertheless required to respond to the complaints referred to it, and there can be little doubt that public-service broadcasters will be under increasing pressure to provide convincing data to establish that they have not been recipients of state aid contrary to Article 92. Moreover, those public-service broadcasters which have entered into commercial ventures to increase their overall revenue will need to ensure that financial assistance provided by the state for public-service activities is not used to cross-subsidize their commercial activities.[110]

---

[110] See, e.g., the steps taken by the BBC to address these concerns in its 'Fair Trading Commitment': BBC (1995).

9

Conclusion: An Appraisal of Judicial Intervention in the Audiovisual Sector

> If social justice would be improved by a less commodified society, then, rather than walling off a few transactions from the pure free market, we should seek to deepen and consolidate the nonmarket countercurrents that cut across the market.[1]

The preceding discussion will have highlighted the many areas of audiovisual regulation in which courts of law have become involved. Their development of the principle of pluralism, awareness of the possible ways in which both public and private power might be abused, and concern for adequate competition across the print and audiovisual media represents a judicial contribution of no small moment. But it is necessary in this final Chapter to stand back and ask how effective judicial involvement in the audiovisual sector has been, or can be, in practice.

The first point to consider is whether courts of law are adequately equipped in terms of access to information and professional expertise to provide regulatory guidelines for the audiovisual field. The technical complexity, rapid evolution, and interlocking nature of the various communication industries exacerbates what in other sectors might seem relatively straightforward regulatory issues. In this respect the judicial process has not always facilitated a proper understanding of the audiovisual industry or the wider ramifications of any given decision. This is illustrated by the 1974 Italian broadcasting case in which the Constitutional Court misunderstood the international system of frequency allocation, despite the importance this system held for the ultimate decision.[2] Greater familiarization with the subject matter clearly reduces the likelihood of such technical confusion being repeated, but the audiovisual world continues to undergo dynamic change, and not only have courts to understand this change, they must also attempt to evaluate the impact which *their* decisions will have on the sector's future development.

The difficulties faced by courts in assessing the dynamics of market development in the context of a specific dispute are illustrated by the 1974

---

[1] M. J. Radin (1989), 178.   [2] Dec. 225/1974 [1974] Giur. cost. 1775.

Italian cable case.[3] Here the Constitutional Court concluded, following information supplied by the Consiglio superiore tecnico delle tele-comunicazioni, that although there was a risk of monopoly in the provision of national cable services, this was not so at the local level, where costs were such that a plurality of competing services could be envisaged. The very nature of cable provision, however, militates against competing services in the same area: the cost and upheaval of laying cable lines along urban streets will lead cable companies to aim to connect the maximum number of households on any given road with the street branch line, avoiding dissipation to competing services.[4] Eli Noam has argued that although there are economies of scale at the level of technical distribution these are moderate, and that the more important factor favouring local cable monopolies is the existence of economies of scope. Where the same firm not only owns the technical infrastructure but also plans and provides the programming services, it can take advantage of existing goodwill, sunk costs, and an ability to cut prices fairly rapidly to warn off potential competition.[5] Moreover, the multichannel nature of cable provision means that any given cable operator has a substantial programme turnover and, owing to the high costs of programme production, will tend to rely heavily on bought-in or satellite programming. Increasing competition for these programmes from additional cable services, and also, of course, from direct broadcasting and microwave services, will inevitably push up programme costs, possibly to the point at which further competition becomes uneconomic. The negative costs of audiovisual competition— heavy promotional expenditure, increased programme prices—under-pinned the merger of the two British satellite services, BSB and Sky, in 1990 after both sides experienced heavy financial losses.[6]

Although the economics of multichannel competition are extremely complex, and there are certainly examples of cable companies 'over-building' networks in the same area, this has, to date, been a relatively rare occurrence. The *economic* significance of this state of affairs should not, however, be exaggerated, for *industrial policy aspirations* and the ability to extract collateral benefits from monopoly operators have led regulators to restrict cable entry to one operator per area, and to capitulate to industry demands for vertical integration of the transmission and programming stages.[7] Such competition as there is within the cable industry thus tends to

---

[3] Dec. 226/1974 [1974] Guir. cost. 1791.

[4] See brief summary of empirical evidence in M. O. Wirth and L. Cobb-Reiley (1987), 404, n. 1.   [5] E. M. Noam (ed.) (1985).

[6] For a general overview of these events see 'The end of BSB' in [1990] *Cable and Satellite Europe*, Dec., 16.

[7] M. O. Wirth and L. Cobb-Reiley (1987) note that the US Cable Act of 1984 permitted municipalities to extract not only 'direct' taxes from cable operators in the form of franchise

focus on the right of 'first entry'.[8] In the light of the foregoing observations the Italian Court's vision of competing 'local' cable services seems at the very least debatable and to raise the perplexing question whether, on its own reasoning at the time, such cable services should not have been placed in public, rather than private, hands.

Nor is this an isolated example, for other judicial conclusions appear equally challengeable, particularly the Italian Constitutional Court's assumption that maximization of 'external pluralism' in the private sector would enhance programme diversity.[9] The view that an increase in competition will of itself lead to greater consumer choice is by no means universally accepted and is brought into question by certain of the strategies adopted by commercial broadcasters to protect their share of the radio and television market.[10] Jay G. Blumler, in a study of the impact of increased competition on American television, concludes that although there has been both a quantitative and qualitative increase in consumer choice, certain non-commercial concerns have been sidelined, there has been a tendency to avoid complexity in news reporting, and those programme genres which are expensive to make but which attract small audiences, educational and documentary programming, for example, are under-represented.[11] The battle for revenue has already toughened attitudes to programme provision in the British market: during the course of 1993, for example, senior ITV directors suggested that current affairs programmes would only survive, whatever their other merits, if they achieved ratings of six to eight million, while ITV's proposal to move the 10.00 pm news forward to 6.30 pm in order to leave the mid-evening free to schedule more lucrative films and drama was dropped only after concerted pressure had been exerted by both the ITC and British Prime Minister.[12] In similar vein, Jacques Chevallier noted at the time of the 1989 French broadcasting legislation: '*[l]'existence de cinq chaînes généralistes ne pouvait manquer de créer les conditions d'une concurrence acharnée, au détriment de la qualité et de la diversité des programmes*',[13] a prediction proven to be

---

fees, but also 'indirect' taxes in the form of 'public services' to be provided by the cable operator. This practice was ultimately brought to an end by the 1992 Cable Act, which prohibited the grant of exclusive franchises.

[8] For an examination of the economics of multichannel bundling see S. S. Wildman and B. M. Owen in E. M. Noam (ed.) (1985), 255–62. Criticisms of early British cable policy, in particular the creation of 'local monopolies', can be found in J. Mitchell (1983) and N. Garnham (1983). [9] Dec. 826/1988 [1988] Foro it. 2477 at 2499, pt. 19.

[10] For academic study on this point see, *inter alia*, J. G. Blumler (1991); R. Collins *et al.* (1988); T. Congdon *et al.* (1992); A. Ehrenberg and P. Barwise (1983); V. E. Ferrall (1989); G. Hughes and D. Vines (1989); and B. Sturgess *et al.* (1995), 29.

[11] J. G. Blumler (1991). [12] J. Dugdale (1993).

[13] J. Chevallier (1989), 62: 'The existence of five generalist channels could not fail but create conditions of relentless competition, to the detriment of quality and the diversity of programmes.'

well founded by the subsequent financial demise of the fifth commercial channel. A 1993 report by McKinsey and Company Ltd noted that '[t]o preserve advertising revenues, both F2 and F3 [the French public channels] have progressively introduced more populist programmes designed primarily to inflate their ratings and attract advertisers . . . Programme diversity has suffered, despite repeated criticism by the industry's regulator.'[14] Nor has Italian broadcasting been immune from these pressures; as Andreatta and Pedde note, both public and private networks have 'directed most of their efforts to acquire foreign, mainly American, motion pictures capable of ensuring a balance in the endless battle to mesmerise prime time audiences'.[15] A failure to grasp the complexities of broadcasting economics may thus lead courts unwittingly to promote the very developments they seek to prevent.

The Italian cable Decision 226 of 1974 also illustrates a rather more general judicial tendency to refer to broadcasting markets as though they are discrete entities, 'out there', waiting only to be discovered: but markets do not exist merely in theory, they operate more or less successfully in a distinct economic and regulatory environment. To say that public ownership or regulation should come into play *only* where 'the market' shows signs of failing is to ignore the way in which modern industrial markets are already shaped and hedged round by legal protections and controls. Indeed, it was the absence of any antitrust regulation to govern the private sector which so greatly troubled the Italian Constitutional Court. Moreover, the various communication industries interrelate at a number of distinct levels—through sophisticated patterns of ownership spanning the whole range of media products and through their competition for advertising revenues or audience loyalty from a common consumer pool—so that a judicial decision concerning one sector may consequently have important ramifications for another, yet a sector not directly considered in the case at issue.

Returning to the Italian cable ruling we can see that the Constitutional Court looked, for the most part, at the cable industry as though it were a distinct market. Yet cable competes with terrestrial, satellite, and microwave services for advertising revenue, subscribers, and programming purchases. If these various relay systems were to be assimilated into a single broadcasting market, then the scope for competitive growth in the cable sector would undoubtedly be assessed differently. It is indeed ironic that it was a subsequent Constitutional Court decision which tolled the death knell for cable development in Italy. Although the 1974 Decision stimulated for a while a marked growth in cable systems, the Constitutional

---

[14] McKinsey & Company Ltd (1993), 13.
[15] E. Andreatta and G. Pedde (1995), 8.

Court's 1976 Decision, which opened the local airwaves to private enterprise, resulted in a rapid shift to the cheaper terrestrial transmission technology.[16]

Such problems may be regarded as teething troubles inherent in any new field of judicial scrutiny, and a greater awareness of these market complexities led the Italian Constitutional Court to call for the compilation of an extensive report on the state of Italian broadcasting prior to giving judgment in its 1988 Decision.[17] Indeed, it would be unfair to represent the Italian Court as blind to the way in which the various broadcasting sectors interrelate: its 1988 Decision, for example, restated concern voiced in the earlier Decisions 225 of 1974 and 231 of 1985[18] that the audiovisual media could eat into the advertising revenues at the disposal of the printed press, though again such concern must be seen in the light of the then rise in advertising revenues enjoyed, albeit differentially, by both the press and audiovisual sectors.[19] A similar awareness of cross-media developments is also evident in the Conseil constitutionnel's discussion of media concentration in its 1986 judgment.[20] The more than ample scope for error in this field serves, however, as a continuous reminder of the need for meticulous analysis of data concerning existing media markets, consumer preferences, technological developments, and potential future trends, if courts are to intervene effectively to realize a given constitutional objective.

Detailed analysis of this kind can be seen in the audiovisual decisions of US courts where there is an established practice of interest-group litigation, of evaluating statistical data concerning the likely impact of a given rule, and, with the consent of counsel for both parties, of submission of written *amicus curiae* briefs prepared by non-parties. In the recent constitutional challenge to the 1996 Communications Decency Act and its restrictions on indecent Internet communications, the American Civil Liberties Union led the action on behalf of some fifty plaintiffs reflecting a wide range of individual and commercial interests.[21] The judges considered the mass of detailed information submitted to them and produced an extensive memorandum on the current state of the Internet. The attorney for the plaintiffs claimed that the judges, who concluded that the indecency restrictions were unconstitutional, the Internet being more akin to telephone communications than broadcasting, had 'done their homework'

---

[16] Dec. 202/1976 [1976] Giur. cost. 1267.

[17] Dec. 826/1988 [1988] Foro it. 2477.

[18] Dec. 225/1974 [1974] Giur. cost. 1775 and Dec. 231/1985 [1985] Giur. cost. 1879.

[19] For a discussion of the interrelation of press and broadcast advertising see EC Commission (1984), 58–60.

[20] Dec. 86–217 of 18 Sept. 1986 [1986] JO 11294 at 11297.

[21] *American Civil Liberties Union, et al.* v. *Janet Reno* and *American Library Association, Inc., et al.* v. *US Dep't. of Justice* [1996] US Dist. LEXIS 7919.

in a way that Congress had not.[22] Such analysis does not, of course, come without its own costs in terms of time and expense, but to expect judges to provide meaningful regulatory guidelines without a firm basis of empirical information is to ask them to resolve disputes literally blindfold.

Access to such information does not, of course, remove the risk of error. In moving into the world of statistics, of market trends, and technological evolution, judges, just as much as politicians, may go badly astray. The temptation in such circumstances may well be to limit oneself to propounding generalized objectives, leaving it to the legislature or regulator to flesh out those objectives with concrete rules. This is particularly so where there is no existing legislation which can be used as a basis for judicial development: the tools at the courts' disposal are primarily negative powers of veto, of holding a law to be unconstitutional, or a contract unenforceable. As Paolo Caretti and others note, the constitutional judge has insufficient power to delineate a new system and render it operative.[23] The Italian Consitutional Court's failure during the 1980s to provide specific indications of the level of concentration which would be acceptable in the private sector was not, therefore, particularly surprising given the absence of any established rules on the matter. Yet, when asked to examine the antitrust provisions of the 1993 Media Law, it was able to confirm that a rule allowing a single undertaking to own three out of the nine national television channels made available for private broadcasting would be unconstitutional. Similarly, the French Conseil constitutionnel, called in 1986 to consider concrete antitrust proposals for the audiovisual industry, was able to highlight specific areas which required further attention.

Where judges do attempt to set out specific regulatory proposals there remains the risk that their directions will be distorted in the implementation stage or quite simply ignored by the government of the day. The import of such rulings is ultimately contingent on factors outside the judicial sphere—on the way in which they resonate within the various political and executive bodies, as well as in public opinion. Thus despite the fact that the Italian Constitutional Court's 'seven commandments' for a constitutional broadcasting order, enumerated in Decision 225 of 1974,[24] quickly found reflection in legge 103 of 1975, the proposals which it made in 1976[25] were studiously ignored by the dominant political parties. In such circumstances judges will frequently be faced with the difficult choice of invalidating existing rules pending reform, thereby creating a regulatory void, or temporarily sanctioning the existing situation on the basis that

---

[22] J. Quittner (1996), 49.   [23] P. Caretti *et al.* (1981), 10.
[24] Dec. 225/1974 [1974] Giur. cost. 1775 at 1789.
[25] Dec. 202/1976 [1976] Giur. cost. 1267 at 1283.

some rules are probably better than none. It was the latter approach which the Italian Constitutional Court chose to adopt in its 1988 Decision, provisionally sanctioning continuation of legge 10 of 1985.[26]

Where there has been a political response, but implementation of the judicial directions appears inadequate, the difficulties inherent in developing a coherent model of the audiovisual industry, of ascertaining cause and effect, emerge again to limit judicial intervention. The Italian Constitutional Court in its 1994 judgment indicated that there was no one single, constitutionally acceptable, system of media antitrust rules waiting to be discovered. Rather, the legislature enjoyed a degree of discretion in framing ownership regulations, and the role of the Court was to ensure that these regulations did not underestimate the constitutional requirements and were generally designed to increase pluralism.[27] Judicial guidelines may thus do little more than set the outer boundaries of executive initiative, and in many cases it will be exceedingly difficult, if not impossible, for courts to challenge the mechanism chosen by the legislature to implement a particular policy. The problem is well illustrated by the American case of *Syracuse Peace Council* v. *FCC*. In *Syracuse* the plaintiffs sought to challenge the Federal Communication Commission's ('FCC') decision to dispense with the fairness doctrine, which required stations to cover controversial issues and afford a reasonable opportunity for the presentation of contrasting opinions on those issues.[28] It was the FCC's contention that the negative effect of the doctrine, its chilling impact on broadcast coverage, could no longer be justified, given the entrance of new operators. In the FCC's opinion the broadcasting market would now provide, independently of the doctrine, suitably diverse programming. Given the probative difficulties of establishing the exact impact of the fairness doctrine on the market and the fact that the FCC had come equipped with significant evidential support for its position, the court declined to find its decision arbitrary or capricious.[29] A degree of judicial deference to rulemaking by legislators or specialized agencies may, of course, be desirable, given their ability to obtain information and consider the wider industrial and policy implications of a particular provision. As Justice Kennedy held in the US Supreme Court judgment in *Turner Broadcasting*, '[a]s an institution . . . Congress is far better equipped than the judiciary to "amass and evaluate the vast amounts of data" bearing

---

[26] Dec. 826/1988 [1988] Foro it. 2477 at pt. 24.

[27] Dec. 420/1994 [1994] Giur. ital. 129 at pts. 14.4 and 15.

[28] 867 F 2d 654 (DC Cir. 1989).

[29] Judge Stephen Williams, speaking of the impact of the doctrine, noted '[w]e are frankly uncertain how anyone could be sure either way. The definitional problems alone are staggering': 867 F 2d 654 (DC Cir. 1989) at 665.

upon an issue as complex and dynamic as that presented here', moreover, '[s]ound policymaking often requires legislators to forecast future events and to anticipate the likely impact of these events based on deductions and inferences for which complete empirical support may be unavailable'.[30]

Do the deference afforded to the legislature in setting audiovisual policy and the complexities of reviewing its implementation render judicial calls for pluralism and diversity empty and misguided? Is the rhetoric of constitutional protection for freedom of information no more than judicial 'fancy talk'?[31] It is indeed possible to argue that, despite the development of pluralism as a key constitutional concept by courts of law, their willingness to open the audiovisual media to private competition, while leaving governments essentially free to weaken the regulatory requirements imposed on new entrants, may ultimately depress standards and reduce, at least in qualitative terms, the degree of audience choice. In Italy, judicial intervention in the mid-1970s led to a rapid and unregulated expansion in private broadcasting, and, despite the Constitutional Court's repeated emphasis on the need for effective antitrust regulations, the Italian broadcasting sector continues to be dominated by two national giants, RAI and the private networks of Silvio Berlusconi. Moreover, the distinct private and public regulatory regimes envisaged by the Court appear to be having little impact on the day-to-day nature of the programmes broadcast, RAI having been criticized for pursuing programming policies which are no different from its commercial rival.[32]

Similarly, although the French Conseil constitutionnel considered the powers granted in 1986 to the CNCL to be adequate for the establishment of a plural private sector, the obligations imposed on the newly privatized TF1 by its *cahier des charges* were considered by many to be minimal, and certain of its 'public-service' activities, religious programming for example, were transferred back to the remaining public channels. Serge Regourd has noted that the *cahier des charges* of the public TF1 ran to 154 articles, while that of the private TF1 to only twenty-one.[33] Yet even the 'light touch' obligations imposed on private-sector operators have become increasingly burdensome in an environment of heightened domestic and international competition, resulting in widespread evasion and pressure for further

---

[30] *Turner Broadcasting System, Inc.* v. *FCC*, (1994) 114 S Ct. 2445 at 2471.

[31] A term employed by R. F. Nagel (1984), 324, who argues at 303 that '[m]uch of what judges [in the USA] do in the guise of protecting speech, despite their efforts and good intentions, may even be dysfunctional and certainly diverts their attention from other important, if less grandiose, considerations.'

[32] E. Andreatta and G. Pedde (1995), 8.

[33] S. Regourd (1987), 368. Though TF1 argued in its 1993 complaint to the EC Commission concerning what it considered the 'double funding' of F2 and F3, that its programme obligations were roughly equivalent to its public-sector 'counterparts'.

relaxation.[34] The *Syracuse* case, discussed above, leads one to question how effectively courts could evaluate, in the name of pluralism, a determined political policy of commercial expansion, with new operators regulated solely by basic antitrust requirements and the rules of fair trading. Moreover, the *Lentia* decision of the European Court of Human Rights, under which state programme regulations designed to further pluralism were regarded merely as legitimate restrictions on freedom of expression, even seems to indicate that such evaluation might not be necessary at all.[35]

But perhaps we expect too much of our courts and the limitations discussed above are no more than the inevitable consequences of the division of powers within society. The issue is surely not whether judges have single-handedly been able to map out a just and democratic audiovisual order, but whether they can contribute meaningfully to this enterprise. Courts of law are limited in their field of action, and there are many structures and practices internal to the mass media, the ability, for example, of those in control of information to set the news agenda, which impede pluralism yet which courts are ill-equipped to address. To remedy these deficiencies we must either look to the political process or seek to change attitudes within the industry: the specific suggestions made by the European Parliament in its 1992 resolution on media concentrations represent a serious attempt to address the often far from apparent ways in which the communication of information to the public may be distorted.[36] Moreover, the subjective and highly personal nature of much audiovisual content militates against judicial intervention in editorial decisions; the search for legal certainty may encourage the development of mechanistic and rigid rules, poorly suited to the mass media.[37]

The primary achievement of constitutional courts throughout Europe has been to give a clear signal that the audiovisual media should not be treated as just another commodity: radio and television have become central mechanisms through which we gain an understanding of ourselves and others. Although such judicial rhetoric can be misleading, imbuing decisions with a weight which, on closer examination, is revealed to be devoid of any practical significance, it can also act as a constraining influence on political decision-making and is open to appropriation by pressure groups and those seeking reform of the existing system. Two

[34] See, in the French context, J. Chevallier (1989), 62, and J. Delisle (1989).

[35] *Informationsverein Lentia and others* v. *Austria* (1994) 17 EHRR 93.

[36] The Parliament called, *inter alia*, for a Freedom of Information Act, the protection of the secrecy of journalist's sources, and a 'Whistleblowers' Act: European Parliament (1992b).

[37] Consider, e.g., the problems encountered in enforcing the fairness doctrine in America, recounted by F. Rowan (1984).

aspects of the case law of the French and Italian courts should, in particular, be noted. First, there is the emphasis on the right of viewers and listeners to programme services which provide diverse and accurate information, information which, as far as possible, should be protected from distortion by either government or commercial influences. Scope for individual participation in the mass media may be limited, but radio and television are nevertheless able to play an important role in reflecting for citizens the political and social environment in which they live. Secondly, state regulation to ensure the provision of reliable and diverse audiovisual services is considered to be legitimate, even essential. There has been no serious move to undermine the licensing system, nor, indeed, the existing rules on programme content. In sum, the French and Italian courts do not regard the realization of a competitive free market, unencumbered by state regulation, to be a goal in itself. Though the legislator is afforded considerable discretion in pursuing the constitutional objectives, and a competitive market in audiovisual goods and services may be one way of ensuring their realization, the judges have emphasized their willingness to scrutinize any given regulatory regime to ensure that it does not undervalue and actually furthers the constitutional requirements they have developed.

It is interesting to contrast these decisions with the approach taken by the European Court of Human Rights, which considers state regulations designed to promote pluralism to be restrictions on freedom of speech requiring convincing justification. The burden is consequently placed firmly on contracting states to establish that such regulations are an effective and necessary means of attaining their objectives. A similar wariness of state regulation is apparent in the Community law context. Member States can potentially be required to justify any non-discriminatory programme or technical requirements which impede the exercise of Community freedoms and will also have to establish that there is no less intrusive way of achieving the same end. Similarly, convincing evidential support will be required where public-service broadcasters seek exemption from the competition rules under Article 85(3) or a derogation under Article 90(2) of the EC Treaty.

Many of the decisions discussed in this book may be thought to reflect key elements of the traditional public-service broadcasting philosophy, and so they do, but it is important to note that these are now considered functional objectives, cut off from any specific system of ownership. Though there may still be room for a distinct public-service sector, subject to specific rules on programme content, this is now just one part of a much larger field in which any financial or operating advantage must be convincingly justified. The challenge for both regulators and courts of law over the forthcoming years will be to adapt these principles to a rapidly changing environment, characterized by new transmission systems and increased consumer choice. Programme providers could, for instance, be given the choice of offering certain programme services or paying a levy into a special fund to subsidize educational or commercially unattractive services. Careful supervision will be necessary to ensure that dominant operators in the market do not curtail access by competitors and that public-service channels, where these are maintained, continue to enjoy adequate finance and means of distribution to meet their social and cultural obligations. The development of universal access requirements in the telecommunications sector may point the way to a more expansive recognition on the part of the European Community of public-service objectives, to be realized by 'old' and 'new' media alike.

The absence of a written constitution in Britain has curtailed judicial intervention in the audiovisual system, and leaves both radio and television services vulnerable to legislative fiat. For those who are in principle opposed to judicial lawmaking, or concerned that the adoption of a charter of rights will inevitably lead to the domination of economic over social interests, this situation may seem eminently desirable. Moreover, the way in which a particular right is interpreted in any given situation will depend, not only on the make-up and outlook of the adjudicating court, but also on the precise manner of its formulation in the governing text. Inevitably, however, as the media market expands and diversifies, there will be increasing pressure to lighten the regulatory load and create a competitive market unencumbered by public-service obligations. In such circumstances it may no longer be sufficient to trust exclusively in the political process to mediate between competing interests. Though it is true that Britain, unaided by judicial intervention, has in the past taught others much about the beneficial uses to which broadcasting can be put, it may now be time to look to the lessons of our European companions and consider in rather more detail the nature of the protection offered by a judicially enforceable constitution for the audiovisual media.

Appendix

1. International and European Community Texts

(i) *The European Convention for the Protection of Human Rights and Fundamental Freedoms, 1950*

Article 10

1. Everyone has the right to freedom of expression. This right shall include freedom to hold opinions and to receive and impart information and ideas without interference by public authority and regardless of frontiers. This article shall not prevent States from requiring the licensing of broadcasting, television or cinema enterprises.

2. The exercise of these freedoms, since it carries with it duties and responsibilities, may be subject to such formalities, conditions, restrictions or penalties as are prescribed by law and are necessary in a democratic society, in the interests of national security, territorial integrity or public safety, for the prevention of disorder or crime, for the protection of health or morals, for the protection of the reputation or rights of others, for preventing the disclosure of information received in confidence, or for maintaining the authority and impartiality of the judiciary.

Article 14

The enjoyment of the rights and feedoms set forth in this Convention shall be secured without discrimination on any ground such as sex, race, colour, language, religion, political or other opinion, national or social origin, association with national minority, property, birth or other status.

(ii) *Treaty Establishing the European Community as Amended by Subsequent Treaties, 1957*

Article 3b

The Community shall act within the limits of the powers conferred upon it by this Treaty and of the objectives assigned to it therein.

In areas which do not fall within its exclusive competence, the Community shall take action, in accordance with the principle of subsidiarity, only if and in so far as the objectives of the proposed action cannot be sufficiently achieved by the Member States and can therefore, by reason of the scale or effects of the proposed action, be better achieved by the Community.

Any action by the Community shall not go beyond what is necessary to achieve the objectives of this Treaty.

Article 52

Within the framework of the provisions set out below, restrictions on the freedom of establishment of nationals of a Member State in the territory of another

Member State shall be abolished by progressive stages in the course of the transitional period. Such progressive abolition shall also apply to restrictions on the setting up of agencies, branches, or subsidiaries by nationals of any Member State established in the territory of any Member State.

Freedom of establishment shall include the right to take up and pursue activities as self-employed persons and to set up and manage undertakings, in particular companies or firms within the meaning of the second paragraph of Article 58, under the conditions laid down for its own nationals by the law of the country where such establishment is effected, subject to the provisions of the Chapter relating to capital.

Article 53

Member States shall not introduce any new restrictions on the right of establishment in their territories of nationals of other Member States, save as otherwise provided in this Treaty.

Article 59

Within the framework of the provisions set out below, restrictions on freedom to provide services within the Community shall be progressively abolished during the transitional period in respect of nationals of Member States who are established in a State of the Community other than that of the person for whom the services are intended.

The Council may, acting by a qualified majority on a proposal from the Commission, extend the provisions of this Chapter to nationals of a third country who provide services and who are established within the Community.

Article 60

Services shall be considered to be 'services' within the meaning of this Treaty where they are normally provided for remuneration, in so far as they are not governed by the provisions relating to freedom of movement for goods, capital and persons.

'Services' shall in particular include:

(a)   activities of an industrial character;
(b)   activities of a commercial character;
(c)   activities of craftsmen;
(d)   activities of the profession.

Without prejudice to the provisions of the Chapter relating to the right of establishment, the person providing a service may, in order to do so, temporarily pursue his activity in the State where the service is provided, under the same conditions as are imposed by the State on its own nationals.

Article 62

Save as otherwise provided in this Treaty, Member States shall not introduce any new restrictions on the freedom to provide services which has in fact been attained at the date of the entry into force of this Treaty.

Article 85

1. The following shall be prohibited as incompatible with the common market; all agreements between undertakings, decisions by associations of undertakings and concerted practices which may affect trade between Member States and which have as their object or effect the prevention restriction or distortion of competition within the common market, and in particular those which:

(a) directly or indirectly fix purchase or selling prices or any other trading conditions;
(b) limit or control production, markets, technical development, or investment;
(c) share markets or sources of supply;
(d) apply dissimilar conditions to equivalent transactions with other trading parties, thereby placing them at a competitive disadvantage;
(e) make the conclusion of contracts subject to acceptance by the other parties of supplementary obligations which, by their nature or according to commercial usage, have no connection with the subject of such contracts.

2. Any agreements or decisions prohibited pursuant to this Article shall be automatically void.

3. The provisions of paragraph 1 may, however, be declared inapplicable in the case of:

—any agreement or category of agreements between undertakings;
—any decision or category of decisions by associations of undertakings;
—any concerted practice or category of concerted practices;

which contributes to improving the production or distribution of goods or to promoting technical or economic progress, while allowing consumers a fair share of the resulting benefit, and which does not:

(a) impose on the undertakings concerned restrictions which are not indispensable to the attainment of these objectives;
(b) afford such undertakings the possibility of eliminating competition in respect of a substantial part of the products in question.

Article 86

Any abuse by one or more undertakings of a dominant position within the common market or in a substantial part of it shall be prohibited as incompatible with the common market in so far as it may affect trade between Member States. Such abuse may, in particular, consist in:

(a) directly or indirectly imposing unfair purchase or selling prices or unfair trading conditions;
(b) limiting production, markets or technical development to the prejudice of consumers;
(c) applying dissimilar conditions to equivalent transactions with other trading parties, thereby placing them at a competitive disadvantage;
(d) making the conclusion of contracts subject to acceptance by the other parties of supplementary obligations which, by their nature or according to commercial usage, have no connection with the subject of such contracts.

Article 90

1. In the case of public undertakings and undertakings to which Member States grant special or exclusive rights, Member States shall neither enact nor maintain in force any measure contrary to the rules contained in this Treaty, in particular those rules provided for in Article 7 and Articles 85 to 94.

2. Undertakings entrusted with the operation of services of general economic interest or having the character of a revenue-producing monopoly shall be subject to the rules contained in this Treaty, in particular to the rules on competition, in so far as the application of such rules does not obstruct the performance, in law or in fact, of the particular tasks assigned to them. The development of trade must not be affected to such an extent as would be contrary to the interests of the Community.

3. The Commission shall ensure the application of the provisions of this Article and shall, where necessary, address appropriate directives or decisions to Member States.

Article 92

1. Save as otherwise provided in this Treaty, any aid granted by a Member State or through State resources in any form whatsoever which distorts or threatens to distort competition by favouring certain undertakings or the production of certain goods shall, in so far as it affects trade between Member States, be incompatible with the common market.

. . .

3. The following may be considered to be compatible with the common market:

. . .

(d) aid to promote culture and heritage conservation where such aid does not affect trading conditions and competition in the Community to an extent that is contrary to the common interest;
(e) such other categories of aid as may be specified by decisions of the Council acting by a qualified majority on a proposal from the Commission.

Article 128

1. The Community shall contribute to the flowering of the cultures of the Member States, while respecting their national and regional diversity and at the same time bringing the common cultural heritage to the fore.

2. Action by the Community shall be aimed at encouraging cooperation between Member States and, if necessary, supporting and supplementing their action in the following areas:

—improvement of the knowledge and dissemination of the culture and history of the European peoples;
—conservation and safeguarding of cultural heritage of European significance;
—non-commercial cultural exchanges;
—artistic and literary creation, including in the audiovisual sector.

. . .

4. The Community shall take cultural aspects into account in its action under other provisions of this Treaty.

. . .

Article 222

This Treaty shall in no way prejudice the rules in Member States governing the system of property ownership.

(iii) Treaty on European Union, 1992

Article F.2

The Union shall respect fundamental rights, as guaranteed by the European Convention for the Protection of Human Rights and Fundamental Freedoms signed in Rome on 4 November 1950 and as they result from the constitutional traditions common to the Member States, as general principles of Community law.

2. French Texts

(i) The Declaration of the Rights of Man and The Citizen, 1789

Article 1

All men are born and remain equal in their rights. Social distinctions may only be based on public utility.

Article 2

The ultimate purpose of every political institution is the preservation of the natural and imprescriptible rights of man. These rights are to liberty, property, security, and resistance to oppression.

Article 4

Liberty is the capacity to do anything that does no harm to others. Hence the only limitations on the individual's exercise of his natural rights are those which ensure the enjoyment of these same rights to all other individuals. These limits can be established only by legislation.

Article 11

The free communication of thoughts and opinions is one of the most precious rights of man; hence every citizen may speak, write and publish freely, save that he must answer for any abuse of such freedom according to the cases established by legislation.

Article 17

Since property is an inviolable and sacred right, no individual may be deprived of it unless some public necessity, legally certified as such, clearly requires it; and subject always to a just and previously determined compensation.

(ii) The Preamble to the Constitution of the Fourth French Republic, 1946

Paragraph 9

Every resource or enterprise the working of which has acquired or is in the process of acquiring the characteristics of a public national service or a *de facto* monopoly, must pass into public ownership.

Paragraph 10

The Nation shall assure to the individual and family the conditions necessary for their development.

Paragraph 13

The Nation guarantees to children and adults equal access to education, professional training and culture. The organization of free, public and secular instruction at all levels is a duty incumbent upon the state.

3. Italian Texts

(i) The Italian Constitution, 1948

Article 3

All citizens are invested with equal social status and are equal before the law, without distinction as to sex, race, language, religion, political opinions and personal or social conditions.

It is the responsibility of the Republic to remove all obstacles of an economic or social nature which, by limiting the freedom and equality of citizens, prevent the full development of the individual and the participation of all workers in the political, economic and social organization of the country.

Article 21

All are entitled freely to express their thoughts by word of mouth, in writing, and by all other means of communication.

The press may not be subjected to any authority or censorship.

Distraint is allowed only by order of the judicial authorities, for which motives must be given, in the case of offences definitely laid down by the press law, or in the case of violation of the provisions which the said law prescribes for identifying responsible parties.

In such cases, under conditions of absolute urgency and when the immediate intervention of the judicial authorities is not possible, distraint may be applied to the periodical press by officers of the judicial police, who shall communicate the matter to the judicial authorities within 24 hours. If the said judicial authorities do not ratify the measure within the next 24 hours, the distraint is withdrawn and is null and void. The law may prescribe, by means of provisions of a general nature, that the financial sources of a periodical publication be made known.

Printed publications, performances and all other manifestations contrary to morality are forbidden.

The law lays down proper provisions for preventing and repressing all violations.

Article 41

Private economic enterprise is open to all.

It cannot, however, be exercised in such a manner as to be in conflict with social utility or when it would be prejudicial to security, freedom and human dignity.

The law prescribes such planning and controls as may be advisable for directing and co-ordinating public and private economic activities towards social objectives.

Article 42

Ownership is public or private. Economic commodities belong to the State, to public bodies or to private persons.

Private ownership is recognized and guaranteed by laws which prescribe the manner in which it may be acquired and enjoyed and its limitations, with the object of ensuring its social function and of rendering it accessible to all.

Private property, in such cases as are prescribed by law and with provisions for compensation, may be expropriated in the general interest.

The law lays down the rules and limitations of legitimate and testamentary inheritance and the rights of the State in relation to the same.

Article 43

For purposes of general utility the law may reserve in the first instance or transfer, by means of expropriation and payment of compensation, to the State, to public bodies or to labour or consumer groups, certain undertakings or categories of undertakings operating essential public services or sources of power or which take the form of monopolies and which are of pre-eminent general interest.

Select Bibliography

ACADEMY OF EUROPEAN LAW (ed.) (1995), *Collected Courses of the Academy of European Law*, iv, Bk. 1 (Deventer: Kluwer).

ALLAN, T. (1991), 'Freedom of Speech and Judicial Review', 141 *New Law Journal* 683.

ALLEN, M., THOMPSON, B., and WALSH, B. (1994), *Cases and Materials on Constitutional and Administrative Law* (3rd edn., London: Blackstone Press).

AMBROSINI, S. (1995), 'Antitrust e informazione radiotelevisiva: incostituzionalità della norma sulle concentrazioni', CXLVII *Giurisprudenza italiana* 129.

ANDREATTA, E., and PEDDE, G. (1995), 'Broadcast Regulation in Italy: Debating New Rules to Join the European Audio-Visual Club', 1 *Entertainment Law Review* 7.

ANNAN REPORT (1977), *Report of the Committee on the Future of Broadcasting*, Cmnd. 6753 (London: HMSO).

AUBY, J.-M., and DUCOS-ADER, R. (1976), *Droit de l'information* (Paris: Dalloz).

—— (1979), *Droit administratif* (5th edn., Paris: Dalloz).

BACOT, G. (1989), 'La Déclaration de 1789 et la Constitution de 1958', 3 *Revue du Droit Public et de la Science Politique* 685.

BADINTER, R., and GENEVOIS, B. (1990), 'Normes de valeur constitutionnelle et degré de protection des droits fondamentaux', 6(3) *Revue française de Droit administratif* 317.

BALASSONE, S., and GUGLIELMI, A. (1983), *Rai-TV l'autarchia impossibile* (Rome: Editori Riuniti).

BALDASSARRE, A. (1986), 'Libertà di stampa e diritto all'informazione nelle democrazie contemporanee', XVII *Politica del Diritto* 579.

BALDWIN, R., and MCCRUDDEN, C. (1987), *Regulation and Public Law* (London: Weidenfeld and Nicolson Ltd).

BALLE, F. (1988), *Médias et sociétés* (4th edn., Paris: Montchrestien).

——, and LETEINTURIER, C. (1987), *La télévision* (Paris: M.A. éditions).

BARBERIO, R., and MACCHITELLA, C. (1989), *L'Europa delle televisioni* (Milan: Il Mulino).

BARBROOK, R. (1995), *Media Freedom: The Contradictions of Communication in the Age of Modernity* (London: Pluto Press).

BARENDT, E. M. (1987), *Freedom of Speech* (Oxford: Clarendon Press).

—— (1990), 'Broadcasting Censorship', 106 *Law Quarterly Review*, 354.

—— (1991), 'The Influence of the German and Italian Constitutional Courts on their National Broadcasting Systems', [1991] *Public Law* 93.

—— (1995), *Broadcasting Law: A Comparative Study* (Oxford; Oxford University Press).

BARILE, P. (1984), *Diritto dell'uomo e libertà fondamentali* (Bologna: Il Mulino).

BARNETT, S. R. (1987a), 'United States Regulation of Transborder Speech', 9 *COMM/ENT Law Journal* 635.

—— (1987b), 'Broadcasting Monopolies and Cable Monopolies under the European Convention on Human Rights and the United States Constitution', in Mestmäcker, E-J. (ed.) (1987), 71.

BARNOUW, E. (1983), 'Propaganda at Radio Luxembourg: 1944–1945', in Short, K. R. M. (1983), 192.

BARR, C. (ed.) (1986), *All Our Yesterdays: 90 Years of British Cinema* (London: British Film Institute).

BARRAT, D. (1986), *Media Sociology* (London: Tavistock Publications).

BARRON, J. A. (1967), 'Access to the Press, a New First Amendment Right', 80 *Harvard Law Review* 1641.

BARWISE, T. P., and EHRENBERG, A. S. C. (1988), *Television and its Audience* (London: Sage Publications).

BEKEMANS, L. (1989), *Economics in Culture v. Culture in Economics* (Florence: EUI Working Paper No 89/389).

BELL, J. (1992), *French Constitutional Law* (Oxford: Clarendon Press).

BELLENGER, C., GODECHOT, J., GUIRAL, P., and TERROU, F. (eds.) (1969), *Histoire générale de la presse française* (Paris: Presses Universitaires de France), i–iii.

BERLIN, I. (1969), *Four Essays On Liberty* (Oxford: Oxford Paperbacks).

BIRN, R. (1989), 'Malesherbes and the Call for a Free Press', in Darnton, R., and Roche, D. (eds.) (1989), 50.

BLACK, J. (1987), *The English Press in the Eighteenth Century* (London: Croom Helm).

BLUMLER, J. G. (1991), 'The New Television Marketplace: Imperatives, Implications, Issues' in Curran, J., and Gurevitch, M. (eds.) (1991), 208.

—— (ed.) (1992), *Television and the Public Interest: Vulnerable Values in West European Broadcasting* (London: Sage Publications).

—— BRYNIN, M., and NOSSITER, T. J. (1986), 'Broadcasting Finance and Programme Quality: An International Review', 1 *European Journal of Communications* 343.

BOLLINGER, L. C. (1976), 'Freedom of the Press and Public Access: Towards a Theory of Partial Regulation of the Mass Media', 75 *Michigan Law Review* 1.

—— (1990), 'The Rationale of Public Regulation of The Media', in Lichtenberg, J. (ed.) (1990), 355.

BOOZ ALLEN and HAMILTON (1992), *Study on Pluralism and Concentration in Media: Economic Evaluation*, final report prepared for the Commission of the European Communities, Directorate General III/F–5.

BOTEIN, M. (1988), *Deregulation and the Public Trustee Concept in U.S. Broadcasting: An Inherent Inconsistency?*, Conference paper given at the Swiss Institute of Comparative Law, Lausanne, 4 May 1988.

—— (1989), 'Can Fibre-Optic Broadband Networks be Regulated?', 17 *Intermedia* 35.

BOYLE, A. E. (1982), 'Freedom of Expression as a Public Interest in English Law' [1982] *Public Law* 574.

—— (1986), 'Political Broadcasting, Fairness and Administrative Law' [1986] *Public Law* 562.

BRANCA, G., and PIZZORUSSO, A. (1975–82), *Commentario della costituzione* (Bologna: N. Zanichelli SpA).

BRIGGS, A., and SPICER, J. (1986), *The Franchise Affair* (London: Century).

BROADCASTING RESEARCH UNIT (1988), *The Public Service Idea in British Broadcasting: Main Principles* (London: Broadcasting Research Unit).

BROWN, L. N., and BELL, J. S. (1993), *French Administrative Law* (4th edn., Oxford: Clarendon Press).

BULLINGER, M. (1987), 'Freedom of Expression and Information: An Essential Element of Democracy', 28 *German Yearbook of International Law* 83.

BURDEN, T., and CAMPBELL, M. (1985), *Capitalism and Public Policy in the UK* (Beckenham: Croom Helm Ltd).

BURGELMAN, J.-P. (1986), 'The Future of Public Service Broadcasting: A Case Study for a "New" Communications Policy', 1 *European Journal of Communications* 173.

BURNS, T. (1977), *The BBC: Public Institution and Private World* (London: Macmillan).

CALABRÒ, A. (1995), 'Il commento di Fedele Confalonieri "Contro di noi la stampa e i magistrati" ', *La Repubblica*, 12 June, 3.

CALHOUN, C. (ed.) (1992), *Habermas and the Public Sphere* (London: MIT Press).

CAMPBELL, T. (1986), 'Introduction: Realizing Human Rights', in Campbell, T. *et al.* (1986), 1.

—— GOLDBERG, D., MCLEAN, S., and MULLEN, T. (1986), *Human Rights from Rhetoric to Reality* (Oxford: Basil Blackwell).

CARDIFF, D. (1986), 'The Serious and the Popular: Aspects of the Evolution of Style in Radio Talk 1928–1939', in Collins, R. *et al.* (eds.) (1986).

—— (1988), 'Mass Middlebrow Laughter: The Origins of BBC Laughter', 10 *Media, Culture and Society*, 41.

CARETTI, P., CHELI, E., and ZACCARIA, R. (1981), 'Tendenze evolutive nei modelli radiotelevisivi e compiti del legislatore', 13 *Il Diritto delle Radiodiffusioni et delle Telecomunicazioni* 491.

CARINGELLA, F. (1993), 'Governo dell'etere e regime concessorio: un binomio (quasi) inscindibile', [1993] *Il Foro italiano* 1340.

CARTER, S. L. (1984), 'Technology, Democracy and the Manipulation of Consent', 93 *Yale Law Journal* 581.

CASSESE, A., and CLAPHAM, A. (eds.) (1990), *Transfrontier Television in Europe: The Human Rights Dimension* (Baden-Baden: Nomos Verlagsgesellschaft).

CASTRONOVO, V., TRANFAGLIA, N., and FOSSATI, L. G. (1979), *La stampa Italiana nell'età liberale* (Rome: Editori Laterza).

CATHCART, R. (1984), *The Most Contrary Region* (Belfast: Blackstaff Press).

CAVE, M. (1989), 'An Introduction to Television Economics', in Hughes, G. and Vines, D. (1989), 8.

CENTRE EUROPÉEN DES ENTREPRISES À PARTICIPATION PUBLIQUE (CEEP) (ed.) (1995), *Europe, concurrence et service public* (Paris: Masson/Armand Colin).

CESARI, M. (1978), *La censura nel periodo fascista* (Naples: Liguori Editore).

CERTOMA, G. L. (1985), *The Italian Legal System* (London: Butterworths).

CHAMBERLAIN, B. F. (1982), 'Lessons In Regulating Information Flows: The FCC's Weak Track Record in Interpreting the Public Interest Standard', 60 *North Carolina Law Review* 1057.

Chapman, J. W., and PENNOCK, J. R. (eds.) (1989), *Markets and Justice* (XXXI Nomos) (New York: New York University Press).

CHEVALLIER, J. (1987), 'Le nouveau statut de la liberté de communication' [1987] *L'Actualité Juridique—Droit Administratif* 59.

——— (1989), 'De la CNCL au Conseil supérieur de l'audiovisuel [1989] *L'Actualité Juridique—Droit Administratif* 59.

CLAPHAM, A. (1993), *Human Right in the Private Sphere* (Oxford: Clarendon Press).

CLUZEL, J. (1988), *La télévision aprés six réformes* (Paris: J. C. Lattés et Licet).

COASE, R. H. (1977), 'Advertising and Free Speech', 6 *Journal of Legal Studies* 1.

COCKETT, R. (1989), *Twilight of Truth. Chamberlain, Appeasement and the Manipulation of the Press* (London: Weidenfeld and Nicolson).

COHEN, F. S. (1935), 'Transcendental Nonsense and the Functional Approach', XXXV *Columbia Law Review* 809.

COLLINS, R. (1994), *Broadcasting and Audio-visual Policy in the European Single Market* (London: John Libbey).

——— CURRAN, J., SCANNELL, P., SCHLESINGER, P., and SPARKS, C. (eds.) (1986), *Media, Culture and Society: A Critical Reader* (London: SAGE Publications Ltd.).

——— GARNHAM, N., and LOCKSLEY, G. (1988), *The Economics of Television: The UK Case* (London: SAGE Publications Ltd.).

COLLINS, T. A. (1987), 'Has the First Amendment Arrived for Broadcasting?', 66 *Texas Law Review* 453.

COMMISSION OF THE EUROPEAN COMMUNITIES (EC Commission) (1984), *Television Without Frontiers: Green Paper on the Establishment of the Common Market for Broadcasting, Especially by Satellite and Cable* (COM(84)300 final) (Luxembourg: Office for Official Publications of the EC).

——— (1992), *Pluralism and Media Concentration in the Internal Market. An Assessment of the Need for Community Action* (COM(92)480 final) (Luxembourg: Office for Official Publications of the EC).

——— (1994a), *Strategy Options to Strengthen the European Programme Industry in the Context of the Audiovisual Policy of the European Union* (COM(94)96 final) (Luxembourg: Office for Official Publications of the EC).

——— (1994b), *Europe's Way to the Information Society. An Action Plan* (COM(94)347 final) (Luxembourg: Office for Official Publications of the EC).

——— (1994c), *Communication From The Commission to the Council and the European Parliament: Follow-Up to the Consultation Process Relating to the Green Paper on 'Pluralism and Media Concentration in the Internal Market—An Assessment of the Need for Community Action'* (COM(94)353 final) (Luxembourg: Office for Official Publications of the EC).

CONGDON, T., STURGESS, B., NATIONAL ECONOMIC RESEARCH ASSOCIATES (NERA), SHEW, W. B., GRAHAM, A., and DAVIES, G. (1992), *Paying for Broadcasting: The Handbook* (2nd edn., Harlow: Addison-Wesley).

COOTER, R., and ULEN, T. (1997), *Law and Economics* (USA: Harper Collins).

COPPEL, J., and O'NEILL, A. (1992), 'The European Court Of Justice: Taking Rights Seriously?', 29 *Common Market-Law Review* 669.

COSTA, J.-P. (1986), *Les libertés publiques en France et dans le monde* (Paris: Editions Sciences et Tecniques Humaines).

COUNCIL OF EUROPE (1991), *Recommendations Adopted by the Committee of*

Ministers of the Council of Europe in the Media Field (Strasbourg: Council of Europe, DH–MM (91)1).

COUSIN, B., and DELCROS, B. (1990), *Le droit de la communication: presse écrite et audiovisuel* (Paris: Editions du Moniteur).

CRAIG, P. P. (1994), *Administrative Law* (London: Sweet and Maxwell).

—— and DE BÚRCA, G. (1995), *EC Law: Text, Cases and Materials* (Oxford: Oxford University Press).

CRAUFURD SMITH, R. (1995), 'Do Human Rights Require Private Broadcasting? The Case of *Informationsverein Lentia and Others* v. *Austria*', 2 *Maastricht Journal of European and Comparative Law* 63.

CRAWFORD REPORT (1926), *Report of the Broadcasting Committee*, Cmd. 2599 (London: HMSO).

CRONAUER, A. (1994–5), 'The Fairness Doctrine: A Solution In Search of a Problem', 47 *Federal Communications Law Journal* 51.

CURRAN, J. (1977), 'Capitalism and Control of the Press 1800–1975', in Curran, J., Gurevitch, M., and Woollacot, J. (eds.) (1977), 195.

—— (ed.) (1978), *The British Press: A Manifesto* (London: Macmillan Press Ltd).

—— (1979), 'Press Freedom as a Property Right: The Crisis of Press Legitimacy', 1 *Media, Culture and Society* 59.

—— (1990a). 'The New Revisionism in Mass Communication Research: A Reappraisal', 5 *European Journal of Communication* 135.

—— (1990b), 'Culturalist Perspectives of News Organisations: A Reappraisal and a Case Study', in Ferguson, M. (ed.) (1990), 114.

—— (1991), 'Mass Media and Democracy', in Curran, J., and Gurevitch, M. (eds.) (1991), 82.

—— and GUREVITCH, M. (eds.) (1991), *Mass Media and Society* (London: Edward Arnold).

——, ——, and WOOLLACOT, J. (eds.) (1977), *Mass Communication and Society* (London: Edward Arnold).

—— and SEATON, J. (1991), *Power Without Responsibility* (London: Routledge).

DARNTON, R., and ROCHE, D. (eds.) (1989), *Revolution in Print: The Press in France 1775–1800* (Berkeley, Cal.: University of California Press).

DEBBASCH, C. (1970), 'La Convention Européenne des droits de l'homme et le régime de l'ORTF', III *Human Rights Law Journal* 638.

DECOCQ, A. (1989), 'Aspects internationaux et européens de la communication audiovisuelle', 2 *Revue Internationale de Droit Comparé* 361.

DE FLEUR, M. L., and BALL-ROKEACH, S. (1982), *Theories of Mass Communication* (4th edn., New York: Longman Inc.).

DELCROS, B., and NEVOLTRY, F. (1989), *Le Conseil supérieur de l'audiovisuel* (Paris: Victoires Ed.).

—— and TRUCHET, D. (1989), 'Controverse: les ondes appartiennent-elles au domaine public?', 5(2) *Revue française de Droit Administrative* 251.

——, and VODAN, B. (1987a), 'Le régime des autorisations dans la loi relative à la liberté de communication', 3(3) *Revue française de Droit Administrative* 386.

—— and —— (1987b), *La liberté de communication. Loi du 30 Septembre 1986. Analyse et commentaire* (France: Imprimerie Sauvegrain).

DELIVET, J. P. (1989), 'Une nouvelle instance de régulation: le Conseil supérieur de l'audiovisuel', *Mediaspouvoirs* 5.

DEPARTMENT OF NATIONAL HERITAGE (1992), *The Future of the BBC: A Consultation Document*, Cm 2098 (London: HMSO).

—— (1994), *The Future of the BBC: Serving the Nation, Competing World-wide*, Cm 2621 (London, HMSO).

—— (1995a), *Media Ownership: The Government's Proposals*, Cm 2872 (London: HMSO).

—— (1995b), *Digital Terrestrial Broadcasting: The Government's Proposals*, Cm 2946 (London: HMSO).

—— (1996a), *Copy of Royal Charter for the Continuance of the British Broadcasting Corporation*, Cm 3248 (London: HMSO).

—— (1996b), *Copy of the Agreement Dated 25 January 1996 Between Her Majesty's Secretary of State for National Heritage and the British Broadcasting Corporation*, Cm 3152 (London: HMSO).

DIRECTOR, A. (1964), 'The Parity of the Economic Market Place', VII *Journal of Law and Economics* 1.

DOCHERTY, D., MORRISON, D. E., and TRACEY, M. (1988), *Keeping Faith? Channel Four and its Audience* (London and Paris: John Libbey).

DOWNING, J., MOHAMMADI, A., and SREBERNY-MOHAMMADI, A. (1990), *Questioning the Media: A Critical Introduction* (London: SAGE Publications).

DOYLE, W. (1981), *Origins of the French Revolution* (Oxford: Oxford University Press).

—— (1989), *The Oxford History of the French Revolution* (Oxford: Clarendon Press).

DROUOT, G. (1988), *Le nouveau droit de l'audiovisuel* (Paris: Editions Sirey).

DRUMMOND, P., and PATERSON, R. (1986), *Television in Transition* (London: British Film Institute).

DUBOIS, J.-P. (1987), 'La loi, le juge et le marché: concession de service public et communication audio-visuelle', 103 *Revue du Droit Public et de la Science Politique* 361.

DUFFY, P. J. (1980), 'English Law and the European Convention on Human Rights', 29 *International and Comparative Law Quarterly* 585.

DUGDALE, J. (1993), 'New Filling for the Doc-u-like', *Guardian*, 4 January 1993, 14.

DWORKIN, R. (1986), *A Matter of Principle* (Oxford: Clarendon Press).

DYSON, K., and HUMPHREYS, P. (1988), *Broadcasting and New Media Policies in Western Europe* (London: Routledge and Kegan Paul).

EHRENBERG, A., and BARWISE, P. (1983), 'Do We Need to Regulate TV Programmes?', 11 *Intermedia*, No. 4/5, 12.

ELLIOTT, P. (1986), 'Intellectuals, the "Information Society" and the Disappearance of the Public Sphere', in Collins, R. *et al.* (eds.) (1986), 105.

—— MURDOCK, G., and SCHLESINGER, P. (1986), *'Terrorism' and the State: A Case Study of the Discourses of Television*, in Collins, R. *et al.* (eds.) (1986), 264.

EMERSON, T. I. (1981), 'The Affirmative Side of the First Amendment', 15 *Georgia Law Review* 759.

ENGEL, C. (1987), 'The Position of Public Monopolies and Cable Monopolies under the European Convention on Human Rights', in Mestmäcker, E.-J. (ed.) (1987), 55.

EPSTEIN, R. A. (1987), 'The Public Trust Doctrine', 7 *Cato Journal* 411.

ERRERA, R. (1986), 'Recent Decisions of the French Conseil D'Etat' [1986] *Public Law* 155.

ETZIONI-HALEVY, E. (1987), *National Broadcasting Under Siege: A Comparative Study of Australia, Britain, Israel and West Germany* (London: Macmillan).

EUROPEAN PARLIAMENT (1990), *Resolution on Media Takeovers and Mergers* [1990] OJ C68/137.

—— Directorate General for Research (1992a), *Mass Media Regulation and the Community* (Economic Series, W2, EN–8–1992) (Luxembourg: European Parliament).

—— (1992b), *Resolution of 16 September 1992 on Media Concentration and Diversity of Opinions* [1992] OJ C284/44.

—— (1996), *Resolution on Broadcasting of Sports Events* [1996] OJ C166/109.

FAWCETT, J. E. S. (1987), *The Application of the European Convention on Human Rights* (Oxford: Clarendon Press).

FEDERAL TRUST (1995) *Network Europe and the Information Society* (London: Federal Trust).

FERGUSON, M. (ed.) (1986), *New Communication Technologies and the Public Interest* (London: Sage Publications).

—— (ed.) (1990), *Public Communication: The New Imperatives* (London: Sage Publications).

FERRALL, V. E. (1989), 'The Impact of Television Deregulation on Private and Public Interests', 39 *Journal of Communication* 8.

FLOWER, J. E. (1971), *France Today: Introductory Series* (4th. edn., London: Methuen).

FOIS, S., and VIGNUDELLI, A. (eds.) (1986), *Codice dell'informazione e della comunicazione* (Rimini: Maggioli Editore).

FORGAN, L. (1990), 'The Right we have Wronged', *Guardian* (media), 26 March 1990, 9.

FOWLER, M. S., and BRENNER, D. L. (1982), 'A Marketplace Approach to Broadcast Regulation', 60 *Texas Law Review* 207.

FROMONT, M. (1989), 'Les jurisprudences constitutionnelles en matière économique aux États-Unis, en République Fédérale d'Allemagne et en France', 3 *Revue Internationale de Droit Economique* 289.

—— (1994) 'The Constitution and Advertising Activities in France' in Skouris, W. (1994), 91.

FURET, F. (1988), *Marx and the French Revolution* (London: University of Chicago Press).

GALGANO, F., and RODOTÀ, S. (1982), *Commentario della Costituzione* (Bologna: N. Zanichelli SpA.).

GARNHAM, N. (1983), 'Public Service Versus the Market', 24 *Screen*, No. 1, 6.

—— (1986), 'The Media and the Public Sphere', 14 *Intermedia*, No. 1, 28.

—— (1992), 'The Media and the Public Sphere', in Calhoun, C. (ed.) (1992), 359.

GENEVOIS, B. (1989), 'Le Conseil constitutionnel et la definition des pouvoirs du Conseil supérieur de l'audiovisuel', 5 *Revue française de Droit Administratif* 215.

—— (1988), *La Jurisprudence du Conseil Constitutionnel: Principes Directeurs* (Paris: Les Editions S.T.H.).

GITTI, F. B. (1994), 'Televisione e libertà d'espressione negli stati uniti d'America' [1994] *Giurisprudenza costituzionale* 4317.

GLASGOW UNIVERSITY MEDIA GROUP (1982), *Really Bad News* (London: Writers and Readers Publishing Co-operative Society Ltd).

GODECHOT, J. (1970), *Les Constitutions de la France depuis 1789* (Paris: Garnier-Flammarion).

GOLDING, P., and MURDOCH, G. (1986), 'Unequal Information: Access and Exclusion in the New Communications Marketplace', in Ferguson, M. (ed.) (1986), 71.

GOLDING, P. (1990), 'Political Communication and Citizenship: The Media and Democracy in an Inegalitarian Social Order', in Ferguson, M. (ed.) (1990), 84.

GOURNAY, C. DE, MUSSO, P., and PINEAU, G. (1985), *Télévisions déchaînées: La dérèglementation en Italie, en Grand-Bretagne et aux Etats-Unis* (Paris: La Documentation Française).

GOURISH, T. R. (1986), *British Railways 1948–1973: A Business History* (Cambridge: Cambridge University Press).

GRABOW, J. C. (1980), 'The Public Broadcasting Act: The Licensee Editorialising Ban and the First Amendment', 13 *University of Michigan Journal of Law Reform* 541.

GRAHAM, C., and PROSSER, T. (1987), 'Privatising Nationalised Industries: Constitutional Issues and New Legal Techniques', 50 *Modern Law Review* 16.

—— (1988), 'Golden Shares: Industrial Policy by Stealth?' [1988] *Public Law* 413.

GUREVITCH, M., and BLUMLER, J. G. (1990), 'Political Communications and Democratic Values', in Lichtenberg, J. (ed.) (1990), 269.

HAAG, M. (1996), 'Developments in EU Telecommunications Policy in 1995' [1996] *Utilities Law Review* 116.

HABERMAS, J. (1979 edn.), 'The Public Sphere', in Mattelart, A. and Seigelaub, S. (eds.) (1979), 198.

—— (1992), *The Structural Transformation of the Public Sphere: An Enquiry into a Category of Bourgeois Society* (Cambridge: Polity Press).

Hall, S. (1986), 'Cultural Studies: Two Paradigms', in Collins, R. *et al.* (eds.) (1986), 33.

HALSBURY (1985), *Halsbury's Laws of England* (4th. edn., London: Butterworth).

HAMELINK, C. J. (1983), *Cultural Autonomy in Global Communications* (London: Longman).

HAMMER, P. J. (1988), 'Free Speech and the "Acid Bath": An Evaluation and Critique of Judge Richard Posner's Economic Interpretation of the First Amendment', 87 *Michigan Law Review* 499.

HAMMOND, A. S. (1995), 'Regulating The Multi-Media Chimera: Electronic Speech Rights In The US', 21 *Rutgers Computer and Technology Law Journal* 1.

HAMON, L. (1987), *Les juges de la loi. Naissance et rôle d'un contre-pouvoir: le Conseil constitutionnel* (Paris: Fayard).

HANCHER, L. (1996), 'Cross-Subsidisation and EC Law', *Utilities Law Review* April, 71.

HARDIN, I., and LEWIS, N. (1983), 'Privatisation, Deregulation and Constitutionality: Some Anglo-American Comparisons', 34 *Northern Ireland Legal Quarterly* 207.

—— and —— (1986), *The Noble Lie: The British Constitution and the Rule of Law* (London and Melbourne: Hutchinson).

HARTLEY, T. C. (1994), *The Foundations of European Community Law* (3rd edn., Oxford: Oxford University Press).

HAYE, Y. DE LA (1977), 'Genesis of the Communication Apparatus in France', in Mattelart, A. and Seigelaub, S. (eds.) (1979), 201.

HAYWARD, J. E. S. (1983) *Governing France: The One and Indivisible Republic* (London: Weidenfeld & Nicolson).

HAZLETT, T. W. (1990), 'The Rationality of U.S. Regulation of the Broadcast Spectrum', XXXIII *Journal of Law and Economics* 133.

HEAD, S. W. (1985), *World Broadcasting Systems: A Comparative Analysis* (Belmont, Cal.: Wadsworth Publishing Company).

HEBDIGE, D. (1988), 'Banalarama, or Can Pop Save Us All?', *New Statesman And Society*, 11 November 29.

HENRY, B. (1986), *British Television Advertising: The First 30 Years* (London: Century Benham).

HEPWORTH, M., and ROBINS, K. (1988), 'Whose Information Society? A View from the Periphery' [1988] *Media, Culture and Society* 323.

HINS, W. (1994), 'Case C–148/91, *Vereniging Veronica Omroep Organisatie* v. *Commissariaat voor de Media*', 31 ev. *Common Market Law Review* 901.

HITCHENS, L. (1994), 'Media Ownership and Control: A European Approach', 57 *Modern Law Review* 585.

HOFFMAN-RIEM, W. (1986), 'Law, Politics and the New Media: Trends in Broadcasting Regulation', 9(4) *West European Politics* 125.

—— (1990), 'Freedom of Information and New Technological Developments in the Federal Republic of Germany: A Case Law Analysis', in Cassese, A. and Clapham, A. (eds.) (1990), 49.

HOGGART, S. (1989), 'Spoilt for Choice', *The Listener*, 5 January, 8.

HOLMES, S. (1990), 'Liberal Constraints on Private Power? Reflections on the Origins and Rationale of Access Regulation', in Lichtenberg, J. (ed.) (1990), 21.

HOLTZ-BACHA, C. (1991), 'From Public Monopoly to a Dual Broadcasting System in Germany', 6 *European Journal of Communication* 223.

HOME OFFICE (1988), *Broadcasting in the '90s: Competition, Choice and Quality*, Cm 517 (London: HMSO).

HOMET, R. S. (1979), *Politics, Cultures and Communication: European vs. American Approaches to Communications Policymaking* (New York: Praeger).

HOOD, S. (1989), 'Yesterday's Man', *The Listener*, 13 July, 18.

HORRIE, C., and CLARKE, S. (1994), *Fuzzy Monsters: Fear and Loathing at the BBC* (London: Mandarin).

HORWITZ, R. B. (1986), 'Understanding Deregulation', 15 *Theory And Society*, No. 1–2, 139.

—— (1989), *The Irony of Regulatory Reform* (Oxford: Oxford University Press).

HOWKINS, J., and FOSTER, F. (1989), *Television in 1992: A Guide to Europes' New TV, Film and Video Business* (London: Coopers and Lybrand Deloitte).

HUGHES, G., and VINES, D. (1989), *Deregulation and the Future of Commercial Television*, Hume Paper no. 12, (Aberdeen: Aberdeen University Press).

IBBOTSON, P. (1993), 'The New Rules Of The Game', *Guardian* (Media), 31 May 1993, 15.

INGBER, S. (1984), 'The Marketplace of Ideas: A Legitimizing Myth', 1 *Duke Law Journal* 1.

JACKSON, T. H., and JEFFRIES, J. C. JR. (1979), 'Commercial Speech: Economic Due Process and the First Amendment', 65 *Virginia Law Review* 1.

JACOBS, F. G. (1992), 'The Protection of Human Rights in the Member States of The European Community: The Impact of the Case Law of the Court of Justice', in O'Reilly, J. (1992), 243.

JENKE, M. (1984), 'Radio: More Programme Services but will there be More Listeners?', XXXV (5) *EBU Review* 33.

JENKINS, J. (1988), 'Death of the Gumshoe', *New Statesman and Society*, 11 November 1988, 12.

—— (1990), *Redeeming Modernity: Contradictions in Media Criticism* (London: SAGE Publications).

JOHNSON, L. (1981), 'Radio and Everyday Life: The Early Years of Broadcasting in Australia, 1922–1945', 3 *Media, Culture and Society* 167.

JONES, T. H. (1990), 'Broadcasting Licenses and Judicial Review' [1990] *Public Law* 156.

—— (1992), 'Judicial Review of the Independent Television Commission' [1992] *Public Law* 372.

JOURDAN, P. (1987), 'La formation du concept de service public', 103 *Revue du Droit Public et de la Science Politique* 89.

JOWELL, J. (1990), 'Broadcasting and Terrorism, Human Rights and Proportionality' [1990] *Public Law* 149.

KARST, K. L. (1975), 'Equality as a Central Principle in the First Amendment', 43 *University of Chicago Law Review* 20.

KEANE, J. (1991), *The Media and Democracy* (Cambridge: Polity Press).

KEELER, J. T. S. (1985), 'Confrontations juridico-politiques: le Conseil constitutionnel face au gouvernement socialiste comparé à la Cour Suprême face au New Deal', 35 *Pouvoirs* 133.

KELLEY, D., and DONWAY, R. (1990), 'Liberalism and Free Speech', in Lichtenberg, J. (ed.) (1990), 66.

KELLNER, D. (1990), 'Advertising and Consumer Culture', in Downing, J. *et al.* (1990), 242.

KLEINSTEUBER, H. J., McQUAIL, D., and SIUNE, K., (eds.) (1986), *Electronic Media and Policies in Western Europe* (Frankfurt: Campus Verlag).

KORFF, D. (1988), 'The Guarantee of Freedom of Expression Under Art. 10 of the European Convention on Human Rights', *Media Law and Practice*, December, 143.

KOSS, S. (1981), *The Rise and Fall of the Political Press in Britain: Vol. 1, the Nineteenth Century* (London: Hamish Hamilton).

Kovar, R. (1996), 'Droit communautaire et service public: esprit d'orthodoxie ou pensée laïcisée', 32(2) *RTD eur.* 215.

Kuhn, R. (ed.) (1985a), *The Politics of Broadcasting* (Beckenham: Croom Helm Ltd).

—— (ed.) (1985b), *Broadcasting and Politics in Western Europe* (London: Frank Cass and Co. Ltd).

Lane, J. E. (1985), *State and Market: The Politics of the Public and the Private.* (London: SAGE Publications).

Lanzillo, R. (1990), *Le communicazioni di massa:* (Turin: G. Giappichelli Editore), i.

Ledos, J.-J., Jézéquel, J.-P. and Regnier, P. (1987) *Le gâchis audiovisuel: Histoire mouvementée d'un service public* (Paris: Les éditions Ouvrières).

Lester, A., and Pannick, D. (1985), 'Advertising and Freedom of Expression', 13 *Intermedia*, no. 2, 25.

Levi, C. (1983), *Cristo si è fermato a Eboli.* (Turin: Einaudi Editore).

Lewis, N. (1975), 'IBA Programme Contract Awards' [1975] *Public Law* 317.

Libois, J.-L. (1983), *Genèse et croissance des télécommunications* (Paris: Masson).

Lichtenberg, J. (ed.) (1990), *Democracy and the Mass Media* (Cambridge: Cambridge University Press).

Lipari, N. (1978), 'Libertà di informare o diritto ad essere informati?', 11 *Il Diritto delle Radiodiffusioni delle Telecomunicazioni* 1.

Locksley, G. (1988), *TV Broadcasting in Europe and the New Technologies* (Luxembourg: Commission of the European Communities).

Long, M. (1995) 'Service public, services publics: déclin ou renouveau?' 11(3) *Revue Française de Droit Administratif* 497.

Longo, G. E. (1992), 'La jurisprudence la plus récente de la Cour de Cassation italienne en matière d'application de la Convention Européenne des Droits de l'Homme', in O'Reilly (1992), 85.

MacCabe, C., and Stewart, O. (eds.) (1986), *The BBC and Public Service Broadcasting* (Manchester: Manchester University Press).

Macedo, S. (1991), *Liberal Virtues: Citizenship, Virtue, and Community in Liberal Constitutionalism* (Oxford: Clarendon Press).

Maley, W. (1986), 'Centralisation and Censorship', in MacCabe, C., and Stewart, O. (eds.) (1986), 32.

Malinverni, G. (1983), 'Freedom of Information in the European Convention on Human Rights and in the International Covenant on Civil and Political Rights', 14 *Human Rights Law Journal* 443.

Mansell, G. (1982), *Let Truth Be Told* (London: Weidenfeld and Nicolson).

Marletti, C. (1986), 'Parties and Mass Communication: The RAI Controversy', in Nanetti, R. Y. *et al.* (1986), 167.

Martini, P. (1990), *No, non è la BBC* (Milan: Arnoldo Mandadori).

Marx, K. (1990), *Sulla libertà di stampa* (Rome: Editori Riunit).

Masclet, J.-C. (1984), 'La loi sur les entreprises de presse', 20 *L'Actualité Juridique —Droit Administratif* 644.

Mathes, R., and Pfetsch, B. (1991), 'The Role of the Alternative Press in the

Agenda-building Process: Spill-over Effects and Media Opinion Leadership', 6 *European Journal of Communication* 33.

MATTELART, A., and SEIGELAUB, S. (eds.) (1979), *Communication and Class Struggle: Vol. 1, Capitalism, Imperialism* (New York: International General).

McGRAW, D. K. (1995), 'Sexual Harrassment In Cyberspace', 21 *Rutgers Computer and Technology Law Journal*, 491.

McKINSEY & COMPANY, INC. (1993), *Public Service Broadcasters Around the World: A McKinsey Report for the BBC* (London: McKinsey).

McWHINNEY, E. (1986), *Supreme Courts and Judicial Law-Making: Constitutional Tribunals and Constitutional Review* (Dordrecht: Martinus Nijhoff Publishers).

McQUAIL, D. (1990), 'Western Europe: "Mixed Model" Under Threat?', in Downing, J. *et al.* (1990), 125.

—— (1991), 'Mass Media in the Public Interest', in Curran, J. and Gurevitch, M. (eds.) (1991), 68.

—— and SIUNE, K. (eds.) (1986), *New Media Politics* (London: SAGE Publications Ltd.).

MESTMÄCKER, E.-J. (ed.) (1987), *The Law and Economics of Transborder Telecommunications* (Baden-Baden: Nomos Verlagsgesellschaft).

MICHAEL, J. (1986), 'Information Law, Policy and the Public Interest', in Ferguson, M. (ed.) (1986), 102.

—— (1990), 'Regulating Communications Media: From Discretion of Sound Chaps to the Arguments of Lawyers', in Ferguson, M. (ed.) (1990), 40.

MICHEL, H. (1989), *La télévision en France et dans le monde* (Paris: Presses Universitaires de France).

MILES, I., and GERSHUNY, J. (1986), 'The Social Economics of Information Technology', in Ferguson, M. (ed.) (1986), 18.

MILL, J. S. (1982 edn.), *On Liberty* (Harmondsworth: Penguin Books Ltd).

MILNER, R. (1983), *Reith: The BBC Years* (Edinburgh: Mainstream Publishing Company (Edinburgh) Ltd).

MILTON, J. (1644), 'Areopagitica: For the Liberty of Unlicenc'd Printing', in Bush, D. *et al..* (eds.) (1959) *Complete Prose Works of John Milton: Vol. II 1643–1648* (New Haven, Conn.: Yale University).

MISSIKA, J.-L., and WOLTON, D. (1983), *La folle du logis: La télévison dans les sociétés démocratiques* (Paris: Gallimard).

MITCHELL, J. (1983), 'The Information Society: Private Monopolies and the Consumer Interest', 54 *The Political Quarterly*, 160.

MONTELEONE, F. (1976), *La radio Italiana nel periodo fascista* (Venice: Marsilio Editori).

MORAN, M. (1988), 'Thatcherism and Financial Regulation', 59 *The Political Quarterly* 20.

MORRIS, C. (1987), *Drawing the Line: Taste and Standards in BBC Programmes* (London: BBC Books).

MORRISON, D. (1987), *Invisible Citizens* (London and Paris: John Libbey).

MOWBRAY, A. R. (1994), 'A New European Court Of Human Rights' [1994] *Public Law* 540.

MURDOCH, R. (1989), *Freedom In Broadcasting*, lecture given at the Edinburgh Television Festival in August 1989.

MULLEN, T. (1986), 'Constitutional Protection of Human Rights', in Campbell, T. *et al.* (1986), 15.

—— and PROSSER, T. (1995), 'An Introduction to Scottish Public Law', 1 *European Public Law* 97.

MUSSO, P., and PINEAU, G. (1989), 'La télévision entre l'état et le marché', 14 *Mediaspouvoirs* 119.

NAGEL, R. F. (1984), 'How Useful is Judicial Review in Free Speech Cases?', 69 *Cornell Law Review* 302.

NANETTI, R. Y., LEONARDI, R., and CORBETTA, P. (eds.) (1986), *Italian Politics: A Review* (London: Pinter Publishers), ii.

NEGRINE, R. and PAPATHANASSOPOULOS, S. (1991), 'The Internationalization of Television', 6 *European Journal of Communication* 9.

NEVOLTRY, F., and DELCROS, B. (1989), *Le Conseil supérieur de l'audiovisuel. Fondement politique et analyse juridique* (Paris: Victoires Editions).

NOAM, E. M. (ed.) (1985), *Video Media Competition Regulation, Economics and Technology* (New York: Columbia University Press).

OECD, Committee on Consumer Policy (1982), *Advertising Directed at Children: Endorsements in Advertising* (Paris: OECD Publications).

O'MALLEY, P. (1981), 'Capital Accumulation and Press Freedom, 1800–1850', 3 *Culture, Media and Society* 71.

O'NEILL, O. (1990), 'Practices of Toleration', in Lichtenberg, J. (ed.) (1990), 155.

D'ORAZIO, G. (1981), *La genesi della corte costituzionale* (Milan: Edizioni di Communità).

O'REILLY, J. (ed.) (1992), *Human Rights and Constitutional Law: Essays in Honour of Brian Walsh* (Dublin: The Round Hall Press).

OWEN, B. M. (1975), *Economics and Freedom of Expression* (Cambridge, Mass.: Bullinger Publishing Corporation).

PACE, A. (1987), 'La radiotelevisione in Italia con particolare riguardo alla emittenza privata', 37 *Rivista Trimestrale di Diritto Pubblico* 615.

—— (1994), 'The Position of Advertising According to the Italian Constitution', in Skouris, W. (ed.) (1994), 213.

—— (1995), 'La television pubblica in Italia', [1995] *Il Foro Italiano* 245.

PALADIN, L. (1987), 'Libertà di pensiero e libertà d'informazione: le problematiche attuali', 7 *Quaderni Costituzionali* no. 1, 5.

PARDOLESI, R. (1988), 'Etere misto e pluralismo (annunciato)', *Foro It.* 2477.

—— (1995), 'Pluralismo esterno (non più d'una rete a testa?) per l'etere privato', *Foro It.* 6.

PARSONS, P. (1987), *Cable Television and the First Amendment* (Lexington Virg.: Lexington Books).

PEACOCK, A. (1986), 'Technology and the Political Economy of Broadcasting', 14 *Intermedia*, no. 6, 35.

PEACOCK REPORT (1986), *Report of the Committee on Financing the BBC*, Cmnd. 9824 (London: HMSO).

PETLEY, J. (1986), 'Cinema and State', in Barr, C. (ed.) (1986), 44.

PEPY, G., and WAHL, P. (1987), 'L'émergence d'une législation multimedia en France', *Mediaspouvoirs*, no. 6, 47.

PILKINGTON REPORT (1962), *Report of the Committee on Broadcasting*, Cmnd. 1755 (London: HMSO).

PINTO, F. (1980), *Il modello televisivo: professionalità e politica da Bernabei alle terza rete* (Milan: G. Feltrinelli).

PINTO, R. (1984), *La liberté d'information et d'information et d'opinion en droit international* (Paris: Economica).

PLOMAN, E. W. (1982), *International Law Governing Communications and Information* (London: Frances Pinter (Publishers) Ltd).

POLLARD, J., and QUARTERMAINE, L. (eds.) (1987), *Italy Today: Patterns of Life and Politics* (Exeter: University of Exeter).

POLTRACK, D. (1985), 'What Happens when Competition Comes—The American Experience', XXXVI(6) *EBU Review* 14.

PORTER, V. (1989), 'The Re-Regulation of Television: Pluralism, Constitutionality and the Free Market in the USA, West Germany, France and The UK', 11 *Media, Culture and Society* 5.

—— (1990), 'Re-réglementation de la radiodiffusion en Europe: le citoyen et le consommateur', XLI(6) *Revue de L'UER*, November.

—— (1991), *Beyond the Berne Convention: Copyright, Broadcasting and the Single European Market* (London: John Libbey).

—— (1993), 'The Freedom of Expression and Public Service Broadcasting', 14 *Media Law and Practice* 46.

—— and HASSELBACH, S. (1991), *Pluralism, Politics and the Media Marketplace: The Regulation of German Broadcasting* (London: Routledge).

POSNER, R. A. (1986), 'Free Speech in an Economic Perspective', XX *Suffolk University Law Review* 1.

POSTMAN, P. (1987), *Amusing Ourselves to Death* (London: Methuen).

POWER, H. (1994), 'Case Notes: *R* v. *BCC, ex p Granada TV Ltd.* [1993] *Times* 31 May; *R* v. *BCC, ex p BBC* [1994] *Times* 26 May, 15 *Media Law and Practice* 130.

PRAGNELL, A. (1990), *Freedom and Control: The Elements of Democratic Broadcasting Services* (Manchester: The European Institute for the Media).

PROSSER, T. (1988), *The Privatisation of Public Enterprises in France and Great Britain. The State, Constitution and Public Policy*, EUI Working Paper No 88/364 (Florence: EUI).

QUARTERMAINE, L. (1987), 'Speaking with One Voice: Society and Mass Media in Post-War Italy' in Pollard, J. and Quartermaine, L. (1987), 1.

QUITTNER, J. (1996), 'Free Speech for the Net', *Time*, 24 June 1996, 48.

RADIN, M. J. (1989), 'Justice and the Market Domain', in Chapman, J. W. and Pennock, J. R. (1989), 165.

RAO, G. (1988), *The Italian Broadcasting System, Legal (And Political) Aspects*, EUI Working Paper No 88/369 (Florence: EUI).

RATH, C.-D., DAVIS, H. H., GARÇON, F., BETTINI, G., and GRASSO, A. (eds.) (1990), *La televisioni in Europa* (Turin: Edizioni della Fondazione Giovanni Agnelli), i and ii.

REGOURD, S. (1987), '*Le service public et la doctrine: pour un plaidoyer dans le procès en cours*', 103 *Revue du Droit Public et de la Science Politique* 5.

—— (1987), '*La dualité public-privé et le droit de la communication audiovisuelle*', 3(3) *Rev. fr. Droit adm.* 356.

RHODES, A. (1976), *Propaganda: The Art of Persuasion (World War II)* (London: Angus and Robertson).

RICHERI, G. (1980), 'Italian Broadcasting and Fascism 1924–1937', 2 *Media, Culture and Society* 49.

ROBERTSON, G., and NICOL, A. G. L. (1984), *Media Law: The Rights of Journalists, Broadcasters and Publishers* (London: SAGE Publications).

ROCHE, D., and DARNTON, R. (eds.) (1989), *Revolution In Print. The Press In France 1775–1800* Berkeley, Cal.: University of California Press).

RODOTÀ, C. (1986), *La Corte Costituzionale* (Rome: Editori Riuniti).

ROLLAND, A., and OSTBYE, H. (1986), 'Breaking the Broadcast Monopoly', in McQuail, D., and Siune, K. (1986), 115.

ROUX, A. (1987), 'La libertà di comunicazione in Francia', XVIII *Politica del Diritto* 365.

ROWAN, E. (1984), *Broadcast Fairness: Doctrine, Practice, Prospects* (London: Longman).

SANDULLI, M. A. (1987), 'Radioaudizioni e televisione', XXXVIII *Enciclopedia del Diritto* 91 (Milan: Giuffré Editore).

SASSOON, D. (1986), *Contemporary Italy: Politics, Economy and Society Since 1945* (London: Longman).

SAUTER, W. (1996), 'The Evolution of Universal Service Obligations in the Liberalisation of the European Telecommunications Sector' [1996] *Utilities Law Review* June, 104.

SAVAGE, J. G. (1989), *The Politics of International Telecommunications Regulation* (Boulder, Colo.: Westview Press).

SCANNELL, P. (1984), 'The BBC and Foreign Affairs 1935–1939', 6 *Media, Culture and Society* 3.

—— (1986), 'Broadcasting and the Politics of Unemployment: 1930–1935' in Collins, R. *et al.* (1986), 214.

—— (1989), 'Public Service Broadcasting and Modern Public Life', 11 *Media, Culture and Society* 135.

—— and CARDIFF, D. (1991), *A Social History of British Broadcasting* (Oxford: Blackwell), i.

SCHLESINGER, P. (1990), 'Rethinking the Sociology of Journalism: Source Strategies and the Limits of Media-Centrism', in Ferguson, M. (ed.) (1990), 61.

SCHUDSON, M. (1992), 'Was There Ever a Public Sphere?', in Calhoun, C. (ed.) (1992), 143.

SCHULMAN, M. (1990), 'Control Mechanisms Inside the Media', in Downing, J. *et al.* (1990), 113.

SCHUCK, P. H. (1983), 'Regulation, Non-Market Values, and the Administrative State: A Comment on Professor Stewart', 92 *Yale Law Journal* 1602.

SCHWARTZ, I. E. (1990), 'La liberté d'expression (Art. 10 CEDH) et la libre prestation des services (Art. 59 Traité CEE) dans le domaine de la radiodiffusion télévisuelle', in Cassese, A., and Clapham, A. (eds.) (1990), 165.

SCOPPOLA, P. (1980), *Gli anni della costituente: fra politica e storia* (Bologna: Il Mulino).

SEDLEY, S. (1995), 'Rights, Wrongs and Outcomes', *London Review of Books*, 11 May, 13.

SENDALL, B. (1982), *Independent Television In Britain* (London: Macmillan), i and ii.

SEPSTRUP, P. (1989), 'Implications of Current Developments in West European Broadcasting', 11 *Media, Culture and Society* 29.

SEYMOUR-URE, C. (1987), 'Media Policy in Britain: Now You See It, Now You Don't', 2 *European Journal of Communications*, 269.

SHAUGHNESSY, H., and COBO, C. F. (1990), *The Cultural Obligations of Broadcasting* (Manchester: The European Institute for the Media).

SHORT, K. R. M. (ed.) (1983), *Film and Radio Propaganda in World War II* (London: Croom Helm Ltd).

SIEBERT, F. S. (1973 reprint), *Four Theories of the Press* (New York: Books or Libraries Press).

SILIATO, F. (1977), *L'antenna dei padroni* (Milan: Gabriele Mazzotta Editore).

SILJ, A. (1988), *East of Dallas: The European Challenge to American Television* (London: British Film Institute).

SKOURIS, W. (ed) (1994), *Advertising and Constitutional Rights in Europe* (Baden-Baden: Nomos Verlagsgesellschaft).

SMITH, A. (ed.), (1979), *Television and Political Life* (London: Macmillan).

—— (1989), 'Reith and the BBC: Built to Last', *The Listener*, 27 July, 10.

SMITH, F. (1996), 'Deregulation of Public Utilities: The Scope of the Exemption in Article 90(2) of the EC Treaty' [1996] *Utilities Law Review*, June, 111.

SORBETS, C., and PALMER, M. (1986), 'France', in Kleinsteuber, H. J. *et al.* (eds.) (1986), 87.

STEPHEN, F. H. (1988), *The Economics of the Law* (Harvester Wheatsheaf).

STEWART, R. B. (1983), 'Regulation in a Liberal State: The Role of Non-Commodity Values', 92 *Yale Law Journal* 1524.

STURGESS, B., AUBEL, M., PISTRE, S., and ARGIMON, L. (1995), *Report on Public Television Financing and Obligations in the European Union* (London: Putnam, Hayes & Bartlett).

SUNSTEIN, C. R. (1993), *The Partial Constitution* (Cambridge, Mass.: Harvard University Press).

SYVERTSEN, T. (1990), 'Public Television in Crisis: Critiques Compared in Norway and Britain', 6 *European Journal of Communication* 95.

TAYLOR, S. M. (1994), 'Article 90 and Telecommunications Monopolies', 6 *European Competition Law Review* 322.

THOMAS, R. (1976), *Broadcasting and Democracy in France* (London: Bradford University Press, in association with Crosby Lockwood Staples).

TRACEY, M. (1988), 'Popular Culture and the Economics of Global Television', 16 *Intermedia*, no. 2, 9.

TORRELLI, M., and BAUDOUIN, R. (1972), *Les droits de l'homme et les libertés publiques par les textes* (Montreal: Les Presses de l'Université du Québec).

TRUCHET, D. (1987a), 'Réponse à un article de S. Regourd: "label" de service public et droit administratif' [1987] *Revue du Droit Public et de la Science Politique*, 501.

—— (1987b), 'Vers un droit commun de la communication?', 3(3) *Revue Française de Droit Administratif* 347.

—— (1989), 'La loi du 17 janvier 1989 sur la communication audiovisuelle ou la fin de l'illusion lyrique', 5(2) *Revue Française de Droit Administratif* 208.

Tunstall, J. (1986), *Communications Deregulation: The Unleasing of America's Communications Industry* (London: Basil Blackwell).

Turpin, C. (1995), 'British Government and the Constitution' (3rd edn., London: Butterworths).

Van Cuilenberg, J. J. (1987), 'The Information Society: Some Trends and Implications', 2 *European Journal of Communications* 105.

Van Loon, A. (1993), 'National Media Policies under EEC Law Taking Into Account Fundamental Rights', 14(1) *Media Law & Practice* 17.

Voisset, M. (1995), 'Le service public autrement: De queslques effets du droit communautaire sur le droit français des services publics industriels et commerciaux', 11(2) *Revue Française de Droit Administratif* 304.

Wachsmann, P. (1987), 'Note (on the 1986 French Audiovisual Act)', 43 *L'Actualité Juridique—Droit Administratif* 111.

Watchtel, D. (1987), *Cultural Policy and Socialist France* (London: Greenwood Press).

Wade, E. C. S., and Bradley, A. W. (1993), *Constitutional and Administrative Law* (11th. edn., London: Longman).

Wade, H. W. R., and Forsyth, C. F. (1994), *Administrative Law* (Oxford: OUP).

Walters, P. (1989), 'The Crisis of "Responsible" Broadcasting: Mrs. Thatcher and the BBC', 42 *Parliamentary Affairs* 380.

Weatherill, S., and Beaumont, P. (1995), *EC Law: The Essential Guide to the Legal Workings of the European Community* (2nd edn., London: Penguin).

Weidenfeld, D. S. A. (1942), 'Broadcasting and the Third Reich', in Mattelart, A., and Seigelaub, S. (eds.) (1979), 272.

Weiler, J. H. H. (1991), 'The Transformation of Europe', 100 *Yale Law Journal* 2404.

Weinberg, J. (1988), 'Questioning Broadcast Regulation', 8 *Michigan Law Review* 1269.

West, W. J. (1987), *Truth Betrayed* (London: Duckworth).

Whish, R. (1989), *Competition Law* (2nd. edn., London: Butterworths).

Whitehead, P. (1988), 'Farewell Auntie', *New Statesman, New Society*, 11 November, 37.

Wilke, J. (1989), 'History as a Communication Event: The Example of the French Revolution', 4 *European Journal of Communication* 375.

Williams, A. (1976), *Broadcasting and Democracy in West Germany* (London: Bradford University Press in association with Crosby Lockwood Staples).

Williams, P. J. (1990), 'Comment: *Metro Broadcasting, Inc.* v. *FCC*: Regrouping in Singular Times', 104 *Harvard Law Review* 525.

Williams, R. (1974), 'Institutions of the Technology', in Mattelart, A. *et al.* (eds.) (1979), 265.

—— (1978), 'The Press We Don't Deserve', in Curran, J. (1978), 15.

Win, P. P. de (1989), 'Freedom Of Expression—Censorship—Self-regulation', XL *EBU Review*, no. 4, 15.

Wirth, M. O., and Cobb-Reiley, L. (1987), 'The First Amendment Critique of the 1984 Cable Act', 31 *Journal of Broadcasting and Electronic Media* 391.

Witte, B. de (1987), 'The Scope of Community Powers in Education and Culture in the Light of Subsequent Practice', in Bieber, R., and Ress, G. (eds.) (1987), 261.

—— (1995), 'The Cultural Dimension of Community Law', in Academy of European Law (ed.) (1995).

WOBER, M., and GUNTER, B. (1988), *Television and Social Control* (Aldershot: Avebury).

WRIGHT, V. (ed.) (1984), *Continuity and Change in France* (London: George Allen and Unwin).

ZACCARIA, R. (1977), *Radiotelevisione e costituzione* (Milan: Dott. A. Guiffré Editore).

ZAGREBELSKY, G. (1977), *La Giustizia Costituzionale* (Bologna: Il Mulino).

Index